Priestess, Mother,
Sacred Sister

Priestess, Mother, Sacred Sister

RELIGIONS DOMINATED BY WOMEN

Susan Starr Sered

New York   Oxford
OXFORD UNIVERSITY PRESS
1994

For Yishai

Oxford University Press

Oxford New York Toronto
Delhi Bombay Culcutta Madras Karachi
Kuala Lumpur Singapore Hong Kong Tokyo
Nairobi Dar es Salaam Cape Town
Melbourne Auckland Madrid

and associated companies in
Berlin Ibadan

Copyright © 1994 by Susan Starr Sered

Published by Oxford University Press, Inc.
200 Madison Avenue, New York, New York 10016

Oxford is a registered trademark of Oxford University Press, Inc.

All rights reserved. No part of this publication may be reproduced,
stored in a retrieval system, or transmitted, in any form or by any means,
electronic, mechanical, photocopying, recording or otherwise,
without the prior permission of Oxford University Press.

Library of Congress Cataloging-in-Publication Data
Sered, Susan Starr.
Priestess, mother, sacred sister: religions dominated by women / Susan Starr Sered.
p. cm.   Includes bibliographical references and index.
ISBN 0-19-508395-4
1. Women and religion—Cross-cultural studies.
2. Women—Religious life—Cross-cultural studies. I. Title.
BL 458.S45 1994
200'.82—dc20   93-35557

9 8 7 6 5 4 3 2 1

Printed in the United States of America
on acid-free paper

PREFACE

The impetus for this study grew out of the fieldwork projects that I have conducted among Israeli women. During the past decade I have investigated women's rituals at Jewish and Christian shrines in Bethlehem, observed and participated in the religious world of elderly Jewish women who came to Israel from Kurdistan, and listened to the fertility, pregnancy, childbirth, and post-partum rituals and beliefs of women in a maternity hospital. By choosing to work with populations and situations in which there is a great deal of sexual segregation, I tried to maximize my contact with women's own concerns, ideas, and rituals.

While conducting my own fieldwork, I also endeavored to seek out studies of other societies in which women have been able to develop some of their own religious rituals and interpretations. Many of the themes that I found relevant to Jewish women's religious lives in Israel resonate strongly with those described in the literature on Christian women in Europe and Latin America, Hindu women in India, and Islamic women in the Arab world. It became increasingly clear to me that when women have opportunities to express their own religious ideas and rites, themes peripheral to men's religious lives emerge as central to women's religiosity.

My work in Israel led me to wonder if similar themes are important to women who have even more control over their religious lives—women who lead or join women's religions (as opposed to women who have some freedom to maneuver within men's religious structures). This book was written in order to explore that question.

In the course of researching this book, I learned about women who have developed or participated in religions that enhance their lives, validate their concerns, sacralize their bodies, and meet their gender-specific needs. I hope to share with readers of this book some of the excitement I felt in finding out about religious situations so different both from the one in which I was raised and from those I encountered in my fieldwork.

Jerusalem, Israel   S. S. S.
August 1993

ACKNOWLEDGMENTS

Writing a book that covers diverse examples and draws upon more than one discipline is always a risk. Many people helped me reduce that risk by taking the time to check the accuracy of my work. In particular, I wish to thank the following people who were kind enough to read sections of this book that deal with their areas of expertise. I. M. Lewis and Yoram Bilu helped me sort out my ideas on spirit possession (Chapter 9). Daphna Izraeli explained the fundamentals of organizational sociology to me (Chapters 11 and 12). Kaja Finkler offered important comments regarding women's illness and healing (Chapter 5). Judith Lorber took the time to read and help me organize the material on the secular benefits that accrue to women who belong to female-dominated religions (Chapter 13). Shimon Cooper demonstrated how classical anthropologists treat social structure and lineality (Chapter 2). And Joel Gereboff offered me a theologian's insights into immanence and transcendence (Chapter 7).

Special thanks go to the experts who were both generous and broadminded enough to share their time and expertise with me. The following people helped me verify the accuracy of my information. Teigo Yoshida and Cornelius Ouwehand (Ryūkyū Islands), Melford Spiro (Burma), Eric Cohen and Gehan Wijeyewardene (Thailand), Laurel Kendall (Korea), Steve Kaplan and Janice Boddy (*zār* cult), Esther Pressel (Afro-Brazilian cults), Starhawk and Julie Greenberg (Feminist Spirituality Movement), Priscilla Brewer and Stephen Stein (Shakers), Virginia Kerns (Black Caribs of Belize), Susan Setta (Christian Science), and Carol MacCormack (Sande).

A number of people read all or parts of the manuscript. In particular, I wish to thank Ross Kraemer, Carol MacCormack, Rosemary Ruether, and Adele Reinhartz. And finally, I continue to appreciate the ongoing inspiration that I receive from Harvey Goldberg and Zvi Werblowsky.

My deepest appreciation to Ariella Zeller, Laini Kavalovski, and Cynthia Read, all of whom helped me pull together this often unwieldy project.

CONTENTS

Priestess, Mother,
Sacred Sister

Introduction

Ethnographic and historical studies of women and religion have thoroughly documented patterns of women's exclusion from positions of significant religious leadership. In many societies women have active religious lives, yet ecclesiastic hierarchies rarely include women, and official or "great tradition" religious concepts generally reflect men's and not women's priorities and life-experiences.

Scattered throughout the world and the centuries, however, are instances of religions dominated by women—in which women have been the leaders, the majority of participants, and in which women's concerns have been central. Through analysis of religions dominated by and oriented toward women, this book explores the questions: What are the cultural, structural, and historical circumstances most likely to allow women to develop autonomous religious systems? What are the salient characteristics of women's religions? Does the fact that women control a religious system mean that there is anything "female" about the content or structure of the religion? These intriguing questions have not yet been seriously addressed by either social scientists or historians of religion.

The key examples developed in this book are ancestral cults among Black Caribs in contemporary Belize, the indigenous religion of the Ryūkyū Islands, the zār cult of northern Africa, the Sande secret society of Sierra Leone, matrilineal spirit cults in northern Thailand, Korean shamanism, Christian Science, Shakerism, Afro-Brazilian religions, nineteenth-century Spiritualism, the indigenous nat cultus of Burma, and the Feminist Spirituality Movement in the twentieth-century United States.

These twelve examples are particularly appropriate for a number of reasons. First, they are all unquestionably female dominated both in terms of leadership and membership; that is, the majority of their leaders and members are women. In none of these religions is there discrimination against women on any level of leadership or participation. Additionally, in all these examples an awareness exists on the part of leaders and/or members that this is a women's religion. And finally, in each case there is some sort of recognition that this religious group is independent from a larger, male-dominated institutional context. All the examples I have chosen to describe are sufficiently well-documented to serve as the basis for wide-ranging comparisons.

I am indebted to the scholars who have researched and written about each of these religious situations. In particular, the work of I. M. Lewis, Janice Boddy, Carol MacCormack, Virginia Kerns, Ann Braude, Carol Christ, William Lebra, Starhawk, Gehan Wijeyewardene, Melford Spiro, and Laurel Kendall has enabled me to ask the sorts of comparative questions that this book addresses.

WOMEN AND RELIGION

Feminist anthropologists have determined that although male dominance is near universal, the forms taken by patriarchy vary from culture to culture. In one society women may be excluded from political decision-making yet wield extensive economic power; in another society women may be barred access to high prestige roles yet still amass a great deal of authority and autonomy through the existence of women's organizations. In general, feminist anthropology has treated religion as the ideological foundation of and justification for patriarchy; through religious doctrine and ritual, women and men are persuaded of the "rightness" of male dominance.

However, in many cultures—including highly patriarchal cultures—it is precisely within the realm of religion that many women find avenues for sacralizing their domestic lives (e.g., through holiday food preparation), acceptable outlets for their frustration with subordination (e.g., through rituals of reversal), or opportunities to celebrate with other women (e.g., at life-cycle rituals). Perhaps because religion frequently emphasizes such internal experiences as belief, faith, and mysticism (all of which are difficult to legislate or supervise), in many cultural situations women have found room to maneuver within the religious sphere.

The study of religion is of profound importance to feminist scholarship because it is so often via religious rituals and ideologies that women and men express their deepest concerns, their truest selves, their fears, hopes, and passions. Studies of women's religious lives—whether utilizing textual, archeological, ethnographic, historical, sociological, or psychological techniques—seek to discover how women construct reality.

Although the academic study of women and religion is still relatively new and lacking in theoretical focus, several patterns have begun to emerge. These patterns, drawn from studies of male-dominated religions, are briefly reviewed below.

THE STUDY OF WOMEN AND MALE-DOMINATED RELIGIONS

Although women are frequently excluded from certain leadership roles (e.g., as priests within the Catholic Church), other sorts of leadership roles tend to be open to women. In particular, women often serve as shamans and charismatic preachers. Among the factors that encourage women's attainment of authority roles are emphasis on personality or supernatural powers rather than on hierarchy or the training of cult/church leaders, and spiritual identity predominating over social categories (Haywood 1983; Weinstein and Bell 1982). These factors are particularly significant in new religious movements, where women often function as founders/leaders, losing their leadership roles as the religion becomes more institutionalized.

Neither the presence of women founders nor devotion to goddesses or female saints necessarily translate into equal privileges for all women in the religious cult. And equality of the sexes in relationship to God may co-exist with complete male monopolization of leadership roles, religious law, and authority in community affairs (as, for example, in traditional Judaism). On the other hand, even within religious frameworks that exclude women from positions of authority, women may be active participants. Australian women, for example, attend church more frequently than men (de Vaus and McAllister 1987) and in many European and North African societies women are the majority of devotees making pilgrimages to the shrines of saints (Mernissi 1977).

David Moberg (1962) has studied gender and religious participation in North America. He found that two factors seem to encourage women and discourage men from joining particular churches. First, churches that offer leadership opportunities for women draw fewer male members. Second, churches (such as Pentecostal and Holiness churches) that encourage highly expressive emotions tend to attract more female than male members. Phrased differently, his findings suggest that women are particularly attracted to religions with female leaders and emotional rituals.

There is evidence that religions of the disprivileged classes—in contrast to aristocratic cults—allow more equality to women. Max Weber (1966 [1922]) has argued that women are more receptive to all religious prophecy except that which is clearly military or political in orientation. Weber contends that members of disprivileged classes are particularly drawn to salvation religions which promise that an individual's true worth will be acknowledged at a future time. In general, disprivileged groups are drawn to religions that assure fair compensation—reward for one's own good deeds and punishment for the bad deeds of others.

Frequently there is greater female participation and influence in religions that teach brotherly love and love for one's enemies. Ross Kraemer, for example, suggests that very few women joined the Qumran religious community because "the entire cosmology, theology, and symbolic universe of Qumran was so pervasively male that no woman would have found it acceptable, let alone compelling. Asceticism as a by-product of cataclysmic war may have been incomprehensible to women. Asceticism derived from less militaristic eschatology, such as that of earliest Christianity, or asceticism unconnected to eschatology, such as that at Mareotis, may have held considerably more appeal for women" (1980b, 306–7).

Women's religious lives are often closely linked to their interpersonal concerns. The network of relationships that seems most relevant to the understanding of women's religiosity is the family. Historical and ethnographic accounts describe women's religious activity as embedded within, complementary to, enriching of, growing out of, and occasionally rebelling against women's familial involvements. An intense concern with the well-being of their extended families characterizes the religious lives of many women. Women who have a great deal invested in interpersonal relationships, and are denied access to venues of formal power, tend to be associated with religious modes that stress relationship. William Christian, studying women in rural Spain, has commented that "Women are more likely to fix on personal patrons [saints] than are men. . . . Such a close relationship carries over into old age when practical requests from the women still center on the children, now grown up, and when there is a deepening of the personal, affective ties between the woman and the divine patron" (1972, 133).

Even within male-dominated religious contexts, women "domesticate" religion by emphasizing rituals and symbols that give spiritual meaning to their everyday lives. In many cultures food is one of the few resources controlled by women, and food indeed plays a central religious role for women cross-culturally. This may take the form of feeding the poor, choosing to give better or more food to certain categories of people, observing food taboos, abstaining from food, or preparing holiday, symbolic, or sacramental foods (Bynum 1987). Food rituals imbue with holiness the everyday domestic work of many women (Sered 1992).

Illness plays a significant role in women's religious paths. Among saints in medieval Europe, fortitude in illness was the one form of asceticism "in which women were not merely statistically overrepresented but constituted an absolute majority" (Weinstein and Bell 1982, 235). In a large number of religious situations women are active in healing rituals. Their involvement may be as participant, healer, or both participant and healer. Women in the United States, for example, are disproportionately represented in cults concerned with health service and therapy (Stark and Bainbridge 1985). Healing tends to blur the distinction between pragmatic care for family members and religious expertise. Women who seek out and join religious groups frequently do so as a result of illness—either their own or that of a family member.

Studies of women and religion are notable for emphasizing ritual instead of theology. As a result, we know a great deal more about what women do than what women believe. This situation may reflect the preferences of researchers, or it may imply an actual tendency on the part of women cross-culturally to invest more energy into ritual than into theological speculations. There is some evidence from Afro-Baptist churches in the southern United States, for example, that men are more interested in theology—the nature of God and the meaning of life—while women are in charge of rituals and caring for the church and congregation (Pitts 1989).

Within patriarchal cultures women are not always at liberty to follow their religious callings. Some religious women (particularly women opting for celibacy) become subject to rejection, ridicule, and even physical harm at the hands of their families, communities, or other authorities. Intensive religious involvement for women may be seen as threatening familial strength, community solidarity, or government control. A recurring motif in the life stories of Christian women martyrs of the Syrian Orient during the fourth to seventh centuries, for example, is gruesome torture as punishment for "refusal to marry, for the common Christian practice of virginity was unsettling in its social impact, eroding as it did the most fundamental aspect of the social and economic order, the family" (Brock and Harvey 1987, 16).

Other external factors that have an impact on women's religious options include elements of the political and economic milieu. Jane Schulenburg (1989), for example, has shown that in seventh-century Europe women's monasteries flourished, at least in part because this was a time of weak and decentralized royal and ecclesiastical authority. Society was open, fluid, peaceful, and prosperous, and the Church was not yet highly organized. Threats to women's monasteries during the eighth through eleventh centuries came both from political events—the Viking invasions—and from economic factors—noble families needed their women for strategic alliances.

The themes and patterns outlined in the previous paragraphs grow out of the existing literature on women and religion, a literature that for the most part looks at religious situations **not** dominated by or oriented toward women. The issues raised by that literature encourage other sorts of inquiries: Are religions in which women are the majority of participants and leaders less hierarchical or less centralized than male-dominated religions? Are women especially drawn to rituals or to altered states of consciousness rather than theological learning? Do women's religions stress positive interpersonal relationships? How do women's religions relate to fertility, menstruation, menopause, and celibacy? When women are in control, are food preparation, illness, or childcare ritual foci? Do women's religions emphasize female symbols or goddesses? Does the presence of a religion dominated by women affect women's status in the society at large? Does the social structure of the society at large affect the occurrence of women's religions? Does female leadership repel male membership?

THE FINDINGS

A preliminary issue that a book of this sort needs to address is the legitimacy of talking about gender and religion in a comparative or universal sense. As an anthropologist I am committed to the idea that religious beliefs and rituals are not inscribed on x or y chromosomes.[1] If that is the case, why would we expect to find trends or patterns in women's (or men's) religiosity?

The answer to that question lies in the fact that there are cross-culturally relevant **social** patterns in women's lives. To begin with, in every known culture adult women grapple with motherhood. Most women are, have been, or try to become mothers, or conversely, make efforts—sometimes even life-threatening efforts—to avoid becoming mothers. Many, if not most women, are concerned with controlling the number of children whom they bear and raise, and with determining the way in which their children are raised. The diverse implications of motherhood, as I demonstrate throughout this book, strongly resonate with women's religious beliefs and rituals.

At this point, it is sufficient to propose that a range of aspects of motherhood could be envisaged as relevant to women's religions. First, we might expect that the physiological processes of fertility—pregnancy, childbirth, lactation—receive attention in women's religions. Second, I would anticipate finding the experience of nurture and childcare—that is, motherhood in the social sense of ongoing and intimate relationships with children of both sexes—to be addressed and possibly enhanced in these religions. In addition, I would expect these religions to in some way exhibit the facility with interpersonal relationships that women develop as a result of being raised by women (Chodorow 1974; Gilligan 1982). And finally, assuming that birthing and raising children have an effect on how women experience the world, I would expect to see some form of "maternal thinking" present in women's religions (Ruddick 1982). These ideas will be referred to repeatedly, especially in Chapter 3, and their validity will be assessed in the Conclusion.

A second pervasive theme in the cross-cultural study of gender concerns male dominance. A great deal of feminist anthropology has been dedicated to the question of whether male dominance is universal. Two major schools of thought have emerged. One school claims that male dominance looks as if it is universal, and concentrates on figuring out why (e.g., Ortner 1974). The other school contends that male dominance is not universal, and concentrates on finding evidence of egalitarian societies (e.g., Sanday and Goodenough 1990).

In recent years, more and more anthropologists have come to the conclusion that it is unhelpful to rate entire cultures as patriarchal or not patriarchal. Cultures are complex—men may dominate in one realm and women in another; and even within a given culture different women have different life-experiences—old women may be much freer than young women, and women of the nobility are likely to exert greater power than poor women. The evidence of women's religions certainly strengthens this line of argument—the very existence of these religions shows that male dominance is not universal or absolute. On the other hand, none of these religions occurs in matriarchal or even fully egalitarian societies. Therefore, when I ask what the common elements of women's experiences are—elements that help us understand women's religions—patriarchy is among them. Yet this does not mean that all women's religions respond to patriarchy in the same way.

Before continuing, I wish to offer a preview of what is surely the most important finding of this study. The impact of gender on religion is quite limited—women's religions are not so very different from men's religions. Female-dominated religions, like male-dominated religions, worship supernatural beings, perform rituals of thanks and appeasement, utilize techniques that induce altered states of consciousness, and provide devotees with persuasive explanations for the ultimate conditions of existence. It is necessary to make this statement precisely because "Woman" in western cultures is so often treated as inherently "Other"—as incomprehensible and mysterious. Having said this, I do believe that the data offered in this book show that gender has a significant—although not absolute or universal—impact on **how** people image supernatural beings, on the **form** and **interpretation** of the rituals performed, on **whether** and **why** one seeks altered states of consciousness, and on the **manner** in which individuals grapple with the ultimate conditions of existence. In short, the material in this book demonstrates that although gender has an important influence on religiosity (and religion has an important influence on conceptions of gender), an individual's religiosity is not determined by his or her sex. Indeed, the two near-universal elements of women's experiences discussed in the previous paragraphs—motherhood and patriarchy—are themselves culturally constructed, and thus intersect with religion in disparate and sometimes contradictory ways.[2]

HOW THIS BOOK IS ORGANIZED

Chapter 1 introduces the key examples and situates each in its historical context and in relationship to other religious options available at the same time and place. Chapter 2 looks at the cultural and social structural settings of the religions, and concludes that women's religions tend to occur in matrifocal societies. In Chapter 3 I show that women's religions address women primarily as mothers. Chapter 4 focuses on one aspect of motherhood—child death— as an impetus for women's religious activity. In Chapter 5 I argue that women (mothers) are dissatisfied with religions that claim that suffering is necessary or unavoidable. As a result, women's religions tend to offer eclectic and persuasive explanations for and solutions to misfortune and illness.

Chapter 6 explores the orientation toward interpersonal relationships found in the ritual complexes of women's religions. Subsections of Chapter 6 deal with food rituals, mourning rituals, and initiation rituals.

Chapter 7, really the pivotal chapter of the book, argues that women's religions are characterized by a this-worldly orientation that does not emphasize the difference between sacred and profane spheres. Chapter 8 asks what kinds of deities and spirits interact with humans in women's religions. Consistent with women's this-worldly orientation, almost all the religions posit highly immanent deities. Chapter 9 concentrates on the most dramatic manifestation of immanence—spirit possession—and explores the connection between women and possession trance.

Chapter 10 turns to the question of gender ideology, asking whether women's religions postulate egalitarian, matriarchal, or patriarchal views of gender. Chapter 11 investigates the life histories and roles of women who are leaders of women's religions. Chapter 12 explores the tendency toward non-centralization, non-standardization, and lack of codification of sacred scripture in women's religions. Chapter 13 asks whether women's religions serve women's secular interests.

Finally, the Conclusion returns to the question of whether there is anything intrinsically "female" about religions dominated by women, and evaluates the differences between women's religious activities in female- and male-dominated religions.

Within each chapter, shorter sections zero in on patterns that are relevant to many or most women's religions. Each section explores in some detail one or more of the key examples. Since information about each religion is scattered throughout the thematically organized chapters, readers who wish to find out about theological, ritual, contextual and structural aspects of a particular religion are referred to the index. I urge the reader not to be overly concerned with keeping track of the many examples; my main aim in this book is to uncover thematic patterns, not to present comprehensive accounts of a limited number of religions. The Appendixes briefly summarize each religion. The Bibliography should be helpful to readers wishing to learn more about particular examples.

In light of the thematic (rather than geographic or historical) organization of this book, it is in order to make a few comments concerning cross-cultural research. A serious challenge to any cross-cultural study concerns the nature of comparisons: To what extent are religions that developed on different continents during different centuries comparable? Anthropologists have long grappled with this issue, and with few exceptions have concluded that without comparison anthropology ceases to be the study of human culture and becomes merely a technique for collecting exotic customs. While the aim of this book is unabashedly comparative, I strive throughout to remain sensitive to cultural context.

I have written this book because I believe that Okinawan and Afro-Brazilian priestesses, Black Carib grandmothers, Burmese and Sudanese housewives, Sande initiates, Spiritualist mediums, Shaker celibates, American Spiritual Feminists, Christian Science practitioners, and Korean shamans do share a common bond—they are all active in religions that address women's concerns and encourage women's religious leadership. Tracing the similarities and the differences among them offers important insights into the intersection of gender and religion.

Notes

1. It is a tenet of anthropology that one always begins by exploring **social** explanations for differences between groups. Only if all possible social explanations fail is it legitimate to turn to biological explanations.

2. It has become increasingly fashionable in academia to share with the readers one's intellectual and personal progression in writing a book. I will take this opportunity to tell the reader that when I began researching this book I did not have any sort of hypothesis in mind; I was simply looking for themes and patterns in women's religions. Once I had finished a first draft, it became clear that motherhood and patriarchy seemed to explain almost all the interesting patterns. As I continued to ponder my data, I realized that these two factors are also what legitimate the expectation that there will be near-universal patterns in women's religious experiences.

1 ❧

The Examples

DEFINITIONS

Women's religions are, from a cross-cultural perspective, anomalous. Despite my growing excitement as I "discovered" more and more women's religions buried in the pages of ethnographic and historical tomes, the fact is that most of the religions of the world are dominated by men. The anomalous status of women's religions leads us to ask when, why, and how they occur.

In the following pages twelve examples of religions dominated by women are presented. The descriptions in this chapter should help the reader follow the thematic analyses in subsequent chapters. (Concise summaries of the main features of each religion can be found in the Appendixes.) But before we begin our journey into the worlds of women's religions, it is worthwhile to point out ways in which these religions differ from one another.

Some of the examples are self-consciously independent religions that exist in a society where the dominant religion is male dominated (e.g., Feminist Spirituality, Afro-Brazilian religions). Others are religious streams that co-exist alongside of, and sometimes intertwined with, male-dominated religions (e.g., zār, Spiritualism, Korean shamanism, Burmese *nat* cultus). Still others are the major religion of an entire society (e.g., the Ryūkyū Islands, the Black Caribs of Belize). And finally, others are sects of otherwise male-dominated religions (e.g., Christian Science, Shakerism).

One problem I faced in writing this book concerns terminology: the experts whose research I rely on use uneven nomenclature to describe their religions. Among the terms used are "cult," "cultus," "sect," "religion," "group," "society," and "movement." In addition, at least one of the examples (Korean shamanism) is probably most accurately described as a "religious situation." Rather than repeat the phrase "religions, religious cults, groups, cultures, sects, societies, and situations that are oriented toward and dominated numerically and in terms of leadership by women," I have chosen to gloss all these terms as "women's religions" or "female-dominated religions."[1] Although my decision may offend some scholars, in light of the fact that all of these terms are etic (imposed from the outside by western scholars) and not emic (the terms used by members of the various religious groups), my decision is defensible—provided that I show each example in its proper societal context. I wish to clarify that I use the term "female-dominated religions" to indicate that women are the majority of participants and leaders, there is no higher level male authority that ultimately directs these religions, and that these religions focus on women as ritual actors. By female dominated I do not mean to imply physical dominance or institutionalized power inequality between men and women. I use the term "women's religions" interchangeably with "female-dominated religions."

Some examples are all-women religions (Sande is a women's secret society), others include some men (Spiritualists do not exclude men, just more women join), and still others include many men yet limit leadership to women (on the Ryūkyū Islands men attend religious ceremonies, yet the leaders are all women). The implications of these distinctions are significant, and it may well be that future studies will narrow down the field of inquiry. In thinking about the religions described in this book, it is helpful to treat the diverse examples as points on a continuum, rather than as a strictly homogeneous group.

In this chapter I am not comparing "women's religion" to "men's religion." There is no such thing as an archetypical "women's" or "men's" religion; I do not believe that religiosity is a biologically determined sexual characteristic. My goals are far more modest: I am comparing specific religions to other religion(s) of the same place and time. Among the questions I ask are: Is this religion the only option available at the given time and place? If not, how is it different or similar to other religions of its day? What is the relationship of this religion to other religions of its day (*nat* religion vs. Buddhism; Thai spirit cults vs. Buddhism; Korean shamanism vs. Confucianism; Afro-Brazilian cults vs. Catholicism; Feminist Spirituality vs. American civil religion; African cults of affliction vs. ancestor worship; Spiritualism, Christian Science, Shakerism vs. Calvinism)? What is the status of this religion—is it the official state religion, a new religion, a persecuted cult? What is the historical and cultural context of this religion? In what way is this religion female dominated?

These religions are not randomly scattered throughout the globe. In fact, all of them are clustered in three loosely defined culture areas.

EAST AND SOUTHEAST ASIA

Four of the women's religions are located in East or Southeast Asia. The similarities among these religions will become apparent as we look at each religion in turn. What I wish to point out here is that unlike most of the women's religions outside of East and Southeast Asia, all these religions seem to be indigenous, probably ancient, religions. While they all have undergone changes in the past century, none of them can be identified as having arisen at a particular point in the historically recorded past; none has a named historical founder.[2]

Japanese scholars speculate that the ancient religion of Japan was dominated by women, and that vestiges of that domination can still be found in modern Japan. According to Teigo Yoshida (1989), the continued religious domination of women in the Ryūkyū Islands reflects the failure of Buddhism to have made much of an impact there. Whether or not Yoshida is correct, it is clear that in East and Southeast Asian societies in which the indigenous religions are dominated by women, men tend to be involved in newer religions. Thai and Burmese men are active Buddhists—many if not most young men enter Buddhist monasteries as novitiates for several years, and Korean men are responsible for Confucianist ancestor worship. In three of the four key East and Southeast Asian examples, men embrace religions that came in from the outside while women dominate the indigenous religion.

I would tentatively suggest two possible historical scenarios. First, it may be that in very ancient times the only religions in East and Southeast Asia were dominated by women. When new religions (Buddhism, Confucianism) were introduced into the area, men were especially eager to adopt the new religions because of their subordinate status in the traditional religions.[3] Alternatively, it may be that in ancient times both men and women were involved in the indigenous religion. For known or unknown social reasons, men more than women were attracted to the new religions, leaving the ancient religion in female hands, where today it has an ambivalent and often inferior status. It is significant that the male-dominated "new" religions of East and Southeast Asia, unlike the female-dominated indigenous religions, preach doctrines of female pollution or subordination.

It is perhaps not unexpected to find that women's religions have continued to thrive in Buddhist countries. In contrast to Islam or Catholicism, Buddhism is relatively tolerant of other religions, and generally allows adherents to participate both in Buddhist and non-Buddhist religious rituals. In East and Southeast Asia it is quite common to find that the men of a family are active Buddhists, whereas the women are dedicated participants in women's religions. Such a situation would probably not be tolerated in Islamic or Christian societies.

The Religion of the Ryūkyū Islands

Religion on the Ryūkyū Islands is inseparable from ethnicity or nationality; the religion has no name, it is simply the religion of the people of the Ryūkyū Islands. The Ryūkyū Islands, of which Okinawa is the main island, extend south and east from the south of Japan. They are a combination of sparsely populated, well-populated, and totally unpopulated islands and coral reefs. The Islands have, at various points in their history, been an independent kingdom, a tributary to China and Japan, incorporated into the Japanese Empire, and occupied by the United States (after World War II). Since 1972 the Islands have been part of Japan. Yet because of the isolation provided by the sea, many old customs have survived. Ryūkyūan culture has been notably unreceptive to outside beliefs, and has typically reinterpreted foreign elements in light of its own, indigenous cultural system.[4]

Ryūkyūan religion is characterized by a highly elaborated ritual calendar and sacred geography. Myriad events, dates, objects and locations are reasons for priestesses to perform religious rituals. Most rituals are directed toward appeasing, notifying, or thanking the divine beings known as *kami*.[5]

The most outstanding feature of Ryūkyūan culture is the belief in the spiritual predominance of women; on the Ryūkyūan Islands women dominate the religious life of the family, community, and (in the past) state. Only women can officially mediate between the supernatural and human beings, women are expected to be much more knowledgeable about religious matters than men, and men are required to participate in religious rituals led by women. It is of interest that the Ryūkyūans have adopted certain Chinese ancestral rites in minute detail—with one exception: in Ryūkyū unlike China the rites are conducted by women. In general, Ryūkyūans are dissatisfied if rituals are conducted by men. Ryūkyūan men do not even pray at the household hearth. Women are so thoroughly associated with the sacred that in the past the rare man who entered the sacred groves had to practice a form of ceremonial transvestism—that is, dress like a woman. This was true even for the chief ministers of state.

While the precise role of priestesses and the exact dates and compositions of rituals vary somewhat from island to island (Mabuchi 1964), the religious culture of the Ryūkyūs is basically homogeneous.[6] Within the household the sister predominates in spiritual matters, and the same is true within the kin-group, cult groups (in the southern Ryūkyū), village, and state. All public and almost all private religious rituals and festivals are conducted by women. In addition, personal problems are often solved by shamans, most of whom are women.

According to the Ryūkyū Islanders, men are spiritually protected by their sisters. The sister of the kin-group head is in charge of domestic rituals; the sister of the village headman is the village priestess; the sister of the king on Okinawa was the head priestess of the kingdom. Priestesses who marry out because of virilocal residence rules continue to return to their natal houses to act as priestesses for their brothers' households.

In contrast to Japan, Korea, and many other cultures in which the mainstream or official religious practitioners (priests) are men while the marginal practitioners (shamans) are women, on the Ryūkyūs both priestesses (*noro*) and shamans (*yuta*) are women. The very few male shamans on Okinawa are men with major physical disabilities that preclude their functioning in typical male roles. These men have a low social status and a reputation for being emotionally disturbed.

Almost all the clients who call on *yuta* are women. Even if the woman is accompanied by a husband or son, it is the woman who communicates directly with the *yuta*. In Ohashi's (1984) study of a middle-sized town in Okinawa, more than half the women had contacted *yutas*, with the percentage increasing as women age. Of women in their sixties, 85% had contacted *yutas*. When the women were asked in what religion they believe, more than three-quarters said "ancestor" (i.e., the traditional Okinawan religion), and among the older women nearly 100% gave that answer.

Douglas Haring noted that the association of women and religion in the Ryūkyū Islands is similar to what we know of early Japan—but in Japan, Buddhism and Confucianism exterminated that association. "Perhaps Buddhism failed to gain wide acceptance in . . . [the Ryūkyū Islands] despite centuries of propaganda because its priests were male" (1964, 121). On the other hand, William Lebra believes that there has been a decline in the power of priestesses on Okinawa beginning in the sixteenth or seventeenth century as a result of contact with China and the influence of Confucianism with its stress on the superiority of males, and the penetration of Japanese Buddhism emphasizing the ancestral cult through the male line. "From the sixteenth and seventeenth centuries, history reveals a persistent effort by the government to reduce the powers of the priestesses" (1966, 117).

It must be emphasized that unlike most other women's religions that are one option in a cultural situation providing two or more religious choices, the Ryūkyū Islands are the only known instance in which the official religion of a people is dominated by and oriented toward women.

Burmese Nat Religion

Buddhism is the state religion of Burma. Alongside of Buddhism, however, there is an earlier, indigenous religion that revolves around appeasement of spirits known as *nats*. *Nats* are propitiated to prevent and cure illness, at key stages in the agricultural cycle, at births, deaths, and marriages, and at Buddhist initiations. Unlike Buddhism, *nat* rituals are dominated by women.

Melford Spiro, who conducted fieldwork in Burma, gives the name "supernaturalism" to this non-Buddhist Burmese religion. Since the concept "supernaturalism" is one that western scholars have imposed from the outside, I prefer to focus on the central element of the indigenous Burmese religion—belief in and rituals concerning *nats* or spirits—and refer to non-Buddhist Burmese religion as "*nat* religion." *Nat* religion is, like Buddhism, an elaborated and articulated system of beliefs, rituals, and practitioners, organized at the household, the village, and the regional levels. Unlike Buddhism, *nat* religion is not a literate tradition—it has no sacred writings—nor is it a world religion—*nat* religion is practiced only in Burma. "Resting on a complex mythological charter, the *nat* cultus consists of an elaborated ritual system under the supervision of socially recognized cult leaders and practitioners. Although, from the Burmese point of view, the *nat* cultus does not constitute a religion, the fact remains that it rivals Buddhism in its elaborate cognitive, ceremonial, and organizational systemization" (Spiro 1967, 40). Buddhism and *nat* religion present radically different belief systems, yet there is little conflict between the two because canonical Buddhism recognizes the existence of spirits and demons, and sanctions their propitiation (Spiro 1971, 4).

Spiro's fieldwork was carried out in 1961–62 in a rural village in Upper Burma approximately 10 miles from the city of Mandalay. Spiro discovered that almost half the men but none of the women claimed not to believe in *nats*. Men and women agreed that women are more involved in *nat* propitiation, that women fear the *nats* more, and that women perform more *nat* rituals. Village *nat* shrines are almost always tended by women, and village *nat* ceremonies are attended almost exclusively by women. Shamans, who become possessed by *nats,* are almost all women. Women also bow to *nats,* while men do not. Villagers explained this difference in terms of the different status of men and women: within the [Buddhist] thirty-one abodes of existence men occupy a higher position than *nats;* women occupy a lower position. Thus women are more susceptible to attack by *nats* than men are. At major *nat* festivals, which attract thousands of people, women outnumber men by at least twenty to one (Spiro 1967, 123).

Every household gives offerings to the *nat* inherited through the mother's matriline and to the *nat* inherited through the father's patriline. According to June Nash (1966), if the parent's *nats* differ, the mother's *nat* is more likely to be inherited than the father's *nat*.[7] Women are more concerned than men about propitiating *nats,* and it is women who give all the food offerings to the *nats*. Men, who are more involved in Buddhism, tend to either cease believing in *nats* or to believe that Buddhism gives them power to overcome the power of the *nats*. Typically, a woman assumes the responsibility for *nat* offerings when her mother, old and dying, pleads with her to carry on the propitiation or beware of the *nat's* wrath.

Although both men and women are involved in both Buddhism and *nat* religion, men are more identified with Buddhism and women with *nat* religion. Even more to the point, specialists in Buddhism (monks) are exclusively male, and *nat* shamans are overwhelmingly (although not exclusively) female. In Burma, almost all male children enter Buddhist monasteries as novitiates for a number of years (usually during adolescence). The time spent in the monastery strengthens men's ties to and knowledge of Buddhism, and reinforces women's perception of Buddhism as belonging to men more than to women. The Buddhist leaders with whom Burmese are acquainted—the monks and teachers—are men.

Spiro believes that Buddhism is the most important cultural force in the Burmese village. Buddhist devotions, holy days, and pilgrimages are observed by almost all villagers. In fact, Buddhism and *nat* religion are so well intertwined that the household *nat* also receives an offering at the ceremony of initiation of boys into the Buddhist monastic order, and, when disaster strikes, a ritual to propitiate the village *nat* may be combined with rituals performed by Buddhist monks. During the rice harvest one of the women of the work group performs a *nat* propitiation ritual for protection against snakes. Immediately afterwards, one of the men leads the group in the worship of a particular Buddha image believed to have the power to cure snake bites (Spiro 1967, 249). In many cases Buddhist and *nat* shrines are adjacent to one another.

On the other hand, the *nats* can be understood as symbolizing opposition to authority; when people participate in *nat* rituals they are, on the unconscious level, expressing their dissatisfaction with official Buddhism. Burmese often feel that Buddhist moral requirements are too strict, and that the consequences of violating Buddhist precepts are too severe. It is significant that *nat* myths often involve anti-Buddhist themes: disobeying Buddhist monks, honoring sensuality.

Spiro has developed a comparative model that highlights some of the central differences between *nat* religion and Buddhism. Whereas Buddhism emphasizes a moral code (right speech, right conduct, etc.), *nats* punish those who offend them regardless of the moral state of the individual, and the charter myths of the individual *nats* have nothing to do with moral behavior. Buddhism, deeply ascetic, teaches that attachment (to people, possessions, one's own body, etc.) is the cause of suffering and that the way to eliminate suffering is to eliminate attachment. *Nat* religion is absolutely involved in this world—with this-worldly passions, this-worldly desires, and this-worldly relationships. Whereas the Buddhist monk renounces sexuality, sexual intercourse with a *nat* is the path to becoming a *nat* shaman. For Buddhists, liberation means dis-attachment from this world; Buddhism teaches that one should abandon family, wealth, glory, comfort. *Nats,* on the other hand, are propitiated solely for worldly ends—health and livelihood; *nats* and *nat* rituals are not concerned with salvation.

At the beginning of the eleventh century King Anawrahta tried to suppress the *nat* cult and enforce Buddhism as the state religion. He did not succeed in eradicating the *nat* cult, but did institutionalize it by appointing the Thirty-Seven "official" *nats,* and establishing a Buddhist *nat* as their overlord.

Both *nat* religion and Buddhism are deeply embedded within Burmese culture. Overlaps occur, but the two religious systems have remained distinct, and neither shows any signs of dying out. However, the two religions are not of equal status—Buddhism is consistently seen as more powerful. Observing Buddhist precepts renders one less vulnerable to harm by the *nats*. Monks are venerated, while shamans may be subject to ridicule and critique. The higher status of Buddhism, coupled with the belief that Buddhism offers magical protection even stronger than that offered by *nat* propitiation, leads one to wonder why *nat* religion continues to flourish. While I cannot provide a complete answer to that question, I would at least like to raise the possibility that the tenacity of *nat* religion lies in the dominant role of women as opposed to women's secondary role in Buddhist rituals.

Korean Shamanism and Household Religion

The Korean religious milieu includes Confucianism, Buddhism, Christianity, and numerous new religions—all dominated by men—and the indigenous household religion—which is the province of women. Women's religion, often called "superstition" or "shamanism," is sometimes considered to be everything that is not Confucian, Buddhist, or Christian. Some of its rituals are led by a shaman, and some are carried out by women alone at home. I will refer to this religious complex as shamanism or women's household religion. Korean shamanism, dominated by women, is a "professional elaboration upon Korean household religion" (Kendall 1983, 166); shamans are the experts in household religion. The Korean shaman is an accepted and recognized religious professional.

Youngsook Kim Harvey contends that in Korea, "The predominant religion is shamanism, despite its lack of organization, coherent doctrine, the outcast status of its practitioners, and a long history of official suppression extending back at least to the fourteenth century" (1976, 189). Shamanism is in practice supported by the majority of Koreans. To get a sense of the extent of shamanism, Harvey (1976) cites a 1932 source that estimates one shaman per 300 residents in P'yongyan, then the second largest urban center. According to a 1972 survey there was one shaman for every 314 people in Korea. A 1982 survey showed that there was only 1 Protestant minister per 1000 people and even fewer Buddhist monks than Protestant ministers (Suh 1989). Despite modernization, urbanization, the proliferation of new religions, and organized suppression of shamanism, shamans remain popular in Korea, and there is evidence that in urban areas their popularity is even increasing.

Women's household religion has received little scholarly attention, yet it is clearly a mainstream and pervasive phenomenon. Lacking ecclesiastical buildings and written doctrines, the religion is centered around the individual person of the shaman. "Scholars of Korean shamanism carefully avoid the term "religion" in defining the *mudang* [shaman] phenomenon . . . but . . . despite its lack of teachings or doctrines, . . . [it] still deserves to be called a religion. . . . It is the basic religious mindset of the Korean people" (Suh 1989, 6–7). In Korean women's household religion, the senior housewife (and because most families live neolocally, almost all women become senior housewives) honors the household gods. Similarly, village women bargain with the gods on behalf of the entire community. Larger rituals are presided over by shamans. At an elaborate ritual, *kut*, the costumed shaman is possessed by a succession of ghosts and ancestors. The job of the Korean shaman is to seek out the gods, engage them in conversation, lure them into houses, and bargain with them. She is an independent practitioner and does not collaborate with any sort of male religious functionary (Kendall 1985). Among the reasons for consulting shamans are to communicate with and placate ancestral spirits, to pick auspicious days for weddings and funerals, and to divine causes of illness, misfortune, and family discord.

Almost all Koreans who consult and hire shamans are women, and women are the most numerous and enthusiastic participants at shaman rituals. At these rituals most participants are women over the age of forty (Janelli and Janelli 1982). Not only the client but also her neighbors and friends actively participate in the shaman's *kut*. The women spend small amounts of money on divinations, they dance, and they form a concerned chorus (Kendall 1985). While this is going on, men gather in other rooms to drink and make derisive jokes about "superstitious women" (Wilson 1983, 124). Korean women sometimes hide from their husbands their involvement (particularly financial) with shamanism.

Male opposition to shamanism is sometimes merely a pose, and when very ill or suffering from prolonged misfortune, many men are perfectly happy to have their wives turn to shamans. Kendall stresses that Korean women and shamans and their rituals are not at odds with men and their goals. Shamans and housewives accept the values of Confucian society: children should respect elders, the living should honor ancestors, sons should be born. "This is often not the case, however, and shamans provide not only explanations but therapies" (1989, 141). It is crucial to understand how closely the various religious streams are woven together. "The same informant might worship at Buddhist temples, visit shaman shrines, and set down rice cake for the household gods" (Kendall 1983, 35). Buddhism, unlike Christianity, Judaism, and Islam, does not make an official demand of exclusive allegiance from its followers. In many Buddhist countries, other religions co-exist alongside, and sometimes intimately intertwined with, Buddhism. Many Korean Buddhists avail themselves of shamans, and even visit Christian churches of various denominations without feeling a conflict of loyalty. According to Kendall, Korean women see the rituals in the shaman's shrine and the offerings they make at the Buddhist temple as parallel. The prayers women make at Buddhist temples and shaman's shrines are the same: for the children, health, and a peaceful family life (1983a, 84).

Northern Thai Matrilineal Spirit Cults

In Northern Thailand groups of matrilineally related kin—people who are "of the same spirit"—make ritual food offerings to spirits known as *phii puu njaa*. *Phii puu njaa* are tutelary spirits who have been inherited from matrilineal ancestors who once served them. According to Cohen and Wijeyewardene, "We are justified in treating the *phii puu njaa* cult as a single cluster of institutional activity" (1984, 250). Since the ethnographic literature reports considerable variations both in cult group rituals and in Northern Thai social structure, the following paragraphs should be seen as an attempt to summarize in a very general way the nature and role of matrilineal spirit cults in the context of Northern Thai family and village life. For specific villages some of these remarks do not hold true.

"The role of women as custodians of the house spirit cult is one aspect of a more general association between women and domestic spirits. Every woman possesses a certain mystic essence, sometimes called a spirit (*phii*) and sometimes a *teewadaa*, which derives from her house and ultimately from her cult group spirit" (Davis 1984, 266). Thai matrilineal spirits are believed to reside in the female body and to succeed from a mother to her daughters. The spirits lodged in a woman's body would be violated if she were to have sex or any bodily contact with an outside man. A man giving money to propitiate his wife's spirits is the crucial element of marriage ceremonies.

"The [Northern Thai] matrifocal kinship system was legitimized by a belief in protector (territorial) spirits . . . . This spirit cult demanded one woman per family to reside in her household until the end of her life to take care of her domestic ancestral spirits. . . . Through this custom, kinship lineages evolved around the female members of related families" (Tantiwiramanond and Pandey 1987, 137).

The ritual constellation surrounding the *phii puu njaa* takes place within the context of extended family groups, also referred to as cult groups. All the matrilineal descendants of a founding ancestress constitute a cult group. Men are formally members of their mothers' groups, but in some families husbands join their wives' cult groups. The median size of the descent group (cult group) is four households (with a range of 1–24). The groups never seem to be more than six generations in depth, and the oldest ancestors remembered are typically a set of sisters. Ideally, the group spirit is lodged in a shrine located in a house site containing the original house, in which a female member of the senior generation currently lives. This woman is both descent group head and ritual officiant.

While in a very few ethnographic accounts men appear as ritual officiants of cult groups, most ethnographers have reported that older women officiate at all cult rituals. (A man, however, may fill in as cult leader after the death of the previous woman leader and until an appropriate young woman of the next generation comes of age.) Typically, men, having little to do with the cults, claim that they are women's business.

There has been scholarly disagreement as to the function of the cults: Some say that the primary function of the cults is to allocate rights to land, and the ritual aspects are secondary. Others argue that the cults serve(d) as an institution of social control, and especially of controlling female sexuality. Andrew Turton contends that descent groups and their cults have important jural and symbolic, rather than economic, functions. He quotes a village headman: "Even within the memory of my mother there were no officials, no law . . . not even a village headman, no single leader, only the old men . . . then the *phii puu yaa* (descent group spirits) were the law . . . though not really law, it was mutual respect" (1976, 214).

In recent times many Northern Thai men and women have moved away from their villages to urban centers. Ethnographers have found that adult women who have moved away from their natal villages and from the authority of their parents remain under the control of their cult group spirits.

In the cities, professional women spirit mediums have begun to replace female family cult leaders. In many instances these mediums claim to be possessed by their own ancestral spirits, thereby guaranteeing the continuation of the traditional cults (Irvine 1984, 316). Gehan Wijeyewardene believes that this contemporary mediumship "had its institutional anchor in the matrifocal spirit cults, though there is no reason to suppose that its practice was confined to these cults" (1986, 153). Although urban mediumship is not an obvious or spectacular phenomenon, most urban Northern Thai probably know how to find a spirit medium, and some people are acquainted with several. During the ninth lunar month groups of women (and some men) get together and dance in public. This festival, according to Wijeyewardene, "establishes the institution as a public, culturally sanctioned one, rather than some vaguely illicit, private practice" (1986, 223).

Although Thais have traditionally been tolerant of other religions, Buddhism is the official religion of Thailand, and the Thai king is required by the constitution to be a Buddhist. In Thailand, as in Burma, the Buddhist temple is the symbolic center of village life, monks are the most prestigious residents of the village, the annual cycle is structured around Buddhist festivals and ritual events, and contributions to monks and the temple take a significant amount of village money.

Buddhism defines women as inherently lower in religious status than men. Women are excluded from the *sangha* (community of monks), while many Thai men become monks, or at least novices, for some portion of their lives. Whereas a man's major merit-making act (in Buddhist terms) is ordination, a woman's is giving a son for ordination. The rationale for excluding Thai women from Buddhist monastic orders is the fear that women would lead holy men astray. In this system, monks are always meritorious whereas the laity are always deficient in merit. This compels the laity (especially women) to be economically active in order to have enough to give food to the monks, whereas monks are exempt from economic activity. Monks welcome women's economic support, but are suspicious of their sexual and reproductive powers. The belief that a son as a monk can accrue special merit for his parents (especially his mother) means that sons and daughters in a family are treated differently. The son is excused from household chores while girls are expected to be active in the house. Sons are given greater consideration. Daughters are taught to serve and yield to elders and males. Being a mother or wife does not give one merit. A mother gains supreme merit only when her son is ordained. Tantiwiramanond and Pandey refer to this as a "merit trap" for women, inducing women to become mothers of sons and depreciating women's economic contributions (1987, 131). A son could repay his debt to his parents by becoming a monk. A daughter could repay this debt only by being a lifelong caretaker of her parents.

Because women were deprived of entry into monasteries, they were also deprived of literacy, which until the twentieth century was acquired only in Buddhist monasteries. Lack of literacy meant lack of access to knowledge of medicine, arts, and lack of social mobility and political participation. "Buddhism became a legitimizing agent for the Thai patriarchy to affirm and sanction the role of women which was limited to reproduction and economic production" (Tantiwiramanond and Pandey 1987, 132). Although women are seen as being on a lower plane of karma than men, in many other ways laymen and women are not greatly differentiated in Theravada Buddhism, and the distinction between male and female appears to be less important in old age as sexual activities wane.

Thai women are very involved in economic activity. Thomas Kirsch (1985) interprets this as reflecting women's lower status in Buddhism; economic activity is one more symptom of being "rooted" in the world. Charles Keyes (1984), on the other hand, argues that popular Buddhist texts portray women as inherently good, especially as mothers. Through their personal experiences of the loss of lovers and children, women are more easily able to understand Buddhist teaching. Kirsch, in return, contends that women's attachment to their children has a negative valuation in Buddhist ideology. According to Tantiwiramanond and Pandey, Buddhism has played a crucial role in subordinating women. "Through religion, women internalized a view of themselves as the subordinate sex in society. A woman not only had to become a mother—to provide fresh labor for the subsistence agricultural system—but also had to bear at least one son—in order to be eligible for 'extreme merit' " (1985, 142).

Wijeyewardene (1970; 1977) contrasts the inner shrine in the Buddhist monastery in which monks conduct rituals from which laymen (and all women) are excluded, with the spirit cult shrine located in the eldest woman's bedroom from which unrelated males are excluded. He believes that the spirit cults are a female response to the male domination of the monastic Buddhism and to Thai ideas about female pollution. However, since there is no reason to believe that Buddhism predates the matrilineal spirit cults (indeed, the opposite is more likely), we can equally well argue that the ease with which Buddhism conquered Thailand constituted a male response to the female domination of household religion.[8]

In a fascinating study, Steven Piker (1972) has looked at how Thai individuals deal with the conflicting beliefs of Thai spirit religion and Buddhism. He found that most people feel that the two sets of beliefs are coherent. One of the most common ways that Thai villagers reconcile conflicting beliefs is by saying that they themselves are not learned in Buddhism and that if one wants to understand these questions one should go to the city and ask the really learned monks.[9]

NORTH AMERICA

The second culture area in which women's religions cluster is North America, specifically during the nineteenth and twentieth centuries. The confluence of a variety of historical and cultural factors has given rise to this cross-culturally rather anomalous situation.

To begin with, neolocal living arrangements combined with high geographic mobility have meant that Americans tend to live outside the sort of closed and powerful extended family groups that could perpetuate kinship-based religions. Individual Americans, including individual women, are relatively free to join new religions. In addition, the cultural pluralism of America has resulted in a situation in which individuals are aware that other people believe in different religions than they themselves do. Unlike in isolated villages or tribes, people know that their own beliefs and rituals are not the only ones that exist.

The well-documented "feminization of American religion" that took place in the nineteenth century has meant that American women are inclined to see religion as their own sphere of action (Welter 1966). Nineteenth-century women's religions grew out of a century of evangelical revivalism that spoke of women's superior moral qualities. It bears emphasizing that in contemporary American culture, religion in general is seen as women's sphere. Studies show that American women are more religious than men both in terms of church attendance and personal faith and commitment to orthodox beliefs (Argyle and Beit-Hallahmi 1975, 71–79). While the feminization of religion is clearly rooted in European religious experience (see Desan 1990), the institutionalization of the process is more characteristic of American religion.

Both in the nineteenth and twentieth centuries the growth of feminism has parallelled the development of women's religions in the United States. It is not surprising that feminist political awareness is reflected in feminist religious awareness.

Christian Science

After decades of struggling with illness and marital difficulties, Mary Baker Eddy discovered the central tenet of Christian Science: The world as we see it with our physical senses is illusory.[10] Therefore, sickness and suffering are illusory. Once the individual understands that this is so, his or her sickness and suffering will disappear. Women have been the majority of Christian Scientists since its founding by Eddy during the second half of the nineteenth century.

Christian Science rejected the Calvinist theology of its day, which emphasized final judgment, endless punishment of sinners and nonbelievers, predestination, and the salvation of only a select few. Christian Science sees itself as part of the Judeo-Christian tradition, and relies heavily on Biblical interpretation. The God of Christian Science is the God of the Bible, and Christian revelation is accepted as true.

Christian Scientists believe that people are already perfect; there is no need for a future salvation. Through Christian Science people are awakened to an understanding of the perfection that is already theirs as children of God. The function of Christian Science ritual is to demonstrate that perfection. People under the illusion that matter is real cannot break with this illusion on their own; they need a mediator to awaken them from their false belief. Jesus was one such mediator, but Christ as the ideal of humankind was not confined to Jesus. Jesus was unusual in that he fully embodied the Christ, but everyone is capable of attaining what Jesus attained. Christian Science endeavors to be a very rational religion; its belief system is "proven" through successful spiritual healing.

In the early years female practitioners (healers) of Christian Science outnumbered males by about five to one (Gottschalk 1973). In the United States of 1926, 55.7% of members of all churches were women, yet 75% of Christian Scientists were women (Stark and Bainbridge 1985, 237). In the United States during the 1950s 87.7% of Christian Science practitioners were women (mostly married women, Wilson 1961, 198). Through the 1950s Christian Science church attendance was made up of more than twice as many women as men (Wilson 1961, 199). A more recent study found the ratio of female to male practitioners to be 8:1 (Fox 1989, 100).

Recruitment to Christian Science is through conversion; even those raised in the faith must make a deliberate decision to accept or reject the religion. There is a formal membership process in Christian Science, and members cannot belong to any other denominations. Christian Science realizes that healing is its best advertisement and its best way of recruiting members. Since the early twentieth century most members have been middle class. Stephen Gottschalk has explicated the affinity between Christian Science and American middle-class beliefs that a person can control his or her own destiny, that it is wrong to submit to undesirable conditions, and that achievement and upward mobility are highly desirable.

A recurrent pattern throughout Christian history has been the labeling of new movements as heretical. Accusations of heresy often coincide with the condemnation of active participation and leadership of women in these movements (e.g., Montanism). Christian Science, especially in the early days, was vehemently opposed by Protestant clergy; it was accused by the medical profession of harming people's health; and Eddy herself was often the target of personal abuse.

As I will later show, Christian Science differs from almost all other women's religions in several ways: Its belief system is complex and unconditionally obligatory, it is based on a large written literature, and the church organization is highly centralized.

Shakers

In 1742 a group known as the Shakers emerged from the multilayered spiritual environment of eighteenth-century England. The early Shakers attracted the local proletariat, particularly from the textile mills of Lancaster. In 1758 Ann Lee, born into a working-class family in Manchester, joined the Shakers, and by 1770 assumed a leadership role. In 1774, having received a vision promising that the millennial church would be established in New York, she took a small group of followers with her and left England for the New World. Believing Ann Lee to be the Savior, in 1776 the Shakers founded a community near Albany. Both in England and in the United States the Shakers were persecuted for their religious beliefs.

Shakers believed the End of Days to be imminent. They saw proof for this in the socioeconomic upheavals of the late eighteenth century, and in the revelation of Ann Lee as the second coming of Christ. They emphasized religious experience instead of doctrine or creed; Shakers were famous for their emotionally stirring and physically active forms of worship (dancing and shaking). In the early years, Shakers made use of the emotional shock brought about by the unveiling of personal secrets. Sermons dealt at length with the regions of darkness in which lost souls suffered in agony.

Shaker communities grew during the late eighteenth and nineteenth centuries, yet Shakerism never became a mass movement. The rural communities served as the ideological, spiritual, and organizational centers of the Shaker religion, although not all Shaker believers renounced their former lives and went to live in Shaker communities. Within these communities, Shaker "brethren" and "sisters" were organized into "families" or administrative units of between thirty and one hundred members, each of which was governed by two male elders and two female eldresses.

Based on records kept by the American Shakers, we have some picture of who joined their agricultural communities. "Though they embraced a radical gospel of millennarian perfectionism, the Shakers were not a dispossessed or socially deviant constituency. . . . sectarian beliefs could appeal to a representative cross section of rural New England society" (Marini 1982, 96). From the perspective of gender, however, it is clear that the Shaker way was not equally appealing to everyone. Whereas almost equal numbers of men and women **joined** the Shakers, far more women than men **remained** in the communities for long periods of time (Foster 1981; Stein 1992).[11] Thus, the reality was that Shaker women outnumbered Shaker men by approximately 2:1 (Desroche 1971, 131), and in some communities there were less than half a dozen brethren between the ages of eighteen and forty-five (Brewer 1992, 630). Shaker communities underwent demographic changes over time, and the unbalanced gender ratio became much more pronounced as the years went on. It is likely that while Shaker theology was equally attractive to men and women, the neat, safe, and ordered life-style was particularly compelling for women. In addition, it may be that the Shakers consciously sought greater female than male membership. William Sims Bainbridge raises the provocative possibility that as the Shakers came to realize that many boys and men would defect, they began to accept fewer and fewer males (1982, 360).

Shaker ideology explicitly addressed issues of gender inequality. They developed a dual form of leadership, with a man and a woman at every level of the hierarchy. In addition, they believed that celibacy would contribute to the breakdown of women's subordination.

Ann Lee was the leader of the Shakers until her death in 1783. After her death, leadership was taken over by men, James Whittaker from 1784 until 1787, and Joseph Meacham from 1787 until 1796. This pattern—the founding of a new religion by a charismatic woman and then institutionalized leadership by men—is a common one in the history of religions. In the case of the Shakers, however, female leadership was resumed in 1796 by Lucy Wright, who retained leadership until her death twenty-five years later. Following Wright, there was no one single leader, either male or female, but rather groups of men and women who led the Society. At certain times, male leadership was in ascendancy. From 1876 onwards, women played increasingly prominent roles in the Society's leadership. During the twentieth century, "Shaker women began to dominate nearly every aspect of the society's life" (Stein 1992, 256).

The mid- to late nineteenth-century religious climate in the United States did not encourage large groups of people to seek radical religious alternatives, and Shaker membership accordingly declined from the mid-nineteenth century on. Because of the celibate Shaker life-style, Shaker membership was limited to adults who had actively chosen to join the Shakers, and to children who were brought by their parents to Shaker communities. Many of these children left the Shakers after adulthood (Stein 1992). Shakerism thrived as long as its religious vision and economic organization appealed to segments of the American and English population. Peak membership was reached in the mid-nineteenth century at nearly 4000 members (Bainbridge 1982).

It is tempting to compare Shakerism to Christian Science—both are Christian-derived religions founded by English-speaking women. A closer look, however, shows some interesting differences. Shakers, unlike Christian Scientists, advocated celibacy and pacifism. Shakers lived in isolated communities where all property was communally owned; Christian Science encouraged its members to mix with the world. Shaker communities were in rural areas, while most Christian Scientists have been urban dwellers. The Shakers attracted mostly (although not exclusively) poor and working-class members, while Christian Science membership has tended to be middle class. Whereas Christian Science provides means of overcoming problems met with in this world, Shakerism prevents its followers from encountering such problems by living in utopian communities. Shakers emphasize the millennium while Christian Science emphasizes healing (see Klein 1979). And finally, the Shakers have all but disappeared while Christian Science still thrives.

Feminist Spirituality and Womanist Theology

Writing about the contemporary Feminist Spirituality Movement(s) of North America and Western Europe is an extraordinarily complex task. As a religious system it is quite new (it began in the 1970s) and still evolving. There are no official sacred texts, no absolute leaders, no required affirmations of faith, no membership dues, and no undisputed agenda of beliefs and rituals. Feminist Spirituality encourages and accepts as valid and legitimate the inspirations, dreams, visions, experiences, and interpretations of individual women. In contrast to many other women's religions that lack self-generated literature (as opposed to studies conducted by outsiders), Feminist Spirituality is an exceptionally prolific religious movement; its corpus of literature includes novels, diaries, descriptions of rituals, sacred histories, and philosophical treatises. Yet none of these writings is considered canonical. The theological and ritual focus of Feminist Spirituality is the celebration of womanhood.

Because women active in the Movement are aware that they are creating a new religion, one of their most important challenges is the search for authenticity. On the one hand, Feminist Spirituality roots its claims for authenticity in the academy: archeology (statues of ancient goddesses), anthropology (studies of primitive cultures in which women are less oppressed than in modern society), history (reports of persecution of women throughout the ages), literary analysis (of books by women authors), and psychology (Kristeva, Jung, Melanie Klein, and others). The very eclectic literature of the Feminist Spirituality Movement has delved into symbols from African religions, African-American traditions, and the Ancient Near East. On the other hand, Spiritual

Feminists focus their search for authenticity on women's dreams, fantasies, intuitions, and direct revelations and encounters with the sacred.

A second challenge faced by the Feminist Spirituality Movement has been to negotiate the relationship between religion and politics. The Movement is clearly a **feminist** (as opposed to women's) movement, and in many groups political action, especially around issues of ecology and women's rights, is perceived as having spiritual elements. Simultaneously, celebrating and strengthening womanhood through rituals is seen as preparing women for political action.

Just as it is difficult to point to a static set of beliefs and rituals and call them "Feminist Spirituality," it is difficult to point to a particular group of women and call them "Spiritual Feminists." A large core of Spiritual Feminists identify themselves as witches and belong to organized covens. Other Spiritual Feminists belong to ritual or study groups that do not identify with Wicca (witch) religion. To further complicate matters, many women who feel a sense of identity with the Spiritual Feminist Movement have retained affiliation with the Jewish or Christian group in which they were raised. Such women would be likely to participate in both Feminist rituals and Jewish or Christian rituals, and to work at effecting feminist change within mainstream Jewish or Christian denominations. Although no one really knows how many Spiritual Feminists there are, Solovitch (1990) has estimated that they number about 100,000 in the United States today.[12]

The Feminist Spirituality Movement offers women rituals celebrating the female life cycle: menarche, first orgasm, birth, and menopause. Other rituals reflect the cycle of nature, and the winter and summer solstices and autumn and spring equinoxes are celebrated by many Spiritual Feminist groups. Starhawk's *Truth or Dare* (1987) includes rituals for building community and rituals for self-knowledge and conquering fear, a ritual for healing from abuse, a body praise ritual, and a ritual of preparation for political struggle.

Parallel to the Feminist Spirituality Movement—which has attracted mostly white and middle-class women—the Womanist Movement has developed among black women.[13] Cheryl Sanders offers the following succinct definition of Womanism: "The womanist is a black feminist who is audacious, willful and serious; loves and prefers women, but also may love men; is committed to the survival and wholeness of entire people, and is universalist, capable, all loving, and deep" (1989, 86).

Womanist theology draws on secular feminism, Christianity, the writings of Alice Walker (author of *The Color Purple*), and African-American folk culture. Unlike white Feminist Spirituality, which is often separatist and anti-male, Womanism affirms black women's "historic connection with men through love and through a shared struggle for survival and for productive quality of life" (Williams 1989, 182). Womanism gives black women the freedom to explore their own history and culture, without being constrained by what white feminists have already identified as women's issues.[14]

Both Feminist Spirituality and Womanism differ from contemporary mainstream Christianity and from American civil religion in several ways. These women's religions embrace non-materialistic value systems, de-centralized organizations, on-going revelation, and female images of divinity.

Spiritualism

Spiritualism, like Feminist Spirituality and Korean household religion, is difficult to pin down. To begin with, Spiritualists are infamous for being unable or unwilling to form a permanent organization to which all Spiritualist groups belong. In addition, a number of somewhat different religious streams in North and South America and in Europe call themselves "Spiritualists." In this chapter I focus primarily on the popular and vibrant Spiritualist movement of nineteenth-century North America. In addition, I draw upon studies of contemporary North American and British Spiritualist groups, and of contemporary Mexican Spiritualism. The core belief of all these groups is that spirits of the dead can communicate with the living. The central rituals are seances at which this communication is carried out.

The founding of Spiritualism as a popular movement is usually said to have occurred in March 1848 when Kate and Margaret Fox, two young sisters who lived on a New York farm, heard loud rappings emanating from within their house. They attributed the rappings to the spirit of a murdered traveling salesman. Although the founding of Spiritualism may be traced to a discrete event, Spiritualist phenomena spread spontaneously throughout large parts of the United States and England. In the half century after the Fox sisters heard their rappings, hundreds of thousands of individuals, mostly women, gathered in private homes and in public lecture halls, and witnessed the ability of some human beings to communicate with the spirit world. Since most people who attended Spiritualist rituals did not belong to any kind of organization, it is not possible to know how many Spiritualists there were during the mid-nineteenth century. Estimates ranged from 1 to 11 million (Moore 1977, 14). When Spiritualism spread to England, it became even more popular than in the United States. There was intense opposition to Spiritualism from Christian ministers, doctors, and scientists. Physicians looked as Spiritualism as an illness. Opponents of Spiritualism were preoccupied both with supposed fraudulence in Spiritualist performances, and with the evil inherent in summoning the dead.

In the beginning Spiritualism was not a full-fledged religion—it presented no new theology. In fact, it was seen primarily as a new scientific innovation—similar to the telegraph. But in response to opposition from Christian denominations, it began to develop a coherent theology. Spiritualist beliefs boil down to two key notions: The human personality survives the death of the body, and it is possible to communicate with the spirits of the dead.

Geoffrey Nelson (1969) has itemized all the forms of spirit manifestations practiced by Spiritualists in 1860: rappings, spirit writing and drawing, trance and trance speaking, clairvoyance and clairaudience, luminous phenomena, spiritual impersonation (behaving with mannerisms of the departed), spirit music, visible and tactual manifestations, spirit intercourse by means of mirror or crystal or water, apparitions of the departed, visions and previsions, dreams, presentiments, spirit influx by which ideas are infused into the mind, speaking in tongues, and possession. Spiritualists see these manifestations as empirical proof of Spiritualist tenets.

Unlike most other religious denominations of the nineteenth century, Spiritualism afforded women equal authority and opportunities. Studies conducted at the time show that the majority of Spiritualist mediums were women, and the popular press portrayed male mediums as effeminate and confused (Moore 1977, 105). June Macklin (1977) found that in 1975 approximately 70% of Spiritualist mediums in the United States were women.

Ann Braude (1989) analyzes women's involvement with Spiritualism in light of the other religious options of the day. Although piety and morality were viewed as female traits, women were forbidden from preaching and sometimes even speaking in mainstream churches. Women could see that most people who attended church were female, but the church leaders were male. In contrast, "If, during a seance, a woman became the principal actor, the instigator and director of the proceedings, it was because she was thought to possess not only genuine spiritual power but also the right to exercise it. Spiritualism validated the female authoritative voice and permitted women an active professional and spiritual role largely denied them elsewhere" (Owen 1981, 6).

During the nineteenth century Spiritualism was popular among the educated and among religious skeptics, as well as among former political radicals who had become disenchanted with the possibility of creating utopia in this world and began to look for utopia in the next. Mid-nineteenth-century Spiritualists tended to support abolition, temperance, women's rights, and social reform. By the end of the nineteenth century, Spiritualism had ceased functioning as a reform movement, those who cared for social reform left the movement, and Spiritualist societies became more and more conservative.

Spiritualist seances typically consist of women mediums helping women clients communicate with departed family members. Contact with the spirits is sought in order to request advice concerning earthly problems, and this aspect of Spiritualism has remained popular today in Great Britain and the United States. Spiritualism does not demand that its members forgo membership in other religions, and Spiritualist groups often choose not to meet on Sunday in order to allow their members to attend church with more conventional Christian denominations. In modern Spiritualist groups most members have been drawn in after having experienced some event that the person considers to be psychic.

In contemporary Mexican Spiritualism, women predominate as clients, healers, and leaders. Although their beliefs are similar to those of American and British Spiritualism, the ritual focus is more on healing than on conversational communication with the spirit world (Finkler 1985b). According to the head of one Spiritualist Temple in Mexico City, Spiritualism is "a total religion, we have our symbols, our laws, and our liturgy" (Finkler 1986, 629).

AFRICAN AND AFRICAN-AMERICAN RELIGIONS

The social and historical contexts of the African and African-American examples are different from those of either the East and Southeast Asian or the

North American examples. While it would be absurdly reductionist to make any sort of global claim about all of Africa, it does seem that a recurrent theme in the ethnographic literature on Africa is gender complementarity—the notion that men and women contribute to the preservation of society in different but equally important ways. Religiously, this often means that men and women have their own somewhat independent rituals, cults, or secret societies. I will present the Sande secret society of Sierra Leone as an example of this cultural pattern. Another characteristic of traditional African religion is its embeddedness in kinship organization and family relations. As we will see, this has rather different implications for men and women.

Knowing that the indigenous religions of Africa often offered opportunities for religious expression and leadership both to men and to women, it becomes interesting to follow the effects of various kinds of changes on this more-or-less egalitarian situation. Throughout much of Africa, Islam has now become the dominant religion. Parallel to growth of Islam with its almost total exclusion of women from Islamic rituals, in some parts of Islamicized Africa women have formed new, non-Islamic (albeit "marginal" in the eyes of male authorities) religious groups. Religious practices involving *zār* possession are the best-documented, yet far from sole, example of this pattern. A question that cannot be fully answered is to what extent women's possession cults (like the *zār*) are new responses to Islam, and to what extent they are leftover from pre-Islamic African religion (as in the model for Southeast Asia presented above). Writing about spirit possession among the Diga of south Kenya, Roger Gomm demonstrates that the traditional propitiation of nature spirits once involved both men and women, but is now almost solely a female concern (1975, 134). Similarly, there is good evidence that what is currently the almost all-female *bori* cult of the Hausa once was the mainstream religion that involved both men and women (Lewis et al. 1991). Although anthropologists and historians talk about the *zār* cult as having originated in Ethiopia during the past 200 years, spirit possession has a long history in Africa. What we may say with some assurance is that while the *zār* cult **in its present institutionalized and predominantly female form** is a new phenomenon, *zār*-type beliefs and practices are neither foreign nor innovative.

An equally interesting question concerns what happened to African religion in the wake of forcible transfer of slaves to America. While all slaves suffered oppression, violence, and culture clash, men and women experienced slavery in different ways. For example, women more often than men were victims of sexual assault. In many parts of America slavery led to the breakup of families, and men more than women were cut off from any sort of family life, while women and children were often able to maintain some semblance of family relationships. Given the embeddedness of traditional African religion in the family, slavery often meant that women more than men continued to observe religious rituals.

In the post-slavery period African-American men have often found it necessary to leave their families in order to obtain employment either in distant cities or as migrant laborers. Again, the result has been that women are more involved in both family and religion than are men.

Variations of this process took place in Brazil and among the Black Caribs of Belize. It is significant that in both these societies women are also more involved in Roman Catholic rituals than men. Like white North Americans, African-Americans perceive religion (whether female dominated or not) as a female enterprise. In contrast to East and Southeast Asia where new religions attracted men, thus leaving the indigenous religion in women's hands, economic necessity forced African-American men to withdraw from both the familial and religious realms, thus leaving religion (albeit syncretic rather than purely indigenous ones) in women's hands.

Sande

The Sande women's secret society exists under various names throughout West Africa, particularly in Liberia, Sierra Leone, the Ivory Coast, and Guinea. Among the Mende, Sherbro and Temne tribes of Sierra Leone nearly 95% of all women undergo initiation into Sande (Margai 1948). Among the Mende (and most likely among the other tribes in which Sande is present) the whole realm of the sacred is controlled by the secret societies. "Most observers of Mende society have been struck by the enormous weight secret societies carry in Mende life. . . . Like the medieval church, Poro [the men's secret society] and Sande provide sanctions for nearly every sphere of secular life. They embody and control supernatural power, lay down rules of conduct, and provide the major source of propitiation for transgressions of sacred and of secular law" (Cosentino 1982, 22).

During initiation rituals, Sande women gather for weeks or months in "bush schools," away from contact with nonmembers and men. Sande initiation is concerned with the cultural construction of fertility and reproduction. Adolescent girls are taught about childbirth, trained in household tasks, and encouraged to cooperate with other women. Sande teaches women what they need to know to function in their community: spinning, weaving, fishing, net making, house and mother craft, first aid, and medicinal herbs.

A central element of initiation is ritual clitoridectomy (see Chapter 6). Another is the appearance of a masked figure who is said to embody Sande spirit. "These masks are representations of spiritual and mythological symbols translated into wood and designed to express a spiritual message so complete that future generations can do no more than learn from its mysteries" (Richards 1973, 76).

Sande chapters are not unified into any sort of central organization. Each chapter owns secret knowledge that is passed on to initiates. Sande chapters also own ritual objects and medicine; that is, "physical substances with effective pharmacological properties and physical substances which link persons with sources of power in the universe" (MacCormack 1977, 95).

Girls are typically initiated into the Sande chapter in their mothers' villages, but, because post-marriage residence is virilocal, transfer to the chapter in the husband's village. Women try to return to their natal villages to give birth in the chapter in which they were initiated. "Sande spreads as women migrate, following marriage, to live virilocally with their husbands' people." (Mac-Cormack 1979, 28).

Women continue to participate in Sande activities throughout their lives. Older women especially may devote a great deal of time to Sande concerns. A men's secret society known as Poro exists in parallel to Sande, and both Poro and Sande leaders may have a great deal of power outside the secret society.

The available ethnographic descriptions of Sande suggest that Sande women do not see themselves as a formal congregation. On the other hand, Carol MacCormack discovered that Sande women in Lungi, Moyamba District, are buried in a great mound in the village. "The mound reminds inhabitants of the power of women to bless and succor, their power existing in unbroken continuity from the living to the ancestors" (1977, 95).

Sande has served as a power base for women both vis-à-vis their own menfolks who can be punished by Sande for infringement of Sande rules, and vis-à-vis outside authorities. For example, Sande women have organized to protest unfair taxes on a number of occasions (see Chapter 13).

Afro-Brazilian Religions

The rich and eclectic twentieth century Afro-Brazilian cults are the most renowned and best-documented examples of religions dominated by women. Known as Candomblé (in Bahia), Umbanda (in large metropolitan areas), Batuque (in Belem), Xango (in Recife), and Macumba (in the southern parts of Rio de Janeiro and Sao Paulo), the cults appeal primarily to women. Anthropologists consider these cults to be syncretic—synthesizing elements of African tribal religions, Amerindian religions, Catholicism, and Kardecism (French Spiritism). The various Afro-Brazilian religions differ among themselves, and I will point out some of the more interesting differences. They are, however, sufficiently similar to be treated as a group.

The most celebrated feature of these cults are public rituals in which mediums are possessed by supernatural beings from an eclectic retinue of African, Catholic, and Amerindian deities, spirits, and heros. Possession is attained through a variety of techniques, most notably dancing, and possessed mediums behave in the manner characteristic of the possessing spirit. What attracts most adherents to the religions is curing, and most people who attend Afro-Brazilian religious rituals do so in order to be healed of a variety of illnesses or misfortunes. There are many supporters or followers who visit cult centers, but never become mediums. These people approach the gods and saints who are incorporated in a medium, and ask for advice concerning particular problems. The petitioner is typically given elaborate instructions about herb baths and candle lighting, and told to make contributions to the medium or cult center.

Esther Pressel (1974; 1980) explains the widespread appeal of the Afro-Brazilian religions in light of the strong historical base of spirit possession religions in both Africa and the New World, the failure of medical facilities to keep pace with developments in other spheres of Brazilian society, and the failure of the elitist Catholic Church to meet the needs of people in the rapidly modernizing Brazil.

In fact, Afro-Brazilian religions do not seem to compete with the Church. Despite Brazil's official Catholicism, true Catholic belief is rather rare; the real religion of most people is Afro-Brazilian religion which **includes** Catholic influenced practices (Landes 1940). For example, mediums honor the saints who are adored by their chief *encantados* (spirits) and place pictures of these saints on their home shrines (Leacock and Leacock 1972). Over 90% of Brazilians are baptized in the Catholic Church, **and** over 50% of Brazilians are either spirit mediums or have attended sessions of spirit groups to obtain spiritual assistance. Babies are sometimes baptized in both Catholic and Afro-Brazilian rituals, and marriages are performed by both religions (Pressel 1974). Not surprisingly, the established Catholic Church is less concerned about the traditional lower-class Afro-Brazilian religions like Batuque and Candomble (as they are seen as part of the superstition of the ignorant poor) and more bothered by the religions that attract the educated middle class (like Umbanda).

John Burdick (1990) has compared the appeal of Umbanda, Pentecostalism, and Roman Catholicism for urban Brazilian women. (Most of his comparisons are true for other Afro-Brazilian religions as well.) Whereas Umbanda and Pentecostalism attract women seeking help with domestic problems, women claim that Catholic priests cannot understand their problems because celibate men do not know anything about domestic life. In addition, Catholic church groups are based in the local neighborhoods, so if a woman shares her problem with the Church group all her neighbors will know and gossip about her. The Church tends to blame people rather than supernatural forces for domestic conflict, a viewpoint that easily leads to acrimonious relationships and guilt feelings. The association of poor Brazilian women with the Church is further weakened by contemporary liberation theology stressing societal rather than individual problems, thus ignoring the day-to-day needs of most Brazilian women. Finally, Marian devotion encourages resignation to suffering, an existential stance many Brazilian women find unappealing.

Pentecostalism and Umbanda, on the other hand, blame supernatural entities for domestic conflict, and provide clear means for coping (expelling the devil in Pentecostalism, spirit possession in Umbanda). Pentecostal and Umbanda rituals are gathering places for people with problems—everyone has problems—so people are not afraid that they will be gossiped about.

But whereas Pentecostal beliefs are absolute and dichotomized (God vs. the devil), Umbanda is ambiguous and multifaceted. In Umbanda humans can influence and bargain with the spirits, and the rituals and beliefs are flexible enough so that one can always find a culprit for one's problems. Whereas Pentecostalism preaches human weakness and total submission to God, Umbanda gives a woman magical tools to get revenge against those who have used the spirits to harm her.

A woman will sometimes ask for help in more than one religion. According to Burdick she is not simply "hedging her bets" or "shopping around." Rather, "In each place she can articulate her predicament in a slightly different way, emphasizing different aspects of the problem" (1990, 167). Catholicism nurtures perseverance, Pentecostalism "letting go," and Umbanda self-help.

The Afro-Brazilian religions documented in the ethnographic literature are composed primarily of women, and the extent to which men are involved varies from group to group. In general, in the more conservative (African) groups men have less of a role, in the newer groups (such as Umbanda) men are more involved. The first cult centers in Bahia were founded by women priestesses. And Lerch (1980) has documented that in Porto Alegre in 1974–75, 80–85% of mediums in Umbanda centers were women.[15]

A number of factors discourage men from becoming mediums. The strong Brazilian masculinity complex is not conducive to obedience to spirits and temple leaders. Women are believed to be "softer" or easier for possessing spirits to penetrate. In the more traditional Afro-Brazilian cults men are not supposed to become possessed at all, and the ritual dancing and singing are seen as feminine activities. There is a popular belief that male mediums are homosexuals (Pressel, 1974, claims that in fact this is probably not true, but people believe it anyway.) In addition, more men than women work at jobs with regular hours and so do not have the time to spend at sessions. When men do find spare time, they have other places (such as bars) to meet friends, whereas women are much more confined to their homes. Lastly, in Brazil all religion is seen as a feminine activity—even the Catholic Church has trouble recruiting enough priests.

Black Carib (Garifuna) Religion

Old women are the religious leaders of the Black Caribs of Belize.[16] Black Caribs, who constitute minority communities in Belize, Guatemala, Honduras, and Nicaragua, are descendants of African slaves and Carib Indians. Black Carib religion is a composite of African, Amerindian, and Roman Catholic elements. Middle-aged and old women dominate the religious life of the Black Caribs of Belize.

The kinship structure of Black Carib communities consists of matrifocal extended families, and households typically revolve around a woman, her daughter(s), and their children. Black Carib children are rarely reared exclusively by both biological parents. Fathers are frequently absent working as migrant wage laborers, and many grandmothers are involved in childcare on a daily basis. As women are "in charge of" kinship, they are also "in charge of" religion. According to Virginia Kerns, whose 1983 study is the best source on Black Carib kinship and religion, informants told her that anyone may take part in ritual—it is just that older women are "more interested" (1983, 167). Black Carib religious ritual is directly related to kinship. The greater part of Black Carib religion consists of rituals aimed at honoring, caring for or appeasing ancestors. The goodwill of ancestors is deemed as necessary to the well-being of descendants. "The ancestral cult . . . when considered in terms of its practical implications, and its role in preserving the traditions of the group, must be regarded as the core of the Black Carib system of belief" (Coelho 1955, 135).

Older women feel that it is their responsibility to perform rituals on behalf of their ancestors. Because a goal of ancestor ritual is to ensure that ancestors will not harm descendants, older women—who stand at the center of the generational chain—are pivotal ceremonial actors. Their ritual responsibility and expertise guarantee that children and grandchildren will be healthy and happy. Typical rituals involve singing, dancing, and feasting, and spirit possession by ancestors. According to Douglas Taylor's 1951 study, at mourning rituals, "The women . . . at a conservative estimate, outnumber the men in the proportion of four to one" (117).

Older Black Carib women are most knowledgeable about religious rituals, and organize and attend many rituals each year. These women have a great deal of autonomy in deciding how to spend their time and money, and they have access to other women on whom they may call for assistance in furnishing rituals. All these factors serve to strengthen the notion that women, and especially older women, are the most suitable ritual leaders.

Sorcery and magic are very much part of the Black Carib religious mind-set. Almost every act of everyday living is accompanied by some magical procedure, and "Every Carib uses some form of protection against sorcery" (Coelho 1955, 166). So-called "love magic" involves bodily secretions concealed in food served by women to men.

Before going on, I wish to clarify that "love magic" is the term used by outsiders and not necessarily by Black Carib women. As a feminist anthropologist, I reject this terminology for two important reasons. First, it implies that it is ontologically distinct from the ancestor religion described above. Yet although different ethnographers have written about the two ritual constellations, it seems to me that they are intrinsically related: both are focused on interpersonal relationships, utilize food in rituals, and are controlled by women. Second, in line with old-fashioned Durkheimian notions of magic versus religion, the words "love magic" imply private, trivial, and possibly even anti-social acts. However, according to the one ethnographer who has carefully recorded these practices, "[Love magic] is institutionalized and direct evidence [for it] is easily found. Practitioners solicit potential clients, the paraphernalia are occasionally seen, and much of the business of magic is simply not hidden. Indeed, to be effective it must have some public aspects" (Bullard 1974, 263). Like ancestor rituals, "love magic," according to Bullard, has a stabilizing influence on marriages and families. On the other hand, Virginia Kerns notes that her informants never spoke of these two sets of practices as being equivalent; in fact, her informants related to them as somewhat antithetical (personal communication 1992). In sum, my own inclination to merge ancestral rites and "love magic" is also somewhat problematic.

Most Black Caribs are Roman Catholics and receive some Catholic education. Knowledge of other spiritual matters is transmitted informally. All rituals for the dead, including Catholic ones, are perceived by Black Caribs as a totality—they are all intended to satisfy the dead and protect the living. The middle-aged and elderly women who are experts at ancestor rituals are also practicing Roman Catholics, and they do not seem to express conflict between

Roman Catholic dogma and their own beliefs. "The typical Carib virtues of flexibility and versatility enabled them to incorporate this non-Christian tradition into their Catholicism, thus achieving, despite the vigorous denunciations of the official representatives of the Church, a synthesis that comprises a coherent and unified body of doctrine" (Coelho 1955, 135).

Catholicism and Black Carib religion differ in terms of leadership (male vs. female), literacy (ancestor worship, unlike Catholicism, does not involve sacred texts), atmosphere at rituals (formal vs. informal), and organizational structure (Roman Catholicism is a centralized, hierarchical world religion, whereas Black Carib ancestor worship is a nonhierarchical, decentralized local religion).

Zār

The *zār* cult of North Africa and the Middle East is essentially women's business. Capricious spirits known as *zār* are prone to attack and possess women, especially married women, who then turn to cult leaders in order to be cured. *Zār* attack takes the form of illness with symptoms ranging from hysteria to physical disorders. Treatment consists of initiation into the *zār* cult, and the appeasement of the possessing spirit by the presentation of gifts to the patient. Treatment means reaching accommodation with the spirit—taming it—not exorcising it. A woman may go through a marriage ceremony with her *zār,* which means a permanent relationship of ritual responsibility. Once inducted into the cult group, the woman participates in ceremonies that promote possession-trance experience among its members, all of whom had been afflicted in the past. Members meet periodically to dance, feast, and incarnate their spirits. While the relationship with the spirit begins with illness, over the years the relationship should become one of complementarity and exchange.

In a Northern Sudanese village studied by Janice Boddy, more than 40% of women ever married and over the age of 15 have been possessed by *zār* spirits. Most afflicted women are between the ages of 35 and 55, two-thirds of whom have *zār* spirits. Thus, from a gynocentric perspective the *zār* cult is far from marginal. Very few men (perhaps 5% of all men) are *zār* adepts. Lucie Saunders (1977) found in her study of an Egyptian village that most women profess to believe in *zār* spirits, and most men profess not to. *Zār* possession is so fully identified with women that among the Egyptian Nubians if the *zār* cult patient is a man he is adorned as a female bride (Kennedy 1978).[17]

Participants in the *zār* cult tend to be individuals of secondary status within their cultural settings. Most scholars agree that the *zār* cult originated in central Ethiopia in the eighteenth century, and then was spread by slaves in Africa and the Middle East (Natvig 1987). Whether the cult is made up solely of women (Sudan), or whether it also includes poor and marginal men (Ethiopia), its members are people who lack access to most leadership or prestige roles in the society at large.

For the most part, the *zār* cult exists in Islamic cultures. (The *zār* also is popular in Ethiopia where most people are Christian and not Muslim.) It is crucial to bear in mind that all the formal roles of Islamic leadership are limited to men, and women are excluded from most important public religious rituals. On the other hand, there are aspects of religious life in which Muslim women are very active indeed. Lois Beck has argued that in those ritual complexes not formally required by Islamic law and tradition, "men do not participate with the intensity, nor in the numbers that do women" (1980, 39). Examples of arenas in which women are active include life-cycle celebrations, beliefs and rituals connected with early Islamic figures (such as Hussain and Fatima) and contemporary saints, pilgrimage to local tombs and shrines, curing and spirit possession cults, charity, and amulets. According to Jane Smith, "[Women's] unorthodox practices served both to further isolate women from the formal rituals of the Islamic community and to give them an arena in which they could feel comfortable and in control. Despite periodic efforts to 'clean up' such heterodox practices, they have been and continue to be a powerful part of the lives of many Muslims, especially women" (1987, 242).

Because women are neither assumed to be acquainted with Muslim liturgy and doctrines, nor expected to have the moral strength to uphold them, women tend to be relatively freer to embrace folk beliefs. In many Muslim societies women have been and continue to be the primary agents in the relationship of humans to the world of spirits; it is women who are experts at warding off evil spirits. Ethnographers have documented the existence of curing and spirit possession cults throughout Muslim societies. Women are active in many of these quasi-Muslim cults (such as the *zār* cult, the *fiqi* cult, and cults of saints) which are characterized by ecstatic and nonformalized rituals.

Women's *zār* activities serve as a counterpart to men's involvement in official Islamic religious practices. Yet while in certain senses complementary to Islamic practice, the *zār* cult is not equal in status to Islam (or Coptic Christianity in the case of Ethiopia). In the Northern Sudan (as elsewhere) the *zār* cult is periodically attacked by the male religious and secular elite. During the last 100 years, the *zār* cult has been described as "un-Islamic innovations," "bad traditions," "superstition," and "backward customs" (Constantinides 1982, 186). Janice Boddy's Northern Sudanese informants report that the *zār* cult became established in the Sudan at about the same time as Islam thoroughly penetrated the villages. (Although much of Africa had been formally Islamic for many centuries, it is only during this century that more than a thin veneer of Islam has penetrated the villages.) "The [*zār*] cult gained ground in virtual tandem with local Islamization" (Boddy 1989, 35). Thus we seem to be seeing a paradoxical situation in which *zār* spreads together with its main opponent. Both *zār* and orthodox Islam in Africa are responses to twentieth-century social changes.

While orthodox Islam condemns the *zār* cult for dealing with devils, opposition is moderated by the fact that *jinn* (spirits) are mentioned in the Koran. Although these *jinn* can be dispelled by reciting the opening of the Koran, because they occupy unexpected places individuals may still be attacked and thus require a *zār* ritual. *Zār* lore abounds with stories of government and religious leaders who attempted to repress the cult until their own womenfolk became seriously ill through *zār* possession. Then they were forced to agree to rituals being held in their very houses.[18]

Similarly, Simon Messing has found that the Coptic Abyssinian priests express passive resistance to the cult—they profess to condemn it but do little to counteract it. "This may be because many priests secretly believe in the cosmology of the *zār* themselves, particularly in spirits that are regarded as Coptic Christian" (1958, 1121).

The ethnographic literature indicates that there is a great deal of local variation regarding the status of the *zār* cult. Lucie Saunders found that in an Egyptian village *zār* was seen as so compatible with Islam that at the opening of public *zār* ceremonies a male leader would read out loud verses from the Koran. Cloudsley (1984), on the other hand, discovered that in Omdurman (Sudan) *zār* is thoroughly frowned on by devout Muslims, and considered a pagan witchcraft ritual used solely by ignorant women. These two conflicting accounts may possibly be reconciled by Boddy's finding that men see *zār* and Islam as conflicting but women regard them both as part of a "general religious enterprise" (1989, 142). Men feel that spirits must be exorcised; women feel they need to be accommodated.

One may be tempted to argue that women's religions develop in situations in which women are excluded from the mainstream or male-dominated religion. *Zār* certainly seems to bear that out: North African women are excluded from public ritual roles both in the mosque and in the Coptic Church. We may recall, on the other hand, that in Brazil the Catholic Church (with the exception of the priesthood) is perceived as a female domain, and rather than being excluded from churches, women are typically the vast majority of participants. I am not convinced that there is any correlation between the occurrence of women's religions and women's exclusion or inclusion in other religions of the day.

A related point concerns the use of the terms "marginal" and "peripheral." The *zār*, like many other women's religions, has been considered to be "peripheral" to the larger society (Lewis 1975). Yet, as a feminist scholar, I am obligated to ask from whose point of view the *zār* is peripheral. It should be clear that in the village studied by Boddy, where most women participate in *zār* rituals, women would be unlikely to consider *zār* rituals as marginal. In an excellent essay dealing with possession cults in the Swahili coastal area of Kenya and Tanzania, Linda Giles argues that "spirit possession should be seen as an integrated part of coastal Islamic belief and practice" (1987, 245). Moreover, she demonstrates that cult performances draw a wide range of spectators of both sexes and all ages; that even many of those who do not attend the ceremonies still share much of the cult belief system; that the range of potential cult members is quite extensive; that there are even more cases of people who profess that they do not participate or even believe in spirit cult activities yet who can be found visiting cult mediums in case of illness or the need for other assistance; and that at least on the Swahili coast the link to societal institutions was quite explicit in former times when the cults played a central role in communal rituals (1987, 246–47).

Snake goddess or priestess from Crete, seventeenth century B.C. (Courtesy of The Museum of Fine Arts, Boston. Gift of Mrs. S. Scott Fitz)

Ryūkyūan priestess praying at shrine. (Courtesy of C. Ouwehand)

Ryūkyūan priestesses holding food offerings. (Courtesy of C. Ouwehand)

Ryūkyūan priestesses arranging ritual food offerings. (Courtesy of C. Ouwehand)

Sande initiates dancing.
(Courtesy of
Caroline Bledsoe)

Sande drummers with a pair
of drums: a "male" and a
"female." (Courtesy of
Caroline Bledsoe)

Sande dancer in submissive pose, bringing tips from spectators to older Sande leaders. (Courtesy of Caroline Bledsoe)

Korean Shaman. (Courtesy of Laurel Kendall)

Shaker sisters and brothers. (From David R. Lamson, *Two Year's Experience Among the Shakers*, 1848)

Shaker ecstatic dancing. (From David R. Lamson, *Two Year's Experience Among the Shakers*, 1848)

Afro–Brazilian medium in costume. (From Leacock and Leacock, *Spirits of the Deep* [Doubleday 1972]. Courtesy of Seth and Ruth Leacock and Doubleday Publishers)

Afro-Brazilian shrine. (From Leacock and Leacock, *Spirits of the Deep* [Doubleday 1972]. Courtesy of Seth and Ruth Leacock and Doubleday Publishers)

Afro-Brazilian religious participants. (From Leacock and Leacock, *Spirits of the Deep* [Doubleday 1972]. Courtesy of Seth and Ruth Leacock and Doubleday Publishers)

Afro-Brazilian dancing. (From Leacock and Leacock, *Spirits of the Deep* [Doubleday 1972]. Courtesy of Seth and Ruth Leacock and Doubleday Publishers)

Entranced Afro-Brazilian medium. (From Leacock and Leacock, *Spirits of the Deep* [Doubleday 1972]. Courtesy of Seth and Ruth Leacock and Doubleday Publishers)

The Fox sisters: Margaret, Kate, and Leah. Nineteenth-century American Spiritualists, they claimed to communicate with the supernatural using table rapping. (Courtesy of the Department of Rare Books and Special Collections, University of Rochester Library)

Woodcut of nineteenth-century Spiritualist séance with table rapping. (Courtesy of the Bettmann Archive)

Priestess Selena Fox leading Mother Earth ritual, on Earth Day 1991. (Photograph by Michael L. Abramson/*Time* magazine)

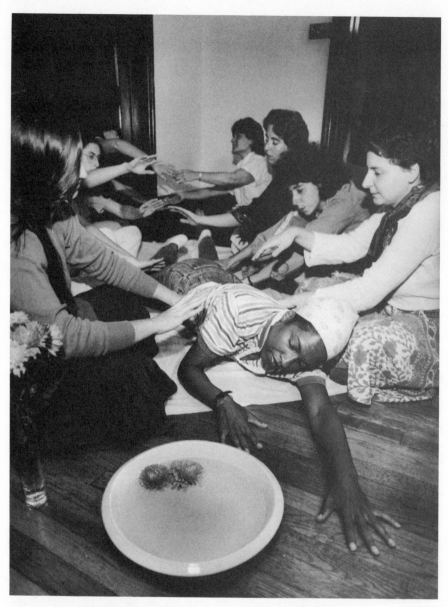

Contemporary spiritual feminist ritual—birth symbolism—on the Jewish women's new moon celebration. (Photo by Ilene Perlman from *Miriam's Well: Rituals for Jewish Women Around the Year* by Penina V. Adelman [Biblio Press, 1990]. Courtesy of Penina Adelman and Biblio Press)

The *zār* cult is spread over a very large geographical area. The functions and the form of the cult vary considerably from country to country, and even from place to place within each country. Ethnographic reports of the *zār* cult come from urban and rural Northern Sudan, Ethiopia, Somaliland, and Egyptian Nubia. While I have tried to be sensitive to the different manifestations of the cult reported for the different societies, the main elements of the cult are similar in all five societies.

RELIGIONS THAT ARE NOT DEALT WITH IN THIS BOOK

Cross-culturally, relatively few religions are dominated by women. The twelve key examples dealt with in this book are, to the best of my knowledge, almost all the female-dominated religions that have been documented in the ethnographic and historical literature. Thus while these examples are not comprehensive, neither are they illustrative of a much larger field. An ongoing difficulty that I faced in selecting and researching the examples around which the book is based concerns the quality and quantity of available information. The contemporary examples are better documented than the historical ones, and several examples are dependent on data gathered by one or two field-workers.

Since the twelve key examples are not the only women's religions that have existed, it is appropriate to explain why I chose these particular religions. First, I preferred not to focus on religious traditions for which evidence is sketchy. I have chosen not to deal with those ancient Near Eastern, Greek, and Roman traditions that seem to have been dominated by women, but for which the only testimony we have is myths and brief inscriptions.[19]

Another category I avoided includes Gnostic groups and medieval Christian heresies for which the historical documentation is based primarily on polemics **against** the religion by the mainstream Christian Church. Since I was able to find twelve religions that had been documented by more impartial observers, I chose not to focus on religions for which the primary sources are groups which opposed the religion, and so can be assumed to present a biased account. The fact that in most cases the written sources were recorded by advocates of male-dominated religions makes these sources even more suspect. For example, the important role of women among the thirteenth-century Guglielmites led the Church hierarchy to condemn the supposed sexual orgies held during their rituals, although it is far from likely that these orgies ever took place (Wessley 1978).

A third category that I, with some reservations, excluded from my list of key examples are African religions similar but not identical to the African religions I have included (see Beattie and Middleton 1969; Lewis 1986). In recent writings scholars have begun to treat the *zār* cult as part of a complex that also includes the West African (Nigerian) *bori* cult (see especially Lewis 1991).[20] For the sake of simplicity, in this book I have chosen to look only at *zār*, although much of what I have written about *zār* is also true for *bori*. The important role of women in African religions has been well documented (if not well publicized) and I found it difficult to select the "best" (most representative, clearly female dominated, and well-documented) examples. In order to avoid working with an unwieldy number of examples, I decided to focus on the Sande secret society and the *zār* possession cult.

I have chosen to exclude religions that were founded by women and/or in whose early days allowed women leadership roles, but which in the course of institutionalization began to exclude women from positions of power. Examples of this are Pentecostalism (Barfoot and Sheppard 1980) and many of the new religions of Japan (Nakamura 1980) and Africa (Jules-Rosette 1979). I have also chosen not to focus on Theosophy, both because in many ways it is similar to nineteenth-century Spiritualism, and because it was founded by both a man and a woman (Helena P. Blavatsky and Colonel Henry Olcott).

I chose not to work with what could more properly be described as clusters of rituals within a male-oriented religion (e.g., pilgrimage in Morocco or childbirth rituals in India) or with streams headed by a woman but which remained within the rubric of male domination (e.g., Beguines in medieval Europe and various devotional cults in India). Similarly, I have excluded folk variations on male-dominated great traditions (e.g., Mexican Spiritism, which is a form of folk Catholicism). In that my working definition of women's religions entails some sort of recognition that this religious group is independent from a larger, male-dominated institutional context, I have also avoided looking at groups of women who organize under the rubric of male domination (e.g., various Catholic celibate orders).

To all these categories of religions I will refer in passing (see Appendix B).

The category I am the most uncomfortable about excluding (and which I hope to deal with in a subsequent volume) includes various tribal religions in which both men and women have active roles, and in which each sex predominates in certain types of rituals. The three main examples I have in mind here are Australian aboriginal religion as described by Diane Bell (1983), indigenous Philippine religion as described by Teresita Infante (1975), and traditional Iroquois religion as described by Annemarie Shimony (1980). Since the goal of the present volume is to try to tease out how women "do" religion when they are in a position of dominance, tribal religions in which men's and women's religious lives are intermeshed proved difficult to work with. Again, I emphasize that my entire typology is artificial. Taking a religion like that of the Ryūkyū Islands on the one hand and one like Islam on the other, we can construct a continuum going from female to male dominance; we cannot construct absolute categories. Since in all known cultures both men and women are "religious"—my twelve key examples are not pure types.

Notes

1. Anthropologists, sociologists, and historians of religion have defined religion in a multitude of ways. One of the most successful definitions is proposed by Clifford Geertz (1969): "Religion is a system of symbols which acts to establish powerful,

pervasive, and long-lasting moods and motivations in people by formulating conceptions of a general order of existence and clothing these conceptions with such an aura of
factuality that the moods and motivations seem uniquely realistic." All the women's
religious situations explored in this book fall well within Geertz's rubric.

2. Laurel Kendall (personal communication) confirms my hunch that there is some
sort of connection among these religious traditions. The same, or a similar, trend
toward female dominance in the religious domain is also probably a characteristic of
certain tribal cultures of the Philippines. I hope to look into this issue further in a future
study.

3. Indian colonization in Burma started in the first century C. E. and in Thailand in
the second century C.E. Buddhism as a dominant religion was introduced into Burma in
the eleventh century and Thailand in the thirteenth. Buddhism was the state religion but
not imposed by force. Missionary monks were responsible for spreading Buddhism.

4. Religious tolerance is characteristic of the Ryūkyū Islands, and Confucianism,
Buddhism, and Christianity can be found on the Islands. Upper-class Ryūkyūans
learned and practiced Chinese ancestral rituals. Buddhist funeral rites from Japan (but
no other elements of Buddhism) became fairly popular on the Ryūkyūs, and monks
were looked at with some disdain. Confucian rituals and status symbols became important in a superficial way and only among upper class families. Even among Catholic
converts, no real break was made with former religious consciousness (Anzai 1976, 62).

5. Ouwehand tells me that the word should be written *kan*, that *kami* is Japanese
(personal communication 1992). However, since all the English-language sources use
the word *kami* I will, with some misgivings, continue to do so.

6. Haring (1964) believes that the Amami Island, have had longer and deeper cultural contact with Japan and China (through Japan) than Okinawa has had. Mabuchi
(1976a) states that belief in the spiritual predominance of the sister survives more in the
southern part of the southern Ryūkyūs than in the main island Okinawa, and is even
rarer in Miyako Island (northern part of the southern Ryūkyūs).

7. Spiro, on the other hand, says that it is normally the father's *nat* who is inherited
(1967, 101).

8. According to Tambiah (1970), it is not only in Thai Buddhism but also in spirit
cults (other than the matrilineal ones treated here) that the ritual specialists are male.
Kirsch (1985, 312), on the other hand, found that while women do support Buddhism
"it is also true that most 'animist' spirit practitioners, displaying a kind of symbolic
'anti-Buddhism,' are also women."

9. In Burma, on the other hand, people do report feeling conflict between Buddhism and *nat* beliefs.

10. Because Mary Baker Eddy exerted an enormous influence over the development
of Christian Science, and because movements founded by women (and women who
found movements) tend to strike observers as sufficiently unusual to need to be "explained," many studies of Christian Science have traced Eddy's life story and shown
how the events and psychological traumas of her life caused her to discover Christian
Science. This fits in with an all-too-common tendency in the scholarly literature to treat
women's religion as somehow psychologically abnormal. Perhaps in reaction, I pay
attention primarily to the key theological and existential concepts of Christian Science,
rather than Eddy's life story.

11. In the early years, men actually outnumbered women in several Shaker communities (Brewer 1986, 215).

12. Starhawk believes that the number is even larger (personal communication
1992).

13. Many Womanist writers do not wish to connect themselves to the predominantly white Feminist Spirituality Movement. On the other hand, most Spiritual Feminists express a strong sense of kinship with Womanism, and generally include articles by Womanist writers in their anthologies.

14. In the past several years Hispanic feminists have begun to produce a body of literature reflecting their own, special religious concerns. Since this budding movement has (at least until now) identified itself with the Christian tradition and the Catholic Church, I will not be dealing with it in the present volume. Among the many interesting ideas given voice in this growing literature are an acknowledgment of women's numerical dominance in the Catholic Church in Latin America, respect for non-Catholic religions (such as Candomble), recognition of the feminization of poverty and the connections between capitalism and patriarchy, use of traditional female symbols such as the Virgin Mary, and an explicit addressing of political issues that affect women's and men's lives (see Tamez 1989 for a sample of this literature).

15. Herskovits (1943) found more equal numbers of men and women in Porto Alegre (southern Brazil) than studies of northern Brazil have shown.

16. Black Caribs are also known as Garifuna. In this book I look primarily at the Black Caribs of Belize because that is the group whose religious and kinship structure has been most thoroughly studied. I have no reason to think that the culture of the Black Caribs of Guatemala, Honduras, and Nicaragua is very different.

17. This is not the case further south, in the Sudan.

18. According to Boddy, in the Sudan women consider *zār* to be part of Islam and not a religion in its own right. Men are more ambivalent: The more educated deny that it is an Islamic practice, and the less educated are not sure (personal communication 1992).

19. Ross Kraemer's newest book (1992) is a brilliant reconstruction of women's religious lives in ancient Greece and Rome. However, much of what she describes seems to be specific festivals rather than full-fledged religions. Even so, much of what she found resonates with what I will be describing in this book.

20. Scholars of African religion have described many local spirit possession phenomena as being similar to or even part of the *zār* cult. It seems to me of the utmost importance to differentiate between spirit possession in which women are possessed by spirits who are exorcised by a male ritual specialist, and spirit possession in which possessed women join an ongoing group of fellow-sufferers who gather to share experiences of possession trance. Among the Digo of South Kenya, for example, spirit possession is officially diagnosed and exorcised by a male practitioner, *mganga* (Gomm 1975). I would treat this a totally different phenomenon from the *zār* cult of the Sudan. There is a tendency among scholars to treat all African spirit possession as if it were one phenomenon, whereas it is far more reasonable to treat spirit possession as a common form of religious activity, which in different African societies is used and interpreted in a variety of ways. The fallacy of treating all African spirit possession as a unified phenomenon could be compared to someone claiming that all European prayer is one phenomenon—that the secretive Latin of a Catholic priest, the speaking in tongues of a Pentecostal woman, and the formal Hebrew daily liturgy of a Jewish man are essentially the same thing.

2

The Social Contexts of Women's Religions

GENDER DISJUNCTION, MATRIFOCALITY, AND A CRITIQUE OF DEPRIVATION THEORY

Just as there is no one historical scenario that explains why women's religions occur, there is no single cultural configuration in which we find all the women's religions, nor a single cultural context in which women's religions are always present. The ethnographic literature suggests that three sets of factors tend to be associated with women's religions. The first of these factors is gender dissonance: situations in which culturally accepted notions of gender are either highly contradictory and/or rapidly changing.[1] The second factor is matrifocality—a cultural emphasis on the maternal role, often coupled with either matrilineality and/or matrilocality. And the third is a relatively high degree of personal, social, or economic autonomy for women.[2]

GENDER DISSONANCE
Nineteenth-century United States (Shakerism, Spiritualism, and Christian Science)

Shakerism, Spiritualism, and Christian Science developed during a period of industrialization and urbanization. As I have shown previously (Sered 1990), modernization affects women's religious lives in complex ways. Although science and new literate religions (such as normative Islam) tend to accuse women's traditional religions of being superstitious magic, rapid cultural change may also mean the introduction of new religious options that women in particular find attractive.

During the nineteenth century (when Shakerism flourished and Spiritualism and Christian Science began) North America was characterized by highly patriarchal cultural norms. Victorian gender ideology and the "cult of true womanhood" proclaimed female passivity, frailty, and weakness (Welter 1966). In addition, as I explain in Chapter 4, nineteenth century women were increasingly expected to be able to guarantee their children's health and welfare, an expectation that most women found impossible to fulfill.

What I have just described sounds more like a situation of women's distress than of gender disjunction. And indeed, Alex Owen (1981) argues that at the end of the nineteenth century and the beginning of the twentieth as women's status improved (e.g., the 1882 married women's property law gave married women control over their own property), Spiritualism (and Shakers) declined.

This argument, however, merits closer examination. Owen shows that during the mid-nineteenth century respectable employment for women began to develop—**and this is the period in which some famous women mediums were able to make a living in Spiritualist circles**. In other words, Spiritualism "took off" when new economic options had begun to open up for women. By the 1890s, when Spiritualism started to decline, many thousands of women had already begun to work for wages in business and commerce. In short, during the mid- and late nineteenth century there was a cultural climate in which women aspired to, and occasionally gained, social and legal equality with men. "The second half of the century was a period of shifting attitudes, holding out a promise of broader and brighter horizons, but it was also a time of anxiety and uncertainty as the old order began grudgingly to give way to the new . . . it is no accident that spiritualism, a movement which privileged women and took them seriously, attracted so many female believers during a period of gender disjunction and disparity between aspiration and reality" (Owen 1981, 4).

American social life in the mid-nineteenth century was fluid. Individuals could change their social roles with remarkable ease. Migrations across the continent, immigrants flooding into the country, and industrialization created a spirit of pluralism and change. American religious freedom meant that religious organizations were voluntary; religious toleration led to the growth of democracy within many of the churches; and the denominations had no effective power to discipline their members (Nelson 1969). In addition, the nineteenth-century Second Great Awakening legitimated public and ecstatic religious roles for women, even within male-dominated Protestant sects.

While men continued to dominate all leadership roles in mainstream Protestant denominations, by the early nineteenth century American iconographic representations of Christ showed feminine characteristics predominating. Louis Kern (1981) has emphasized the dissonance in nineteenth-century American religious culture: On the one hand women were morally "better" than men (i.e., less materialistic, more pious), but on the other hand they were not allowed to exercise the power that could be expected to derive from moral superiority.[3] Kern demonstrates that nineteenth-century men had ambivalent feelings about women. Women were simultaneously the source of salvation from the materialistic world, and secretive, sexual beings. He concludes that this period was characterized by intense sexual ambivalence and anxiety caused by social, cultural, and economic changes.

I would argue that Shakerism, Spiritualism, and Christian Science "took off" not at a time when oppression of women was at its peak, but during a time in which sex roles and gender ideology were changing. Nineteenth-century America (like late eighteenth-century England) was characterized by an intellectual climate of radical ideas and spiritual turmoil. Many new religious groups emerged during this period; science and technology became a real alternative (in the eyes of many people) or threat (in the eyes of many other people) to religion; and population shifts meant sudden and intense cultural contacts.

The emergence of Shakerism, Spiritualism, and Christian Science seems to have less to do with distress or deprivation than with gender disjunction—disjunction between ideology and practice, combined with a situation in which cracks had opened up in the old ways—in which new social and intellectual options began to be available.

West Africa (Sande Secret Society)

West African cultures posit official ideologies of male dominance. On the other hand, West African women traditionally have had active and sometimes dominant economic roles. Women have farmed, sold surplus food at local markets, engaged in trade, and accumulated money and other resources. As David Rosen has argued, "West African women maintain a separate sphere of production and exchange which provides them with the ability to carry out a wide variety of economic transactions independently of male household members. . . . the situation in West Africa, unlike elsewhere in the world, is one in which women as well as men mediate the relationship between the peasant community and outside society" (1983, 37). While modernization has had certain negative consequences for African women (Boserup 1970), it has "provided new opportunities for Kpelle [a West African group among whom almost all women belong to Sande secret society] women to acquire independence and prestige. Where cash cropping is possible or wage labor opportunities are available, women can remain unmarried because cash from marketing or from wage-earning lovers allows them to hire farm labor, pay house taxes, and buy household necessities themselves, a pattern noted as well by studies in other parts of Africa" (Bledsoe 1980, 3).

Ideologically, West African legal systems give rights in women's reproductive and productive services to men (fathers, husbands, etc.). On the other hand, in actuality, many women are independent. For example, among the Nuer over half the women of marriageable age are not under any man's legal control (Bledsoe 1980). In parts of West Africa women have a long history of political activity that even includes serving as chiefs of towns. Among the Mende and Sherbro tribes, women can be household and descent group heads, positions of importance and power in managing the group's land and a basis for community influence. In one Sherbro community, 23 of the 39 household heads in 1970 were women (Hoffer 1972, 154).

An interesting West African twist on kinship organization is that while men want as many wives as possible to enhance their political and economic status, many head wives also want junior wives for companionship and help with the chores. Sometimes the wife is the one who actually chooses the secondary wives. The Kpelle believe it is important for co-wives to get along well, whereas husbands and wives are not expected to really love each other, just to cooperate. First wives often enlist their friends or younger sisters to be junior wives for them (Cosentino 1982).

On the one hand, Sande membership must be seen in the context of cultures in which women control important economic resources. On the other hand, West Africa is far from matriarchal. It can more accurately be described as a situation of gender disjunction—ideology (patriarchal) and reality (fairly egalitarian) clash. We will return to West Africa and the Kpelle later on.

MATRIFOCALITY

In a fascinating study of women and religion in the Greco-Roman world, Ross Kraemer has drawn on the work of anthropologist Mary Douglas to explain why in certain societies positions of religious activism and leadership are open to women and in others they are not. Douglas developed a system of classification in which human social experience is described in terms of two factors: group and grid. Group refers to the degree to which individuals feel themselves to be part of a community, to the degree to which the individual is incorporated in the group in shared households, work, resources, and leisure-time activity. Grid refers to the extent to which rules and regulations govern an individual's activities. Kraemer concludes that in the Greco-Roman world a strong group and low grid constellation is correlated with increased religious authority and options for women. When women are well incorporated into associations of some kind, and when rules and hierarchy are relaxed, women become more religiously active (1992, 199). To a large extent, Kraemer's observations are also true outside the Greco-Roman world. As we saw above, women's religions are often associated with societies that are undergoing rapid cultural change; that is, low grid societies. As I will show now, women's religions are also associated with matrilineal and matrilocal societies in which group—for women—is very strong.

Before I begin it is helpful to clarify the terminology I will be using. A term that is crucial to my argument is matrifocality. Traditionally, anthropologists have believed that matrifocal societies are rare, certainly far rarer than our sample of women's religions would suggest (see, Table 1). Exactly how rare we do not know because, as both Marvin Harris (1985) and Nancy Tanner (1974) point out, researchers have treated them as aberrations. Anthropologists have been inclined to assume that normative societies are patrifocal; for a society to be described as matrifocal there had to be a very dramatic absence of male presence. Feminist anthropologist Sylvia Yanagisako argues, however, that matrifocal does not necessarily mean that the husband is absent from the house; it is sufficient for the mother to be the **focus** of the household (1979: 178). Yanagisako expands the category of matrifocality to include far more situations that have hitherto been recognized, and certainly includes practically all the cultures in which female-dominated religions occur.[4]

Nancy Tanner (1974, 131) defines matrifocality as a kinship system in which the structurally, culturally, and affectively central role of the mother is seen as

Table I. *Female-Dominated Religions and Matrilineality, Matrilocality, or Matrifocality—Summary*

Country	Summary
Burma:	Clearly matrifocal with a matrilineal bias. Some evidence for official matrilineality in earlier centuries.
Northern Thailand:	Matrilocal with a matrilineal bias.
Ryūkyū Islands:	Bilateral kinship; evidence of matrilocality in former times.
Korea:	Matrifocal with some evidence of former matrilocality.
Sudan (Zār):	Recent shift toward "budding" matrifocality. Evidence of matrilineality in former times (see below).
Brazil:	Matrifocal.
Belize:	Matrifocal and often matrilocal.
United States:	Officially neolocal and bilateral, yet evidence of a matrilineal bias.
West Africa:	Matrifocal and often de facto matrilocal.

legitimate. In addition, according to Tanner, matrifocal societies are character-ized by relatively egalitarian relationships between the sexes, and relatively equal valuations of men's and women's economic and ritual statuses. These attributes certainly describe the social contexts of most women's religions.

For the purposes of this book, I find it most helpful to define matrifocality as a complex of traits rather than as a uniform or absolute organizational type. The cultures addressed here are sufficiently different from one another to demand the use of somewhat flexible conceptual constructs. The complex of traits that make up matrifocality include: identifying women primarily as mothers rather than as wives, absence of adult males from the household, matrilocality, matrilineality, structural authority vested in mothers, maternal control of key economic resources, decision-making authority vested primar-ily in the hands of mothers, and household groups in which members are defined in terms of their relationship to the mother. For a society to be considered matrifocal it does not need to exhibit all these traits; it needs to exhibit many of them. Similarly, societies that are patrifocal may exhibit one or two of these traits.

Nancy Tanner's insistence on structural and not only affective features pre-vents expanding the concept of matrifocality to include societies in which the mother-child bond is the strongest emotional bond, but in which women have no real structural power. Thus, for example, neither Tanner nor I would con-sider a society matrifocal in which children are far more attached to their moth-ers than their fathers but in which women have no economic or social authority. It is of interest to note that in many societies of that sort, women are more religiously active than men, but men dominate positions of religious leadership (e.g., the Catholic Church in Mexico; see Fromm and Maccoby 1970). The evidence suggests that intense mother-child bonds facilitate women's religious involvement, but without structural recognition—typically in the form of matrilocality or matrilineality—these bonds do not promote women's religious leadership.

Matrilineality refers to a system of reckoning descent through the female line.[5] Matrilineal kinship is, statistically, far more rare than patrilineal kinship. In George Murdock's (1967) sample of 1179 societies, 558 had patrilineal kin groups while only 164 had matrilineal kin-groups. In the same sample 71% percent of the societies were patrilocal or virilocal (the wife lives with the husband or with the husband and his family). In Marvin Harris's words, "Patrilocality and patrilineality are the statistically 'normal' mode of domestic organization" (1985, 281). As we will see, most female-dominated religions occur in societies that are neither patrilocal nor patrilineal.

In addition, according to Harris, because men are so reluctant to relinquish control over their sons (and, I may add, their women), matrilineal societies are more often avunculocal (sons at maturity go to live with their mothers' brothers, thus allowing a core of related male kin to live together) than matrilocal. Since none of the matrilineal societies in which women's religions occur is avunculocal, the matrilineal and matrilocal nature of these societies is statistically even more outstanding.

In the following sections I will briefly summarize aspects of kinship organization in cultures in which female-dominated religions are located. I believe that each of these situations can be construed as matrifocal. In certain examples the matrifocality receives clear definition through matrilineality and matrilocality. In other examples matrifocality runs as an undercurrent through an officially patrilineal and patrilocal society. What I wish to draw attention to is that even in the latter situations, the female-dominated religion comes into play at the point of matrifocality.

Northern Thailand (Matrilineal Spirit Cults)

The Northern Thai matrilineal spirit cults in which related women give offerings to their matrilineal ancestors are a prime example of the matrifocal context of women's religions. Formal Thai ideology—reinforced by Buddhist belief and practice—posits male superiority (see Davis 1974). Although Thai women are active in many spheres, there are certain crucial jobs from which women are excluded. The village headman is always male, as are Buddhist monks and officials in charge of irrigation.

Still, in comparison to most other known cultures, Northern Thai men's and women's work is quite interchangeable. Both sexes work in the fields. Women are particularly involved with communal transplanting and harvesting of rice and in selling their goods at rural markets. Both men and women perform household chores, and it is not uncommon for Northern Thai men to cook their families' meals. Care of small children is carried out by women, girls, men, and boys (Hanks and Hanks 1963). Children of both sexes are treated with affection; the same ceremonial procedures are carried out at the birth of a boy or a girl. In general, Thai culture tends to minimize sex differences.

In Southeast Asia, according to Penny Van Esterik, "Both in the gardens of shifting cultivators and the wet-rice paddies of lowland agriculturalists, women's labor has been critically important" (1982, 8). In Thailand women not only work hard, but also contribute to decision making in rural farming communities. They are involved in market trading and entrepreneurial activity. History and myth support the idea of powerful female political and legal figures in Southeast Asia's past. More recently many women have left their villages to work on road building crews, at factories, in services, and as prostitutes. Women have a great deal of independence and authority, and often are responsible for managing the financial affairs of their households.

Shulamith Potter (1977) has described Northern Thai social structure as conceptually female centered, a system in which the significant blood ties are those between women. While there is broad agreement in the ethnographic literature regarding Northern Thai matrilocality, not all writers concur that Northern Thai kinship organization is truly matrilineal. For the purposes of the present book, it is sufficient to note that there seems to be a matrilineal bias that emerges particularly clearly in the context of the domestic spirit cults (Wijeyewardene, personal communication 1992). Northern Thai matrilineal spirit cults are an intrinsic part of a matrilocal and matrilineally oriented household organization.

While there is variation among villages and among families, newly married couples are typically expected to live with the bride's parents for one year, after which they move to another house in the same compound as that of the bride's parents. Female kin rely on each other for assistance with both agricultural and domestic work. Postmarital living arrangements reinforce the strength of women's identification with and loyalty to their own families. This has continued to be the case in urban areas, where married daughters often live near their mothers (Hanks and Hanks 1963).

Matrilocal residence is both the ideal and reality; in the village studied by Potter it occurs in 73% of all marriages. Daughters and sons inherit equally but it is customary for sons to sell out their rights in the land to their sisters. In a family with several daughters, the youngest daughter and her husband are expected to continue living with her parents, caring for them in their old age, and finally inheriting the house upon their deaths. When the family land is not sufficient to support additional households, married sisters and female cousins move off as a group with their husbands to new lands. "Thus, male individualism and rivalry is dampened among these households and neighborhoods organized around co-operating females" (Hanks 1984, 106). Divorce, which can be initiated by either partner, is frequent and typically it is the husband who goes away while the wife keeps the land.

Gehan Wijeyewardene speculates that the Northern Thai preference for matrilocality reflects a previous era in which men were subject to military conscription and corvee labor. Until about fifty years ago, Northern Thailand was characterized by small population, malaria, epidemics, warfare, and wild animals. There was abundant irrigable rice land, yet a shortage of labor to farm that land. Men were often absent hunting, in feudal services, or in warfare. Warfare and migration have always made the Northern Thai, especially the men, mobile. In traditional Thailand peasant men (the majority of the population were peasants) owed four months yearly labor to feudal lords. A recurrent theme in the development of Thai culture is the scarcity of labor in relation to land. Women were the key asset for the continuity of peasant society (1984a, 288).

Northern Thai explain the ideological underpinnings for their matrilocal household system by saying that two women with different spirits (women of different matrilineal cult groups) cannot share the same roof. The implication is that when a man marries he cannot bring his wife (who has a different spirit) to live with his mother. Instead, he must go to live with her family. Childrearing practices reflect and reinforce the notion that boys are destined to leave their natal homes, while girls are expected to remain with their natal families. When a boy is born, the mother is enjoined to recuperate by lying next to the fire for 29 days; when a daughter is born she should lie near the fire for 30 or more days. The shorter period for boys is said to ensure that they will be able to wander abroad; the longer period for girls is said to ensure that they will remain at home.

In Chapter 1, we saw that women's dominance in economic activities reflects a cultural assessment of women as more rooted in worldly attachments—an assessment with clearly negative implications in a Buddhist society. According to Thomas Kirsch, "The institutions of uxorilocal [matrilocal] residence, female ultimogeniture, and gaining access to land through a wife's family reflect this grounding ('attachment') of women in the home locale and rural life, a limitation of women's options and mobility compared to the situation of young men" (1985, 313–314). What Kirsch does not add is that this very attachment to land and family **strengthens** women's role in the matrilineal spirit cults.

Shulamith Potter has argued that although Northern Thai culture is matrilineal and matrilocal, women are not more powerful or influential than men. Thailand is not a feminist utopia (witness, for example, the widespread prostitution); gender inequality affects many spheres of life; and gender dissonance results from Buddhist assessments of women as rooted in this world. On the other hand, women dominate the kinship system. As we will see, this is a theme that recurs in many women's religions.

Belize (Black Carib Religion)

The next example is one that even more strongly emphasizes the role of women in kinship organization, and the interplay between women's dominance in kinship and in religion. Black Carib family and household organization is matrifocal; that is, families revolve around a woman and her children. The mother–child, and especially the mother–daughter link is the most important and the most stable in Black Carib society. Mothers look after their daughters' children, daughters care for aging mothers, old women organize rituals on behalf of their ancestors. If the focal woman leaves the household permanently, because of death or any other reason, the household is likely to break up. Other household members come and go with much less effect. In short, each resident's primary tie is to the focal woman (Kerns 1983, 129; see also Gonzalez 1969, 1983; Helms 1981).

Fathers are expected to provide financially for their children, yet many are unable to. In any case, the bottom line is that mothers and mothers' mothers see to it that children are not neglected. Women, who must care for their children, can rarely do so single-handedly. The public sphere does not provide mothers with lucrative employment, nor does the government force fathers to support children. Women learn at an early age that they must depend on others—in particular kin. The ritual complex of Black Carib women tests, strengthens, and dramatizes kin ties.

In both the cities and villages of Belize approximately 50% of children under the age of fourteen live with both biological parents, 25% with their mothers but not fathers, and 25% with other relatives, most typically a grandmother or maternal aunt (Sanford 1974). Even when the biological mother is present in the household, the child may be cared for and 'mothered' by another relative. Childcare is the responsibility of kin, not only of the mother, and whoever is most interested in enacting the social role of mother is likely to do so. The reason for the absence of the mother is almost always that she is away working. "The ideal role of the strong and nurturing mother can thus be fulfilled whether one is a genetrix or not" (Sanford 1974, 398).

In contemporary Belize Black Carib men rarely work together. Women's work (financial and ritual) is much more cooperative than men's. In Black Carib villages men are frequently absent for long periods of time, either working or looking for work in the cities. Women, left to care for children, have various economic strategies. They expect and often receive financial help from their husbands and sons. They garden, take in laundry, and sell cakes, candles, and dried fish in nearby markets.

Most daughters, at some point in their lives, turn to their mothers for assistance. Daughters return to their mothers' houses for a number of reasons: financial problems, marital problems, mistreatment, unemployment, the need to go to the city to find a job (Kerns 1983, 112). Because absent children are expected to send financial support to their mothers, mature women often serve to redistribute financial resources among siblings.

Black Carib women are quite independent of men. Their labor and sexuality are not treated as the property of men, nor are women under the authority of men. Women choose their own spouses and leave unsatisfactory ones at will. They control their own money and own their own property. Spouses generally keep their finances separate. The kinship system is officially bilateral, yet although all kin are expected to help each other, it is primarily women who are responsible for the networks of reciprocity. Most daughters stay in the same communities in which they grew up. Most marriages are among residents of the same village, and women show a marked preference for living with their own rather than with their spouses' kin (Kerns 1983).

Marriages are either legal or extra-legal, long term or short term, and no stigma is attached to extra-legal relationships. Most marriages begin with

emotional and physical attraction, and women do expect fathers to acknowledge paternity. When a marriage dissolves, relationships with in-laws are
generally preserved. Because most people have more than one spouse during
their lives, networks of affines tend to be large (Kerns 1983, 113–116). The
result is that village Black Carib women rarely interact with anyone who is
not kin (in some sense). Boys and girls play freely with each other, yet from a
fairly young age boys and girls (and men and women) show preference for
congregating with their own sex. Throughout their lives, men develop ties
with friends, while women's bonds are with kin. In short, cultural expectations for women and men are different. Men have more contact with the
outside world than women do. Women have more intra- and intervillage
contact with other Black Caribs (Kerns 1983, 93). The picture we have
painted here is of villages in which women are the permanent residents, and in
which women—linked together by bonds of kinship and mutual help—raise
and support children.

Black Carib children of both sexes are socialized to be independent, to be
able to take care of themselves, and also to be generous to their kin. Men are
expected to do much of the heavy work of building houses and clearing fields,
yet for reasons of expedience many tasks are performed by both sexes (Kerns
1983, 93). Black Carib society does discriminate against women in certain
ways. Although men and women are expected to enjoy and seek sexual pleasure, women are expected to control their sexual urges at various points in the
life-cycle, especially after birth. (Virginity before marriage is neither expected
nor desired.) Women are praised for sexual restraint; men are admired for
sexual conquests and for "breeding" many children with many women. From
a young age girls are dressed more modestly, and their behavior is more
monitored and controlled than is boys' (Kerns 1983, 90–92). Boys have fewer
responsibilities and spend less time at home.

Within Black Carib communities there is little official or authoritarian leadership of any sort. Most property is personal and portable, few people own any
productive land, and inheritance is not considered an important means of
acquiring property (Kerns 1983, 76). We may assume that absence of the sorts
of centralized, male-dominated institutions that characterize many other societies has facilitated the important role played by women in Black Carib religion. More important, however, is the kinship system, which encourages
dependence on female kin and autonomy from male dominance.[6]

Upper Burma (Nat Religion)

Researchers have considered the kinship structure of Burma to be bilateral—
individuals are equally affiliated with the families of both of their parents.
Melford Spiro (whose ethnographic work in Upper Burma is considered authoritative), however, found a definite matrilineal and matrilocal slant. "Although kinship distance is a function of biological distance, there is some
suggestion that within the same degrees of genealogical distance the kinship tie
to females is conceived to be stronger than that to males. There is no

doubt . . . that this is the case at the affective level . . . but even at the cognitive level there is some reason to believe that, because of the importance of the womb, the (biological) stuff of kinship is believed to be transmitted more through females than males, and that, consequently, more of it is shared with females than with males" (1977, 46).

The Burmese term for the biological family is *mitha su*, literally "mother-child group." The same term is used for the descent group, which, according to Spiro, implies that the founding female contributes more than the founding male to its common kinship. While each person belongs to both the father's and the mother's descent group, Burmese say that they **feel** closer to their maternal kin (1977, 65).

Residence patterns are typically neolocal. However, as in Thailand, it is the custom for newlyweds to reside for some period of time with the bride's parents, and the youngest daughter is expected to remain with her parents after her marriage. For both parents the attachment to daughters is said to be stronger than to sons (Spiro 1977, 81). Statistically, there are more households of parents and married daughters than of parents and married sons. While there is a preference for village endogamy, in the past it was the custom in inter-village marriages for the husband to move to the wife's village.

Spiro found that fathers are viewed more as figures of authority and mothers as figures of affection. The tie between mother and child is believed to be stronger because of pregnancy and nursing. In partial exchange for this nurturance, in Buddhist initiation the son "worships" his mother before his father, and the merit he acquires from becoming a novice is transferred to his mother. " . . . if cultural expressions are to be taken seriously, the mother may be said to be viewed as the pivotal person in the family" (Spiro 1977, 84). In the case of divorce, children are almost always given to the mother, not the father.

Mothers and daughters are especially close, and grown daughters and mothers visit each other constantly. Mothers take care of daughters' children. The mother-daughter bond is the core of the Burmese family. In many ways, the mother-daughter relationship is seen as threatening to the wife-husband relationship; men feel that women neglect their husbands for their mothers. It may well be that this feeling is strengthened by lengthy sexual taboos: There is a taboo on sex after the fifth month of pregnancy and while the woman is nursing. Sons are demonstrably emotionally attached to their mothers, yet "the women of the matriline comprise an especially close circle" (Spiro 1977, 89).

As we might expect, gender dissonance is a feature of Burmese culture. Despite the dominant role of women in Burmese families, ideology accords men a superior status. The Burmese view of marriage is that the man "owns" the woman's sexuality; there is no notion that the woman "owns" the man in the same way (Spiro 1977, 150). Girls—not boys—are expected to be virgins when they become engaged. Men may have extramarital affairs, but not women. Polygyny is permissible but rare (each co-wife has her own house). Burmese women wish to be reborn as men—a higher incarnation and an easier life (no pain of menstruation, pregnancy, or childbirth, and less housework.)

Men (not women) are believed to possess a sort of psychospiritual essence known as *hpoun*. *Hpoun* is a man's source of strength and power. Contact (including indirect contact) with the vagina is seen as a threat to *hpoun*. The loss of *hpoun* means that a man's powers decline, and that he is subordinate to his wife and children. According to Spiro (1977, 266), men fear women's desire to control them. They believe that women are temptresses and sorceresses, and that women use magical techniques to dominate men. Men are attracted by women but view their sexuality as a snare.

Burmese women are quite free and independent in most ways. Women control the family economy and most retail trade. Proprietors of shops and bazaars are preponderantly women, and women are well represented in large business enterprises and in all professions except engineering. Women participate in agriculture and receive the same wages as men for the same work. Legally men and women are equal and inherit equally. Women can own property, enter freely into marriage, and initiate divorce. In modern Burma women vote and are active in politics, and in traditional Burma a daughter could succeed to the hereditary headmanship. In comparison to China or India, the status of women is high: there is no footbinding, purdah, veil, child betrothal, or widow immolation. Women have freedom of action and are involved in both domestic and public society.

Spiro found that in many and possibly most marriages women are the dominant partners (1977, 277). Despite the ideology of male superiority, women make most of the major and minor decisions, and control the family's purse (the husband turns over his earnings to his wife and she doles it out; men are believed to be irresponsible with money and to squander it). Women are expected to be more responsible for the family. In short, Burma presents a clear picture of matrifocality.

There is some evidence that Burma kinship structure was once truly matrilineal. I. C. S. Furnivall (1911) has argued that the custom of widowed queens marrying a succession of men who upon marriage become kings is a vestige of matrilineality. At the beginning of the twentieth century, when Furnivall conducted his fieldwork, it was still the custom in Burmese villages for the groom to live with or near the bride's family.

Ryūkyū Islands (Indigenous Religion)

Observers of the Ryūkyū Islanders have been impressed by their lack of aggression and militarism, and their high level of interpersonal cooperation (Mabuchi 1968; Lebra 1966).[7] They have also noted that the status of women in traditional Ryūkyūan society is high—certainly higher than in China or Japan (Hopkins 1951; Lebra 1966). For example, division of labor on the basis of sex is rather flexible and easily crossed.

The kinship system is usually described as patrilineal and patrilocal. A number of scholars, however, have argued that this organization is rather new (Ota 1989). In the past, brideservice (the groom working for the bride's family) was commonly practiced, lasting for approximately two years, and matrilocal residence often continued until the first child was born. According to Takenori

Noguchi, the practice of a husband temporarily staying with his wife's family is still common on at least some of the Ryūkyū Islands (1966, 27). Robert Spencer reports that in ancient times a woman, having high economic value, did not go to live with her husband but stayed and worked in her parental home, with her husband coming from his parental fields to stay with her nights. According to the Ryūkyūan scholar Shimabukuro Genichiro (quoted in Spencer 1931, 96), this was still the custom in parts of Okinawa as late as the beginning of the twentieth century, and Toichi Mabuchi (1967) found that in the southern Ryūkyūs the kinship system is explicitly bilateral.[8]

Although nowadays a woman typically goes to live with her husband's family, it is not unusual for her brother or her parents to move in order to live near her. In general, cognatic rather than agnatic kinship is important in people's daily lives (Noguchi 1966, 28). Village endogamy is very much urged and in some areas required. Thus patrilocality is attenuated by the fact that all residents of a village are related to each other through multilayered kinship ties. In addition, as we will see in Chapter 10, sisters regularly return to their natal families to perform rituals.[9]

To summarize, despite the inclination on the part of anthropologists to label the Ryūkyūs as patrilineal and patrilocal, there is good evidence that until quite recently the typical kinship pattern was bilateral and matrilocal.

Korea (Women's Household Religion and Shamanism)

A somewhat parallel situation has been described for Korea. On the one hand, Korea is a well-known patrilineal and patrilocal society. Confucian ancestor worship means that male children are especially valued, and the first-born son inherits the house and most of the property. On the other hand, it is likely that Korean society was matrilocal until fairly recent times (Kendall 1985).

Korea became a Confucian society rather recently (by the seventeenth century).[10] Until then, kinship was not exclusively patrilineal and daughters could inherit. Husbands lived in the wives' homes for a number of years. A married woman would eventually establish her own home, or join her mother-in-law's home—but as a matron and mother, not as a young and powerless daughter-in-law. Still today, daughters continue their relationship with their natal families after marriage—many women give birth at their mother's homes; mothers may give their married daughters financial help on the sly; daughters attend shaman's *kut* rituals at their mothers' houses.

In contemporary Korea most couples have their own homes and within the household women have a great deal of power (Lee 1984). The mother is in charge of housekeeping, controlling storage, and supervising the daily life of the family members (food, clothing, and sleeping). According to Youngsook Kim Harvey, despite the official "patriarchy" of Korean society, the Korean man "is an outsider in the heartland of his own household. His formal authority is hardly ever challenged, but his actual authority within the household is much curtailed, for, like the king who knows only what his ministers choose to tell him, he is often ignorant about his domestic affairs" (1976, 190). It seems that the matrifocal household, rather than the patrilineal family, functions as the socially and economically significant unity in Korean society.

Household religion and shaman's rituals reinforce women's pivotal position in the household. "While dramatically acknowledging a woman's affective ties to her own dead kin, a *kut* also reaffirms bonds between a woman and her living kin. Like natal ancestors, living mothers, sisters, brothers, and brothers' wives may be present when a woman holds a *kut* in her own home. . . . The pattern of participation by living and dead . . . reveals a chain of households linked by out-marrying women" (Kendall 1983, 106).

Brazil (Afro-Brazilian Religions)

Urban Brazil may seem at first glance to contradict my proposed correlation between women's religions and matrifocality. The introduction of a wage and market economy and the elimination of artisan jobs as the result of industrialization has hurt many women. Although in recent years there has been an increase in education and employment for women, women are still heavily employed in the service (especially domestic service) fields, with all its attendant problems. Women tend to work in the informal sector of the economy, where there is no job security or protection, and employment tends to be low paid, temporary, and with no chance of advancement. Whereas the informal sector is transitional for men—men tend to move on to better jobs—it is permanent for women (Lerch 1980). Brazilian women suffer from a patriarchal ideology, a sexual double standard, and economic discrimination.

On the other hand, many urban Brazilian women live for many years quite independently of men. The dissolution of extended families in urban centers means that fathers and brothers have limited control over daughters and sisters. And the ease with which men leave wives and girlfriends means that many women are in charge of their own finances, social interactions, and mobility. "[A]mong poor urban populations the proportion of women who head their own households without a male breadwinner present is high and steadily increasing" (Merrick and Schmink 1983, 232).[11] Let us note that the female-dominated Afro-Brazilian cults are a predominantly *urban* phenomenon. Significantly, in Bahia, which is one of the most important centers of Afro-Brazilian religions, households are typically headed by the mother, not the father. Ruth Landes explicitly associates the high status of women in the Afro-Brazilian cults with the authority Brazilian women have in the home, and with the history of slavery, which recognized women and not men as family heads (1947).

Twentieth-century United States (Feminist Spirituality)

The Feminist Spirituality Movement has developed in a demographic climate of late marriage, frequent divorce, and single-parent families in which the parent is almost always the mother. Combined with typical American neolocal household arrangements, this means that many women are the heads of families and households (Lopata 1987). Although American women certainly suffer from economic discrimination, both single and married women are legally entitled to control their own finances.

American families tend to be organized around the mother. Psychologists have noted that for American children of both sexes the mother is the most important figure (Baruch and Barnett 1983, 601). Daughters especially see their mothers as role models. Bert Adams has observed that, "The close mother-daughter bond may be extended further to indicate that females play a more dominant role in the kin network than males. Young wives (in comparison to young husbands) tend to express a closer affectional relation to all degrees of kin, are in slightly more frequent contact with siblings and secondary kin, and are more likely to feel that kin are an important part of their lives" (1969, 169–170). Jessie Bernard has pointed out that mother-daughter relationships constitute the major component of old women's lives, "due to the matriarchal emphasis on kinship relations in America" (1975, 150–151; also see Yanagisako 1977; Hagestad 1984).[12] And finally, Miriam Johnson points out that the parents of the young middle-aged (the population from which most Spiritual Feminists are drawn) often consisted of a mother whose family of origin was of a higher socioeconomic class than that of the father. In this kind of situation, the father's greater economic contribution could be neutralized by the mother's class "superiority" and equal education. In light of the general American tendency toward greater emotional ties between mothers and children than between fathers and children, Johnson makes a claim for white middle-class families leaning toward matrifocality (1988, 241).

A further element in the cultural setting of the Feminist Spirituality Movement is the large number of lesbians among both leaders and participants. Although demographic information is not available, we do know that many Movement writings are by women who identify as lesbians. Lesbians are, on the whole, a population of women who control their own finances and who run their own households,[13] and lesbian families are excellent examples of matrifocal families.

Another Look at West Africa (Sande)

West Africa is not a clear-cut example of matrifocality, yet I believe that enough elements of the trait complex are found to justify including it in the discussion here. "An analysis of Kpelle [a society in which Sande secret societies are situated] consumption units reveals that nonkin members of a consumption unit usually have ties to the woman in charge of the cooking pot" (Bledsoe 1980, 113). Women use kin ties to their own advantage. Although women do not have legal authority over their children, they do have moral authority. Men and women informants told Bledsoe that they "revered their mothers above everyone else and felt morally obliged to support them in their old age" (1980, 114).

Among the West African Kpelle, if a woman bears a child out of wedlock the child is considered hers unless the father has paid compensation to the mother's family. There is no stigma on these children and "in a sense children are a form of property that fathers must pay for and maintain if they are to be considered the legal 'owners' " (Bledsoe 1980, 91). In other words, patrilineality needs to be actively created; unless that happens, children are considered part of their mother's families.

Kpelle husbands have ongoing economic obligations to wives' parents. Although the official ideology is virilocal, in actual fact only wealthy men can afford to pay **brideprice** (a payment to the bride's parents in return for her contributing her productive and reproductive capabilities to him or his family). In reality, most men perform **brideservice** (living with or near the wife's parents and contributing his productive capabilities to their household). Using demographic data, Bledsoe shows that it is far more often the wife's than the husband's parents (and especially the wife's mother) who lives with a married couple (1980, 108–109). Classical anthropologists would probably not consider these last two traits to be indicative of matrifocality. Yet, in light of arguments made by Tanner and Yanagisako (see above, page 46), it is reasonable to interpret them as part of the matrifocal complex. It would be unwise to ignore the day-to-day reality that a mother, her adult daughter, and the daughter's children live together and most probably form the core household group. In sum, the ethnographic evidence portrays Kpelle society as matrifocal and de facto matrilocal.

Regarding the Mende of Sierra Leone (another society in which Sande is found), Harris and Sawyerr note the importance of the mother's brother who "seems to have considerable authority perhaps even more than one's natural father" (1968, 129). This piece of information is important in light of the classical anthropological contention that a critical role for the mother's brother is typically a characteristic of matrilineal societies. In addition, the Mende believe that the physical parts of a child are derived from the father's semen, but the spirit derives from the mother. "This accounts for the psychic connexion which, it is assumed exists between mother and child" (1968, 129). Harris and Sawyerr have also found that matrilocal residence is common among the Mende. "In the days before any bride-price was paid, men married only one wife by working for the parents of the bride. Even after the custom of paying a bride-price had been established, there was a time when young men, who could not provide an adequate sum to this end, adopted the earlier practice of going to live and work for the parents of the bride. . . . The young man, anxious to marry the girl, was then absorbed into the girl's family as a son of the house. . . . When the Sande ceremonies were over, the girl's mother or one of her sisters would inform the man that he might cohabit with the girl, and they began life together as man and wife. . . . In such matrilocal marriages, the wife's family was dominant" (1968, 129).

Haiti (Urban Vodou) and Ancient
Japanese Shamans

We will now look at two additional examples that strengthen the case for the association between women's religions and matrifocality. In both examples, we can trace the historical circumstances that accompanied the emergence or decline of female dominance.

Haitian Vodou has evolved in the direction of female domination. In the Haitian countryside men are the vast majority of Vodou priests; in the city as many women as men are in positions of religious leadership. This trend is even more conspicuous in New York, where Haitian Vodou seems to be almost entirely a female-led enterprise. Because this development has been so rapid, it is possible to identify the social structural changes that have accompanied the modification of religious leadership.

Karen Brown has looked at the alterations in Haitian life resulting from the move from the countryside to the city. In rural Haiti typical households consist of extended families headed by an older male. In the cities, in contrast, women have better chances than men of finding employment. Urban young male unemployment may be as high as 60%, and white employers prefer hiring women for repetitive factory jobs. Moreover, urban women have continued the market tradition of rural women, and many if not most are involved in small-scale commerce of some kind. "The urban woman spun away from the rural extended family frequently ends up not only in charge of her house and her children—as she might well have been in the country—but also solely responsible for their financial support" (Brown 1989, 262). What is being described here is a household arrangement characterized by absence of adult males, female control of economic resources and decision making, and primary ties revolving around women (often two generations of adult women). Clearly, the shift from male to female dominance in Haitian religion occurred alongside the shift from patrifocal to matrifocal households.

A similar historical shift seems to have taken place in Japan. In classical Japanese mythology great shamanesses (*miko*) often married or were possessed by heavenly *kami* or gods (Hori 1968, 70), and shamanesses had pivotal political and ritual roles (1968, 112). Significantly, Hori argues that the **role of the miko changed with the transition from matrilineal to patrilineal society.** Under Chinese influence, the *miko* lost their important political role, and became part of folk rather than official or great tradition culture (1968, 187). Instead of practicing as independent religious specialists, they began to function as assistants to Buddhist mountain ascetics, and as village diviners, dancers and singers, and reciters of ballads. In a process the reverse of that which occurred in Haiti, in Japan the shift from female to male religious dominance occurred alongside the shift from matrilineality to patrilineality.

Luvale of Zambia: Matrilineality and Virilocality

A last brief example further clarifies the association between kinship arrangements and women's religion. In Zambia, women of the Luvale tribe "participate in a system of curing that is run for women by women" (Spring 1978, 166). Because of the high infant mortality rate and the high incidence of illness among Luvale women,[14] mothers undergo spirit possession rituals for their own illnesses and on behalf of their sick children.

The Luvale are a matrilineal people who practice virilocal residence norms. In other words, women move away from their natal families at marriage, yet children belong to their mother's lineage. **The ancestral shades or spirits that afflict women belong to their own lineages and not their husband's.** Anita Spring asserts that "[S]pirit possession and ritual become the vehicle for bonding women of a matrilineage. Along with membership, ritual expertise is passed down through matrilineal lines" (1978, 182). We see here how the women's religion is concerned with matrilineality, in a society in which women do not live in matrilocal households. Matrilineality is what is "picked up" in the female dominated religion.

The spirit possession ritual for childbearing, for example, begins with public all-night drumming, dancing and singing in front of the patient's home. Cult members and relatives gather to aid the patient by singing and teaching her the appropriate dances. The ritual leader invokes the "ancestral shades" who are believed to be located within the patient's body and to have caused the sickness. The shades appear via the possessed patient who dances in standardized movements associated with the cult. Afterwards the patient continues to take medicines and observe food and behavioral taboos. Following recovery the possession ritual is repeated and the patient is initiated into the cult. Through this ritual, bonds are formed among fellow and former sufferers, and misfortune is concretized and cured. "It may be a unique situation that, in a matrilineal society, women may gain access to ritual power through their own ancestors, who were themselves women" (Spring 1976, 111).

According to Spring, female models of interrelatedness may be intensified in matrilineal cultures. "Undoubtedly, there is a feminine ideal of community among . . . the Luvale . . . whose realization is prevented by virilocal residence. However, female rituals that transcend residential separation involve all women in a community of concern for themselves, their children, their mothers and grandmothers, and the whole body of female members of Luvale society, both alive and departed" (1978, 188).

In matrilineal societies it often seems to be the case that even when the formal or great tradition religion is male dominated, women gather in the context of female-dominated cult groups or ritual constellations. Another example of this phenomenon has been documented for the virilocal, matrilineal Tulu speakers of India among whom large numbers of people—almost all women—gather annually to propitiate the foundress-goddess Siri, sing her legend, and become possessed by her or by members of her family (Claus 1975).

MATRIFOCALITY AND RELIGION: SOME CONCLUSIONS

A pattern has begun to emerge: Women's religions are most often found in societies in which women control important resources, in which families are focused upon mothers, in which kinship is matrilineal.[15] It bears emphasizing that these societies are not matriarchal, nor are they even fully egalitarian. In all the cultures dealt with in this chapter we found ideologies of male dominance, uneven sexual mores, or other "unfair" beliefs and practices. Given that these societies are not really egalitarian, the dominant position of women in the family becomes even more significant.

Melford Spiro has argued that family and religion "are related to one another in a systematic relationship which holds for no two other sociocultural systems" (1984, 35). Religious systems, in Spiro's view, are metaphorical expressions of family relations. "[R]eligious symbols often represent the transformation and elaboration, at the **cultural** level, of fantasies and cognitions that are found at the **psychological** level, which in turn are produced by family relations at the **social** level" (1984, 36). The examples presented in this chapter certainly bear out the association between kinship and religion: Family and household arrangements, more than any other social structural element, are correlated with the rise and existence of female-dominated religions. To my mind, this is hardly surprising. As Clifford Geertz has eloquently shown, religion is how people come to terms with the "ultimate conditions" of existence, with birth, suffering, and death. Birth, suffering, and death, of course, also constitute the very essence of kinship and domestic relations. Thus we find that in societies in which kin ties center on mothers, mothers have powerful roles in religious activity.

Three sets of factors provide insight into the association between women's religions and matrifocality or matrilineality. First, in several instances we have seen that the female-dominated religion is concerned with ancestor worship, and that the ancestors are solely or primarily matrilineal ancestors. Women's religions and matrilineality reinforce one another through the institutionalization of matrilineal ancestor worship. It must be pointed out, however, that this is only one possible scenario. In many matrilineal societies there is no female-dominated religion, and many female-dominated religions do not concern themselves with matrilineal ancestor worship.

Second, as I will show in greater detail in Chapter 3, women's religions tend to sacralize the maternal role. This meshes well with the fact that matrilineal and matrifocal societies also emphasize maternity. On the other hand, sacralization or idealization of the maternal role is not unique to female-dominated religions; it is also a feature of, for example, Catholicism and orthodox Judaism. In short, matrilineal ancestor worship and the sacralization of maternity provide some but not all of the answer to why women's religions are found in matrifocal/lineal/local societies.

Third, we note with interest Alice Schlegel's findings that the combination of matrilineality and matrilocality correlates with women having greater control over their persons and property, and with the availability to women of positions of importance outside the home (1972, 98–99). Schlegel concludes that when women are more independent at home, they are also more important in the society at large. And, "Even when female autonomy is low, my general impression is that it is higher in matrilineal than in patrilineal societies within any given culture cluster" (Schlegel 1972, 141). Thus matrilineality and matrilocality can be seen as allowing women the autonomy to develop their own religions.[16]

It may be more useful to turn the question around and instead of asking why women's religions occur in matrifocal and matrilineal societies, asking why they rarely occur in patrilineal societies. In patrilineal societies men are extremely (sometimes even obsessively) concerned with guaranteeing that the children whom their wives bear are truly their progeny. While it is likely that men in many societies wish to avoid raising other men's children, in patrilineal societies the issue is more acute—a man's children are the ones who will continue his patriline. Mistaken incorporation of a child who is not really his into his patriline can be a grievous affront to a man's ancestors, and can leave him without "true" descendants to perform ancestor rituals on his behalf when he dies. When the basic social link is along the male line, guaranteeing the soundness of that line becomes a key social problem. As a result, patrilineal societies develop various means—including religious means—to control women's fertility and thus to ensure that the patriline is "true." Among the most common means are virginity tests, modesty rules, and sexual taboos. As I will show in later chapters, these sorts of beliefs and rituals are rarely found in female-dominated religions. Quite to the contrary, in women's religions what we often find is that women's control of their own fertility is somehow sacralized or institutionalized. Apparently, religions that sacralize or institutionalize women's control of their own fertility are anathema to patrilineal societies.

THE *ZĀR* CULT AND DEPRIVATION THEORY

One of our key examples—the *zār* cult—seems to be an exception to the patterns laid out above. We now turn our attention to this extraordinarily fascinating case.

I. M. Lewis has argued that women's possession cults are peripheral religious movements that function as "thinly disguised protest movements directed against the dominant sex. They thus play a significant part in the sex-war in traditional societies and cultures where women lack more obvious and direct means for forwarding their aims" (1975, 31). Lewis's theory is an example of deprivation theory—the notion that people who are deprived of satisfaction in other areas of their lives turn to religion as compensation or as an outlet for their frustration. While Lewis himself has backed off from deprivation theory in the new edition of his classic *Ecstatic Religion* (Second Edition, 1989), deprivation theory has been, and continues to be, widely used to explain women's religious participation.[17]

Deprivation theory suggests that when women suffer from intense subordination in political, ideological, economic, and social realms, membership in marginal (female) religions may serve as a safety valve. By periodically participating in exciting religious rituals, women blow off enough steam to enable them to continue functioning in an overall cultural context that denies them the freedom to control their own lives.

Zār is the very example that inspired Lewis's ideas about women and religion. As I will show in greater detail in Chapter 13, *zār* beliefs and rituals are situated in highly patriarchal cultures. Women who participate in the *zār* cult are undoubtedly oppressed in almost every sphere of life. If we accept that *zār* beliefs and rituals attract women because of their subordinate status, we would expect that when there is a change in women's status for the better *zār* would decline, and for the worse *zār* would increase. Pamela Constantinides (1982) provides us with a test case: In rural Sudanese villages social and kinship ties overlap, and seclusion of women is often irrelevant because there are few unrelated males from whom women need to be secluded. Women engage in gardening work outside the household, attend life-cycle events, and can band together to pressure their husbands into protesting against a man who wants to divorce his wife. When a woman moves to town her range of social activity is more limited, and she loses the support of female kin. Whereas men who have moved to town can join work associations, sports clubs, Muslim brotherhoods, and political parties, these options are unavailable to women. And indeed, Constantinides has found that in the Sudan *zār* is particularly popular among women in urban environments.

Thus far everything that I have written is common wisdom concerning both women and religion, and the *zār* cult. Yet I suspect that this is not the entire story.

Historical documentation for *zār* religion is problematic. While some scholars trace its inception to eighteenth-century Ethiopia, it is clear that similar beliefs and rituals involving spirit possession are not new to Africa. What may be new is the organization of these beliefs and rituals into an identifiable "cult" rather than their being an intrinsic and inextricable part of the broader cultural setting. Given the rapid crystallization and spread of *zār* religion in the modern era, it is crucial to note that *zār* tends to grow together with male migration from villages to cities. Could it be that as more and more men leave the villages, the social organization and kinship structure in the villages shifts toward matrifocality?[18]

Here I would like to quote at some length from Janice Boddy's study of the *zār* in a Sudanese village. "Today more men native to Hofriyat live outside the village for most of the year than live within it. However, adult women are far less mobile. Whereas the nonresidency rate for males between the ages of fifteen and forty-nine is 63 percent, the comparable rate for women is only 25 percent" (1989, 39). Boddy describes a typical contemporary family history: After the wedding the groom goes back to the city to work while the bride "remains in her natal household until after the births of several children. . . . The ratio of adult women to adult men in Hofriyat is understandably high: 2.2:1. **Yet it is a situation which many women say they prefer**" (1989, 40–41, my emphases). Boddy found that in Hofriyat there "is an explicit preference for women who are near relatives to live together" (1989, 41). Even women who live with their husbands' kin generally return to their own mothers' homes during pregnancy, remaining there for a prolonged period after the birth, often extending such visits to quasi-permanent residence. Boddy explicitly refers to the growing "tendency toward matrilocal residence and matrifocal groupings" (1989, 83) in the village she studied.

Village women manage the household and maintain informal networks of exchange of food, childcare, support, and information with other women. Women have a great deal of say regarding whom their children marry because in this highly sexually segregated society only women can provide information about potential brides. Women prefer their sons to marry girls from their own family, not from their husband's family. And indeed, mother's brother's daughter marriage is more frequent than father's sister's daughter. This preference serves to strengthen the bonds among matrilineally related women.

Women spend a great deal of their time socializing and visiting, especially with sick neighbors and relatives, new mothers, girls and boys after circumcision, and mourners. Women mostly socialize with other women, yet they also maintain strong social ties with their brothers and sons (relations with husbands tend to be weaker). Rural Northern Sudanese women, according to Boddy, are far from social isolates, yet they are highly active in *zār* religion.

I would argue that *zār* possession both mirrors and enhances the matrifocal leanings of the Northern Sudanese village.[19] *Zār* affliction is transmitted along the maternal line, particularly in cases in which the *zār* has been turned into a powerful protective spirit (Messing 1958). Thus mothers and daughters or sisters may share the same spirit; "[T]hese bonds resemble the alignments of descent" (Boddy 1989, 241).

In the preceding paragraphs I have tried to show that in the villages *zār* is associated with matrifocality. Yet we began this section with reference to the *zār* cult among urban women, and with an assumption that because of their greater social deprivation they have greater need of *zār* involvement. Now let us try to rephrase the same bit of information. According to I. M. Lewis's most recent book, "The implicitly rebellious, feminist tome of Ethiopian *zār* is, perhaps, most clearly evident in towns where **a high proportion of marginalised single women, living autonomously** as beer sellers and prostitutes, are heavily involved in *zār* coteries (my emphases)" (1991, 3). In other words, *zār* flourishes among urban women who live in matrifocal households!

Could it be that the same woman whom one researcher sees as lonely and deprived, another researcher sees as independent and autonomous? In reality, the same woman may well be both lonely and autonomous. The question is which side of the coin—deprivation or independence—more convincingly explains women's religious participation. In light of the other examples of women's religions that we have seen in this chapter, I unequivocally argue for independence.

Deprivation theory would lead us to expect that in highly patriarchal societies women have more of a need to use religion as an emotional outlet. In relatively egalitarian societies women would either have less need for religious activism and so be content with lower level membership roles in male-dominated religions, or the mainstream religion itself would offer women meaningful roles and so obviate the need for an autonomous women's religion.

While this hypothesis sounds eminently plausible, I believe it to be untrue. In thoroughly patriarchal societies women are unlikely to have the intellectual, financial, or social freedom to establish or join women's religions. A far more common religious strategy in very patriarchal cultures is for women to "domesticate" religion—to reinterpret aspects of the dominant male religion in ways that they as women find meaningful.

Elderly Kurdish Jewish women in Israel, for example, are deprived by almost every measure of social and psychological deprivation: they are poor, old, sick and illiterate in a culture that values money, youth, health, and education; they are women in a man's world; they are pious members of a religious system that relegates women to the sidelines ritually and theologically. As I have shown in an earlier book (Sered 1992), these women do not establish an alternative, female-dominated religion. Instead, they modify and reinterpret Jewish rituals, symbols, institutions, and beliefs in directions that give meaning to their role as mothers and protect the children for whom they, as mothers, are responsible. Similar religious strategies and emphases have been noted for Muslim women (Beck 1980; Jamzadeh and Mills 1986; Ladislav 1988), urban Hindu women (Beech, 1982), rural Hindu women (Thompson 1983; Wadley 1980), Spanish Christian women (Christian 1972), and Christian women in rural Greece (Danforth 1982).

An even more serious problem with deprivation theory is one that it shares with almost all functionalist interpretations of religious behavior: It assumes that people (and, it seems, especially women) behave religiously because of social and psychological reasons rather than for religious reasons. Leading deprivation theory proponents Rodney Stark and William Bainbridge (1985, 417) claim that American women more than men join novel religious movements, and in particular deviant religious movements, because of their relative deprivation in career and other public opportunities, and because of their solitary confinement in the nuclear family which turns women into social isolates. The essence of their argument is that women join religious groups for nonreligious motives. My own fieldwork among elderly Kurdish Jewish women in Israel suggests that this formula glosses over the actuality that many women do have nonreligious options that would also give them a chance to get out of the house. The Kurdish women, for example, had access to a number of programs for senior citizens, yet chose to attend a senior citizens' day center at which almost all the activities, lectures, and tours deal with religion. Put differently, religiously active women should be understood as having **chosen** to be religiously active (unless in a specific instance there is clear evidence to the contrary).

A number of recent studies have begun to challenge deprivation theory in regard to women's religiosity. Arvind Sharma (1977) has asked how and why women in ancient India became Buddhist nuns. Out of a total of 68 women for whom he found textual information, at least 42 indicated that it was the spiritual attraction of Buddhism and not some form of personal, familial, or social deprivation that led them to become Buddhist nuns. Sharma found that deprivation theory explained only a small number of the cases.

Contrary to what deprivation theory would lead one to expect, the West African example cited at the beginning of this chapter suggests that some economic independence may be a "good" setting for women's religions. Nineteenth-century America shows that situations of social change may lend themselves to the formation of women's religions. All the examples indicate that gender disjunction or gender dissonance (manifested either as rapidly changing gender relationships or as important discrepancies between gender ideology and practice) is a feature of societies in which there are women's religions. But the examples that provide the most meaningful paradigm are those that show matrifocality (and especially matrilineality and matrilocality) as a significant social structural correlate of women's religions.

Matrifocality, more than any other element of the social structure, seems to provide women with a sense that their roles are powerful and important, with the opportunity for groups of related women to congregate on a regular basis, with an absence of ongoing male supervision of women's activities, and with access to vital social and economic resources.

The goal of this chapter was to explore in what types of societies women's religions are found. In looking for the "cause" of religious behavior in social structure, and especially kinship organization, we have followed along well-worn conceptual paths. Women's religious behavior has traditionally been treated as especially rooted in social structure (rather than in abstract thinking). A close look at the situations described in this book, however, suggests a dynamic interplay between religion and other aspects of human experience. The examples developed in this chapter leave us wondering whether female-dominated religions develop in matrifocal societies, or whether matrifocality is a structural expression of an ideology of female power.

The significant point, to my mind, is that women's religions not only occur in matrilineal and matrifocal societies, but that they also emphasize and preserve matrilineality and matrifocality. In officially matrilineal societies such as Northern Thailand the connection is obvious, but in the other examples it is perhaps of even greater interest. Sande membership, for instance, ensures that a married woman retains her ties with her natal family. Sande women return to their mother's chapters (where they themselves were initiated) to give birth. Women's religions typically tie into the society at the point of matrifocality or matrilineality, strengthening and dramatizing that point.

In addition to the features of matrifocality that we have spelled out, Nancy Tanner has noted two other characteristics of matrifocality: **a woman's role as mother is more important than her role as wife, and the role of mother is ritually elaborated**. In most female-dominated religions, as in most matrifocal societies, a woman's identity as mother predominates over her identity as wife. To a large extent, women's religions center around the ritual elaboration of the maternal role. In the next chapter we will see how this works. We will look more closely at the multidirectional borrowing of contexts, needs, and meanings between women's familial lives and women's religions. Women's religions not only occur in matrifocal societies, but motherhood is what brings many women to women's religions, and in these religions maternity is a potent symbol.

Notes

1. This does not mean that gender consonance is a cross-culturally "normal" situation. It simply means that women's religions seem to occur in situations in which the degree of gender dissonance is greater than usual.

2. The reader may notice that I have avoided using the words "patriarchal" or "egalitarian" in laying out the social contexts of these religions. Cross-culturally, gender inequality takes a multitude of forms. Evaluating particular cultures as less or more patriarchal is a complex and often delicate task. In recent years many feminist anthropologists have concluded that the most interesting question is not "Is this society sexist?" but rather "What manifestations of patriarchy are most apparent in this culture?" For the purposes of this book (and with some misgivings), I define as "highly patriarchal" societies in which women do not exert control over their own time, bodies, fertility, finances, and mobility. "Egalitarian" (or relatively egalitarian) societies are ones in which women are free to make important decisions regarding their own lives, and have input into decisions that affect the society as a whole. The majority, although not all, of the women's religions are located in relatively egalitarian societies.

3. This is not an unusual scenario. Moral superiority often correlates with structural inferiority.

4. Some anthropologists, including Nancy Tanner, now believe that the "original" or "core" human family is the mother-child unit (cf. also Gough 1968) and that other kinship systems are superstructures that build on or partially negate this matrifocal core. While I suspend judgment regarding the absolute truth of this claim (I do find it tempting), such a universalistic notion of matrifocality does not help us understand the particular societies in which female-dominated religions occur. What is relevant for our purposes is that in these particular societies matrifocality is **explicit**.

5. Anthropologists formerly used a much stricter definition of matrilineality and patrilineality, basing their conceptions on African systems of unilineal descent. We now know that the African models are not particularly useful outside Africa. In Southeast Asia, for instance, the notion of unilineal descent is problematic. On the other hand, in many cultures children are identified as belonging primarily to either the mother's or the father's kin-group. They inherit rights, obligations, and loyalties almost completely from one side or the other. It is in this broader, non-African sense that I use the term matrilineality.

According to Yanagisako, anthropology traditionally labeled household organization "according to the tie between its most genealogically 'close' members, because it is presumed that this relationship forms its structural core. If it contains two adult brothers, their wives and children, it is thus labeled a fraternal-joint family or household. . . . Yet obviously there is more to 'family structure' than genealogical composition" (1979, 185). Yanagisako's observation allows us to de-emphasize the patrilineal ideology of, for example, Korea, the Ryūkyū Islands, and the Northern Sudan, and look instead at the actual relationships and power distribution in the households. In all three cases, letting go of an overemphasis on genealogy allows us to see the actual matrifocal household arrangements.

6. In a recent paper Janet Chernela (1991) has re-examined one of the most notorious elements of Black Carib culture—couvade. Generations of anthropologists have been fascinated by cultures in which husbands imitate their wives' pregnancies and labor pains, or observe pregnancy or postpartum taboos along with or instead of their wives. Chernela explains couvade among Black Caribs of Honduras in terms of their belief that the father and the infant are inseparably linked because they share the same soul and because the baby is created out of the father's blood (the mother just nourishes it). Since the bond between the father and child is so strong, injudicious acts on the part of the father may injure the infant. Thus men must abstain from strenuous work when their babies are small. During this extended time, a woman's brothers (rather than her husband) are providers to her offspring. Couvade, by strengthening the economic ties

between sisters and brothers and by limiting the role of husbands, serves to underscore the matrifocal nature of Black Carib society.

7. There is little criminality, suicide, or violence on the Islands. During Sho Shin's reign (fifteenth–sixteenth century) the army was disbanded, and private use and owner-ship of arms outlawed.

8. During the past five or six generations there has been a tendency not to record women in genealogical records; before then women were always recorded. William Lebra sees this as evidence of the increasing stress on the male line in modern Okinawan society (1966).

9. A further bit of information that I am not sure how to interpret is Noguchi's observation that on Ikema Island wives are often older than their husbands (1966, 27). Since this arrangement is, from a cross-cultural perspective, anomalous (cross-culturally, husbands are far more often older than wives, and this age difference is typically reflected and enhanced through norms of male dominance and female subordination), we may wonder if there is some connection between female religious dominance and familial dominance that could be linked to wives being older than husbands.

10. Confucian ideology was known long before, and Neo-Confucian philosophy was adopted as a social blueprint in the fifteenth century, but the transformation of institutions took quite a bit longer (Kendall, personal communication 1992).

11. More urban than rural Brazilian households are headed by women. Merrick and Schmink (1983) estimate that between 1960 and 1970 one out of every five urban households was headed by a woman, and that number is increasing. Households headed by women show a higher incidence of poverty—44.9% fall below the poverty line, compared with 27.4% of households headed by men. There are several factors that contribute to the feminization of poverty in Brazil: in female-headed households it is unlikely that there is a second earner, women lack access to the formal sector job market, female-headed households have less access to basic government services such as the government sponsored health program (Instituto Nacional de Previdencia Social), and working mothers suffer from the lack of day care facilities.

12. The precise cultural constellation I have just described is true for late twentieth-century America, yet there is historical evidence that American society of the nineteenth century was also characterized by neolocality and by particularly strong bonds among women. Carol Smith Rosenberg, in a fascinating essay entitled "The Female World of Love and Ritual," has demonstrated that in the late eighteenth and nineteenth centuries, intimate and close female relationships were socially acceptable and normal parts of life. Close and trusting and loving female relationships included sisters, friends, mothers and daughters, young children, and mature women. Social networks tended to be single sex, and women shared in one another's birthings, deaths, weddings, vacations, and educational experiences. All of this should be seen as part of the background to the emergence of female-dominated religions in nineteenth-century America.

13. This is not meant to belittle the discrimination lesbians suffer in many areas of American life.

14. Luvale women, according to Anita Spring, have few live births, many genital and urinary-tract diseases, barrenness, and frequent miscarriages and stillbirths. Many women suffer from chronic abdominal pain, dysmenorrhea, and fevers caused by bacte-ria and parasites. These diseases are seldom fatal, but do cause infertility and weak health. The women are particularly susceptible to bilharziasis, a disease that affects the genitalia, because they enter stagnant pools of water to catch fish with drag baskets. Almost half the adult women reported symptoms consistent with either gonorrhea or bilharziasis (see Chapter 5 for more on women and illness).

15. One female-dominated religion that is located in a truly patrilocal and patrilineal society is the religion of the Tetum of Timor Island. David Hicks describes the complex series of birth rituals (some performed by men and some by women) that culminates in a rite in which "[T]he infant's agnates place themselves on one side of the mat facing their affines, opposite. With the baby between, agnates and affines commence to lampoon each other, with the women cupping their hands into nearby pitchers, and flinging water at those on the opposite side of the mat [i.e., their in-laws]" (1984, 48). This rite seems to indicate a certain discomfort with the patrilineal identity of the newborn baby.

16. Not all matrilineal societies include female-dominated religions. The Hopi—the very society studied by Schlegel—is an example of a matrilineal and highly egalitarian society in which men dominate the religious domain. Women do have active roles in the religion, but men's roles are more prominent (Schlegel 1977).

17. "Lewis bashing" has become a favorite pastime of some anthropologists. While I do not agree with everything that Lewis wrote about women and religion, he is one of the very few scholars who has even tried to develop cross-culturally meaningful models for looking at women's religious lives. It is worth pointing out that the bulk of his work on women and religion was completed before the introduction of feminist ideas into the academy.

18. The link between male migration and women's religion is intriguing and needs further research. Regarding Mexican Spiritualism, for example, Kaja Finkler reports that more adherents than non-adherents are unmarried and more are members of families in which at least one person migrated in search of wage labor at some point (1986, 633).

19. Boddy cites evidence suggesting that in the past Northern Sudanese society was not patrilineal. "From well before the Christian millennium until at least the fifteenth century AD, and perhaps for some centuries thereafter, matrilineality with preferred endogamy and adelphic succession were predominant structural principles in the region of Sudan stretching north along the Nile from Khartoum to the Dongola Reach" (1992, 7).

3

Maternity and Meaning

In the previous chapter we have seen that family organization, more than any other aspect of social structure, sets the stage for women's religions. A range of identities describe women's familial relationships: daughter, sister, wife, co-wife, mother, grandmother, aunt, cousin, niece. In different cultural situations, and throughout the life cycle, various of these identities become most salient for specific women. The implications of this seemingly obvious statement are important.

According to anthropologist Karen Sacks (1979), in African societies characterized by a patrilineal kin corporate mode of production, young women—**daughters** in their natal groups and **wives** in their affinal groups—have a uniformly low status. As a woman ages, she becomes a **sister** in her own group (her brothers also age and so her key relationship is to her brothers who have now replaced father as decision makers and resource allocators) and a **mother** (of adult children) in her husband's group. Because mothers and sisters (as opposed to daughters and wives) control their own and other people's labor, these roles entail higher status. Sacks looked only at African societies, yet it is likely that the distinction between mother and wife holds true in many other cultures as well. For example, in Northern Thailand a woman's status as mother is significantly higher than her status as wife (Mougne 1984; see also Martin 1990 on Mexican women's use of motherhood as a source of spiritual and political strength). Miriam Johnson cites studies carried out in the United States indicating that in young children's fantasy play both boys and girls depict wives as helpless, yet they depict mothers as nurturant and efficient (1988, 198).

Religions, like all social institutions, tend to address individuals through only one or two of their possible identities. In male-dominated religions women receive attention when they impinge on male space or interests. Not surprisingly, male-dominated religions—institutions in which adult men are in charge—deal with and define women primarily as wives. As a result, much of the discourse regarding women concerns menstrual pollution and taboos as they affect husbands (a woman's children and even her parents are rarely affected by her menstruating). Male-dominated religions also relate to women as daughters, especially in the sense of daughters whose virginity must be guarded over.

In female-dominated religions neither wife nor daughter is the most salient aspect of women's identity (which is not to say that women are **never** addressed as wives or daughters). Instead, women receive attention primarily as mothers, grandmothers, or sisters. It is typically in these roles that women join these religions; women's concerns as mothers, grandmothers, or sisters are addressed by these religions; women's roles as mothers, grandmothers, or sisters are highly elaborated and dramatized in these religions; and mothers, grandmothers, and sisters have prominent mythic and symbolic roles.

In Chapters 10 and 13 I look more closely at women as sisters. The remainder of the present chapter is dedicated to exploring the religious significance of motherhood in women's religions. In light of the discussion of social context in the previous chapter, it is clear that the accent on women as mothers in female-dominated religions is associated with the matrifocal nature of the cultures in which these religions are located. Matrifocal societies tend toward structural arrangements that de-emphasize a definition of women as wives and give prominence to women as mothers.

MOTHERHOOD AND RELIGION

Motherhood is a multifaceted experience, both in terms of how a particular woman feels and behaves as a mother during the course of her life (pregnant women and great-grandmothers experience motherhood in different ways) and in terms of how different cultures construct motherhood. That women give birth is biological fact. The ways in which cultures interpret that fact are infinitely variable. Still, the intense and powerful psychological, social, and biological experiences of motherhood are central in the lives of most women. Religions (male dominated and female dominated) address issues of motherhood. Religions may tell women how many children to have, when, and with whom; religions may tell women that celibacy is preferable to fertility; religions may tell women that infertility is a punishment from the gods; and religions may tell women how to raise and educate their children. Cross-culturally, religions interpret the experiences of motherhood.

Many male-dominated religions recognize that motherhood gives women power. This realization leads to beliefs and practices such as subincision (in which men cut their penises in order to mimic women's natural functions), belief in virgin mother goddesses or male gods or heroes who create out of their own bodies (Adam and Eve; Zeus and Athena), couvade, and glorification of male supremacy (see Kittay 1983).

Motherhood is a fundamental image, a key ritual focus, and a chief theological concern in women's religions. In some women's religions motherhood is believed to bestow upon women deep spiritual insights. In others motherhood is what led women to be dissatisfied with the male-dominated religions practiced by their fathers or husbands. And in still other female-dominated religions motherhood is what shapes women's ritual roles. Through ritual and theology, female-dominated religions enhance, dramatize, and strengthen women's identities as mothers.

In contrast to male-dominated religions where mothers are typically envisioned from the perspective of children (and especially sons; see Chapter 8 on mother goddesses as projections of male infantile fantasies), in female-dominated religions the concern with motherhood is from the perspective of the mothers themselves.

Psychologist of religion Diane Jonte-Pace has used psychoanalytic object relations theory to develop a multidimensional understanding of the connection between mothering and religion. According to Jonte-Pace, object relations theorists have suggested that "the psychological capacity for religious experience lies in the relational maternal-infant matrix out of which a sense of selfhood and otherness emerges" (1987, 319). This capacity, according to theorists, is rooted in the early experience of symbiosis before the infant discerns the existence of a separate self.

While object relations theory is useful to feminist analysis, it is crucial to bear in mind that like all psychoanalytic theory, it locates religiosity (together with almost all other elements of personality) in early stages of psychological development. Motherhood, however, is an experience of **adult** women. Alexandra Kaplan and Janet Surrey critique most existing theories of psychological development on just that point. They suggest that women's capabilities for relationships should be examined not only in terms of the early precursors of this relational capacity as developed within the mother-daughter relationship, but also in terms of the development of this relational capacity throughout the life cycle. They propose a model of psychological growth that underscores "development as a dynamic process of growth *within* relationship" (1984, 87).

The evidence of women's religions highlights the relevance of developmental models. In this and the next chapter I present women who, because of their adult experience of child death, became dissatisfied with the religion in which they were raised. It is difficult to interpret this sort of process within a model that situates religion in infancy. Psychological development does not end with early adulthood, and in the second part of the present chapter I show how grandmothers differ from mothers in their experience of religion.

Before we continue, let me clarify that I do not claim that the mother-child bond is intense, loving, and momentous in all cultures; I do claim that this is the case in the societies in which women's religions are situated. Let me also clarify that I have not found that in all female-dominated religions women are seen only as mothers. As Diana Burfield (1983) has pointed out, in Theosophy maternal feelings seemed not to be emphasized, and several female leaders were childless. On the other hand, in the vast majority of known women's religions, motherhood so clearly emerges as the pivotal theme that I feel justified in organizing my own observations around the notion of motherhood.

Ritual Control of Fertility—Sande

In women's religions childbirth is not merely a biological event. Motherhood is vested with important cultural significance, and rituals express and validate the emotional and symbolic meanings of motherhood. In many women's religions, theology and ceremony provide women with some measure of control over fertility.

Sande rituals give social definition to motherhood, and teach that definition to young initiates. The gender ideology taught by Sande stresses gender distinction (women and men are clearly different), respect for women's bodies, dependence on fellow women, and preserving women's secret knowledge and power.

During the Sande initiation period girls are fed abundant quantities of high quality food. Fatness is seen as linked to beauty, prosperity, health, and fertility. Carol MacCormack (1982, 125) suggests that in geographical regions (such as Sierra Leone) where there are periodic food shortages, the deliberate fattening of young women combined with the belief that full-bodied mature women are more beautiful has a selective advantage in terms of promoting fertility and decreasing infant mortality. This is a crucial consideration in a society in which women give birth to many children (often eight or more), and more than half are likely to die at a young age. In addition, Sande rules prohibit sexual intercourse while a woman is lactating, ensuring some spacing of children. Sande women know that they control a scarce and important resource: offspring. Sande women also know that they can withhold that resource if their husbands violate Sande laws.

Initiated Sande women "do not have sexual intercourse in any place, at any time, with any person they wish, as animals do. Such 'natural' behavior would be a grievous offense to ancestral spirits, whose wrath might rain disease and infertility on the people and the land. Successful bearing and rearing of children is informed by Sande knowledge about hygiene, nutrition, medicine, and myriad other practical techniques rather than being a careless matter of doing what comes naturally. . . . Rather than being uncontrolled reproduction machines, Sande women, with their secret knowledge, public laws, legitimate sanctions, and hierarchical organization, bring women's biology under the most careful cultural control" (MacCormack 1977, 94).

According to Carol MacCormack, a central function of Sande is to provide women and men with a cultural rather than a purely biological understanding of fertility. Sande beliefs and ceremonies are a striking example of how a women's religion empowers motherhood.

At the Center of the Web—Korean Mothers

Almost all the women's religions enhance and support women's familial involvement and provide women with concepts and rituals that interpret motherhood from a gynocentric perspective. In the following paragraphs the household-oriented religion of the women of Korea is presented. The crucial point, as shown by Laurel Kendall, is that for Korean women it is not the formal definition of family (in the sense of official patrilineality) but rather a relationship-based informal conception of family (in the sense of all people dead and alive with whom the woman has ties that she herself perceives as familial) that has meaning in the female ritual sphere.

Korean women are marginal in formal Confucianist and Buddhist ritual. A daughter who marries out of her natal family is no longer part of that family, and as a wife in her husband's family she has only minor and limited ritual obligations. From the point of view of children, mother's relatives have no ancestor rituals. "Some informants even say that a man's natural mother is entitled to [Confucianist] ancestor rituals only because she is the wife of his father—it does not matter that she bore him" (Janelli and Janelli 1982, 120). In Korean men's rituals, family hierarchy and patrilineal kinship relations are critical.

Women's household rituals and shaman's *kut*, on the other hand, include the extended bilateral family. Various ancestors and relatives who are irrelevant to men's rituals are important to *kut* (dead children, matrilineal relatives, husband's married sisters, etc.). In women's household religion, mothers have key ritual and theological roles. A great deal of women's ritual life revolves around domestic rituals aimed at safeguarding the well-being of their families. As a mother with her own household a woman comes into her own religiously. The household religion of Korean women has to do, above all, with women's role as mothers. Illness of a child or other family member is often the reason for a Korean woman to make a food offering to the household gods or to consult a shaman.

Whereas both men's and women's religion in Korea are oriented toward family, male religion treats family as a hierarchical ladder linking generations of men to their ancestors. In the female religion family is envisioned as a web of varied relationships—a web in which a mother/housewife stands at the hub. Korean men's religious rituals revolve around generations of fathers. Korean women's rituals revolve around mothers.

Symbolic Motherhood—Shakers, Black Spiritual Churches, and Tensho-Kotai-Jingu-Kyu

Moving from concrete motherhood to more symbolic treatments, we find that the Shakers used imagery that reflected maternity. Founder Ann Lee described herself as having "labored" until she received the gifts of God and the Gospel. When Lee experienced her soul's encounter with God, "I felt as sensibly as ever a woman did a child, when she was delivered of it. Then I felt an unspeakable joy in God, and my flesh came upon me, like the flesh of an infant" (quoted in Kern 1981, 73). Later Shakers also used childbirth metaphors in regard to Ann Lee. Sarah Lucas, for example, described Lee's role in delivering believers "from the fetal condition of our natural and worldly life" and birthing souls "out of the world state into the Christ state" (quoted in Kitch 1989, 137).

According to Shaker traditions, Ann Lee embodied the highest ideals of motherhood. "She was depicted as a concerned, loving, solicitous individual who developed deep personal relationships with her followers—her children" (Stein 1992, 22).[1]

Images of laboring and pregnancy and nurturing children were important symbols for Shakers, and many of the early Shaker converts regarded Lee as their mother. Procter-Smith (1985, 148) quotes a song about Ann Lee written in the 1820s (in this song "Mother" is Ann Lee):

> Mothers love is like an ocean
> Mothers love will make me free
> Mothers love it is so wholesome
> I can skip and dance and play
> Mothers love it beautifies me
> Mothers love is pure I know
> Precious love o how I prize thee
> Mothers love come round me flow.

Sally Kitch persuasively argues that for the Shakers the "metaphor of spiritual motherhood is a positive symbol for women because it transforms qualities that have been perceived as liabilities of female gender symbolism into strengths. . . . The metaphor of spiritual motherhood reveals the cultural value hidden in traditional female characteristics, personalities, and experiences" (1989, 138). We will return to this theme in Chapter 10, where I show that many women's religions accept prevalent notions of femininity, while reinterpreting as strengths traits defined as weaknesses in the society at large.

Female founders of religions are often called Mother, and utilize maternal symbols to explain their religious roles. For example, Mother Catherine, one of the early leaders of the New Orleans Black Spiritual movement, claimed, "I got all kinds of children, but I am they mother. Some of 'em are saints, some of 'em are conzempts (convicts) and jailbirds; some of 'em kills babies in their bodies; some of 'em walks the streets at night—but they's all my children. God got all kinds, how come I cain't love all of mine" (quoted in Jacobs and Kaslow 1991, 167).

To take one last example, Mrs. Kitamura, the foundress of the new Japanese religion Tensho-Kotai-Jingu-Kyu, realized her special calling when she became conscious of a mysterious spiritual force or soul residing in her abdomen. At first she believed that this strange inner force, which annoyed her and compelled her to do queer things, was an evil spirit, but it later identified itself to her as the Absolute God of the Universe. This God is referred to by Mrs. Kitamura and her followers as "God-in-her-abdomen" (May 1954, 123). In light of our previous examples, I am not surprised that a woman who "gives birth to" a new religion does so by discovering the deity residing within her belly.[2]

Motherhood and Spiritual Intuition—
Spiritualism and Feminist Spirituality

A number of women's religions posit that motherhood enables women to intuit spiritual truths and reach higher levels of ethical understanding. "Spiritualists and Women's Rights advocates shared the belief that women's experience as mothers gave them a heightened sense of values which justified their departure from tradition. As mothers, they objected to the fate of their children in the theology preached by men and in the society controlled by men" (Braude 1985, 427).

The contemporary Feminist Spirituality Movement has emphasized the notion that because women are mothers they understand love, relationship, and spirituality in ways that men do not. One of the most developed feminist works to deal with motherhood from a religious perspective (or, more precisely, to deal with religion from the perspective of motherhood) is Kathryn Rabuzzi's book *Motherself* in which she contrasts the mythic, male quest for selfhood with the "way of the mother." "Through the natural processes of childbirth women inherently possess means for experiencing the mysteries associated with the ancient earth mother goddesses such as Demeter. Like the 'dead' seed of grain buried for a season in the ground, the human seed planted in the woman's body also forms new life. Rather than cause for guilt, this is reason for joyous wonder. Emergence of life from the womb—whether that of woman or earth—incorporates the essence of women's mysteries. . . . Childbirth really means participating in the mysteries of the Goddess" (1988, 200). Rabuzzi argues that through giving birth women participate in and come to understand cosmic creation.

Spiritual Feminists explore the relationship between mother goddesses and real women. (This theme will be examined in more detail in Chapter 8.) Writings of the Feminist Spirituality Movement claim that human religiosity originated in the awe felt by early humans contemplating women's powers of childbirth. "The mysteries of female biology dominated human religious and artistic thought, as well as social organization, for at least the first 200,000 years of human life on earth. . . . The first human images known to us . . . are magic images of the mysterious power of the female to create life out of herself, and to sustain it" (Sjoo and Mor 1987, 46). Monica Sjoo and Barbara Mor imagine what early humans were thinking and feeling when they designed and celebrated the Goddess. "As we read the powerful magic signs of the Great Mother's celebration, we can read these first women's powerful discoveries and celebrations of themselves. The religious beliefs, the mysteries and rites developed by ancient women, grew organically out of women's supreme roles as cultural producers, mothers, and prime communicators with the spirit world. The mysteries of creation, transformation, and recurrence—the primal mysteries of all religions—emerged from women's direct physical and psychic experiences of these mysteries: in bleeding, in growing a child, in nursing, in working with fire, in making a pot, in planting a seed" (1987, 50).

In contrast to white Spiritual Feminists, black Womanist theologians have emphasized the historical experience of nurturing more than the symbolic meaning of childbirth. "For the womanist, mothering and nurturing are vitally important. [Alice] Walker's womanist reality begins with mothers relating to their children and is characterized by black women (not necessarily bearers of children) nurturing great numbers of black people in the liberation struggle" (Williams 1989, 183).

GRANDMOTHERS—EXPERT MOTHERS

In many cultures the grandmother role is an extension of the mother role. Grandmothers, like mothers, nurture and raise the young. This is especially so in matrifocal societies, where households typically revolve around a senior woman, her daughters, and their children. While **participants** in women's religions are mothers, **leaders** tend to be grandmothers.

The available literature on women in male-dominated religions suggests two rather different sorts of reasons why older women are ritually active. Ideologically, postmenopausal women (unlike younger women) would not be excluded from sacred places and activities because of menstrual pollution (Gutmann 1977). Pragmatically, older women are more likely to have the necessary free time and autonomy to dedicate to religious leadership (Sered 1992).

Writing about women in Morocco, Susan Davis reports that women are thought to become expert practitioners of magic as they grow older. Old women may actively seek contact with the spirit world. Certain old women are healers and are believed to know magic that helps wives deal with unsatisfactory husbands. "Not that a woman would ever threaten her husband openly; but all men know that angry women, and especially angry older women, are dangerous" (1982, 117). The scenario presented by Davis is a common one in male-dominated religious cultures—old women, and especially widows, are suspected of being independent of male control and run the risk of being accused of witchcraft. In women's religions, on the other hand, the enhanced religious activity and prestige of older women lies in their superior knowledge of rituals and theology—erudition that they have accumulated over the years of their lives. Unlike in Morocco, this female expertise is judged as beneficent. And unlike in, for example, Jewish societies, this expertise is institutionalized (see Chapter 11).

Ritual Expertise—Black Carib Grandmothers

In Black Carib culture women "plug in" to the religious system as mothers and grandmothers. "Female responsibility to lineal kin serves as an organizing principle of Black Carib kinship and ritual, and as the focus of female unity and collective action. Maternal obligations are primary, broadly defined, and life long. As mothers, women share common concerns and a valued identity, one that commands respect (not only from their children). Motherhood connotes strength, the capacity and duty to protect others. Women act together to achieve this end" (Kerns 1983, 182).

Black Carib women of all ages exhibit concern for their children's health. This concern is manifested through ritual and more pragmatic procedures. Observers have noticed that among the Black Caribs childless women are usually less involved in ritual affairs, having fewer resources and less incentive to take part in ceremonies (Kerns 1983, 77).

For Black Carib women, as for women around the world, infant mortality has been a major emotional and religious concern (see Chapter 4). Virginia Kerns reports that some older women in Belize tell of having borne a dozen children of whom less than half survived to adulthood, and even today many women lose at least one child (1983, 95). "Their major responsibility as mothers, at any age, is to care for their children and protect them" (Kerns 1992b, 97). It is typically grandmothers who have the knowledge and the resources— both medical and spiritual—to protect children.

Women (as opposed to men, in Black Carib culture) are responsible for preserving the health of children and grandchildren. Women are in charge of searching for cures when a child is sick. They are in charge of observing precautions on behalf of their unborn children while pregnant. A woman's behavior and her child's well-being are seen as inexorably intertwined. Among the culturally recognized sources of illness (see Chapter 5) is taboo behavior on the part of the mother of the afflicted individual. For example, a pregnant or post-partum woman may endanger her child's health by consorting with a man other than the father of that child (see Staiano 1981). A woman who does not fulfill her ritual responsibilities endangers her children's health. Yet (and here is where we see one of the more distinctive features of Black Carib culture), female infidelity is not seen as a violation of male property rights, but rather as a dereliction of maternal duty (Kerns 1992b, 99).[3]

For women, ritual is a matter of maternal and filial duty. From a young age women teach their children a sense of responsibility and gratitude toward mothers. In return, Black Carib women represent their children to the ancestors at placation rituals. Black Carib culture is a potent example of an ongoing situation in which motherhood and religion overlap. Yet it is as grandmothers that the mothering-religion complex emerges most forcefully. **Most women begin to become ritual experts when their own mothers die.**

Among the Black Caribs, women of childbearing age must follow certain restrictions, in particular ones having to do with mobility. The capacity to bear children carries a social cost. Older women are more mobile and more socially visible. The loss of fertility is accompanied by the loss of many constraints. (Kerns 1983, 193). Older women are responsible for enforcing the behavioral constraints that are incumbent on younger women. In old age women enjoy increasing autonomy and freedom of movement as they are freed both from household chores and suspicions of improper sexual conduct. "Immunity from supernatural harm is said to increase with age" (Kerns 1992b, 106). In addition, older women have access to money sent them by children employed in the cities. And finally, older women tend to know more about both reproductive processes and rituals.

Old age is more difficult for men, for whom loss of independence is a difficult issue. Women have spent their lives developing bonds of interdependence, and in old age may cash in on some of the rewards of years of nurturing others. They expect and receive support from grown children and grandchildren, and many old women manage to accumulate more money than they had been able to accumulate when younger.

Kerns (1983, 190) found that many older Black Carib women admit that they once thought little of rituals but have now come to understand their value. The central ritual constellation of the Black Caribs concerns death and funeral ceremonies for lineal ancestors. These ceremonies, organized by older women, protect the health and well-being of their descendants. Older Black Carib women are the ritual leaders, and they may badger anyone who is reluctant to sponsor or attend appropriate rituals. It is usually the eldest living woman relative who organizes the ritual. The organizer collects funds, sets the dates, informs others, purchases supplies, and oversees preparations. Smaller rituals are attended only by old women, and old women have informal networks of reciprocity among themselves in organizing rituals (Kerns 1983, 171–176).

In sum, as Virginia Kerns shows, "Older women, who act together to enforce . . . rules . . . that support moral and social order, have a perceived power to protect and preserve, and so to serve the common good" (1992b, 107). It could be said that the religious power of Black Carib women does not even end with their deaths: Douglas Taylor (1951, 98) notes that the Dominica Caribs mourn longer for a mother (three years) than for a father (two years).

Family Representatives—East and Southeast Asian Senior Women

In several female-dominated religions the senior woman of the household or the lineage is in charge of rituals on behalf of the family. In Okinawan (Ryūkyūan) religion, "Calendrical dates and calendrical fortunes are closely watched by the senior female in the household, who is usually familiar with the details concerning each member's personal calendar history" (Lebra 1966, 49). The senior woman announces forthcoming rites, prepares the ceremonial offerings, places them on the altar, and prays. Similarly, Burmese women make large ceremonial offerings to their own and their husband's *nats* (spirits) once a year. Alternatively, the family may give a contribution to an older female relative who knows better than they how to make the offerings. The offering to the *nat* of the paddy fields is made by the work gang leader, who is usually the eldest of the women who transplant and harvest the rice (J. Nash 1966).

In Northern Thailand shrines to the *phii puu njaa* (spirits) are located in the stem house; that is, in the house where the founding ancestress of the family or cult group lived. Other branches of the family usually live nearby. The entire cult group shares a spirit (some ethnographers refer to this as the clan spirit), which is conceptualized as divided among the individual households of the cult group. In each generation, one family member—typically the eldest woman— is responsible for presenting the offerings to the spirits. Within each household, the eldest woman is responsible for caring for the household spirit. If members of a cult group move far away from the stem house, they are expected to build a new shrine at the home of the eldest woman of their group.

Nature and Nurture

Grandmothers as expert mothers epitomize the theme of nurture rather than the theme of nature. Grandmothers are experts not because they continue to be fertile, but because they are specially knowledgeable about how to take care of children. The Womanist emphasis on the social aspects of motherhood is more in line with the majority of women's religions than is the Spiritual Feminist emphasis on the mysteries of the biological process of birthing (see above).

Female-dominated religions offer women conceptions of motherhood that are not merely biological. Female-dominated rituals spiritualize motherhood and proclaim that motherhood has social value. It is not only the biological ability to give birth that empowers women in female-dominated religions, and birth is rarely glorified or even especially ritualized. Female-dominated religions honor women less in their role as birthers than in their role as nurturers. I see it as significant that the one women's religion to ceremonialize the physicality of birthing—Sande—in fact **socializes** fertility and birth. In women's religions mothers are powerful beings whose social bonds with their children give them ritual and spiritual strength. It is instructive that Shakers—a women's religion that requires celibacy—still use motherhood imagery in talking about spiritual progress.

THE MEANING AND IMPLICATIONS OF MOTHERHOOD

In this chapter we have begun to look at the implications of women's identity as "mother." Unlike in male-dominated religions, in women's religions the content of that identity is described from an adult and gynocentric perspective. In subsequent chapters we will see the myriad ways in which motherhood affects women's religious choices. But before we go on, it is necessary to clarify what I mean by motherhood. The meaning of motherhood is not as indisputable as it seems at first glance. Surrogacy cases have surely shown us that motherhood, like gender, is culturally constructed.[4]

There are two overlapping yet distinct aspects to motherhood: physiological and social. The physiological aspects include conception, pregnancy, childbirth, lactation, and maternal mortality. A central question in this book is whether these physiological processes receive particular attention in women's religions. The discussion of motherhood in this chapter does **not** indicate that this is the case.[5]

The social aspects of motherhood consist of the activities, rights, responsibilities, relationships, and social statuses that make up motherhood in particular cultural contexts. Because the social content of motherhood is infinitely variable, I would expect to find that women's religions relate to an assortment of social aspects of motherhood. I would not expect to find motherhood treated identically in all women's religions, and the evidence we have presented thus far indeed supports that assumption.

On the other hand, I would expect to uncover certain similarities, rooted in the fact that social arrangements lead women in most cultures to be more involved in childcare than men. Nancy Chodorow (1974; 1978) has explored the social-psychological implications of women's greater responsibility for childcare. She argues that girls develop their sense of self and gender identity in the context of ongoing, intimate, daily contact with their mothers. Girls learn not only what their mothers do, but what their mothers are, how their mothers feel, and how their mothers react to a multitude of situations. Boys are also raised primarily by mothers. This means that boys develop their sense of self and gender identity in a situation in which the male role model is often absent. The growing boy may know what his father does (or he may only have a vague sense of what his father does)—his father hunts, plows, directs traffic, assembles machinery parts—but he doesn't know what his father **is**. Raised by women, the growing boy at some point realizes that he is not female but he does not really know what it is to be male. He comes to define maleness as not-femaleness, and to see femaleness as something to be rejected (inferior, polluted, etc.). Unlike his sister, he develops his sense of self in a negative way.

The ramifications of Chodorow's argument are twofold. First, it explains why in so many cultures women and female pursuits are considered less good, less noble, or less pure than men and male pursuits. And second, it explains why women seem to have an easier time with interpersonal relationships than men do. In Chapters 6 and 10 I discuss these matters as reflected in women's religions.

While I believe that Chodorow's theory is on the whole valid, it situates the roots of "culture" entirely in the preoedipal experiences of sons and daughters.[6] By highlighting the role of motherhood in shaping adult women's religiosity, I am implicitly critiquing psychological and psychoanalytic theories that situate religion in infantile experiences. Recent studies have clarified the numerous ways in which pregnancy and motherhood are growth experiences for women. Since certain of these findings have important implications for women's religious lives, I will briefly review two of the more interesting studies.

In a fascinating inquiry into the psychological dimensions of pregnancy, Myra Leifer has demonstrated that the personality does not become fixed by adolescence, but continues to change and grow throughout the life cycle. Leifer followed a group of women throughout their first pregnancies and post-partum period. "From a psychological perspective . . . the emotional turbulence of pregnancy may be a positive phenomenon when viewed within a developmental perspective" (1980, 42). According to Leifer, the intense emotional changes during pregnancy reflect significant reorganizations in personality as a woman moves toward the developmental stage of parenthood. Pregnant women appeared to be more open to their inner experiences than other women. "Looking back on their pregnancies, almost all the women felt that despite the difficulties and strains, pregnancy had been a unique and valuable experience and that they had changed considerably in the course of these nine months" (Leifer 1980, 25). Although Leifer does not raise the issue, it seems to me that there are religious ramifications to her discovery of the inner orientation of women during pregnancy; pregnancy is a time of concentrated emotional and spiritual growth for many women.

Mary Hales (1990) investigated mothers who were parenting second or subsequent children, and found that second-time parenting brought about changes in many of the mothers. Some of the more common changes included more assertiveness in getting their husbands to share in homemaking, increased inner-directedness and greater control over children, an enhanced sense of competence, achievement and endurance, an increased appreciation of their own rights and needs, and a deepening appreciation of femaleness. Again, although Hale did not write about religion, I suspect that in the religious domain these characteristics translate into leadership ability (see Chapter 11), a sense that one does not have to passively submit to fate (see Chapter 5), and a recognition of the power inherent in femaleness (see Chapter 10). The evidence from women's religions strengthens both Leifer's and Hale's understandings of intra-psychic processes of motherhood.

A useful complement to these ideas can be found in Sara Ruddick's writings regarding "maternal thinking." Ruddick begins by pointing out that because most mothers are young women, their adult psyches are strongly shaped by the maternal practices in which they engage (1983, 236). Ruddick's work gives specific and explicit consideration to how the experience of mothering affects the ways in which mothers (that is, most adult women) think. Although her writings make no pretense at cross-cultural applicability, I have found it useful to "test" her ideas against what I have learned about women's religions around the world.

First, according to Ruddick, mothers are concerned with preserving the lives of their children. The theme of responsibility for the health and lives of children is indeed central in women's religions. More specifically, "Faced with the fragility of the lives it seeks to preserve, maternal thinking . . . implies a profound sense of the limits of one's actions and of the unpredictability of the consequences of one's work" (1982, 80–81). Somewhat surprisingly, the theological implications of this statement are not borne out by the data on women's religions. Contrary to Ruddick's expectations, women's religions teach that individuals have a great deal of control over their own and their children's destinies. On the whole, they do not posit capricious and all-powerful deities. Instead, they provide many different rituals designed to ensure children's well-being.

Second, mothers not only preserve life but also foster growth and welcome change. A mother realizes that her child continuously grows and changes, and "her realistic appreciation of a person's continuous mental life allows a mother to expect change, to change with change" (Ruddick 1982, 82). In line with Ruddick's expectations, we in fact find that women's religions tend to preach flexible ideologies, ideologies that recognize and sacralize change (see Chapter 12).

Third, according to Ruddick, mothers try to raise children who will be acceptable to the next generation. Mothers take on the values of the subcultures to which they belong and of the men with whom they are allied. One of the most interesting patterns in women's religions is the tendency to accept the dominant patriarchal ideology of the culture in which the religion is located (while reinterpreting that ideology in ways that empower women— see Chapter 10).

Fourth, women on the whole remain peaceful in situations in which they are powerful, namely, in battles with their own and other children. Ruddick writes, "I can think of no other situation in which someone with the resentments of social powerlessness, under enormous pressures of time and anger, faces a recalcitrant but helpless combatant with so much restraint. It is clear that violence—techniques of struggle that *damage*—is by definition inimical to the interests of maternal work" (1983, 243).[7] We find that women's religions indeed praise harmonious interpersonal relationships, and offer women help in coping with the emotional conflicts created by the situation Ruddick describes. Many female-dominated religions offer women concrete assistance that ameliorates conflict and powerlessness (see Chapter 13). Furthermore, forceful missionizing is not a component of any known women's religion. This finding certainly resembles Ruddick's realization that mothers rarely use violent force against their children, even though the physical possibility (and the temptation) surely exist.

Fifth, Ruddick believes that women are more attracted to concrete thinking and men to abstract thinking.[8] For Ruddick, abstraction refers to the disposition to simplify, dissociate, generalize, and sharply define. Its opposite— concreteness—respects complexity, connection, particularity, and ambiguity. Ruddick roots women's concreteness in the experience of motherhood. "Concreteness can be seen as a mix of interwoven responses to a growing, changing child. . . . A mother attends to a particular child and understands her as best she can on a given day, tolerating both the ambiguity of the child's actions and the tentativeness of her own interpretations. She will eschew generalization, not only because children are very particular beings to whom she attends, but also because they confound prediction. . . . In short, her thinking will be 'holistic,' 'field-dependent,' 'open-ended,' not because of any innate sex difference, but because that is the kind of thinking her work calls for" (1983, 249). (We will return to this notion in Chapters 7 and 12.) It does seem to be the case that the belief systems and moral frameworks of women's religions are contextual and "field dependent." These religions do exhibit a high tolerance for ambiguity. They do focus ritual and thought on specific individuals rather than on generalized categories. And they most certainly bear in mind the "moral and human significance" of any plan or doctrine (1983, 250).

And finally Ruddick, like Carol Gilligan (1982), finds that women are more concerned with sharing responsibility than with claiming rights. One of the clearest patterns to emerge in this book is that women's religions are consistently more attentive to interpersonal relationships than to rules, valuing caring more than abstract justice (see Chapters 6 and 7).

Motherhood has received remarkably little attention from theologians, and the hypotheses I have laid out in the preceding paragraphs grow out of social psychological literature, not out of theological discourse. In a rare article by a theologian, Bonnie Miller-McLemore (1992) draws attention to one more relevant aspect of motherhood—mothers typically lack the space, time, energy, money, and solitude to articulate and record their ideas. Realizing this leads us to surmise that elaborately written theological tracts will not be a feature of most women's religions. In Chapter 12 we will see that this indeed is the case.

Empathy is another consequence of motherhood considered by Miller-McLemore. Mothers' enhanced empathy has two somewhat discrete antecedents. First, "Ultimately, to lactate when another thirsts teaches a certain empathic, connected knowing" (1992, 242). And second, "Somehow, through the mutual understanding learned and practiced over and over in the intense moments of attachment with a little, developing person, one who has truly cared for a child gains new modes of relating and new empathy for others—parents, other children, one's spouse, the oppressed" (1992, 246). If Miller-McLemore's impressions are correct, we should expect to find that women's religions offer institutionalized support for all categories of weak and oppressed people, and encourage members to develop empathy. In fact, although most women's religions encourage members to preserve excellent relations with their families and communities, few of the religions urge members to devote time or money to helping unknown unfortunate individuals.

Motherhood—culturally constructed in various shapes—does not impact upon religiosity in a uniform manner. What is present in all the women's religions is direct, emphatic, and serious addressing of the diverse implications of motherhood. Yet I wish to clarify once again that when I speak of motherhood as interacting with women's religious lives, I am building on evidence that points to the social far more than the biological aspects of motherhood. Recent research by psychologists and sociologists indicates that the parenting role shapes both men's and women's characters in rather similar ways, regardless of men's and women's very different biological contributions to parenthood. In a fascinating study, Barbara Risman (1987) compared the personality traits of single mothers, single fathers, and married parents. She found that responsibility for childcare was strongly related to such "typically" female traits as nurturance and sympathy in both men and women. In other words, single fathers with primary responsibility for childcare were more like mothers than like married fathers.[9]

In this chapter we have looked at a wide range of religious ramifications of motherhood. We have seen symbolic and practical aspects of motherhood reflected and dramatized in women's religions. Of all of these many facets, there is one that so dominates discussions of women's religions as to warrant a separate and detailed analysis. That facet is child death, which we will look at in Chapter 4.

Notes

1. Ann Lee's title is "Mother," but, according to Jean Humez, anecdotes portraying Lee's relationship to her followers do not present a picture of a warm, nurturing,

maternal figure. To the contrary, Lee is most commonly portrayed as stern, authoritative (yet devoted), and even bordering "on the sadistic" (1992, 94). Reconciling the title with the descriptions, Humez argues that, "As a pious, working-class Englishwoman of her day, the historic Lee would likely have held what to modern minds would seem an unacceptably severe attitude toward children. The more sentimental ideal of all-loving motherhood with which we moderns are so familiar had simply not yet been invented" (1992, 95).

2. Many Japanese believe that the soul area is the abdomen (rather than the chest or the head as many Westerners believe). I find it interesting that Mrs. Kitamura taught women to have their babies naturally, that is, without the aid of physicians or midwives (May 1954, 131). While on the one hand this advice is difficult or even dangerous for some women, for other women it leads to a strong and positive self-image of themselves as mothers.

3. According to Kerns, given the rather fluid nature of heterosexual relationships in Black Carib society, publicly celebrated female fidelity is a potent means to ensure paternal acknowledgment, which in turn assures "a child a full set of kin . . . and an unambiguous social identity" (1992b, 99).

4. In the Baby M case, for example, U.S. courts declared the wife of the biological father, rather than the biological mother, to be the baby's legal mother (Chesler 1989).

5. Until recent decades in the West (and still today in many parts of the world), childbirth has been a direct confrontation with death and large percentages of mothers died giving birth or in the immediate post-partum period. I have not found that women's religions address this issue head on. On the other hand, the central role of healing in women's religions (see Chapter 5) may be assumed to reflect concern with maternal mortality.

6. A theory as all-encompassing as Chodorow's is bound to draw criticism. Some critics have contended that Chodorow's work is methodologically problematic because it is based on clinical practice that relies on verbal recall, effectively ruling out the possibility for the therapist to access memories of the first year of the patient's life. Yet it is precisely these early months that are critical to Chodorow's theories (Rossi 1981, 495). Moreover, the patients who supply the psychoanalyst's "clinical evidence" differ in many respects from the general population. Since Chodorow's research deals with the development of healthy adults and not psychiatric patients, the use of clinical illustrations for her evidence raises difficulties.

Chodorow does not ask why it is that all known societies have found it useful or at least not harmful to have men and women "reproduced" in this manner (Laub Coser 1981, 488). Further objections to her ideas concern the historical and cross-cultural applicability of a model that situates fathers out of the home and mothers as the primary caretakers of young children. Unfortunately, Chodorow chose not to examine social structural conditions causing women to become the primary childrearers (Bart 1983, 150). Tavris (1992) has suggested that the traits Chodorow associates with women are in fact traits shared by all subordinates, whether male or female. A number of critics have drawn attention to Chodorow's lack of attention to factors of class, race, and ethnicity (Lorber 1981, 483, Bart 1983, 150–151, Rossi 1981, 493–494).

Another, perhaps crucial, objection is that gender may not be as significant a part of an individual's identity and sense of self as Chodorow claims. Psychological studies in cognition, behavior, and even emotion consistently show men and women to be more similar than different (see Hyde 1990).

Chodorow has tried to correct some of these deficiencies in her later work (Chodorow 1989). In any case, the quantity of attention (both critical and laudatory) paid to Chodorow's work is a tribute to the importance of her ideas. In this book, I have tried to apply Chodorow's ideas cross-culturally, outside of the psychoanalyst's couch, and have found most of her ideas useful in helping me understand women's religions.

7. In contrast to Ruddick's ideas, Macaulay argues that there are "far too many studies with no gender differences to support any theory that strong biological factors, deeply ingrained personality traits, or well-learned gender roles make even a majority of women reliably or consistently very much less aggressive than men" (1985, 192).

8. I am not convinced that Ruddick is correct in this assertion. It is unproven and probably unprovable that cross-culturally, or universally, women and men have different cognitive styles. Regarding all of Ruddick's ideas, one should bear in mind that she does not bring empirical, scientific evidence as proof. Ruddick is more of a philosopher than a scientist, and tends to exaggerate the differences between men and women.

9. The single fathers in her study had custody of their children through circumstances beyond their control (e.g., widowhood); they were not a self-selected group of "feminist" or "feminine" men.

4

When Children Die

Young children are especially vulnerable to illnesses and accidents, and in many cultures mothers are not provided with adequate resources to safely birth and raise children. Cultural decisions regarding allocation of resources may lead to high maternal and infant mortality rates. And even in the best of circumstances, all mothers know that their children's health and well-being are not guaranteed. (Even we middle-class Westerners never know when a drunken driver will run over our child while walking home from school.) Biology—carrying a baby in one's womb, childbirth, and lactation—combines with social structure—prolonged and intensive childcare—to ensure that most women love their children and are vitally concerned with their children's health and well-being.[1] Most adult women devote a great amount of time and energy to childcare, and women's emotional ups and downs tend to be related primarily to family happenings, while men's tend to be connected to work (cf. Hagestad 1984, 38, on American women). Not surprisingly, women's religious lives often reflect occurrences within the family. In situations where male-dominated religions do not offer women adequate help with their problems and worries as mothers, female-dominated religions that address the ramifications of mother-love and child death attract many women.

We Westerners find it comfortable to believe that Third World women do not love their children as much as we do; that African and Asian women do not care as much as we do when their children suffer and die (cf. Dally 1982, esp. pp. 28–29). While anthropology of emotion is a relatively undeveloped field, I see no evidence in the ethnographic record to support such a belief. The literature certainly shows that both abortion and child death take an emotional toll on women regardless of their socioeconomic status. On the other hand, I would not assert that all mothers feel the same toward their children. The model of one-on-one nurture we know in the West is far from universal, and it is likely that in cultures in which the vast majority of children die before the age of five parents develop different modes of relating to their children than in cultures in which the vast majority of children survive. "Different modes" could include both reluctance to becoming overly emotionally involved with the baby and heroic measures to ensure the child's survival.

One might claim that infanticide is evidence that mother-love **as we know it in the West** is not universal. Yet I insist that not even infanticide should automatically be taken as evidence of lack of maternal feeling. To the contrary, infanticide is often practiced by women who realize that they will not be able to take care of their other young children if the new baby lives. And I suspect that in cultures in which women practice infanticide, women's experience of infanticide is reflected in their religious lives.

In this chapter I focus on the religious implications of child death. My argument is not that child death leads women to "escape" into religion. My argument is that child death encourages women to ponder existential and theological questions. As part of that process, some women change their religious beliefs and affiliations.[2] In sum, although Western-style mother-love is not universal, child death is something with which women in all cultures must grapple, albeit in different ways. Encouraging motherhood, rejecting motherhood, and the loss of motherhood are important to women, and all of these themes surface in women's religions.

MATERNAL RESPONSIBILITY

Women's religions plug into the mother-love and child death dynamic in a number of ways: They offer consolation to grieving mothers (Spiritualism), they provide means of controlling fertility (Sande, Shakers), they ensure that mothers receive support from their families (Thai matrilineal spirit cults, Black Carib religion), and they encourage women to organize and demand social change that will enhance maternal and infant health (Feminist Spirituality).[3] We begin with several brief examples that show some of the ways in which women infuse their responsibility for their children with a religious dimension.

Burmese women are bothered by men's skepticism concerning *nats*, and urge men to stop making comments that will offend *nats* and so cause the *nats* to harm their families. One informant explained to anthropologist Melford Spiro that she as a woman needs to be more concerned with *nats* because she is responsible for her children—if the *nats* are angered they will cause her children to fall ill. "All she asks is that they not harm her children; so let him (her husband) keep his peace" (1967, 59).

The infant mortality rate among the Luvale tribe of Zambia is especially high—between 20% and 33.3% of all children die within the first year of life. The Luvale believe that ancestors send illness and death to children whose mothers have not behaved properly, either in terms of social behavior or ancestral devotion. According to Anita Spring (1978), this belief serves to institutionalize the stronger grief reactions experienced by bereaved mothers as opposed to bereaved fathers. Fathers never undergo spirit possession on behalf of their sick children. Since the spirits who afflict Luvale women belong to their matrilineages, we can see a multigenerational maternal responsibility for child health and illness.

Kaja Finkler has studied the attraction that Spiritualism holds for lower-class, rural Mexican women (see Chapter 5 for more on Mexican Spiritualism). One typical devotee, Lupe, began to suffer from vague chronic illnesses shortly after her marriage at age fifteen. In interviews with Finkler, she attributed her illness to the difficult life she had with her husband who beat her, and to her mother-in-law. "The first attack [of illness] she experienced coincided with the death of her firstborn infant at four months of age. She held herself responsible for its death. . . . During one irradiation [Spiritualist treatment], God called Lupe up to stand before Him. He told her that the baby's death was not her fault but rather that it was His will, that she was being tested, and that it was her duty to serve Him in His house" (1985b, 29ff.). Lupe's biography is especially significant in light of Finkler's finding that the vast majority of Spiritualist "temple patients—especially regulars—have suffered the death of a child, whereas only three out of nineteen controls [people from the same village who do not attend a temple] have known a similar loss" (1985b, 72). Death of a child is the single most common attributing event offered by temple patients to explain their illnesses, **but only among women patients**. "None of the men [at the Temple] related their symptoms to the death of a child, whereas over 24% of the women did, even though in at least one instance a man had lost four infants" (1985a, 39). Finkler explains women's greater adverse reaction to child death in terms of the fact that a rigid sexual division of labor means that successful mothering is a basis for women's self-esteem. Both the bereaved mother herself and her husband hold the women culpable for the tragedy.

Brazil—A Case Study

Matrifocality means that mothers (and not fathers) are seen as ultimately responsible for children's health and well-being. In urban Brazil the typical pattern of plural mating—serial common-law marriages in which one man visits but rarely supports a number of households consisting of women and children—strengthens the perception that it is women and not men who are accountable for the survival of children.

Many poor urban mothers lack the resources to adequately care for their babies, and infant mortality rates are appallingly high. The Catholic Church in Brazil, dedicated to liberation theology, no longer provides bereaved mothers with spiritual scripts that help them make sense out of the loss of their children. "Traditionally, the local Catholic church taught . . . [that] . . . if an infant died suddenly, it was because a particular saint had claimed the child. . . . The infant funeral was, in the past, an event celebrated with joy. . . . The new theology of liberation imagines a kingdom of God on earth based on justice and equality, a world without hunger, sickness, or childhood mortality. At the same time, the church has not changed its official position on sexuality and reproduction, including its sanctions against birth control, abortion, and sterilization" (Scheper-Hughes 1989, 16).

Worry about their ability to care for their children is often what draws women as clients and as mediums to the Afro-Brazilian cults. Two of the three women mediums interviewed by Esther Pressel reported having lost a child shortly before joining the cult.[4] One of the mediums became involved with the spirits after her young child died; another after she lost four children. Pressel records in detail the biography of a medium whose first spiritual experience was at age eight. She moved from a small town to a city at age seventeen, married and bore three children. Her older daughter died and her boy was killed in a car accident the following year. Her husband began to act strangely and lost his money; he had a mistress. A friend suggested that she go to an Umbanda center for help. A spirit there told her she needed to be a medium because her dead mother had a mission to fulfill through her.

This medium's story incorporates a number of common patterns in women's religious life stories: child death, a history of suffering because of the double sexual standard of patriarchal culture, the role of her mother in her decision to become a medium, the "matrilineal" character of her mediumship, and the long and gradual process of becoming a medium (see Chapter 11 on leadership).

RESPONSES TO CHILD DEATH— NINETEENTH-CENTURY UNITED STATES

The United States in the nineteenth century presents an excellent case study of the connection between motherhood and infant death and women's involvement in religion. It is also one of the best-documented examples of the cultural construction of mother-love and the intersection of mother-love and religion.

To understand what happened in the nineteenth century, it is necessary to go back to the colonial period. During the colonial period, friends and kin shared in childcare, and Divine Providence was the explanation for infant death. Seventeenth- and early eighteenth-century motherhood meant almost continuous illness and death of children. Parents loved their children yet did not expect that caring for them properly would cure illness, avert accident, or prevent death. Children were God's temporary gift to parents. Women's diaries and letters display feelings of powerlessness over infant and child health and safety (Dye and Smith 1986).

During the second half of the eighteenth century a move began toward more affectionate, nuclear families in which children became the focus of indulgent attention and mothers became defined as the moral and physical guardians of their children. By the early 1800s the mother was seen as the most important force shaping and preserving a child's life, replacing God as the one responsible for a child's welfare, and replacing the network of kin and friends who had formerly looked after children. During the nineteenth century ministers, educators, physicians, and social commentators built up the notion that motherhood is a full-time job for which women are especially fitted by nature. The increasingly private and isolated nature of the family in the nineteenth century encouraged very strong mother-infant bonds. Although American women had always been more involved in daily childcare than had men, in the early nineteenth century changes in the organization of the labor force tended to increase their share even more (Dye and Smith 1986).

In the wake of technological advances, American families began to believe in the responsibility and power of humans to ensure children's health. At the same time, the infant mortality rate stayed high (it even may have risen due to urbanization). These circumstances created anxiety for many nineteenth-century women. Nineteenth-century mothers (unlike eighteenth-century mothers) recorded their children's idiosyncracies and developmental milestones. "But beneath this delight lay the ever-present fear that their children might die. In the first days and weeks after giving birth, many mothers appear to have been frightened by the intensity of their feelings for infants whose lives seemed so fragile" (Dye and Smith 1986, 340). By the late nineteenth century women more and more believed that good mothering should and could ensure a baby's survival, and mothers worried incessantly about their children. Nancy Dye and Daniel Smith, writing about the nineteenth century argue that, "Living beyond the time of unquestioned confidence in the providential power of an omnipotent God and before that of public health advances and reliable medical help, women experienced motherhood in solitude—sole possessors of all the delights and fears that come with raising children" (1986, 346).[5]

"Death literally occurred in woman's sphere. Most people died at home in bed, attended by female relatives. In New York City in 1853, 49 percent of those who died were children under five, who presumably had been under primarily female care. Women, who were expected to focus their lives on the nurture of family members during life, were also expected to feel losses through death more deeply than men, who might turn their attention to other duties. Middle-class women remained at home by empty cribs and unoccupied seats at the dining room table and produced and purchased a variety of memorial artifacts, from postmortem photographs to jewelry woven from the hair of the deceased. Etiquette prescribed longer periods of mourning for women than for men" (Braude 1989, 52).

Nineteenth-century evangelical revivals stressed the importance of early religious and moral training in attaining salvation. This placed an even heavier burden on mothers: If a child were damned, it was not solely because of predestination, but also because his or her mother failed in her duty.[6] Throughout the eighteenth and nineteenth centuries women's diaries and letters suggest that at least some women were dissatisfied with the mainstream Calvinist doctrine that proclaimed that dead babies, like all individuals who have not undergone an authentic conversion experience, are denied entry into heaven.

Three of the female-dominated religions available to nineteenth-century American women addressed the issue of infant mortality head on, yet came up with rather different answers. Spiritualism told women: Your dead children are happy in a good place, you will certainly be reunited with them when you die, and you can even communicate with them now through seances. Shakerism told women: If you don't want to grieve when your children are sick and die, if you don't want to see your beloved children suffer, become celibate—stop having children. And Christian Science told women: Matter is illusory, suffering is illusory, and by joining with us we can heal you and your children of pain and disease.[7]

Spiritualism

Against this background of high child mortality rates, maternal love and responsibility, and Calvinist theology, we can trace the history of a rather typical
nineteenth century middle-class family who became involved in Spiritualism.
Ann Braude tells about an American woman, Annie Denton Cridge, who was
griefstricken after losing her first child as an infant. Yet her grief was assuaged
by the fact that during his final moments she saw the spirits of her own dead
parents above his bed "waiting to bear his sweet spirit away." She saw his spirit
withdraw from his body and "with the help of his grandparents assume a
spiritual body. Since then, she held her child in her arms everyday. He weighed
nothing and within a week had recovered from the illness that took his life"
(1989, 1).

Alex Owen relates the history of a British Spiritualist family of the same era:
Five children died, some in infancy and some in childhood, and one child was
stillborn. Of eleven pregnancies only four children survived. "Gradually a
trusting relationship developed between the earthly family and its spirit members, the spirit children evolved into separate and distinct personalities, and
their communications became increasingly serious and meaningful" (1981, 82).
During seances a child who had died a number of years earlier informed the
family of the welcome that the newly dead baby received in Summerland. This
must have brought much needed comfort to the bereaved parents, and especially the mother. "Through Louisa the Theobalds learned, to their great joy,
that their babies were safe and continued to grow and develop in the spirit
land. . . . When baby Percival died in 1870 at the age of six-and-a-half months,
the spirit children were anxious to emphasize the suffering the convulsive
'tubercles of the brain' had caused him and the improvement already registered
in his new life" (1981, 84). The spirits recognized that parents felt guilty
because of the death of children (If only I had/had not . . .), and the spirits
made efforts to tell the parents that they were not to blame. An excellent
example of the manner in which Spiritualism related to child death can be
found in the Funeral Service for Children (*Twentieth Century Formulary of Songs
and Forms* by W. C. Bowman [1907], cited in Ward [1990]): "Tis vain to bid the
sorrowing heart dismiss its grief; but to those who mourn so deeply and so
sadly o'er this coffin we may offer the sure consolation that 'it is well with the
child.' "

"The more a woman's identity derived from her family relations, the more
she must have been devastated by the irreversible separation from family members at death. Although many nineteenth century Christians leaned toward the
Spiritualist position that individuals retained their personal identity after death,
Spiritualism went further than any other religion in promising to prevent the
severance of family relations. Spirit messengers painted rosy pictures of life
after death, in which reunited families picnicked by babbling brooks. . . . The
possibility of communicating with lost children was a great appeal of Spiritualism to bereaved mothers" (Braude 1985, 427). Ann Braude quotes from one
woman comforting another on the death of a baby: "But one thing I know,

that in the other world your baby and mine will know us—their mothers, else God were not God" (1989, 54).[8]

Shakers

Shaker leader Ann Lee was born to a working-class family in Manchester, England, in 1736. She was the second of eight children, and her mother, like many women of her day, died in childbirth. Ann was sent to work in a cotton factory as a child, at age fourteen or fifteen she became involved in religion, and at twenty-two joined a Shaker sect. She was pressured by her family to marry (against her will and her religious beliefs) and bore four children, all of whom died in infancy or early childhood. Ann Lee was not so different from other women of her time: High birth rates and high infant mortality rates in eighteenth-century urban England (possibly as high as 68.6%, see Dally 1982, 25–26) meant that women spent most of their adult years pregnant and mourning. Unlike most women of her time, however, Ann Lee interpreted the deaths of her children as punishment for her having engaged in sexual relations with her husband. At age thirty-four she had a vision that led her to assume leadership of the Shakers. The essence of the revelation was the necessity for celibacy in order to follow Christ.

For the Shakers, celibacy was a solution to the pain and suffering women endure as mothers.[9] Shaker celibacy freed women from the hideous threat of death in birth. "If she [Ann Lee] repudiated marriage because it exploited women, she had only two logical choices sexually: chastity or promiscuity. In an era without effective birth control, the choice of the latter would have condemned women to suffering and death" (Klein 1979, 367). It is highly significant that although Shaker women in general outnumbered Shaker men,[10] the sex imbalance was particularly large in the childbearing age group. Women aged twenty to forty-four outnumbered men two to one (versus the ratio of three to two for other age groups) in nineteenth-century Shaker communities (Kitch 1989, 202). In addition, many Shaker converts were mothers with small children, suggesting that the Shaker life-style was particularly compelling for women struggling with raising children in a society not overly conducive to the needs of mothers and children (Kitch 1989, 202).

The Shakers were clear in their wish not to propagate for the sake of providing factories and armies with new workers and soldiers. In later Shaker writings a Malthusian theme appears: The unrestrained generation of the human species will overpopulate the earth; voluntary celibacy is the way to ensure adequate space and resources for earth's creatures. The Shaker view of history led them to "conclude that it was necessary to remake society on the basis of a new type of human relationship . . . since the economic evils were based on 'biological' evils, only a new kind of biological relation would make it possible for them to refashion society and its economic structure" (Desroche 1971, 39).

Shakerism grew out of the Christian world view in which the sinful act of the Fall in Genesis was sexual, and marriage was an imperfect solution for the basest human instincts. Shaker writings argue that the marital (sexual) relationship violates the laws of God and nature; those who live by the flesh would suffer in the world to come. The Shakers envisioned a new type of relationship between men and women: Instead of husband and wife—an unegalitarian relationship in which women are exploited—Shaker men and women lived as brothers and sisters. The Shakers themselves, unlike many other millennarian groups, believed that the millennium had already arrived, that Ann Lee was the second coming of Christ. Their celibacy was understood as part of the process of human divinization in Christ (Whitson 1983, 156).

"Shakers are convinced that a free sharing in both temporal and spiritual gifts is not really possible except among the celibate simply because the married have a properly exclusive concern for each other and their children. . . . While other attempts at communitarianism quickly failed (Owenism, Harmonism, Oneida Perfectionism, Amana, and many more) largely because of conflicts in family/children values, the Shaker communes survived the better part of two centuries" (Whitson 1983, 158). Celibacy allowed a fuller commitment to nonviolence; without an obligation to defend children or spouse, Shakers were free to avoid violence even in instances where non-Shakers felt forced to use violence to protect their children.[11]

It is of interest to briefly refer to another communal, Christian, celibate, female dominated religious group that emerged in Texas during the nineteenth century—the Sanctificationists, or Women's Commonwealth. We need feel no surprise to learn that Martha McWhirter, the founder of the Sanctificationists, received a vision instructing her to embrace celibacy shortly after the deaths of her brother and two of her children (Kitch 1989, 49). Unlike most other women's religions, however, the Sanctificationists did not employ metaphors of spiritual motherhood, nor did they encourage special bonds between mothers and children. Members shared in childcare and nurturing responsibilities. It is likely that at a time when many mothers lost one or more child, diffusing maternal affection served women's interests well.

DEAD CHILDREN AS TUTELARY SPIRITS—THE CASE OF CANTONESE SHAMANISM

Among Cantonese Chinese there are women shamans known as *mann seag phox*—"old ladies who speak to spirits." According to anthropologist Jack Potter's description (1974), these female religious specialists deal solely and expertly with interpersonal relationships, among the living and between the living and the dead. They intercede between the villagers and the supernatural world by sending their own souls to the supernatural world where they communicate with deceased members of village families. They also know how to predict the future and to recapture the kidnapped souls of sick village children. In particular, they care for the souls of girls who die before marriage, and they protect the life and health of village children by serving as fictive mothers. Potter describes one ritual: Speaking through a shaman, a deceased first wife appeared at a gathering in which the second wife was present. The ghost assured the second wife that she would not bother her, that she was visiting because she was lonely. She spoke with several women in the audience, expressed anxiety about her children, and admonished the second wife to take good care of them. This anecdote is a good example both of a religious response to women's fears that death will separate them from their children, and of the sacralization of maternal nurturing: The mother in this anecdote continues to voice concern for her child even after her own death.

The three *mann seag phox* whom Potter studied became shamans after severe crises, including deaths of children. One shaman had lost five daughters and two sons. The second lost three daughters and one son. Each was visited in her dreams by her children's spirits who urged her to become a shaman. "Deceased children, who mediate between their mother and the supernatural world, are essential to a career as a spirit medium" (Potter 1974, 226). The parallels between Cantonese shamanism and American and British Spiritualism are instructive. One of the most interesting aspects of Spiritualism is the role of dead children as spirit guides (as intermediaries between their mothers and other spirits). Both in the case of Spiritualism and in the case of Cantonese shamanism, women's religions provide solace to bereaved mothers and transform the very fact of their bereavement into spiritual power.

Of particular interest is Potter's description of how one of the shamans works—she always begins by calling the spirits of her dead children "because she is powerless without their help" (1974, 220). The dead children are the intermediaries through whom she contacts the more powerful deities on her altar. Sometimes the children's spirits refuse to enter their mother's body, in which case she is powerless. The spirits may be very young and prefer to go off and play. They may also be uncooperative when they feel slighted. The ceremony ends when the shaman scatters rice around to feed her tutelary spirits (her children) and gives her clients rice to take home to the patient. Clients are typically women who have come on behalf of their children.

KOREAN SHAMANS VERSUS KOREAN NUNS

Korea is one of the few societies in which women seeking professional religious paths have more than one available option. Hesung Chun Koh (1984) has compared the life-stories of five Korean Buddhist nuns to the life-stories of six Korean shamans. Each of these individuals was free to choose the type of religious specialist role that appealed to her; family preference was irrelevant.

Both nuns and shamans tend to be the first born or eldest daughter. Shamans typically came from lower middle-class families who had declined in wealth during the shaman's teen years; nuns came from middle- or upper-class families. Both shamans and nuns experienced role conflict. Nuns tended to enter monasteries in their early twenties; religion became important to them during their teens when their families pressed them to make decisions (such as marriage) regarding their adult female roles. Shamans found their callings in their mid-thirties, when they were already married and had children, and often when despite their own desires to do what proper women do, their husbands did not function as proper husbands (i.e., they did not earn money to support their households).

Finally, both groups of women reported recent loss of beloved relatives: **for the nuns it was typically a parent, grandparent, or fiancé; for the shamans it was typically a child.**[12] I believe that this distinction is a crucial one. While all religions address "ultimate" issues of life and death (Geertz 1969), women's religions particularly address maternal grief at the death of children.

I find interesting the difference between the way that dead babies are treated in Korean women's shamanistic and household rituals, and how they are treated—or more precisely **not** treated—in men's Confucianist rituals. As we saw in Chapter 3, Confucianist ancestral rites only acknowledge patrilineal ancestors who left male progeny. Women's household rites and shaman's seances, on the other hand, relate to other categories of dead relatives—including babies and children.

MEN, WOMEN, AND CHILD DEATH

In this chapter I have not tried to show that men do not love their children, that men do not mourn for their children who die, or that men do not interpret child death in religious terms. I **have** suggested that because of a variety of social (and possibly biological) reasons, women's grief at child death tends to be longer lasting and especially likely to lead to religious responses.

Several recent studies have compared mothers' and fathers' responses to child death. Although all these studies have been conducted either in North America or Western Europe, they do suggest trends that may be applicable in other cultural situations. First, fathers seem to grieve for shorter periods of time than mothers, and to express more of a desire to get on with their lives. A typical mother's reaction is reported by Dyregrov and Matthieson: "I have not recovered my own self following the death. I am much more anxious for everything, and I think about illness and death every day" (1987, 9).

Mothers have been found to feel higher anxiety, self-reproach, sadness, and sleep disturbances and to report more thoughts of the child. Fathers find it more difficult to talk about the death, and both parents agree that the mothers' grief is stronger and more intense (Dyregrov and Matthiesen 1987).

Mothers are more likely than fathers to suffer from increased health complaints following child death (Dyregrov 1990, 269). As we will see in Chapter 5, women's religions offer diverse ritual and nonritual means for treating vague and chronic somatic symptoms—the very sorts of symptoms commonly experienced by bereaved mothers.

A variety of theories have been advanced to account for the differences between bereaved mothers and bereaved fathers. Some writers emphasize gender differences in emotional responses in general, arguing that women report a larger proportion of interpersonal situations as stimulating emotions than men do, or arguing that men and women have different styles of coping with stress (see Dyregrov 1990, esp. p. 275 for an overview of the literature). Differences in response to child death are then interpreted as one manifestation of this global difference.[13] Other writers accentuate the different work experiences of men and women, pointing out that because men are more likely than women to return to work outside the home after the death, men are forced to "get on with it" and not continue to brood and mourn (Rando 1986, 26). Women, on the other hand, are surrounded by objects, activities, and other sensory stimuli that remind them of the dead child (Schatz 1986).

A third approach has highlighted the special strength of the mother-child attachment. During pregnancy the baby is physically part of the mother; breast feeding continues this physical bond; and social arrangements in which women have primary or exclusive responsibility for childcare reinforce that connection. Especially during the first year of life, the psychological boundaries between the mother and child overlap. Simon Rubin has found that many bereaved mothers continue to think of their deceased infants as developing children (he terms it a "phantom child syndrome") and points to the "permanent presence of the child in the maternal experience" (1984–85, 351). "When people ask me how many children I have, said Mrs. G., I answer four; and if they ask further, I explain that three are living and one passed away" (Rubin 1984–85, 351; see also Pine and Brauer 1986, 71, on "enshrinement" of dead children).

The studies cited here indicate a number of differences between fathers' and mothers' responses to child death, differences that have implications for women's religions. That mothers are more affected both emotionally and in terms of their day-to-day lives is reflected in women's religions' explicit appeal to maternal sorrow. Of equal interest is the "phantom child syndrome" described by Rubin. Can we understand the role of dead children in the rituals of Spiritualists and Cantonese Shamans as a sacralization of this phenomenon? In studies conducted by Western psychologists, bereaved mothers are unwilling to unequivocally part from their children. Women commonly believe that their children continue to live in some form, in some sphere.[14] It is of interest to us that most women's religions elaborate on these beliefs—describing pleasant hereafters, and encouraging communication between this world and the next. Gehan Wijeyewardene shows that the Northern Thai spirit cult, like Western Spiritualism, denies death. "In the eschatology of the *caw* [spirit], it almost seems that *Nirvana* has been completely abolished, life is eternal" (1986, 201). I see it as especially significant that Korean women's religion acknowledges the spiritual presence of dead children (as restless ghosts and spirits), whereas Korean's men's religion is concerned solely with adult ancestors who died after producing male offspring.

The most important piece of information we can learn from psychological studies of parental response to child death is that mothers, more than fathers, report never "getting over" the death of the child. For many women, being the mother of a dead child remains a—or the—core element of personal identity; memories of the child do not fade; sorrow does not ebb; life does not "go on." For these reasons, women seem especially likely to seek religious interpretations of and responses to child death.

The literature suggests that in addition to grief, sadness, and anger, bereaved parents try to find meaning in the loss. "Comparative cultural studies demonstrate that the level of material abundance necessary to sustain life and induce a sense of well-being is indeed minimal. . . . What most people cannot tolerate for extended periods is the lack of a satisfying framework through which they can make sense out of what they perceive to be inequity or other misfortunes" (Williams 1980, 150). Because the death of a child, particularly of an infant or young child, seems so incomprehensible, psychologists believe that searching for meaning is a healthy way to recover from such tragedy. Vanderlyn Pine and Carolyn Brauer cite studies showing that the existential search for meaning on the part of bereaved parents may ultimately lead to positive growth outcomes. Bereaved parents have reported developing a stronger faith, more compassion and care toward others, and an increased sense of the preciousness of life (1986, 73). Thus I would argue that involvement in women's religions that offer meaningful interpretations of child death (and techniques for avoiding deaths of other children) provides more than emotional support or compensation; it offers expertise in reassessing and coming to terms with the existential "meaning of life". Participation in women's religions provides bereaved mothers with opportunities for intellectual and spiritual growth. Ann Lee, for instance, questioned accepted theological doctrines in light of her experiences of child (and maternal) death. For Ann Lee, that process culminated in religious innovation and leadership.

Infant mortality is one of the most dramatic concerns of women's religions, but the sorts of theological questions raised by it also arise in regard to other situations of suffering and illness. We will pursue this theme in Chapter 5.

Notes

1. A cautionary note is in order: It must not be assumed that all women share a common experience of motherhood. Some women choose not to have children, some women wish to have children yet are unable to do so. Some women thoroughly enjoy rearing children, some women enjoy raising children when they have adequate financial and social support, and some women find childraising a difficult, even agonizing process.

2. In a recent newspaper interview, Israeli author Yehudit Rotem described the process leading up to her rejecting the ultra-orthodox Jewish world into which she was born and raised and in which she lived as a married woman for twenty years. In the first paragraph of the article we read that "Two children died in infancy and another was stillborn, but pictures of the remaining seven—her greatest assets, she calls them—cover almost an entire wall of her tiny Ramat Gan office" (Surie Ackerman, "The Other Side of Sisterhood," *Jerusalem Post Magazine*, August 21, 1992, p. 12). Somehow I am not surprised to find that a woman who has made a "career" out of personal religious change is also a bereaved mother.

Another example of the religious significance that women allot to child death comes from contemporary Japan, where rituals for aborted fetuses are commonly performed by women (Werblowsky 1991; see also Ferichou 1991, 216, on child death and women's spirit possession cults in Tunisia.)

3. On the Ryūkyū Islands the religious response to infant death is notably different from other women's religions. According to Noguchi (1966, 28), dead infants (up to

three years of age) are "hated and thrown into ravines, without their remains being accorded 'bone-washing' and a tomb."

4. Pressel points out that we do not have a large sample of life histories of mediums (personal communication 1992).

5. By the twentieth century, women in clubs and organizations began to act in the public sphere to turn infant mortality from a private tragedy into a public social and political issue. Twentieth-century mothers share responsibility for child welfare with public health officials, the medical profession, and the state.

6. Dally cites several examples of mainstream Protestant interpretations of child death from this period. "In Massachusetts, when Cotton Mather's daughter fell into the fire and burned herself badly her father wrote: 'Alas, for my sins the just God throws my child into the fire,' (1982, 44–45). Other fathers interpreted child death as a test of faith.

7. Some women who stayed within the mainstream male-dominated denominations also sought religious means for coming to grips with child death. Debra Campbell (1989) has shown that the life-stories of nineteenth-century Protestant women indicate a correlation between women's conversion experiences and the deaths of their children.

8. Not only child death but also adult death led many women to Spiritualism. Nelson (1969) shows that the popularity of Spiritualism in England in 1916–18 reflected the large number of women who had been bereaved in World War I and wished to contact their dead.

9. The question of why celibacy appeals to men necessitates a more extensive analysis than I am prepared to present in a book dealing with women's religions. In the case of the Shakers, the millennarian message proclaiming that celibacy was part of the process of human perfection was probably equally compelling to men and women.

10. The male-female ratio changed over the years. In the early years, the sect was not nearly as "feminized" as it later became (I thank Priscilla Brewer for pointing this out to me, personal communication 1992).

11. Unlike Spiritualists, Shakers did not pay particular attention to sustaining relationships with dead children. On the other hand, Ann Lee's ability to interact with the spirit world was a matter of great importance to early Shakers. Early Shakers were concerned with assisting their dead relatives on the path to Redemption. According to Humez (1992, 93), Lee is frequently remembered as speaking of witnessing the passage into the resurrection of the souls of dead relatives of living Shakers.

12. In the belief system of Korean shamanism, deceased people remain in the physiological state they were at the time of death. Therefore, dead children never become adults.

13. Rosenblatt, Salsh, and Jackson suggest that women may not experience a death more strongly; it may be that women are used (and allow themselves to be used) as the persons who publicly symbolize the loss that everyone (men and women) have experienced. This may be because it is seen as out of character for high status persons (e.g. men in patriarchal societies) to self-mutilate, cry, or be self-indulgent in the face of loss (1976, 27).

14. In light of Rubin's findings, it is not surprising that American women report a significantly greater belief in the life hereafter than men (Keller, Sherry, and Piotrowski 1984).

5

Misfortune, Suffering, and Healing

The most conspicuous similarities among women's religions emerge in the realm of suffering and healing. Whereas all religions deal in some way with explanations of and solutions to suffering, women's religions are characterized by the particular emphasis placed on illness and curing.[1] This emphasis is manifested theologically (elaborate explanations for suffering), ritually (key rituals are often healing rituals), in terms of membership (members often join because of illness), and in terms of leadership (a history of illness is typically part of the path to leadership). Almost all the women's religions devote a great deal of attention to suffering—especially illness—to the extent that some of the religions have been "accused" of being not much more than healing cults.

Why do women create or join religions that deal with healing? First, as primary childcare providers, most women are concerned with children's health and function informally as domestic healers. In women's religions, this informal role is enhanced and formalized. Second, as subordinate members of sexist societies, women more than men seem to suffer from persistent and recurrent conditions such as headaches and dizziness that are not amenable to treatment by either folk or modern medicine. In addition, women bear the brunt of culturally assigned responsibility for infertility and all the physical consequences of pregnancy and childbirth.

Women's religions advance ideological approaches that declare that suffering is **not** necessary to the human condition—that it has discernable causes and can be alleviated and avoided. Reflecting the insistence that suffering can and should be avoided, these religions offer a variety of healing techniques, including spirit possession, and eclectic approaches to suffering and healing that allow the religion to be used as one of a number of culturally acceptable solutions for suffering.

Let me say from the outset that I have not found any particular healing technique to be unique to women's religions. What is striking about women's religions is the **accent** on healing and, in most cases, the **multiplicity** of healing procedures. In addition, the healing approaches of women's religions tend to be characterized by a holistic mind-body-spirit approach: Ill bodies reflect emotional and spiritual distress, physical healing means that psychic tension has been allayed. This trait is especially noteworthy in the women's religions that are situated in Western cultures in which the mainstream world view is highly dualistic. Both Western Christianity and Western medicine posit models that split the body from the soul, bestowing care of the body on physicians who typically pay little attention to the patient's overall emotional or spiritual state, and bequeathing the soul to priests and ministers who, with the exception of "fringe" sects, are disinterested in bodily healing. In contrast, in women's religions curing is typically a combination of healing interpersonal relationships, healing relations with the gods or spirits, and healing physical symptoms (Carol MacCormack, personal communication).

Women's religions rarely differentiate between illness and other types of suffering. For the Korean shaman, for example, misfortune includes all sorts of bad luck, illness, and financial loss. Also for Christian Scientists illness includes not only bodily illness, but business problems, problem relationships, and finding lost articles. "Nonphysical and minor problems constitute the greater part of the [Christian Scientist] practitioner's work" (Fox 1989, 110). In Northern Thai cities, women mediums are consulted for such matters as arthritis, back problems, goiters, social problems, business problems, and care of children (Wijeyewardene 1986). And on Okinawa, although the majority of the people who consult *yuta* (shamans) do so for health problems, the roles of the *yuta* include giving advice regarding plans, business, and wedding dates; interpreting unusual experiences such as dreams or accidents in religious terms (neglect of rituals, etc.); communicating with relatives after death; leading exorcisms to guide lost spirits to the tomb; leading rituals of thanks to the house deity; and teaching traditional rituals (Lebra 1966, 79).

WOMEN AND ILLNESS

Women are associated with illness and healing on two levels: As primary caretakers of children they feel themselves responsible for their children's well-being, and as women carrying, bearing, and tending children in an imperfect world, they themselves are often ill. The connection between women and illness has been investigated from a number of perspectives (cf. Whelehan et al. 1988). As victims of institutionalized oppression in sexist societies, women may indeed be ill more often than men. In many cultures men have access to important resources that are denied women through food taboos or notions of serving men first. Practices such as forcing very young girls to marry, and prohibitions on birth control and abortion take their toll on women's health. Furthermore the stigmatizing of infertile women—treating childlessness as a female illness—causes many otherwise healthy women to be perceived as ill.

Feminist sociologists have argued that patriarchy actually makes women ill. Women in patriarchal cultures may have no avenue available to them other than illness for expressing their dissatisfaction with their lives. As Harriet Lerner (1989) has pointed out regarding American society, both men and other women are more comfortable with women who feel sick than with women who are angry. In general, women receive far more positive responses when they define their problems in medical terms than in political terms.

It has been well documented that women all over the world utilize health-care facilities of every type more than men, although men suffer from serious disabilities and injuries more than women (Nathanson 1979). In the United States, males in all age groups die at a higher rate than females and suffer higher death rates from heart disease, cancer, accidents, suicide, homicide, diabetes, and almost everything else. Yet even when diseases due to reproductive functions are excluded, women suffer more from acute and nonfatal chronic conditions than men. Women report more depression and are treated more for mental illness. They report more minor ailments such as headaches, dizziness, and stomach upsets. Women use more prescription and over-the-counter drugs than men. They restrict their activities due to health problems about 25% more days per year than men, and spend about 40% more days per year in bed (Powell 1988).

Women's overwork, burn-out, and frustration often lead to chronic ailments which do not respond either to modern or herbal medicine. Especially in cultures that do not differentiate between physical and nonphysical ailments, these are precisely the sorts of symptoms women seek to alleviate through ritual means. Thus rural Mexican men and women exhibit similar emotional states when faced by acute impairments, but different responses when faced with chronic conditions. The chronic conditions are typically what bring women to Spiritualist temples for treatment (Finkler 1985a).

In previous chapters we have looked at how the experience of motherhood shapes women's religious activities and ideas. In this chapter we draw attention to the connection between motherhood and illness. Judith Hibbard and Clyde Pope (1987) conducted a study of gender roles and interest in health in the United States. They found that not only are women in general more likely than men to engage in health protective behaviors, **mothers of young children** are more interested in health than those women with older or no children in the household.

"What is missing in the understanding of mothering is the extent to which it is a painful relationship and an exhausting, often thankless, occupation. . . . In the United Kingdom, research has demonstrated that up to 50% of mothers with small children (under age five) have symptoms of intense emotional distress on a regular or continual basis. . . . Women are five times more likely to be diagnosed as mentally ill in the first year after their first child's birth than at any other time in their lives" (Knowles 1990, 4). An even more interesting statistic for our purposes comes from the Haj Yousif area of Khartoum (one of the centers of the *zār* cult) where 40.3% of mothers of three to fifteen-year-old children described themselves as being anxious or depressed, and about one-third of the women interviewed believed in *zār* (Rahim 1991, 138).[2]

In many cultures mothers complain of somatic symptoms rather than psychological ones. Research has shown that stress and emotional distress influence the functions of the immunological system, and that social and psychological factors are linked to delayed recovery from infectious diseases. Life crises, and most especially loss and bereavement, have been shown to correlate with chronic illness (Finkler 1985, 50). Kaja Finkler suggests that subjectively perceived stressful life events play a crucial role in illness expression "especially when they are culturally and collectively accepted to be stressful" (1985b, 29). Finkler's insight into the illness-causing role of bereavement allows us to identify another element in the connection between child death and women's religion. Child death may lead to chronically ill mothers who are incurable through physical means. This is a population from which women's religions often draw members.

There is also a positive side to the motherhood-illness connection. The strengths that women acquire through grappling with motherhood may be incorporated into their repertoire of healing skills. Carol McClain has explored the role of women as healers cross-culturally and found that in many instances women who become "ritual or other specialized practitioners of medicine . . . infuse powerful female symbolism, including the metaphor of maternal nurture, into their healing practices" (1989, 6).

A more direct way in which motherhood figures into the religion-illness equation concerns the key biological transitions in women's lives: menarche, pregnancy, birth, lactation, menopause. In many cultures these events are interpreted in a health context, and lead women to seek the services of health practitioners. Simultaneously, these same events may be interpreted in a religious context, and lead women to seek the services of ritual practitioners. Put differently, motherhood is often understood as both a fundamental physical crisis and a fundamental spiritual matter.

WOMEN'S RELIGIONS AS HEALING CULTS

Zār: *Reapportioning Responsibility for Infertility*

Muslim women in North and East Africa spend most of their time in domestic units with other women and children. Looking at Muslim women's religious activities (Islamic and non-Islamic) in the general context of their lives, Lois Beck concludes that their various religious responses address their particular problems as women. Much of the activity around pilgrimage to holy tombs and saints, for instance, has to do with problems of fertility and child mortality (1980).

Recruitment to the *zār* cult is typically through illness. Although the dramatic possession rituals are the most flamboyant element of *zār* religion, the true emphasis in *zār* cults is on curing, not ecstasy (Saunders 1977). Women suffering from illness inflicted by *zār* spirits need to join *zār* ritual groups to bring the spirits under some control—in order to alleviate their symptoms. Possession rituals function as techniques to bring about healing. The Egyptian Nubia, for example, use the *zār* ceremony to cure a range of emotional and chronic physical disorders. Patients most frequently treated through *zār* are those suffering from *wasswassa*—a state brought on by the death of a close relative or by a frightening meeting with a spirit. The symptoms of this state

are apathy, withdrawal from human company, minimal communication, refusal to work, a desire to die, lack of appetite, and sleeplessness. Other common complaints are unlocalized pain, weakness, and listlessness. John Kennedy
argues that *zār* cult initiation "seems particularly tailored for alleviation of the
hysterias, anxiety-produced problems, and psychosomatic ailments apparently
related to living conditions in Nubia" (1978, 203).

In North and East Africa if a woman fails to conceive, or miscarries, or bears
a stillborn child or a daughter, or loses an infant, it is her ability to procreate and
not her husband's that is called into question. Not surprisingly, many women
who join the *zār* cult do so because of fertility and childbirth problems. According to Janice Boddy, *zār* possessed women have been pregnant more times than
nonpossessed women, and have lost more children than women who are not
possessed (1989, 172). In the Northern Sudanese village in which she carried
out fieldwork, one of every two possessed woman has had both fertility and
marital difficulties, whereas only one in five nonpossessed reported both types
of problems. In light of Chapter 4's discussion of mother-love and child death,
it is significant that a number of women linked the onset of *zār* possession to the
death of an adult daughter, usually in childbirth (Boddy 1989, 237).

Zār possession as an explanation for women's fertility problems removes
responsibility and blame both from the afflicted woman and from Allah (who
is supposedly beneficent); instead, the *zār* spirits are deemed to be the guilty
party. Furthermore, the fact that the afflicted woman's husband must pay for
her *zār* initiation serves to reallocate the burden of infertility more evenly
between husband and wife.

Mexican Spiritualism:
Patriarchy Sickens Women

Kaja Finkler presents a convincing case for the relationship between women's
subordination and women's illness in rural Mexico. In recent years, high
school education for all children has become the goal of most families, a goal
that creates economic and psychological stresses and an increased workload
for women in particular. "In view of the traditional sexual division of labor,
women continue to carry out the incessant daily household activities, but
now lack the help previously received from their daughters. Moreover, because of the expanding need for cash, many women attempt to supplement
their spouse's income by petty commerce, or washing laundry for others"
(1985b, 39). Increased industrialization has led to nuclear families becoming
more common. While the nuclear family does eliminate certain sorts of stress
between women, it also eliminates the possibility for sharing the workload.
More important, in the nuclear family there is greater emphasis on the male-
female dyad, which often means an increase in tension between the spouses.
"Significantly, extreme tension between spouses are reflected in the numerous
illnesses which are attributed by the women to anger and dissension between
spouses. . . . While dissension between males and females is inherently stressful to both sexes, the men can more easily remove themselves from the

situation by leaving the house and dissipating the emotional strains in the *cantina* (liquor serving station) with their cohorts. Rural Mexican women lack such escapes and outlets. . . . women remain relatively isolated and require permission from their spouses to leave their households" (Finkler 1985b, 40). Compounding this difficult situation is the high rate of alcohol consumption by men that results in both a financial drain on the household and increased likelihood of wife-beating.

Finkler found that 58% of the clientele of a typical Spiritualist temple were women, 27% children, and only 15% adult males (1985b, 58). Women in particular complained of suffering from nerves (associated with chronic illness).[3] Many of the disorders bringing clients to the temple are directly associated with interpersonal strife, particularly between men and women. "In fact, the majority of problems presented to Spiritualist healers concern conflicts between men and women" (1985b, 61). Even more to the point, many of the temple patients perceive this connection: "Many women tend to link their symptoms to the onset of their marriage and to abuse by their husbands when they return home drunk" (1985a, 40). Indeed, temple patients were far more likely than other women to report difficult relationships with their husbands, and to report that their husbands behave violently when inebriated.

In addition, we saw in Chapter 4 that the high infant mortality rates in rural Mexico mean that many women spend their adult years grieving for their dead children. Oppression and bereavement combine to set the stage for women's religious involvement.

Afro-Brazilian Religions:
Illness as the Path to Recruitment

Illness is typically the path of recruitment to membership and leadership roles in Afro-Brazilian religions, and healing consultations are the initial source of contact for most people. Diana Brown (1986) interviewed Umbanda mediums and found that 62% had originally sought out their present center for aid in resolving some kind of personal problem, most typically a health problem.

Afro-Brazilian mediums are consulted regarding illness, marital problems, business decisions, drinking problems, unemployment, interpersonal quarrels, and insanity. Illnesses for which supernatural curing is sought are typically chronic illnesses—ailments that did not respond to home remedies. Ritual efforts to treat all of these sorts of problems are referred to by the same term, *cura* (curing). Esther Pressel (1974) quotes one of her informants in Brazil as telling her that the most common complaint that brings people to Umbanda is headaches.

We can easily understand the attraction of spiritual curing in isolated and primitive societies. It is more difficult for us to understand why Brazilian urban dwellers choose to attend Afro-Brazilian rituals when they are ill. Surely there are more efficacious medical options available in Rio de Janeiro! The reality, however, is that in poor, urban neighborhoods in Brazil few people have the resources to fully utilize Western health care: doctors and medicine are expensive. In addition, many of the diseases from which people suffer cannot be fully cured by Western medicine (e.g., malaria, leprosy, tuberculosis). In these cases, spiritual curing offers hope of miracles. And where the Catholic Church offers sick people only prayers and vows, Umbanda and Candomblé mediums provide cures that have been ordered specifically for the given situation by the spirit world.

The Failure of Modern Medicine: Japan, A Case Study

During the past century there has been a flowering of new religions in Japan, many of which have been founded by women and almost all of which have more female than male members. On the whole, these religions have a great deal to do with healing; most offer explanations and remedies for illness, and teach that illness is indeed curable. One may wonder why religious healing should be so attractive in modern Japan where, unlike in Brazilian shanty-towns, modern medicine (and even socialized medicine) are readily available.

Edward Norbeck (1970) argues that religious healing is encouraged by deficiencies in modern medical practice in Japan. Modern Japanese medicine tends to ignore psychological aspects of therapy. Relations between urban physicians and patients are remarkably impersonal. Socialized medicine means that health care costs less, but it also means that many more people seek medical services and that poorly paid physicians treat vast numbers of patients. Average Japanese citizens cannot make appointments for medical care, but must wait in crowded waiting rooms to be treated briefly in an assembly-line fashion by an overworked physician. In contrast, in the new religions ill people (mostly women) receive a great deal of personalized attention; the roots of illness are sought in the specific karma or life experiences of the individual; and healing is effected through rituals involving notice and concern on behalf of the leader and the group.

Spiritualism: Women Make the Best Healers

Studies of North American and British Spiritualism show that it is at stressful periods, and especially periods of illness, that women begin to meet spirits. "Spiritualists . . . consider themselves beset by a variety of disabilities" (Skultans 1974, 27). June Macklin (1974), writing about the appeal of twentieth-century Spiritualism, underscores that modern medicine, touted as infallible, in fact often fails. Mediums in Macklin's study had reason to doubt modern medicine—they or their kin had suffered from ailments that doctors could not cure. In addition, many of their physical complaints were interwoven with difficult social or marital situations. While in the secular world illness made one dysfunctional, in the Spiritualist world sickness is seen as making a good medium, and many women became mediums after long and severe illnesses. "Every pain we suffer helps unfold our medium powers . . . all suffering is friction to the material covering of the soul, that makes the gem shine brighter within" (Moore 1977, 121). Spiritualists see the gift of healing as one of the highest expressions of psychic power, and one that is accessible to everyone. Women are however, on some level, better suited than men to act as healers, and the majority of medical mediums have been women (see Chapter 11).

Feminist Spirituality: Sexism and Suffering

Two women's religions explicitly acknowledge the connection between sexism and suffering. The Shakers taught that suffering is caused by continuing procreation—a process from which women in particular suffer.[4] Their solution was a radical one: the formation of celibate communities.

The Feminist Spirituality Movement teaches that suffering, in a global sense, has been caused by patriarchy that brings with it militarism, rape, conquest, and disregard for nature. The solution to global suffering is the dismantling of patriarchy. Rituals focus on healing women from the effects of patriarchy, and Feminist Spirituality groups have devised rituals to heal women who have been victims of rape and other forms of male violence.

Although curing is not institutionalized in the Feminist Spirituality Movement, many Spiritual Feminists are involved with alternative healing systems such as crystals, massage, home births, and aromatherapy. The impetus for this involvement comes from a number of directions. On a political level, feminists (including Spiritual Feminists) are unwilling to grant a health-care monopoly to a capitalist and male-dominated medical establishment. On a philosophical level, feminists are wary of the Western medical tradition that tends to see women's bodies as pathological and that cures through attacking germs or tumors rather than through cooperating with the body. And on a personal level, many contemporary women suffer from ailments that modern medicine simply cannot cure. In many instances, these ailments are dismissed by physicians as trivial and psychosomatic. Spiritual Feminists are inclined to believe that the physical and nonphysical are intertwined, and that all conditions should be treated on physical, emotional, and spiritual planes.

"THERE ARE CERTAIN THINGS THEY CAN DO"

In contemporary urban Korean society a variety of biomedical and religious options are available to a sick individual. Thus it is significant that so many women turn to shamans when misfortune strikes. The job of the Korean shaman is to divine, explain, and remove the cause of suffering. Shamans typically explain that misfortune is caused because the household gods became affronted by neglect or pollution, and so dropped their defense of the family, thus allowing ancestors to grow restless and dangerous. Youngsook Kim Harvey quotes one shaman talking about how she sees her role: "We give them hope. . . . They see it's not so bad . . . **There are certain things they can do** [my emphasis]" (1976, 196).

Suffering is a core concern of all religions. In various ways, religions endeavor to explain why people suffer, and to offer solutions for suffering. Differences among religions are manifested in how much attention is given to the problem of suffering, and in the content of the response to suffering. In the previous section I argued that because women more than men tend to suffer from the sorts of chronic illnesses that are unresponsive to **medical** treatment, women are especially likely to seek alternative solutions. In addition, in many cultural situations the male-dominated **religion** does not offer women adequate responses to suffering. Female-dominated religions, on the other hand, tend to address head on such specific aspects of women's suffering as infertility and child death.

In women's religions ideas concerning the causes of illness and misfortune are highly elaborated. Most of these religions offer clear, persuasive, and dramatic solutions to human suffering. Most women's religions teach that suffering does not need to be passively accepted. In contrast, many (not all) male-dominated religions teach that suffering is the will of the gods, preparation for bliss in the next world, punishment for acts in this or previous lives, or the unescapable essence of the human condition.

In his classic sociological study of religion, Max Weber (1966, Chapter 9) overviews the solutions that religions throughout the world offer to the problem of suffering. Weber summarizes the four principal responses as follows: (1) messianic eschatology—a future revolution in this world, (2) heaven and hell (retribution and reward in the world to come), (3) dualism, and (4) transmigration of souls. I find it interesting that most women's religions do not propose any of these solutions. The Shakers, for example, employed messianic theology and imagery, but for them the messianic revolution had already happened. Notions of an afterlife are certainly recurrent in women's religions, but hell—a place of eternal punishment and suffering—is foreign to the generally positive views of human nature and the universe offered by women's religions. As we saw in Chapter 4, hell as the repository of unbaptized babies was particularly repugnant to nineteenth-century American women. Dualism—a split between essential good and essential evil, a cosmic war between good and evil—is also alien to women's religions. As we will see in Chapter 8, most of these religions posit a multiplicity of good, bad, and indifferent supernatural beings, but none posits an entity that is thoroughly evil. And finally, while most women's religions believe in some sort of continued existence of the soul after death, most seem to lean toward a belief that ancestors retain their identities rather than a belief in transmigration of the soul.

In the following sections we will see in more detail how women's religions address the problem of suffering.

Christian Science: Disease Is Not Real

Nineteenth-century North America provides a particularly illuminating case study of the approach of women's religions to suffering and healing. I quote here at some length from Ann Braude's wonderful analysis of women, religion, and medicine in the nineteenth century.

Orthodox religion and orthodox medicine reinforced a similar worldview in which human beings in their natural state were seen as flawed from birth and in need of assistance from officially sanctioned authority figures trained in a specialized body of knowledge. While orthodox clergy portrayed the human soul as inevitably prone to sin, orthodox physicians portrayed the human body, especially the female body, as inherently prone to disease. Just as ministers traditionally found a tendency toward sin in woman's moral anatomy because of Eve's instrumental role in tempting Adam into disobedience in the Garden of Eden, so doctors associated woman's physical anatomy with a tendency toward pathology. The emerging male medical establishment alleged that a disease-prone reproductive system governed woman's physiology, resulting in inevitable physical frailty that dictated a severely restricted sphere of action. Regular doctors joined the clergy in asserting the appropriateness of women remaining within their "sphere," the clergy basing their arguments on the Bible, the doctors basing theirs on the body. Doctors and ministers agreed that both physical and spiritual ill health in women resulted from disobedience. They prescribed obedience to a male authority figure as a cure for the degenerative tendencies of body and soul. . . . [On the other hand] Spiritualists [and Christian Scientists] opposed orthodox medicine with the same fervor with which they opposed orthodox theology, and with some of the same arguments. Because they viewed each individual as embodying the image of God and the laws of nature, they viewed health, like godliness, as the natural condition of human beings, which only misguided human intervention could destroy (Braude 1989, 143–144).

To my mind, two points here bear emphasis. While Victorian doctors blamed women's physiology (especially sexual physiology—ovaries and uterus) for all emotional and physical problems (Smith-Rosenberg 1985c), nineteenth-century female-dominated religions not only saw women as essentially sound, but blamed external forces for the problems women suffer. And second, as the nineteenth century progressed, people more and more believed that doctors should be able to alleviate illness and suffering. In fact, however, physicians were not very successful at healing, and many of their treatments were actually harmful (e.g., blood-letting, or requiring that post-partum women stay in bed for weeks). The spiritual healing techniques provided by women's religions were a reaction to the unsuccessful and often intrusive male-dominated medical establishment.

Of all of the women's religions, Christian Science provides by far the most intellectually sophisticated explanation for illness and suffering. The first generations of Christian Scientists expressed disenchantment with the orthodox Christian idea of resignation to suffering as the will of God in this life. They felt that it is impossible to reconcile the suffering and evil in this world with a benevolent and omnipotent deity. Therefore, the suffering and evil must not be real. According to Christian Science there is no final judgment after "death;" there is no heaven or hell. If God is good and all-powerful, He does not want people to suffer.

"True Christianity, [Mary Baker Eddy] taught, must have a practical healing and redemptive effect. She discouraged passivity in the face of suffering of any sort and utterly opposed the belief that man must acknowledge the cycle of fatality. . . . Indeed, Christian Science itself stood for her as the means whereby man could rise up and take control over his own destiny. She saw redemption as including the redemption of the body. . . . According to Christian Science, one cannot attain final spiritualized consciousness while submitting to any form of suffering" (Gottschalk 1973, 154).

Christian Science does not heal merely in order to lessen discomfort; rather, because disease proceeds from the illusory belief in the reality of matter, healing through spiritual power destroys that false belief.[5] By overcoming disease (and eventually death, although not in our times—mankind has not yet attained sufficient spiritual growth), one proves the power of the Spirit to destroy the false beliefs of mortal mind.

Against this background, we can now understand the life history of Mary Baker Eddy. Eddy was born into a middle-class rural New England family and as a teenager began to feel dissatisfaction with contemporary Calvinist notions of original sin and predestination. Her first husband died of yellow fever, and her second husband felt that her son was too wild and rough for her to take care of, and so sent him to live with another family. After losing her son, Eddy became chronically ill. Her second husband left her, her health deteriorated, she almost died, and then one day, while reading the Bible, she was healed. She spent the next decades healing and teaching. She died in 1910 at the age of ninety. For Christian Scientists of both the nineteenth and twentieth centuries, Mary Baker Eddy serves as a role model of someone who successfully overcame illness, pain, and suffering (Williams 1980).

Because Christian Science teaches that disease does not really exist, Christian Scientists have sometimes been blamed for cruelty or disregarding human suffering. However, the official position of Christian Science is that although evil and suffering are in fact not real, people do perceive them as real and it is wrong to ignore suffering. A Christian Science practitioner can only heal, according to Eddy, if the healing is impelled by true affection.[6]

In conclusion, I fully agree with Mary Bednarowski's assessment that, "The appeal of Christian Science for women lay primarily in its stress on self-help rather than helplessness, and on the possibility of healing without dependence on the dictates of doctor or clergy" (1980, 218).

Burmese Buddhism versus Nat Religion

The contrast between nineteenth-century American women's religions and Calvinism/official medicine is in many ways identical to the contrast between Burmese *nat* religion and Buddhism. The differences between male-dominated Buddhism and female-dominated *nat* religion in Burma emerge dramatically when we look at how the two systems deal with suffering. According to indigenous Burmese belief, *nats* (together with ghosts, demons, and witches) are potentially harmful. Human suffering is caused by supernatural beings who have not been propitiated, whose territory has been invaded by humans who did not ask permission, or who sometimes are simply capricious. The solution to suffering is to perform the proper rituals to appease the *nats*. *Nat* religion absolves humans of responsibility for causing suffering; individuals are the victims of *nats*, witches, and ghosts. Humans can, however, learn to alleviate suffering through religious rituals.

Therevada Buddhism, on the other hand, explains suffering in this life as the result of karma—the consequences of one's deeds in previous existences. What one should do in this life is strive for a better situation in the next life. The way to do this is to follow Buddhist precepts, to transcend the cravings and desires that produce wrong action. Buddhism teaches that each individual is ultimately responsible for his or her suffering in this world; it was one's own behavior in previous lives that has caused one to suffer in this life. And although there are certain Buddhist rituals that are apotropaic in aim, the bulk of Buddhist teaching and ritual does not offer an immediate solution to suffering; the best one can hope for is less suffering in subsequent incarnations.[7]

Buddhist explanations of and solutions to the problem of suffering are not sufficient in the eyes of many inhabitants of Buddhist lands. Because Buddhism interprets suffering as an unavoidable aspect of this worldly existence, and locates both the cause and solution in other lives (past and future), individuals concerned with alleviating misfortune **here and now** are not offered much help. *Nat* religion, on the other hand, offers both compelling explanations for and immediate solutions to human suffering. "While the *nats* do not control decisions or impose patterns of action, all the exigencies of daily living and the crises in the life cycle are interpreted in terms of them" (J. Nash 1966, 127). Indeed, the most common sign of *nats'* displeasure is illness. When someone falls ill, Burmese villagers suspect that they have aroused the anger of household *nats*. "A stream may flood and drown the people along its bank, a tree may fall and kill the person walking in its path. The forest is trackless, and it is easy to lose one's way and die of privation; wild beasts are unpredictable and may attack a harmless victim. None of these events occurs by chance" (Spiro 1967, 47).

Steven Piker contends that Buddhism embodies universalistic, categorical, and all-inclusive explanations of the causes and results of events, whereas magico-animistic beliefs (spirit cults, *nat* religion) are particularistic, fragmented, and ad hoc in the explanations they offer (1972, 215). In Chapter 7 I propose that the "particularistic explanations" are what make "magico-animistic beliefs" especially attractive **to women**.

TECHNIQUES OF HEALING

In women's religions suffering has meaning; illness is more than bad luck or bad fate. Healing rituals of women's religions are dramatic antidotes to resignation in the face of suffering. Because healing is so crucial in women's religions, it should not come as a surprise that many offer a variety of healing techniques. The message of women's religions is that suffering is not inevitable, that individuals can and should seek means of alleviating suffering, and that we (the shaman, the cult group, the priestess, etc.) offer a range of healing procedures. Anthropologists have suggested that magical or religious curing lends itself to the "law of accumulation." Since healing rituals endeavor to be as effective as possible, healing practitioners accumulate many and diverse rituals in order to maximize the possibility of efficacy (Bastide 1978, 278).

One of the noteworthy patterns found in women's religions is openness to the use of healing systems other than those offered by the religion itself (see Table 2). I would offer two explanations for this finding. First, as I shall show in Chapter 12, women's religions generally do not teach that "only our way is true." Aggressive missionizing, for example, is almost never a part of women's religions. Second, healing is so crucial to women's religions, and the sorts of illnesses that members suffer from tend to be so difficult to cure, that prohibiting use of other healing systems might easily backfire and cause women to forsake membership in order to continue searching for all-too-elusive cures.

In two fascinating studies of the effects of foreign influences on Okinawa (Ryūkyū Islands), a team of Japanese scholars found that in the realm of curing there is co-existence—Okinawans are perfectly willing to use Western medicine and *yutas* (shamans) simultaneously (Ohashi, et al. 1984; Matsui, et al. 1980). The scholars prophesy that Western medicine will not conquer Okinawa because the biomedical model of disease is limited to answering the question of how a disease occurs. It is unable to explain why a disease happens to the specific individual. A typical modern Okinawan pattern is to consult a physician for treatment and a *yuta* for explanation.

This pattern is common in women's religions, and gives us insight into why these religions often pay little attention to actual symptoms. Women's religions excel at diagnosing and healing the underlying cause of suffering, not its temporal manifestations.[8]

AFFIRMATION AND AUTHORITY

Writers in a number of disciplines (medicine, psychology, anthropology, sociology, history of religions) have found it remarkable that religious healing systems often do accomplish their therapeutic aims. A thorough examination of how, in the eyes of Western scholars, these healing rituals "work" lies well outside of the issues I wish to deal with in this book. Various scholars have explained the success of healing rituals in terms of the social support the patient receives, emotional catharsis, the use of evocative symbols that intensify the faith of the participant, trance that frees the patient from social norms and superego control, and the manipulation of the world of fantasy (the subconscious).

Two features of healing seem to be particularly salient in women's religions. First, in these religions a central element of healing rituals is group acknowledgment that one's suffering is real. Typical scenarios begin with a woman whose family is reluctant to acknowledge that she is in distress; women who come to female-dominated curing religions are often considered malingerers or hypo-

Table 2. *Eclectic Healing Techniques*

In Afro-Brazilian religions misfortune can be a sign that one should be initiated, a punishment for infringement of religious rules, the actions of an *exu* (spirit of the dead), or caused by a sorcerer. Responses to suffering include propitiatory sacrifices, retreats, baths, fumigations, shakings, dusting with protective powders, and divination (Landes 1940b, 262).

Black Carib women understand a variety of reasons that people become ill: germs, sorcery, lack of practical caution (such as wearing insufficient clothing), angry ancestors who were not properly treated through ritual, and taboo behavior on the part of the individual's mother. Various causes of illness legitimate various solutions to illness: Western medicine, bush medicine, and ancestor rituals.

Black Spiritual people of New Orleans commonly mix healing therapies: physicians, patent medicines, home or folk remedies, and healing rituals at church.

The fertility knowledge owned by Sande women includes a wide variety of empirically tested herbal medicine, amulets, and more "magical" remedies and prohibitions (MacCormack 1982, 127). The Sande system is inherently flexible; new information is easily absorbed; and Sande midwives are eager to learn more about hygienic techniques that will reduce maternal and infant mortality.

Regarding the Northern Sudan, Janice Boddy (1988) describes the following steps likely to be taken by a sick person: advice from family members, home remedies, patent medicines, Western doctors, and *feki Islam* (male religious specialists) who perform divinations and provide charms. If spirits are found to be the cause of the distress, the *feki Islam* will perform an exorcism. However, since the *zairan (zār* spirits) are immune to Islamic ritual techniques, women patients may then consult a female *zār* practitioner. Yael Kahana (1985) found that in Ethiopia *zār* is not turned to after other cures have failed, but together with other cures, all of which are seen as complementary.

When an Upper Burman is sick he or she consults many sorts of experts: monks, astrologers, *natkadaws* (*nat* shamans), and doctors (M. Nash 1966). Kunstadter notes that in Southeast Asia several medical care systems are available; religious eclecticism is the norm. Illness is caused by various categories of spirits, soul loss, sorcery, sin, germs and more (1978, 187–188).

Spiritualists accept multiple models of illness: social, spiritual, psychological, and organic; and eclectic approaches to treatment: spirit healing, herbs, psychological insight, and social manipulation of difficult situations. Spiritualism sees itself as complementary to orthodox medicine, not as a full-fledged alternative to it. Health advice ranges from simple and practical (eat vegetables), to American Indian remedies, to seances (Skultans 1974).

The Korean shaman functions within a health system in which there are many options. Sick people typically turn in this order to various practitioners: pharmacist, Chinese-style herbalist, hospital. The shaman often actually urges the client to also see a Western or Chinese doctor (Kendall 1985, 94).

The Shakers did not engage in healing per se, yet they were very concerned with health. In addition to emphasis on neatness and cleanliness, Shakers experimented with various health regimens, including a wide range of medical and manipulative therapies (herbs, hydropathy, bloodletting, faith healing, Grahamism).

On the Ryūkyū Islands reasons for misfortune include insufficient ancestor ritual, priestess or shaman failing to acknowledge her call to office, improper ritual action, defiling a sacred place, violating social values, crimes of violence, and improper behavior on the part of one's ancestors (while they were alive). A wide range of solutions are available to deal with this wide range of causes.

chondriacs. In the context of the women's religion, on the other hand, the sufferer receives communal, often public affirmation of her perception of reality. I am arguing that in addition to the emotional support chronically ill women receive from joining a group, women receive cognitive support. In patriarchal cultures the dominant model of reality is one that reflects and expresses **men's** perceptions. Women often have their own alternative model of reality, but this model receives far less social confirmation than men's models, for the simple reason that the dominant social institutions are based on men's models. Religious healing often offers a model of reality that "fits" women's experiences and so allows them to move beyond illness to strength.

A second and related feature is the role of the healer; in very few of the religions is the healer treated as an absolute authority. Women are allowed space to negotiate explanations and cures that correspond to their own perceptions. For example, clients waiting to consult with a Korean shaman behave as though at an informal social gathering, offering comments and cluckings of the tongue, and the shaman sometimes uses this audience to muster a consensus support for her advice (Harvey 1976). The shaman brings in a divination tray—an ordinary tray of the type used for everyday Korean meals. On the tray is a mound of rice, some coins, and a bell rattle to summon the shaman's visions. She tosses the rice and coins, and the patterns suggest the client's concerns. The shaman describes a situation (based on the rice and coin configurations, and on what the gods told her) and asks for confirmation. As the divination continues, the shaman brings together her own visions and information from the client. "They [the friends and relatives present at the divination] sigh sympathetically for the woman whose divination reveals an adulterous husband, unruly child, or pitiable ghost. . . . Not for them the confidential atmosphere of the Western doctor's or analyst's office. The confessional's anonymity is missing here. The women enjoy each other's stories and accept each other's sympathy" (Kendall 1985, 74). And as David Suh points out, "This is a religion of dialogue between the *mudang* [shaman] and the 'congregation'—a lot of give and take between them" (1989, 22).

Leacock and Leacock have observed similar forms of behavior at an Afro-Brazilian curing ritual (1972, 253). Half a dozen clients sat in the medium's living room. A woman who had come to consult the medium on behalf of her sick husband knelt in front of the medium and whispered to her about the problem. Another client leaned closer to hear, and soon all the clients joined the conversation. The medium (entranced) prescribed certain herbs for the husband, and the other clients commented on the appropriateness of the herbs. The contrast between this style of healing and the style of western medical doctors must be striking to Brazilian or Korean women, who have access to both [male] Western physicians and [female] religious healers.

I am struck by the social nature of healing rituals in women's religions. As we will see in the next chapter this sort of communal healing is consistent with the great emphasis placed on interpersonal relationships in almost all the rituals of women's religions.

Notes

1. I am not claiming that male-dominated religions do not give attention to illness and healing. Healing is certainly one of the dominant themes in, for example, the life of Jesus. Dissident religious movements, whether male or female dominated, often use healing to recruit new members. (I thank Kaja Finkler for pointing this out to me, personal communication 1992.) And while healing is a dominant theme in most women's religions, it is not central to all women's religions. The Christian "heresy" Guglianism (a female-dominated cult that advanced a female pope), for example, interpreted suffering as a necessary manifestation of the unredeemed world, and did not offer followers ritual means for alleviating suffering in this world.

2. It is crucial to bear in mind that a variety of studies have failed to find elevated rates of psychopathology among participants in religious groups or among nonbiomedical practitioners (see Finkler 1986, 632, for an overview of the literature).

3. In the part of Mexico in which Finkler carried out fieldwork many people suffer from parasites that cause vague, chronic symptoms.

4. At the time that Shakerism emerged, the workday in Manchester and similar cities averaged fourteen hours, and children were hired in the factories and mills from the age of four. Working conditions were horrible, discipline in the factories was strict, and workers—including numerous pregnant women and young girls—were forced to work at a pace that often resulted in broken health.

5. The immediate cause of disease is usually fear (terrifying images or thoughts impressed on the body), but the basic cause of disease is false belief. Christian Scientists also believe that certain individuals can harm other people through a process known as animal magnetism or mental malpractice.

6. Despite Christian Science's well-publicized refusal to turn to other healing systems in cases in which spiritual healing has not proven effective, Christian Scientists do use surgeons to set broken bones, acknowledging that surgery is difficult to effect through spiritual healing.

7. Buddhism (especially "folk Buddhism") does provide rituals aimed at alleviating present suffering, but it seems to me that the emphasis is far more on alleviating future suffering in the next life (Spiro 1971, esp. Chapter 6). Indeed, as Spiro shows, Burmese informants were quite vague concerning how Buddhist apotropaic rituals are even supposed to work.

8. Kendall makes the same point concerning Korean shamanism. Underlying illness (especially serious or prolonged illness) are angry gods and restless ancestors. "While the *mansin* [shaman] concedes the efficacy of medicine for herself and her clients, medical expense is [interpreted as] another aspect of household affliction" (Kendall 1985, 94).

6 ∾

Rituals and Relationships

RITUALS OF THE RYŪKYŪ ISLANDS— A CASE STUDY

The most striking feature of Ryūkyūan religion is the sheer number of rituals performed by the priestesses. Since neither the kami *(gods) nor ancestors are inherently benevolent, humans must work hard in order to be rewarded with health, livelihood, and fertility; good relations with the* kami *demand time and attention.*

C. Ouwehand (1985) documents forty one rituals that make up the agricultural cycle. The rituals dramatize a few basic themes: thanksgiving for the harvest, securing prosperity of crops and of human beings for the next year, warding off evil spirits, and bridging the preceding to the following agricultural cycle. Priestesses visit ritual sites before the day of each main ceremony in order to inform the kami *that the ceremony will take place, and to request their attendance.*

*Within the household, ancestors are informed about matters of importance to the family: births, deaths, business transactions, and marriages. Ancestral rites are performed regularly by the kin-group for their ancestral spirits.[1] Household rites center on the hearth (*kamado*), and the hearth spirit is a messenger between the family and higher* kami*. It is always the wife who conducts* kamado *rites. Many rituals are performed by sisters to safeguard their brothers (see Chapter 10).*

Fishing and sea rituals include various rites for ensuring the safety of the fishermen and the abundance of sea harvest.

Rites of passage include installation and retirement rites for priestesses, and marriage, birth, naming, and death rites.

*In parts of the Ryūkyū Islands the priestess (*noro*) annually entertains a god as lover in secret rites that precede the harvest festival (Haring 1964, 50). In some communities there are rituals welcoming deities who have come from mysterious worlds to bring fertility and prosperity.*

*Priestesses (*noro*) are engaged to pray on behalf of sick individuals, or people facing crises or challenges. They also preside over rites preceding new ventures such as selecting locations for tombs, building new houses, starting on journeys, and launching boats.*

RITUAL, THEOLOGY, AND GENDER

Ritual is the outward face of religion. Through ritual, people give expression to their beliefs, their myths, and their hopes and fears. Successful and persuasive ritual strengthens people's conviction that their religious institutions are powerful and true. Ritual serves to consolidate disparate individuals into a group, and ritual serves to link that group to other, supernatural realms. Ritual is a tool for eliciting altered states of consciousness in participants. And rituals are among the most widespread means used by human beings who wish to manipulate their environment, ward off misfortune, and ensure well-being for themselves and their loved ones.

The existing literature on women and religion enables us to direct our attention to a number of questions regarding the nature and role of ritual. Are women's religions ritually rather than theologically oriented? Are women's rituals particularly expressive emotionally?

Walter Pitts (1989) studied one American Afro-Baptist congregation in which the membership is 75% female and the clergy is all male. He found a sexual division of religious labor: men are interested in theology (the nature of God and life) whereas women are in charge of rituals and caring for the church and congregation. Pitts has suggested that the association of men and theology versus women and ritual is in keeping with the traditional African model of gender and religious activity (personal communication).

I, on the other hand, am inclined to believe that all people, male and female, **think about** existential issues (of course some individuals are more "intellectually inclined" than others). Gender difference, I suspect, lies in proficiency at **talking about** or **writing about** these issues in a language that ethnographers or historians can understand, and in institutionalized access to acquiring that proficiency. The elderly Kurdish Jewish women among whom I conducted fieldwork in Israel are extraordinarily inarticulate. Most do not even know one language adequately for prosaic purposes, and traditional Jewish teaching about sacred matters certainly was not available to women of their generation. Partway through my time in the field however, I began to see that the women used an eloquent language of hand gestures and food rituals to express complex theological and philosophical notions. These old women have taught me to be suspicious of reports of women's religiosity that minimize theology.

Neither all women's religions nor all women are located at the "highly ritualistic" (as opposed to the "highly theological") end of the religion continuum. Christian Science, for example, stresses study—"science"—rather than ritual, and their church services are plain and unceremonial. Moving backwards by half a millennium, the Beguines, monastic women in medieval Europe, chose a life-style that emphasized service to the poor over a cloistered life of prayer and ritual.

When scholars say that women are more concerned with ritual than with theology, the implication often is that ritual is somehow less noble, important, or sophisticated than theology.[2] While men sit and ponder and write about complex metaphysical problems, women jump up and down and ask the spirits to cure their children of the flu. This sort of dichoto-mous and androcentric thinking is of little use in grappling with women's religions.

With these words of caution in mind, an overview of women's religions shows that a strong emphasis on ritual is indeed typical.[3] There are several women's religions that could essentially be described as constellations of ritu-als: these religions lack a standardized belief system, formal membership proce-dures, rules and regulations, and recognized leaders. The clearest example of this model is American Spiritualism. In fact, an "overemphasis" on ritual has been one of the criticisms most commonly leveled at nineteenth-century Spiri-tualism. The principal feature of Spiritualism is the seance—a dramatic ritual in which mediums establish contact with spirits of the dead. June Macklin has observed that in the modern Spiritualist movement "the philosophical and religious aspects of the system are not a primary concern" (1974, 411).

An emphasis on ritual, however, does not mean that women's religions are simplistic. Human beings have many ways of articulating their beliefs; writ-ing theological treatises is but one. If we abandon a dichotomy between ritual (magical, superstitious, ignorant) and theology (philosophical, abstract, un-selfish, moral), we begin to see that rituals may express very complex belief systems. Spiritualist seances, for example, explicate and reinforce the notion that material reality is not the only reality; that all living creatures are eter-nally connected with one another; that what one person does affects everyone and everything forever; that people are not specks of dust, disappearing into nothingness when they die; that love has meaning; that human relationships are sacred.

WOMEN, RITUALS, RELATIONSHIP, AND COMMUNITY

Religions dominated by women tend to have an interpersonal rather than an individualistic orientation. Women's religions rarely include hermits or yogis dwelling in mystical isolation on mountaintops (although in male-dominated religions there are women who choose isolated spiritual paths). Far more typi-cal of female-dominated religions are rituals and belief systems well designed to strengthen bonds among people. This is consistent with Carol Gilligan's (1982) contention that women's experiences lead them to understand morality in terms of webs of relationship and interpersonal caring and responsibility, whereas men's experiences lead them to understand morality in terms of ab-stract issues of rights and justice.

In many societies women are especially responsible for caring for children and for old people. Relationship is often the core element of women's daily experi-ences. Women's religious lives serve to sacralize those experiences; women's rituals tend to reflect the interpersonal orientation of women's profane activities.

"[A]ll [Haitian] Vodou healing is the healing of relationships" (Brown 1991, 331). Karen Brown observes that, "In her cures Alourdes [a Vodou priestess] puts problematic human relationships into a tangible, external form, where they can be worked on and ultimately transformed. When a love relationship is desired, she binds two dolls face to face. When the dissolution of a relationship is sought, she binds them back to back. For restive, 'hungry' spirits, she prescribes a meal of their favorite foods. To treat a violent marriage, Alourdes makes a charm for the wife by filling a jar with ice ('to cool him down') and molasses ('to make him sweet')" (1991, 348).

Feminist psychologists offer a number of persuasive explanations for women's interpersonal orientation. One of these, developed by Nancy Chodorow, has already been summarized in Chapter 3. Carol Gilligan (1982, 23) writes that, "The elusive mystery of women's development lies in its recognition of the continuing importance of attachment in the human life cycle. . . . The myth of Persephone . . . remind[s] us that narcissism leads to death." A similar idea has been expressed by Belenky, Clinchy, Goldberger, and Tarule: "Men, valuing distance and autonomy, are more exclusionary. To them, 'we' clearly means 'not they'. Women, valuing connection and intimacy, are much more likely to be inclusionary, finding 'they' and 'we' to be intertwined and interdependent" (1986, 45).

Women's religions illustrate and clarify these ideas. In Northern Thai matrilineal spirit cult rituals, for instance, women ask ancestors to guard over descendants, and descendants fulfill their obligations to the ancestors. These rituals highlight dependency and interconnectedness. I find it interesting that Northern Thai descent group spirits punish intragroup conflict through sickness. The offense is brought out into the open, apologies are made to the spirit, and solidarity is expressed in the communion of food offerings. The descent group's spirits do not necessarily punish the particular individual who has committed an offense; instead, another member of the group may be afflicted by illness or misfortune in a sort of "communal punishment." The solution, then, is not individual but rather communal rituals in which all members participate. "The spirits are here identified as a single source of morality that determines the well-being, health and fortune of all members of the descent group, irrespective of actual men or women" (Tanabe 1991, 191).

The importance of harmonious interpersonal relationships in Ryūkyūan culture can be seen in the traditional way of determining who had committed a crime. In this ritual each member of the village must find a nonrelative to be his or her close partner. Whoever could not find a partner was assumed to be the guilty party (Lebra 1966, 131). Like most women's religions, Ryūkyūan religion is essentially communal and the major rituals are carried out in the context of the family and community. As in North Thailand, supernatural punishments for ritual neglect or misconduct do not always affect the specific individual who was guilty of the breach in behavior; rather, other members of his or her family may suffer as well. Relations among the priestesses are particularly cordial—they believe that discord will harm their relationships with the *kami* (gods). And they try to provide a positive example of cooperation for the people on whose behalf they serve.

Similarly, Korean shamans use horoscopes (personal year fate) to link individual affliction to the supernatural state of the household. When the gods are angry and the household's defenses are lowered, the individual who will suffer is the one whose horoscope indicates particular vulnerability; this is not necessarily the one who committed the improper act. "Religious practice in Korea is not for the individual but for the family unit" (Lee 1984, 186). *Kut* (shaman's ritual) emphasizes the inclusive solidarity of the extended bilateral family. The goal of Korean shamanistic ritual is to discern which household god was offended, and to carry out the appropriate ritual action to "patch up the relations between human and spirit and restore the integrity of the house" (Kendall 1983, 99).

David Suh offers the following analysis of Korean household and shaman's religion: On the one hand, the living want the dead to be totally dead and go away. On the other hand, they continue calling the dead back through the shaman's trance to ask for blessings. "Dead or alive one cannot escape a tight relationship with family and community" (1989, 14). Suh stresses the community centeredness of shaman rituals. "The *kut* is a family affair, if not an affair of the whole village. . . . [T]he entranced *mudang* (shaman) will give the whole family didactic instruction . . . admonishing them to mutual cooperation, filial piety, loving each other, sharing the wealth generously among the relatives and so on. Basically, the *mudangs* seem to believe that the basic cause of sickness and misfortune in the family is a lack of giving, care and concern and love among the members of the family. . . . The *mudang kut* brings about a renewed spirit of love among the members of the family" (1989, 18).

An even clearer instance is that of the American Shakers. Shaker religion had meaning only within the context of Shaker communities where individuals could rely on the physical and emotional support that developed among sisters or brothers "in the gospel" (Procter-Smith 1985, 68). According to Stephen Marini, the Shakers understood that "it was their community—the sharing of goods, spiritual gifts, and discipline—that had the most impact on New Englanders" (1982, 88). Thus, hospitality was a key feature in Shaker evangelism, and all visitors were offered food and lodging.[4] Furthermore, "Shaker worship exceeded all other forms of Christian worship for full and equal congregational participation" (Procter-Smith 1985, 162).

Spiritualism is characterized by its emphasis on interpersonal bonds that continue even after death. June Macklin quotes a medium leading a Spiritualist service: "I want each and every one of you, as is my usual custom, to sit in a little silence for a moment, and ask your spirit loved ones to come and visit with you this afternoon. You know they like to be invited especially, just the same as you and I do from day to day by our friends and loved ones here" (1974, 404). Spirits can atone for sins committed while on earth, so they frequently apologize for improper conduct toward those left behind, which serves to reestablish good relationships. Kin spirits transmit messages of love, and are characteristically concerned and supportive. Spirit messages not only strengthen ties between the living and the departed, but also enhance relations among the living who often are told by the spirits to mend their relationships with friends and relatives. In Spiritualist groups, "The client is treated as a significant individual, worthy of the special and unique attention of the caring powers" (Macklin 1974, 413). Spiritualism highlights the importance and significance of the individual and that person's relationships. In the Spiritualist view people are not simply cogs in the wheel; each person can affect his or her own destiny. People and their relationships matter.

Similarly, the essence of the Feminist Spirituality Movement is interpersonal relationship. "Earth-based spiritual traditions [such as Spiritual Feminism] are rooted in community. They are not religions of individual salvation, but of communal celebration and collective change. Community includes not just the human but the interdependent plant, animal, and elemental communities of the natural world" (Starhawk 1987, 23). In recent years a key political concern of the Feminist Spirituality Movement has been ecology. "With many spiritual feminists, ecofeminists, ecologists, anti-nuclear activists and others, I share the conviction that the crisis that threatens the destruction of the earth is not only social, political, economic, and technological, but is at root spiritual. We have lost the sense that this earth is our true home, and we fail to recognize **our profound connection with all beings in the web of life**" (Christ 1989, 314; my emphasis).

And to take one final North American example, among the nineteenth-century Sanctificationist sisters, dreams were the chief form of spiritual inspiration and divine communication. However, dream interpretation was a group activity which, according to Kitch (1989, 180), fostered group cohesion.

As we have seen in Chapter 5, women's religions devote attention to illness and healing, and offer persuasive explanations for why people suffer. It is significant that these religions, for the most part, blame neither the individual sufferer nor her friends and neighbors for the illness. The *zār* cult, for example, offers cures and explanations for illness that are far less socially "hot" than many other possible explanations (such as sin, sorcery, or the evil eye). *Zār* possession does not cast blame on either the sufferer (she did not ask the *zār* spirit to bother her) or on neighbors or acquaintances (other people cannot manipulate *zār* spirits in order to hurt someone else).

An almost identical argument has been made by Kaja Finkler regarding Mexican Spiritualism. She demonstrates that Spiritualism differs from other Mexican models of illness in that it denies the existence of witchcraft and attributes affliction solely to impersonal spirits. Like most other women's religions, Spiritualism does not hold the individual liable for her illnesses—suffering is caused by external forces. Thus, "Spiritualists make an important statement about human interaction and the shaping of illness. . . . the great importance Spiritualists attach to amiable social relations is evidenced by their shifting the onus of an illness from one's neighbors, friends, or relatives to impersonal spirits. . . . many patients recognize the advantages of an ideology that stresses positive social interaction" (1985, 52–53).

The remainder of this chapter will explore the theme of relationship in ritual in the contexts of initiation, mourning, and food rituals.

INITIATION

Sande Initiation Ceremonies

In Sande secret societies the key ritual complex is initiation into the group. For Sande women, initiation (rather than marriage, first birth, etc.) is the most important ritual girls and women participate in. During the prolonged initiation period, young women learn to rely on the group; they learn group secrets, group myths, group sacred knowledge; and they promise never to speak ill of other Sande women. Initiates undergo a painful physical procedure that marks them as members of the group and when it is time to give birth they return to the group in which they were initiated. Sande is a multifaceted secret society with various functions and goals, but as a system of myth and ritual it only has meaning within the context of the group.

Among the Kono of Sierra Leone initiation into Sande is preceded by several weeks of parading and dancing by groups of female participants known as the "little Sande"—adult women and their young female children. The "little Sande" is led by a masked and costumed figure—the spirit *Nao*—who is the incarnation of the power of the association.[5] The "little Sande" is the main public organizational means by which women are drawn into the activities of the Sande. Each day and night women parade and dance, and as the actual initiation approaches, the crowd of dancers becomes larger and more vocal. Finally, the "little Sande" leads the initiates into the secret Sande bush encampment (Rosen 1983).

Initiation classes may consist of as few as three or as many as several hundred young women, depending on the place and the year. At the start of the initiation period, young women sponsored by their mothers or other kinswomen leave the village and enter the Sande "bush"—typically a secluded forest clearing. The girls remove their clothing (symbolizing shedding childhood), paint their bodies with white clay (possibly symbolizing the lochia with which babies are covered when they are born), and dress alike in short skirts and beads (the uniform clothing symbolizing group rather than individual identity). During the time that they are in the grove men may not see them or approach them sexually.

The initiation process takes a child (the word used by the Mende is a neutral one in terms of sex) and in ritualized stages turns her into a woman. Early in the process, when the initiates appear in public they are dressed androgynously and behave awkwardly. The women conducting the rites berate them for their inabilities, and make a show of instructing them. Later on, initiands are called by a word meaning "virgins" or "maidens" and they are the subject of lewd speculation by men. The final time that they are brought to the village they are called brides and sit in a special building where they are admired by women and receive gifts from their future husbands and visits from kin in other villages.

During the time that the initiates are in the bush they learn songs, dances, and stories. The stories concern both practical matters and mystical ones, and often end with an ethical or philosophical dilemma that the girls and women discuss. The girls learn the philosophies and myths of the group, while also learning spinning, fishing, cooking, and mothering skills. In recent years, anatomy, sanitation, and first-aid have been added to the curriculum.

The power of Sande derives both from the secret knowledge and ritual objects owned by the chapters, and from the founding ancestresses, to whom offerings are made on ritual occasions. The Sande initiation ritual dramatizes the notion that all are descended from a common ancestor and so are culturally one family.

Genital Mutilation

We now turn to a topic I wish I could sweep under the carpet. In Sande—one of the most "feminist" female-dominated religions (see Chapter 13)—the central ritual complex involves clitoridectomy of adolescent women.[6]

I will begin this discussion with observations and analysis provided by Carol MacCormack, the foremost feminist scholar who conducted fieldwork among Sande women. According to MacCormack, the gender ideology taught by Sande stresses sex distinction (women and men are clearly different), respect for women's bodies, dependence on fellow women, preserving women's secret knowledge and power, and a cultural rather than a purely biological understanding of fertility. Sande training stresses their value as women to society. "In this institutional setting women dramatically pass on a strong, positive self-image to other women" (MacCormack 1977, 98).

The central element of Sande initiation is surgery in which the clitoris and part of the labia minora are cut away. Sande women believe that this procedure makes women clean and helps women bear many children. Carol MacCormack (1977, 98) and Donald Cosentino (1982, 24) both interpret this to mean that by removing the clitoris, which is analogous to the male penis, Sande women are made totally female; any sexual ambiguity is cut away. Sande women explain that a woman who has not undergone clitoridectomy will not be respected; even though she is physiologically mature she will remain in the status of immature girl. At the end of the initiation period the girls are washed in a herbal solution. They are now women, "in knowledge-able control of their own sexuality, eligible for marriage and childbearing" (MacCormack 1977, 99). Symbolically, the surgery dramatizes the role of culture—in this case Sande officials—in ensuring reproduction and defining womanhood. In addition, according to MacCormack, "Shared pain and risk of death from infection in initiation helps to bond initiates together into a cohesive group" (1979, 32).

MacCormack's comments about Sande initiation reflect a perspective that anthropologists call emic—an insider's interpretation in which ideas are presented from the point of view of the members of the culture. In dealing with clitoridectomy, however, I do not believe that an emic interpretation is sufficient; an etic—from the point of view of the outside researcher—approach is also called for. I am not convinced that MacCormack's interpretation explains why Sande women—women who belong to a well-established and powerful organization that has scores of means to control fertility at its disposal—opt for a painful dismembering of women's bodies. From an emic point of view Sande genital operations empower women and dramatize women's command of fertility; from an etic perspective clitoridectomy is a culturally condoned procedure for mutilating women's bodies. While Sande seems, on the face of it, to proclaim a highly egalitarian philosophy, from a Western feminist perspective, female genital mutilation is a form of collaboration with patriarchy (Daly 1978).[7]

I would like to raise several possible (and complementary) interpretations that may help reconcile these two such different views. First, Sande initiation serves to reinforce old women's control of young women. Clitoridectomy—performed by old women on young women—is part of the process by which old women gain that control (Bledsoe 1980).[8] Thus, for old women it is indeed an empowering procedure; for young women it is painful mutilation pure and simple.

Second, as I suggest below (see pp. 136–38), blood rituals serve to establish uniquely strong interpersonal bonds in nonmatrilineal societies. Because blood ties are so enduring, Sande initiation binds women more closely to one another than to their fathers or husbands. In other words, in societies in which the primary social organization is along the male line, a dramatic and bloody communal ritual can serve to establish equally compelling connections among women. This female bonding has important consequences in the patrilineal and virilocal societies in which Sande is located. In short, Sande clitoridectomy can be seen as a somewhat feminist response to a patriarchal cultural environment.

Third, given that genital mutilation is so widespread in Africa (Sanderson estimates that some form of female genital mutilation exists today in thirty-two out of the forty-eight African countries; 1981, 32), it may be that Sande initiation—in which the mutilation is carried out in a group (rather than individually) and consists of clitoridectomy (rather than the more severe and crippling pharaonic circumcision or infibulation)—is not as oppressive to women as it seems from the perspective of Western culture.[9]

My final suggestion returns to the theme of motherhood. Studying the Northern Sudan (where infibulation rather than the milder clitoridectomy is the norm), Janice Boddy has proposed that genital mutilation does not so much enhance fertility as it "socializes" fertility. Genital mutilation de-emphasizes sexuality and sexual pleasure, and so emphasizes childbearing. Seen from this perspective, infibulation is part of a system of curbing women's sexual desire in order to preserve their chastity in a culture in which the dignity and honor of a family are defined by the women's sexual conduct (1989, 74). Although clitoridectomy does not curb sexual desire or preserve chastity in the way that infibulation does, I would argue that both procedures serve to sever maternal from sexual functioning, and in so doing emphasize maternity. This line of reasoning fits in well with the maternal focus of women's religions in general. I would like here to refer back to Karen Sack's ideas concerning the low status of wives cross-culturally (see Chapter 3). If Sacks is correct (and I think that she is), given that women as mothers consistently have a higher status than women as wives, it may be that women in certain situations opt to downplay their identities as wives in order to enhance their identities as mothers, even at the expense of sexual enjoyment.[10] By splitting off maternity from sexuality, clitoridectomy serves to raise the status of women through accentuating the part of women's identities that is most culturally esteemed.

Truthfully, I do not know if any of these interpretations are correct. What I can say with more certainty is that Sande initiation has meaning **because** of the ritual exclusion of men (cf. Jedrej 1976). In the very specific context of Sande, genital mutilation highlights and dramatizes the fact that this is a **women's** secret society and that the physical fact of femaleness has social meaning. It may well be that Sande genital mutilation is the battle ground on which the diametrically opposed implications of women's motherhood—male ideologies of female inferiority and female self-knowledge as powerful and complete— vie for dominance.

Zār Initiation

On the face of it, Sande is the only women's religion in our sample that provides a group initiation ritual for most local women. It is tempting to say that what differentiates Sande initiation from, say, zār initiation is that the former occurs fairly automatically at a certain stage in the life cycle, whereas the latter is a ritual solution to the physical, social, or psychological disturbances suffered by particular ill-adjusted women. However, studies suggest that at least in some communities almost all women are initiated into the zār cult during their childbearing years. Therefore, I am led to speculate that zār initiation may not be so different from Sande initiation. Anita Spring's observation regarding women's reproductive rituals among the Luvale of Zambia seems to hold true for zār initiation as well: These rituals do not occur randomly or in response to individual sickness, but are coordinated with life and reproductive cycles (1976, 112).

Once a woman is diagnosed as afflicted by spirits, she is believed to be in danger until the specific possessing zār is identified. Therefore, neighbors will not leave the afflicted woman alone. They sing, dance, and drum in front of her, promising to bring her whatever she desires in an effort to make her react. As in several other women's religions, healing comes about through **joining** the group.

At the beginning of the zār initiation ritual, the initiate is confined to a dark room for several days. Her husband may not see her and she may not wash. Later, she washes and is reintegrated into the community. The ritual includes singing, drumming, dancing, and incense (techniques to invoke trance), fortune-telling and prescribing cures for the audience, animal sacrifice, and a communal meal. During the initiation the patient is referred to as the bride of the zār, and the entire ceremony has ritual, symbolic, and linguistic parallels to weddings. The core of the zār audience is women who have been initiated in the past, and so are obligated to continue attending rituals to appease their spirits. The result of initiation is the establishment of a community of women who are or were fellow sufferers.

Female Initiation: Cross-Cultural Perspectives

Anthropologists and historians of religion have written a great deal about boys' initiation, but very little about girls' initiation. In his classic *Rites and Symbols of Initiation*, Mircea Eliade concluded that girls' initiation ceremonies are less widespread, less developed, and less dramatic than boys'. Typically, each girl is initiated at the time of the individual, discrete physiological event of first menstruation, whereas boys are initiated together with the other boys of the same age group (1958, 41ff.). The implication is that boys' initiation has to do with creating "male bonding" whereas girls' initiation is concerned with more personal matters.

In some cultures initiated women form a female secret society (like the Sande). Sometimes these secret societies terrorize, threaten, or strike men whom they encounter, just as men's secret societies often terrorize women. According to Eliade, this is because women's mysteries might be endangered by the presence of men. "The tension is always between two different kinds of sacrality, which are the foundations of two different and polar world views— masculine and feminine" (1958, 80). Although I greatly admire Eliade's work (and even see my own work as growing out of his approach) I find it hard to accept his assumption that men and women have sacred modes that are "polar opposites" of one another. All recent psychological studies of sex differences show that men and women are far more similar than different from each other (Hyde 1990). And indeed, Eliade's phenomenological approach is not popular among contemporary anthropologists who object to broad generalizations not grounded in specific cultural contexts.

Bruce Lincoln has also looked at female initiation from a comparative perspective. He asks the critically important question: Who is in charge of initiating girls: men or women? "It is society as a whole that acts, and thus the initiand experiences both the repressive force of men (who may cut her, rape her, or simply force her to run, work, or stay up all night) and the support of her fellow women (who may dress and adorn her, bring food to her, or keep vigil with her)" (1981, 93). Although Lincoln does not make the point explicit, the implication seems clear enough: Women's initiation creates or perpetuates networks of women linked on the one hand by mutual social support and shared experience of sacrality, and on the other hand by a sense that men are the "other."

Initiatory segregation of girls (i.e., elaborate initiation rituals) is most common in cultures where women's status is relatively high, and the rituals often express joy at menarche. Bruce Lincoln has reached the same conclusion: "My general sense is that the presence of women's initiation in a given culture is a mark of the importance of women within the culture and of the culture's willingness to recognize this publicly and institutionally" (1981, 91).

Another well-known cross-cultural study of female initiation (or, more properly, female puberty rites) was carried out by Judith Brown (1963). Brown reached two conclusions with important implications for our present inquiry. First, female initiation rites occur in societies in which women do not leave

their natal homes after marriage, because, according to Brown, in these instances there is more of a need to proclaim their changed status at adulthood. If
the bride stays at home instead of moving away, ritual encourages family
members to shift their view of her from girl to woman. Second, female initiation rites occur in societies in which women make a notable contribution to
subsistence activity, because, Brown says, their future importance to the life of
the society requires that girls be given special assurance of their competence. I
am impressed by Brown's findings, but not by her interpretations. In light of
Chapter 2's discussion of the contexts in which women's religions occur, I
would argue that **the occurrence of female initiation rites in matrilocal societies reflects the presence of an ongoing female culture that is celebrated by
women who control substantial economic means.**[11]

FUNERAL RITUALS

Cross-culturally, women are active in mourning rituals (see, e.g., Seremetakis
1991 on Greece). The goals of mourning rituals are typically threefold: to
provide social support for the mourners, to ease the passage of the departed,
and to symbolically explore and explain the existential meaning of death and
separation. Death rituals are often highly emotionally charged. Laurel Kendall
describes the part of Korean *kut* known as *chosang-gori,* the ancestors' sequence,
when the ancestors of the house appear in the person of the possessed shaman.
"Manifesting a sobbing ancestor, the shaman clutches at the shoulders of a
child, grandchild, sibling, or spouse and laments death and separation. Tears
course down the cheeks of both shaman and client" (1983, 97).

In most women's religions there is a conscious awareness that the most
significant and permanent human relationships are those that radiate from
mothers. This is the meaning of the matrifocality we discovered in Chapter 2.
In cultures in which female-dominated religions occur women do the "work"
of nurturing relationships, and that "work" is lauded, spiritualized, and often
institutionalized. Women, whose interpersonal bonds are deemed culturally,
spiritually, and personally significant, tend to be preeminent mourners. In
death rituals, bonds with ancestors and descendants are pondered, mytholo-
gized, dramatized, and ultimately either sundered or amplified.

Mourning rituals have to do with entanglement and separation. In the following paragraphs we will see how two women's religions use diametrically
opposed strategies to express and work out these emotions.

Tensho-Kotai-Jingu-Kyu:
Cutting the Ropes that Bind

Our first example is extraordinary in that it highlights severing relations with
the dead, rather than strengthening them. Tensho-Kotai-Jingu-Kyu, a new
Japanese religion, teaches that ancestors are capable of harming their descendants. Avoidance of such harm is not through propitiation or commemoration,
but through symbolic severing of the ties binding ancestors to their descen-

dants. Members of Tensho relate that they were attracted to the religion because it promises alleviation of suffering (particularly ill health), family troubles, and economic problems. Suffering is believed to be the consequence of a variety of negative supernatural interferences, including malignant ancestors. All ancestors who have not been redeemed through Tensho practice are believed to suffer intense agony, and to cause illness and misfortune for their descendants because of "their attachment to living people" (Kerner 1976, 212).

Tensho teaches that persons in this life are linked by karma both with their ancestors and other household members (including dead fetuses) and with other compatriots from their own past lives. "The curing of illness caused by spirit possession is accomplished by breaking the ties between suffering individuals and the afflicting spirits" (Kerner 1976, 213)—through "cutting the karma" of the afflicted person. Mrs. Kitamura, the founder of Tensho, was believed to possess a special capacity to release individuals from their karmic bonds. Devout members of the sect have the ability to a lesser degree, and all members can perform this severing themselves through ritual, prayer, and dance.

Central to Tensho belief is the destruction and abandonment of the traditional ancestral soul tablets and the household "god shelf" on which they are normally placed in Japanese households. Ancestors are no longer considered to participate in the ongoing life of the family. Once redeemed (and that is what one must do in order to avoid personal suffering), ancestors no longer are linked to their descendants.

Parallel to the severing of ties with ancestors is severing of ties with living friends and relatives who are not members of Tensho. Members are warned not to interact with unconverted family members. They are told that this is necessary for their health and well-being. Sect marriages are often arranged between Japanese members and members living abroad, which means that one of the spouses is forced to leave his or her family. Children of members are not infrequently given in adoption to totally unrelated members. Members living abroad often adopt Japanese children. The newly adopted children are expected to leave their natural parents free of sentimental attachment to them. "Tensho therefore redefines the nature of social ties" (Kerner 1976, 215).

In sum, even though the **content** of Tensho's relationship with ancestors is different from that of other women's religions, the extent of its **concern** is most typical.

Black Carib Mourning Rituals:
Binding the Ropes that Were Sundered

Relationships among Black Caribs continue long after death. The recently dead rely on the religious practices of their descendants to allow them to make progress on the road to the highest heavens. Spirits may stay on earth if their relatives fail to perform the appropriate rites. "The road to the world of the dead is long and arduous, and the spirits will ask for more baths to refresh them and offerings of food to restore their forces before they arrive there"

(Coelho 1955, 145). Along the way, the spirit stops frequently to greet friends who died earlier, but who have been unable to travel as rapidly. The living family is kept informed of the journey's progress through omens and dreams until the spirit finally joins the "blessed souls." The family dead who have been admitted to the category of "blessed souls" are under obligation to advance the earthly affairs of their descendants (Coelho 1955, 140–146).

Black Carib women mourn kin for six months or a year (depending on the relationship). Older women who outlive many kin spend a significant portion of their adult lives in mourning. Mourning includes refraining from drinking alcoholic beverages, dancing, quarreling, and wearing bright colored clothes. Men and children do not mourn formally (Kerns 1983, 156).

Among the Black Caribs, death and sickness are not suffered alone. Large crowds are required at rituals for the dead, and ancestors who are dissatisfied because of a small turnout may demand that the ritual be repeated. Virginia Kerns has noted that a large crowd makes both the organizer and the deceased feel appreciated (1983, 173). Rituals for the dead are designed to meet the needs of the dead and thus protect the living from illness, misfortune, or death at the hands of neglected and resentful spirits. Offerings and prayers—centered on remembrance—prove to the dead that the living care about them.

"Ritual is so common as to be almost an aspect of daily life in Black Carib villages" (Kerns 1983, 147). In one village Kerns found that over a one-year period, a collective death-related ritual of some kind was held on 102 days. (This does not include the Roman Catholic holidays or other communal calendrical holidays.) Ancestor rituals are carried out both on predetermined anniversaries and in response to a death or sickness thought to be caused by the spirit of a dead person. Only a few rituals are absolutely obligatory.

Although Black Carib death rituals have a solemn purpose, there is a festive ambience, which includes song and dance. Virginia Kerns' informants told her that they enjoy the rituals for the dead (1983, 170). The rituals involve a great deal of preparatory work—mostly involving food which is shared among female kin and neighbors. Black Carib mothers expect to be thanked for food by young children—and to be financially supported by grown children. Ancestors have the same expectations. Rituals express gratitude to the ancestors and provide them with offerings of food and rum.

Kerns (1983, 154–156) describes the preparations for the ninth-night wake. Early in the morning women grate coconut and express the liquid to make bread. Other women mix flour, coconut milk, and yeast, and knead it. Additional women prepare dried coconut husks and firewood to bake the bread. It takes most of the morning to make the large quantity necessary for the ceremony. Here is how Taylor describes the food at an ancestral ritual: "The cooks, relaying one another from the hall, have been busy all night preparing the ancestors' favorite dishes . . . and by now [the second day of the ceremony] the various contributions have been set out and tastefully arranged on the offering tables. . . . Besides the crabs and other sea food caught by the *adugahatiu*, there is meat from the cows that have been sacrificed and from the pigs that have been slaughtered, together with corn-cakes, rice, chickpeas, and quantities of cassavas (*areba*) and manioc beer" (1951, 125).

At the *dügü* ritual the ancestral spirit is the guest of honor at a feast that lasts for three days and nights of drinking, eating, and dancing in the temple. Preparations may last for as long as a year. Enormous quantities of food for sacrifice and eating are purchased. All food and drink must be offered to the dead, or shared and distributed among the living; none may be retained by the sponsors. If the sponsors are "greedy" or "stingy" they will fall ill—victims of ancestors.

At rituals there is also food (bread, rum, and so forth) intended to be eaten by participants. The sharing of food and strong drink with the living and dead is a central ritual act. "It provides the quintessential expression of trust and kinship, and it tangibly demonstrates generosity to the living and gratitude to the dead" (Kerns 1983, 149).

FOOD RITUALS

Emphasis on food and food preparation is one of the clearest and most common themes in the ritual systems of women's religions. Cross-culturally, food is an especially sacred symbol because it is ingested—incorporated into the body of the believer.

On the Ryūkyū Islands, most rituals include offerings of food and incense to the *kami* (gods) or to the ancestors. Alcoholic beverages distilled from rice, millet, or potatoes are also offered. Formerly, one of the ceremonial tasks of priestesses was to prepare the alcoholic beverages; fermentation was induced by their chewing the grain and allowing saliva to act as a catalyst.

Food offered to the ancestral spirits and *kami* is similar to, yet more varied than, food eaten by mortals. Arrayed at shrines are dozens of individual bowls containing small amounts of various delicacies prepared by the priestesses. Ouwehand (1985, 132–134) lists the following items (I have only cited a few): bowls of holy water from a shrine well (each bowl with different herbs and leaves), incense, rice cakes, dried fish, rice water prepared in a special way, a mixture of garlic, herbs, vinegar, bean sprouts, and sesame seeds, crab legs, salted crabmeat, rice wine, fish soup, and a soup made with bean curd. After large ceremonies, priestesses and their entourage spend the afternoon feasting, drinking, and dancing. Food offerings are never wasted and leftovers are brought home. Within the home, women make offerings to the ancestors and the hearth *kami* at least twice a month. These offerings coincide with the morning meal and are consumed by the family.

Moving to a very different example, for the Shakers, "The only Eucharist was a collective consumption of what had been collectively produced; and for them it was these economic practices which day by day fashioned and refashioned the Family body in which the blood of the Spirit circulated. Thus it was that the Shaker meal transformed communism into a religion. It was their custom to eat in silence and to kneel in silent prayer before and after every meal" (Desroche 1971, 210).

Many Korean household rituals involve food offerings. The most basic ritual *kosa* consists simply of leaving offerings in particular places, bowing stiffly, rubbing the hands together, and making a personal petition. The types of foods offered as *kosa* are, in the eyes of the women, snacks or delicacies. "As a tasteful accompaniment to their wine, she [the housewife] gives them each [each god] a dried fish" (Kendall 1985, 115). *Kosa* is offered after bad dreams, when a child is ill, and at calendrical rituals. Certain gods, or more important occasions, merit more elaborate dishes. After the food has sat out for a half hour or so, it is distributed to family and neighbors. For Korean women's household rituals, according to Lee (1984), the foods must be prepared personally by the housewife. The fact that in the home the senior woman offers *kosa* shows that the house is women's space and women represent the household before the household gods (Kendall 1985, 124). Men do not make offerings to household gods, and their offerings to ancestors are often prepared by women.[12] Moving from domestic ceremonies to more public ones, ethnographic descriptions of the shaman's *kut* show an abundance of food and drink.

Among Burmese women, the basic obligation to *nats* is to provide them with food offerings; such offerings are made at every life crisis. Precise rules govern which foods to offer at which occasions. When a child is seven years old thirty-seven small fish are fried and offered to the Thirty-Seven *Nats*. The various domestic *nats* are known to have food preferences. For example, the Taungbyon brothers like betel nuts, while Ma Negale likes duck eggs. At wedding ceremonies bananas and pineapples are offered to the *nats* of the bride's and groom's families. Sometimes guests eat the offerings. At regional *nat* rituals all the *natkadaws* (shamans) bring *nat* images which are lined up and the *nats* are offered bits of food (M. Nash 1966).

Also in Sande ceremonies, libations are poured to the ancestresses, and food offerings are prepared for them. In the Black Spiritual churches of New Orleans feasts are prepared in honor of saints, and the saint's altar is decorated with, (e.g., in the case of St. Joseph's feast) rich cakes, cross-shaped Italian breads, baskets of fruit, bottles of wine, seafood (including jumbo shrimp, soft-shelled crabs, crawfish, stuffed oysters, and crabs), and other delicacies (Jacobs and Kaslow 1991, 118). Preparing feasts necessitates major cooperation from other church members, and an organizer will request and cajole donations from friends and relatives.

A rather different use of food has been described among Black Carib women. According to Kenyon Bullard (1974), Black Carib men and women have opposite financial agendas: she wants him to give her money for the household and children; he wants to spend money on alcohol, other women, and gambling. Therefore, women use ritual means to ensure a man's continuing presence in and economic contributions to the home. A woman's "love magic" involves secretly putting some of her bodily secretions into his food. Knowing that women can and do perform such rituals creates an ambivalent attitude toward food. Men love to eat and are dependent on women for food (women control food preparation and distribution), but they are scared of what women have put into the food. Highlighting the ways in which these food rituals enhance interpersonal relationships, Bullard emphasizes that "love magic" encourages men to follow through with co-residence and financial support after a casual sexual relationship.

Northern Thailand: A Case Study

In Northern Thailand food offerings to the *phii puu njaa* (spirits) are made on a variety of occasions. At regular intervals, the spirits are asked to forgive any offenses committed against them and to continue to protect the family they are associated with. When a daughter of the household marries, offerings are made to gain the approval of the spirits of the bride and groom. The essential element of the marriage ceremony is offerings made to the spirits to ensure that the spirits of the bride's cult group cause no harm to members of her group because a man from another cult group has joined the household. Spirits are propitiated when members of the family have fought among themselves, mistreated the shrine, or failed to perform the proper offerings to the spirits.

Ongoing loyalty to the family/cult group is encouraged by the belief that if the spirits are abandoned, members of the family will turn into witches. Loyalty to the spirits means loyalty to the group itself. At certain vital rituals it is required that all member households are represented, or at least that all members who live within walking distance attend. After the offerings to the spirits are made and accepted, the cult members share the leftover food. The communal meals in which both cult members and spirits participate contribute to the sense of group solidarity.

The most important annual event for the group is an offering made soon after plowing has begun in the ninth month. At this time of year demands for labor are made on close kinsmen. It is also the time of year when the health of the villagers tends to be poorest, since rice is in short supply and the beginning of the wet season gives rise to various fevers. Kin group solidarity is a priority—it is believed that conflicts may lead to sickness that is interpreted as punishment by descent group spirits for failure to cooperate.

This is how Andrew Turton describes the annual offering: "The sacrifice [offering] is made in the stem house and is attended by all women of the group and some or all of their unmarried children of both sexes. Affines and married consanguineal males may attend but seldom do. Each member household contributes a chicken (in some cases pork), rice, and the basic ritual offering, common to nearly all types of sacrifice, of a small banana leaf cone containing flowers, popped rice, candles and possibly incense. The food is cooked, offered by the ritual officiant to the spirit and then eaten by those present. If a member household cannot be represented at the sacrifice a small parcel of the cooked food will be sent to it afterwards" (1984, 278). During the annual offering (which lasts for several hours), the house and housesite are ritually closed by a white cotton thread and gates and shutters are closed, signifying the group identity of the participants.

Animal Sacrifice versus Communal Meals

In most cultures, women prepare food. Thus it is not surprising that food rituals are important to women. Food is a resource that women control, and food rituals sacralize women's everyday activities of cooking and serving. By sharing food with the gods, profane work becomes elevated to sacred ritual. Even in male-dominated religions women are often responsible for preparing ritual foods (although the public food ceremony is typically conducted by men; e.g., Jewish women cook for the Sabbath and men recite the *kiddush*).[13]

Food rituals in women's religions share several significant characteristics. To begin with, the foods used in female-dominated religions are not served in small symbolic portions. No Catholic Church style Eucharist ceremonies have been reported here. Instead, we have seen large quantities of elaborately prepared food. The food rituals are public and communal. They involve both supernatural and natural domains—both gods and people eat. Food rituals create bridges between this world and other worlds. Sharing food emphasizes good relationships with the living and the dead and the spirits, an emphasis in line with the other sorts of rituals described in this chapter.

The classic scholarly discussion of food rituals is found in W. Robertson Smith's study of ancient Semitic religion. Smith concluded that animal sacrifice was the earliest way that humans conversed with the gods; cereal offerings were simply an accompaniment to animal sacrifice.[14] In ancient Israel all animal slaughter was seen as ritual sacrifice, and meat was never eaten except as a religious act. The sacrificial meal was an act of communion, a social act in which people and God ate together. Eating and drinking collectively was a symbol and confirmation of fellowship and mutual social obligations. Kin are people with whom one eats, and who are sealed together in a bond of mutual obligation. When an animal is slaughtered and kin assemble to eat it, the communal eating is de facto a ritual of solidarity. Why is this so? Smith suggests that kinfolk, God, and the sacrificial victim were believed to share the same blood. By ingesting some of the life blood of the sacrificial animal, the blood bond among people is strengthened. At a more advanced stage of cultural development, the part of the animal that goes to God came to be burnt. As people acquired a more transcendent notion of the nature of the divine, the gods came to be understood as inhaling the smoke rather than eating the meat.

In light of Smith's emphasis on animal sacrifice in ritual meals, it is significant that in women's religions food rituals rarely include animal sacrifice; in those cases where there is animal sacrifice it is a rather minor part of a larger ritual that includes many other elements; and in no cases have we seen burnt offerings sent up to the heavens. Instead, in women's religions cooked and mostly vegetable foods are shared by members of the group.[15]

Male-dominated religions in patrilineal societies wrestle with the frightening knowledge that the most significant societal bonds (kinship) are artificial (patrilineal). Why? Because in patrilineal cultures the blood ties among kin are hypothetical: Men postulate "common blood," but uncertainty remains.[16] This is why (and here I base my ideas on those of Robertson Smith) sharing the blood of the sacrificial animal (originally the totem—which was believed to be a relative of all members of the clan) has important ritualistic connotations—it dramatizes, indeed it **forges,** the blood ties between the members of the group. By ritually killing an animal and then sharing in its consumption, groups of men ingest common blood. In many male-dominated religions, kinship is "created" by sharing the blood of animals.[17]

A similar argument has been made by Nancy Jay who reviews a range of African societies and concludes that there is indeed an affinity between blood sacrificial religion and patrilineal social organization. Sacrifice serves as evidence of patrilineal descent and functions to constitute and maintain patrilineal descent systems (1985, 285). She brings examples of societies such as the Nuer, Dahomey, and Tallensi among whom the actual word for patrilineage translates as "people who sacrifice together." Among the cases Jay cites is the West African Yako who organize themselves into both patrilineal and matrilineal descent groups. **Only the patrilineages practice sacrifice.** I quote here from Jay at some length:

> Paternity never has the same certainty [as maternity], and birth by itself cannot be the sole criterion for patrilineage membership. Nor can any enduring social structure be built only upon the shifting sands of that uncertain relation, biological paternity. Jural paternity (paternity in terms of rights and obligations) and biological paternity may, and often do, coincide, but it is jural paternity that determines patrilineage membership. Some sacrificing societies, such as the Romans or the Nuer, distinguish between biological and jural paternity in their vocabulary, for example, the Latin distinction between *genitor* and *pater.* **It was the *pater* who was significant sacrificially.** (1985, 290–291, my emphases).

In women's religions, which as I have shown in Chapter 2 tend to occur in matrifocal or matrilineal societies, the bonds between people are already empirically "in the blood" and animal blood is not needed to strengthen, prove, or dramatize that bond. Most women's religions do not confront the sorts of problems that can be solved by animal sacrifice. Significantly, in Northern Thailand the annual sacrifice occurs at a point in the agricultural cycle in which blood (kinship) ties are insufficient: the labor of outmarrying males is sorely needed at this time. Even so, in the Northern Thai case the emphasis seems to be on the sharing of a mostly vegetable meal, not on the spilling of blood. Similarly, among the Black Caribs animal sacrifice seems to be a rather peripheral part of ancestor rituals; much more emphasis is given to the preparation and serving of the ancestor's favorite foods.

In two women's religions, however, there are spectacular blood rituals. First, at *zār* cult initiations animal sacrifice is followed by a communal meal. Second, in the Sande secret society the initiate sheds her own blood—through clitoridectomy—in the communal initiation ritual. **The only two women's religions to perform blood rituals carry out these rituals both in the context of initiation and in the context of patrilineal and patrilocal societies. Sande and *zār* women, like men in Robertson Smith's ancient Near East, create**

interpersonal bonds through blood rituals. The case of Sande is particularly instructive: Initiated women become Sande "sisters."

Sande and *zār* are the only two instances of women's religions (from among our twelve key examples) that occur in patrilineal, patrilocal societies. Nineteenth-century America and England were bilateral and neolocal; most other women's religions occur in matrilineal or matrifocal societies. Thus, kinship (blood) would not be problematic because kinship ties are self-evident. **In most women's religions creating or strengthening blood ties is not an issue.** What food rituals do dramatize in women's religions is **social** ties, and that is why elaborately cooked food is so important. Offering delicious and attractively prepared delicacies to the ancestors or gods is a way of socializing or domesticating the deity.[18]

We may ask why the Shakers who self-consciously and articulately created synthetic "families" of brothers and sisters did not use some sort of blood ritual or animal sacrifice. I believe that the answer is given by the Shakers themselves: They not only deny the importance of blood ties (biological family) but see in blood ties much of the root of suffering in this world. Shakers wanted neither biological families nor blood sacrifice. It is by transcending biological family that Shakers find spiritual and material contentment. As we saw above, Shaker food rituals contribute to that process, but not through ritual blood sacrifice, and not even through the common Christian symbolic sacrifice of the Eucharist.[19]

The one question that remains is why in women's religions food for the deity is eaten by human participants and not sent up as burnt offerings. I believe that this is consistent with the interpersonal emphases of women's religions. In the elaborate food rituals of women's religions the accent is on socializing with the gods. Immanent deities are invited to partake of tasty treats; smoke is not sent away to transcendent deities. In women's religions neither people (shamans) nor offerings (food) ascend; rather, gods, spirits, and ancestors descend and join in the communal, human experience. This pattern is most clearly articulated in rituals of spirit possession, which will be explored in Chapter 8.

LIFE-CYCLE RITUALS

Anthropologists and historians of religion categorize rituals into three major groupings: rites of solidarity, rituals of affliction, and rites of passage. In this chapter I have shown that almost all the rituals of women's religions fall within the rubric of rites of solidarity: dramatizing and strengthening interpersonal bonds is an important ritual focus of women's religions. In the previous chapter I demonstrated that rituals of healing that highlight and resolve suffering and affliction have a momentous role in women's religions. Turning to the third category of rituals—rites of passage—we are confronted with something of a puzzle. **Rites of passage are relatively rare and unelaborated in women's religions.** Maternity is consequential and respected, yet birth rituals are close to non-existent. To take one example, among the Northern Thai pregnancy and birth are enveloped in ceremony, but these ceremonies seem to have nothing to do with the female-dominated matrilineal spirit cult (see Hanks 1963). I have found no discussion of birth rituals in the ethnographic literature on most of the other women's religions, and given the excellence of the ethnographies available, I do not believe that this absence reflects some sort of anti-natality bias on the part of the ethnographers. Birth is simply not a focus of ritual in most women's religions. Maturation rituals also receive little attention in women's religions. Ironically, contemporary Jewish and Christian feminists are constructing rituals to celebrate women's physiological passages, yet most female-dominated religions ignore menarche, menstruation, and menopause. Marriage ceremonies also play a very minor role in female-dominated religions. And finally, despite women's fame as mourners cross-culturally, with one or two exceptions (especially Black Caribs) we do not find that female-dominated religions particularly emphasize death or funeral rituals.

A number of factors taken together can explain the remarkable absence of life-cycle rituals. To begin with, women's religions do not seem to pay very much attention to women's bodies in any context. As I argued in Chapter 3, although motherhood is consequential in these religions, what receives notice is the social aspects (nurturing) rather than the physiological aspects (lactation, pregnancy) of maternity. Nurture, a lifelong process, does not lend itself to rites of passage. Similarly, as I argue in Chapter 11, old women are often leaders in women's religions, but the definition of "old" is a social one rather than a physiological one: Women who are freed of household responsibility and who have accumulated religious wisdom are leaders, menopause does not seem to enter the picture.

Could it be that the emphasis on women's bodies in male-dominated religions has more to do with men's concerns than with women's? All the so-called "unique" or "exceptional" female physiological processes are neither unique nor exceptional from the perspective of women. It is men who would find menstruation anomalous; women would more likely take it for granted. I am reminded here of an interview that I conducted with a post-partum woman at an Israeli hospital in the context of a research project on the cultural construction of childbirth. We had been discussing whether birth is a miracle when my informant quite severely put me in my place, telling me: "Well the baby is in there, isn't it? It has to come out somehow. What's the big miracle about that!" (see Sered 1991). Women's religions are characterized by concern with social ties, not with biological facts. Not surprisingly, other women whom I interviewed in the course of the same project stressed that the miracle of birth was not the physiological process but the opportunity to get to know and take care of a new human being. To quote one more informant, "A miracle, yes, when I saw how he looks around, how he was a person already."

The absence of birth ceremonies in most women's religions stands in contrast to for example, rural India, where birth is highly ritualized (see Wadley 1980). I suspect that the de-emphasis of blood taboos in female-dominated religions (see Chapter 10) partially accounts for the de-emphasis of birth rituals. In many male-dominated religions birth rituals focus on distancing spirits attracted to childbirth blood, or disposing of the "polluted" afterbirth. Let me add that an alternative explanation for the lack of elaboration of childbirth rituals is Starhawk's suggestion that "birth itself is such a powerful experience that it doesn't seem to require a lot of ritual . . . when it's happening—it just takes over, creating its own ritual" (personal communication 1992).

The arguments I have just made explain why the biological events in women's lives may not receive much ritual notice in women's religions. It does not explain why wedding ceremonies are marginal in women's religions. Marriage is the social tie par excellence, and as such we would expect it to receive ritual recognition in women's religions. It is useful here to turn to the excellent theoretical work on reproductive rituals carried out by Karen Paige and Jeffrey Paige. Paige and Paige argue that the elaboration of reproductive rituals has to do with men's interest in controlling women's reproductive power. Rituals accompany the pivotal times in which women's reproductive potential is transferred from one group of men to another.

Women's religions do not ritualize the transfer of rights in women's bodies from one group of men to another. This is not to say that there is no marriage in societies in which female-dominated religions occur; with the exception of the Shakers all women's religions are made up primarily of married women. However, female-dominated religions do not, for the most part, feature rituals that legitimate men's control of women's bodies. (We will have more to say about this in Chapter 13.) I find it significant that one of the very few women's religions to even offer a wedding ceremony is Spiritualism, in which the wedding ceremony is modest, unembellished, and totally reciprocal. Rights over women are not reallocated among men in Spiritualist weddings (see Ward 1990).

Two women's religions do include dramatic life-cycle rituals, and we have already dealt with both in some detail in this chapter. Among the Sande puberty and childbirth are hubs of ritual activity. I have already suggested an explanation for this somewhat unusual (in terms of women's religions) situation: Sande rituals create blood ties among women in a patrilineal society. In other words, among the Sande there are exceptionally compelling social reasons for life-cycle rituals.

Among the Black Caribs the dead lie at the heart of the ritual world. To my mind, the most interesting feature of the Black Carib mourning rites is their duration. These mourning rites are not rites of passage: they do not take place immediately after death, nor do they ritualize the passage of the deceased into the next world. Quite to the contrary, these rituals continue for years after the death of a family member, and highlight the **lack** of passage of the deceased. These rituals are aimed at retaining the deceased as an ongoing presence among the living.

The absence of rituals that underscore change fits in with the proliferation of rituals that underscore continuity in women's religions. This is consistent with Nancy Chodorow's claim that female psychological development in general is more continuous than male development. In line with Chodorow's ideas, I suggest that rites of passage may better reflect male spiritual and emotional patterns than female ones. We will return to these ideas in greater detail in the next chapter.

Notes

1. Family tombs traditionally were the focal point of the social unit; upper-class tombs were among the most prominent features of the landscape. Many of these were shaped in domes, said by some to resemble a turtle's back and by others to represent the womb from which all men must come (Kerr 1958, 218).

2. Max Weber bears a large share of the responsibility for the idea (or for "proving" the idea) that highly ritualistic religions are not as "good" as other religions. He claimed that pure ritualism is not very different from magic, and may even lag behind magic on an evolutionary scale. His argument is that rituals have no lasting effect upon the participant—it is an "essentially ephemeral subjective state [that] is striven after" (1966, 152).

3. Not all women's religions are characterized by ecstatic and exciting rituals. Okinawan ritual is highly stylized and may strike the observer as purely perfunctory. According to Lebra (1966), Okinawan rituals emphasize proper performance and decorum, rather than sincerity and emotionalism. Typically, prayer consists of chanting, offerings, and softly rubbing the hands together.

4. This was true both in the permanent Shaker settlements and when Shaker leaders were away from home on evangelical tours. "By supplying hospitality and continuous informal evangelism, the Shakers added another dimension to the evangelistic effort. . . . [I]nstead of relying on traditional notions of church discipline to organize converts, they simply incorporated families of new Believers into the traveling community on the spot" (Marini 1982, 93).

5. During certain ceremonies, Sande ancestresses appear in the form of masked figures. The masks are highly sacred, and members and nonmembers alike express reverence and awe toward them. If a man molests a Sande girl or infringes Sande rules, a masked Sande member arrests him. While wearing the mask of the Sande she personalizes the spirit or protector of the Society and everyone obeys her. Although everyone knows that "regular" people are underneath the masks, it is forbidden to watch the Sande "ancestress" unmask. Sande masks are representations of complex spiritual and mythological messages (Richards 1973).

Okinawan priestesses also wear (or wore) masks at certain ritual occasions. At annual rites in which deities visit the village, the deities are sometimes represented by villagers wearing costumes and masks.

The previous generation of anthropologists believed that throughout the world men use masks as parts of rituals which act out why women have been rightly deprived of the authority that resides in the ownership of masks. According to this theory, men created secret societies that used masks as aggressive means to take power from early matriarchies. These men's secret societies terrorize women by using masks representing spirits. Recently Elizabeth Tonkin (1983) and Henry Pernet (1982) have made the argument that women's role in men's mask rituals is not as passive as ethnographers have assumed; women's screaming in fright on seeing the masks is ritualized and symbolic, not real fright. Neither Tonkin nor Pernet, however, describe rituals in which **women** don masks. Further research is needed to uncover the meaning of women's masking rites.

6. I am limiting my comments here to clitoridectomy, but many of the questions

that I raise are even more relevant regarding infibulation, a far more severe procedure that often causes permanent pain and dysfunction.

7. Feminist scholar Mary Daly has looked at African genital mutilation in a cross-cultural context of atrocities committed against women's bodies. In common with Indian suttee, Chinese footbinding, and European witchburnings, genital mutilation betrays an obsession with female purity, a pattern of proliferation from an elite to the upwardly aspiring lower echelons of society, a ceremonial setting that misfocuses attention away from the actual cutting, an ideology that says that for a woman to be normative she must suffer the slicing away of part of her anatomy, and the legitimation of the whole procedure by outside scholars who treat it as a "custom." Daly indicates two other characteristics that are particularly relevant here: the total absence of men at the execution of the mutilation, and "the use of women as token torturers" (1978, 163). Yet, as Daly point out, the women themselves say that they carry out the mutilation because no man will marry a woman whose genitals have been left intact (also see Lightfoot-Klein 1989). Daly leads us to question the facile observation that women perpetuate genital mutilation; she suggest that the women themselves realize that the real perpetrators are the men.

8. Kennedy sees excision (genital mutilation) among the Nubia as reflecting and strengthening social principles of sex separation, male dominance, and **age-generation dominance.** He argues that the mixture of social support and pain and fear instilled by these procedures are "ideal for intimidating a child, suppressing sexual and aggressive Oedipal desires, and inculcating docility" (1978, 162 my emphasis). According to Kennedy, "Sexual fears, anxieties concerning fertility responsibility, and a clear-cut impression of her social subordination to men are forcefully stamped into a young girl's consciousness" (1978, 165).

9. Sanderson (1981) presents a number of possible explanations for genital mutilation, none of which is really provable but many of which are interesting. (1) Female excision may have been a substitute for human sacrifice at one time. (2) Female excision may be a kind of "tribal badge" when people were naked. It distinguished them ethnically from other groups and demonstrates status. (3) A severe test of loyalty or bravery for a neophyte. (4) To please men who dislike the sight and feel of unexcised female genitalia, or increase the man's sexual pleasure because the vaginal aperture is minuscule. (5) An exaggerated form of cleanliness or purification. (6) To control female sexuality.

10. The issue of the symbolic separation between women's sexuality and fertility in many cultures warrants more attention. In Africa we see that sexuality and fertility are ritually detached, and preference is given to fertility. I suggest that in the United States this separation has taken the unusual form of preference for sexuality and a general devaluation of fertility. The American penchant for both pornography and hysterectomies is the mirror image of Sande clitoridectomy.

11. Brown also suggests that genital mutilation and other painful puberty rites for boys and girls occur in societies with patrilocal residence *and* an exclusive mother-infant sleeping arrangement. She interprets these rites as having to do with sex identity conflict. I would tend to see both as having to do with breaking up the strong mother-child bond in order to allow the patrilocal (patriarchal) culture to repeat itself in the next generation (Brown actually hints at this kind of interpretation).

12. Men can also offer *kosa*—for example, when a new office building is opened. (Kendall 1985).

13. I refer the reader to Caroline Bynum's fascinating discussion of food rituals among medieval Christian women (1987, esp. pp. 189–194).

14. This is because sacrificial worship was standardized while the Semites were still nomads who did not have agriculture and so did not have cereal as part of their ordinary diet (Smith 1972 [1889]).

15. There is a problem in the ethnographic literature in that some scholars use the word "sacrifice" for vegetable offerings followed by a communal meal (see the preceding section on Thailand for an example of this sort of terminological muddle). I do not consider vegetable offerings or communal meals to be sacrifice. I treat sacrifice, as did Smith, more narrowly as rituals that focus on the ritual killing of an animal.

16. The problematic nature of kinship in patrilineal societies may also be solved by religious injunctions concerning the control of women. By ensuring that girls remain virgins until they marry, and that wives do not have contact with other men, husbands can have some level of assurance that the children to whom their wives give birth are really their own. Another solution to the "problem" of patrilineality is boys' initiation rituals, which symbolize a return to the womb and rebirth as a member of the male community. Please note that my analysis of patrilineality as inherently problematic is almost exactly opposite to William Divale's (1984) argument that matrilocality is inherently temporary and problematic because it does not allow fraternal interest groups to function.

17. I am particularly impressed with David Hick's description of Tetum religion, a religion almost totally dominated by women. Among the very few roles for men are a sacrifice performed by a male rainmaker (1984, 85). Priestesses, as far as I can ascertain from Hick's description, serve a great deal of cooked food, but they do not perform ritual sacrifices. Hicks also describes the wedding ceremony in this patrilineal, patrilocal society. As part of the ceremony the father of the bride makes reference to two kinds of trees that "exude a reddish secretion villagers liken to blood" (1984, 58). This "blood" is an allusion to blood covenants that unite individuals, clans, and princedoms in this patrilineal society.

18. The association between men and blood rituals and women and food rituals turns out to be far broader than I imagined when I first wrote this chapter. For example, in a comparison of Turkic (including Kazakh, western Turkman, and Karakalpak) versus Tajik (including Tajik, Uzbek, and Uabek) shamanism in Central Asia, Russian anthropologist V. Basilov notes that among the former only men become shamans, while among the latter almost all shamans are women. For our purposes, what is most fascinating is that although the two types of shamans are similar in many ways, only the former engage in bloody rituals such as jumping barefoot on sabers, hammering a dagger into the flesh of the shaman, pricking the patient with a knife, and striking their heads and chests. Bloody rituals are wholly absent from Basilov's portrayal of Tajik (female) shamanism. In Tajik (female) shamans' rituals, flour and foods made of flour are used as ritual snacks of which the spirits also partake (1976, 151–152). Skipping half a continent, we find that Taiwanese male shamans, who in most other ways resemble Korean and Japanese female shamans, engage in frenzied, bloody rituals such as raking their foreheads and backs with long nails, and piercing their mouths with needles. Significantly, their Korean and Japanese female counterparts do not perform similar acts of bloodshed (Suzuki 1976). And, while in Mitsuo Suzuki's report of Taiwanese male shamanism there is no mention of food rituals, food plays a crucial role in Korean shamanistic rituals.

19. The lack of blood sacrifice among the Shakers really needs no explanation; blood sacrifice was simply not part of nineteenth-century American religion. On the other hand, the absence of blood sacrifice metaphors and symbolism does warrant interpretation.

7 ≋

The Sacred in the Profane

THIS-WORLDLY VERSUS OTHER-WORLDLY RELIGIONS

Looking in from the outside, academicians try to understand the basic orientations of religious movements. One of the standard categories used by historians of religion to evaluate religions is "this-worldly" versus "other-worldly." This-worldly religions emphasize life in the here and now, relationships between people, and the alleviation of suffering in this world during this lifetime. Other-worldly religions focus attention on life after death, future redemption, and mystical truth. Although no religion is totally this-worldly or totally other-worldly, many scholars find that this terminology is useful in showing us where particular religions invest the most energy, thought, and time.[1] The orientation of a religion is most clearly reflected in its rituals. Other-worldly religions may be less ritually rich, or may direct their rituals toward self-perfection and future salvation. This-worldly religions concern themselves with the elaboration of a rich ritual repertoire focused on concrete problems. This does not mean, however, that this-worldly religions do not posit the existence of another, supernatural plane.[2] This-worldly religions either understand the supernatural plane to be integrated with the natural world, or they pay little attention to the too-distant supernatural plane.

Women's religions, attentive to alleviating suffering in the here and now, are characterized by a this-worldly orientation. Indeed, in these religions the focus is so much on the here and now that there is almost no elaboration of creation stories or end-of-the-days scenarios. In some women's religions the this-worldly orientation is explicit; in some it is disguised by other-worldly jargon. In all the women's religions devotees learn to sacralize profane experience, to enhance the quality of their current lives, to comprehend the supernatural already present within the natural world, and to invite the divine into their lives or even into their bodies.

Buddhism versus Women's Religions

To begin, it is of interest to compare Buddhism to the women's religions that are situated in Buddhist societies. As we saw in Chapters 1 and 5, Buddhism makes a radical distinction between worldly (which is mere illusion) and other-worldly (which is reality). Attachment to the world means being involved with all sorts of impurities that prevent salvation. Salvation, in Buddhism, is salvation from the world. Buddhism, in Melford Spiro's words, "is a religion, par excellence, of other-worldly asceticism" (1971, 9).[3]

Women's religions in Buddhist societies challenge the other-worldly inclination of Buddhism. The goal of the Burmese *nat* cult, for example, is to avoid suffering while remaining in the world; one must accept the world and strive for its rewards. Similarly, the Northern Thai matrilineal spirit cults are entirely focused on this world and its problems and relationships. Ryūkyūan religion is also characterized by an emphasis on ritual rather than on metaphysical speculation. Almost the only myths are etiological ones explaining the origin of particular customs. "The range of speculative interest in nature and the supernatural seems pragmatically limited to those areas directly related to man's survival and well-being" (Lebra 1966, 42).

Korean shamanism does not describe heaven or hell—except for occasional borrowing from Buddhist or Christian depictions. There is no good or bad place to go after death, there is no reward or punishment for souls based on what they did in this life, and there is no notion of rebirth of the soul. David Suh argues that Korean shamanism is totally this-worldly in its affirmation of the importance of the living and life in this world. Even though this world is filled with pain and suffering, life is precious. "Religious salvation in the *mudang* [shaman's] religion is not a release from the life of this world. The *mudang* does not pray for a better life in another world, but for *this* life in *this* world" (1989, 21).

The new Japanese religion Tensho-Kotai-Jingu-Kyu was founded by a woman and attracts mostly women followers. In one of the first English-language field studies of this religion, anthropologist L. Carlyle May wrote that the founder "Mrs. Kitamura has not disclosed intricate doctrine concerning life after death, heaven, and hell mainly because she is primarily interested in building God's kingdom on earth for the benefit of living people" (1954, 127).

The Individual and the Community: Afro-Brazilian Religions and Feminist Spirituality

The this-worldly orientation of women's religions is also true outside Asia. In her study of the Afro-Brazilian cult in Bahia, Ruth Landes found that people believed that only life (and not death) is good, and that the best future for a soul is to be reincarnated soon in a living baby. Notions of an afterlife are barely developed. In general, the Afro-Brazilian religions are devoted to curing illnesses and solving financial and social problems. Rituals have a pragmatic and instrumental focus (1947, 217).

In Afro-Brazilian religions the this-worldly focus concerns the individual and improving his or her immediate life circumstances. Feminist Spirituality, on the other hand, is a this-worldly religion in which concerns are communal and rituals are directed toward broad-based social change. In the writings of the Feminist Spirituality Movement a recurring theme is the empowering of women here and now. Movement writings make almost no mention of heaven, hell, redemption, or the afterlife. The thrust of Feminist Spirituality is that experiences of the sacred are available immediately, that the spiritual task of human beings is to make this physical world a peaceful, harmonious, clean, and safe place for all creatures. The Movement's involvement with ecological issues is perhaps the clearest indication of the emphasis placed on this world as the locus of human action. One Spiritual Feminist writer put it this way: "Meditating individually and collectively, we build a vision that helps us create the kind of world we want to live in. . . . Simultaneously, we become the kind of people we want to see living in our world" (Iglehart 1982, 303).

This-Worldly Religions in Other-Worldly Disguise

Both Christian Science and Shakerism devalue life on this earth, yet both believe that it should be as pleasant as possible. On the one hand, Shakers withdrew from the world to their rural communities. On the other hand, for the Shakers heaven was already in this world—in the peaceful, neat Shaker villages. "The spiritual and the earthly were not two mutually exclusive spheres, but were a unified whole, with the earthly life containing glimpses of heaven even in its most mundane aspect [such as cleaning]" (Procter-Smith 1985, 201–202). For the Shakers the redemption had already occurred, here in this world. It is of interest that although Shakerism demanded celibacy, asceticism was not part of the Shaker platform: Believers were well fed and clothed, and enjoyed the society of co-believers. According to Sally Kitch, "Shakers . . . extolled the importance of physical and emotional comfort to a spiritual quest" (1979, 80). In the first important Shaker written work, *Testimonies of the Life, Character, Revelations and Doctrines of Our Ever Blessed Mother Ann Lee, and the Elders with Her* (published 1816, quoted in Stein 1992, 27), the editors explain that Ann Lee and the other Shaker founders had made it a point to instruct their followers in temporal matters because "such affairs impinged directly on spiritual development."

When I began reading about Christian Science I felt as if there were two different religions going by the name of Christian Science. One religion was paradigmatically other-worldly, teaching that matter is illusory. The other religion was extraordinarily this-worldly, dedicated to alleviating personal suffering and illness in this world through ritual healing. Christian Science has a paradoxical relationship to this-worldly concerns. Since the world is unreal, Christian Scientists do not need to separate themselves from the world, but rather to learn to see it as an illusion. Physical matter is unreal; death, sin, suffering and disease are unreal; only the Spirit exists and man is wholly Spirit.

Ironically, however, Christian Science draws attention to the physical through spiritual cures of bodily ailments. Thus Stephen Gottschalk (1973) argues that Christian Science is essentially a pragmatic religion: Its theory is related to practice, the truth of an idea is to be tested by the actual consequences of believing in it. Christian Scientists are not ascetic; they believe that individuals can and should avoid physical suffering.

Christian Science has a vague and unemphasized eschatology; the spiritual goal of Christian Science remains in this world—not to prepare people for heaven. Although Christian Science interprets social problems in spiritual terms, it does not teach that people must wait for an apocalypse before social problems can be dealt with. The greatest this-worldly achievement of Christian Science is the *Christian Science Monitor*. The newspaper concerns itself almost solely with such this-worldly matters as politics, war, and economics. Christian Science believes that social problems, like health problems, are caused by mental processes and can be healed through prayer. Unlike true other-worldly religions, Christian Science is concerned with solving social and health problems, and Christian Scientists give substantial funds for direct relief in disaster situations (such as floods and fires).

Turning to a less-known example, in the 1920s a black woman named Leafy Anderson founded the black Spiritual religion of New Orleans. Leafy Anderson's spirit guides, spirits who are still popular today, included Father John (a healer), the Biblical Queen Esther, and Black Hawk (an eighteenth- to nineteenth-century native American leader who in recent years has become associated with Martin Luther King). According to Claude Jacobs, "Researchers have characterized black churches such as . . . [black Spiritual churches] . . . as 'other worldly' in orientation and largely composed of women who have 'given up hope that the socioeconomic problems characterizing their daily lives can be solved by any effort on their part' (Thompson 1974:159). My data indicate that some reassessment of this position is needed. In the New Orleans black Spiritual churches, spirit guides such as Father John and especially Queen Esther and Black Hawk are symbols of protest and empowerment for the largely female membership who must confront problems that range from personal illness to . . . an oppressed groups's concern for righting 'a long history of wrongs' " (1989, 66). If I may take the liberty to interpret Claude Jacob's fascinating findings, spirit possession in the black Spiritual churches of New Orleans is not about escaping into the world of the spirits, but rather about inviting the spirits into this world in order to empower church members.

Christian Science, Shakerism, and black Spiritual churches are examples of this-worldly religions disguised by other-worldly costumes or rhetoric. Spiritualism is another religion that on the surface seems obsessed with the next world. Yet, according to Laurence Moore, "Spiritualism, despite the interest it generated in a life after death, was not necessarily otherworldly in its outlook. It too closely defined the spheres of the afterlife in terms of what went on here. The people who contacted the spirits of the dead were in no particular hurry to join them" (1977, 86). Spiritualism taught that one should enjoy this life while in it, but not to fear death. Death is just a state through which one must pass to reach the next existence. In Spiritualism the "other-world" is an extension of "this-world." Even messages from the spirits tend to deal with this-worldly and personal rather than theological or philosophical matters. Spiritualists can be said to have rejected any distinction between natural and supernatural; spirit is a tangible presence in the everyday world. It is interesting that critics of Spiritualism (of which there were many, see Chapter 12) **censured** Spiritualism for camouflaging its this-worldly focus inside other-worldly trappings. These critics, according to Moore, "failed to see anything spiritual in the average seance, and this was a complaint raised within the movement as well. Too often sitters ordered the heavens down to earth, never encouraging their own souls to soar any higher than the furniture flying around the room" (1977, 17).

A Question of Gender?

Given that female-dominated religions address women primarily as mothers, it makes sense to begin interpreting these examples by situating the link between women and this-worldly religion in the mother-child relationship and "maternal thinking" (see Chapter 3). Grounded in particular relationships with particular children, mothers are unlikely to find a wholly other-worldly religion appealing. To borrow Carol Gilligan's language (see below, page 155), people whose "moral voice" speaks of care and responsibility would necessarily seek to bring the spiritual down to earth, rather than seek to escape earthly interpersonal obligations and gratifications.

While I disagree with most of Erik Erikson's ideas about gender, certain of his thoughts regarding women and religion provide food for thought. Specifically, he compares religious rituals that seek to form links with the Ultimate with the rituals of interaction that all mothers exercise in relation to newborn children. According to Erikson, rituals make the goodness and presence of the infinite within the finite relations and facts of the everyday world, actual and immediate to both child and religious follower (1968; also see Doyle 1974). To phrase his ideas somewhat differently, the ritual task of both mother and of women's religions is to insert the sacred into the profane and draw attention to the unity of the two. In both cases, the ritual process itself is centered on interpersonal interaction (see Chapter 6).

SACRED AND PROFANE

One of the most fascinating features of the Northern Thai matrilineal spirit cults is their embeddedness in everyday life. One ethnographer who spent two years in a Northern Thai village remarked that the cults were so inconspicuous that "I might have spent my entire period in the village without being aware of their existence" (Mougne 1984, 300). As Gehan Wijeyewardene has pointed out, in normal circumstances the spirit cult tends to be so invisible that a number of well-respected anthropologists have not even mentioned them, or simply noted them briefly, commenting that they suspected people were trying to keep them away from these rituals (personal communication 1992).[4] The rituals have to do with warding-off misfortune and illness, with practical matters like ploughing and intragroup relationships, and with food and food preparation. Similarly, Wijeyewardene found that the shrines of urban Thai mediums are typically the front rooms of their houses and the mediums tend to be consulted regarding everyday matters. "[T]he ritual activity of the medium is concerned with this world" (1986, 163).[5]

In this-worldly religions the supernatural is immanent (see Chapter 8); devotees do not need to leave the profane world in order to experience the supernatural.

The clearest implication of the this-worldly orientation of women's religions is the use of commonplace—"profane"—locations, individuals, concerns, and instruments in "sacred" rituals. As I demonstrate in the next few examples, the physical sites, implements, and goals of women's religions tend to be indistinguishable from daily life.

Sacred Geography

According to William Lebra, in Okinawan religion "all things, animate and inanimate, are conceived as possessed of indwelling spirits. Consequently, a rigid dichotomy of sacred and profane does not exist, such distinction being merely one of degree" (1966, 45). Each village has a sacred grove that males are not allowed to enter.[6] The hearth of each house is also believed to be sacred. Various trees, beaches, caves, and piles of rocks are ritual sites. Although sacred geography is a fundamental element of Ryūkyūan religion and there are myriad holy places on the Ryūkyū Islands, ritual sites do not look very different from ordinary structures or natural formations. The sacred grove is a common-looking clump of trees with a censer. The traditional style for constructing shrines was no different from other buildings, and shrines contain no special decoration. The community hearth and the household hearths are made up of three stones and a simple shelf for offerings. There are no religious carvings or statuary. Household rites use no special ritual paraphernalia and household rituals are carried out by the senior female member rather than by a trained priestess. In the yard outside the house are other lesser ritual sites where prayers and incense are offered. In short, the domestic quarters are both profane and sacred space.[7]

Similarly, the ritual objects and symbols of Korean women's religion are so fully embedded within the home as to be almost invisible to the eye of the observer. Jars of grain in particular places, for example, are offerings to gods and ancestors. Household gods live inside the very structure of the house (the roof beam, etc.). Every house, rich or poor, has its own gods. The Korean shaman's inner room in which she performs divination rituals looks like the main room of any prosperous village home. In the room are clothes, dishes, cosmetics, toys, a television, and so on. The domestic appearance of the shaman's ritual space makes sense in light of Kendall's observation found that, "A woman's participation in shaman ceremonies is an extension of her ritual responsibilities in the home" (1983, 99).

In England, "Leading spiritualists had always emphasized the importance of the domestic base as the backbone of the movement, and the home circle was revered as the focus for spiritual values and family harmony. The family represented the perfect milieu for uplifting manifestations" (Owen 1981, 75). In these domestic seances, home furnishings played a central role. Across America people gathered around their dining room tables and tried to communicate with spirits. The home, as opposed to the church, was seen by Spiritualists as the true locus of religion. This ideology put religion squarely in women's sphere.

The cult house of the Afro-Brazilian religions also has no special architectural features, and most groups simply use space in the home of the cult leader. A marked feature of these cults is the lack of absolute distinction between sacred and profane. Consultations take place in the kitchen or living room; food offerings for the gods are prepared in the same pots in which the cult leader cooks for her family; a television table is converted into an altar at the beginning of the ritual. Ruth Landes (1947) has described a cult house in Bahia, Brazil. The chief priestess (also called "Mother") and lesser priestesses live there, so it is in fact a sort of neighborhood center, where people make both social and religious calls. The mother and priestesses live in the house (*candomblé*) in order to be in the company of the gods they tend and to serve clients who need their intercession with the gods. Unlike Catholic priests who embody the other-worldly, these priestesses only rarely withdraw from common life.

Sacred Work

Within religions that are dominated by men, women tend to be ritually active in the domestic domain: educating young children in religious values, preparing holiday meals, laundering surplices. This is consistent with Michelle Rosaldo's (1974) notion that gender inequality grows out of and reflects the association of women with the domestic sphere and men with the public. In female-dominated religions—located in societies that are not egalitarian—women are also associated with domestic work. The difference is that domestic work is interpreted as sacred and powerful.

Shaker communities, for instance, sacralized all of life, and everyday work became metaphors for sacred work. In particular, the rituals and songs of the period of Mother Ann's Work raised the everyday activities of women to the level of spiritual activity. In purification rituals Shakers spent the night scrubbing and cleaning the village. Marjorie Procter-Smith cites one of the songs sung during these rituals (1985, 188):

> Bow down low, bow down low,
> Wash, wash, clean, clean, clean, clean.
> Scour and scrub, scour and scrub
> From this floor the stains of sin.

During and after the period of Mother's Work, "[O]ne implication of the luxuriant growth of ritual mysticism was the universal sacramentality of the world in which anything and everything was potentially capable of manifesting Divine Reality . . . the possibility of consecrating the world, transforming it to share the New Creation" (Whitson 1983, 20).

Sacred People

> In daily life the priestesses of Hateruma [Ryūkyū Islands] are hardworking peasants who as sisters, mothers, and grandmothers fulfil an important social role in which they do not differ from other women. The difference is only observable when they perform their religious functions. In performing the rituals—the invocations of the *uyan* (gods), the wishes to the *uyan*, the soft rubbing of the hands, the offering procedures, the incantations—these women who are so normal in profane life undergo an extraordinary metamorphosis. The natural authority and the genuine seriousness and certainty with which the ritual acts are carried through never fail to make a deep impression on the outsider and even on those who have long been familiar with them (Ouwehand 1985, 127).

The overlap of the sacred and profane, and of the public and domestic, is a recurring theme in depictions of leaders of women's religions. Sande leaders, for example, teach domestic skills in a setting that is most explicitly sacred and non-domestic—the bush. Afro-Brazilian religious leaders begin as women suffering from personal problems, and as mediums they are involved with individuals coming to the temple seeking assistance with domestic worries (bad husbands, sick children, etc.), but as priestesses who head Centers they carry out a sacred function in the public domain. Most villages in Burma have at least one shaman who is responsible for the village *nat,* participates in regional festivals, and is hired to perform private rites (often to divine why someone is ill). Village shaman, however, is a very part-time role—shamans are also housewives and farmers, indistinguishable from other village women.[8] Similarly, Margery Fox (1989) found that there is usually a considerable overlap of friendship ties between Christian Science patients and practitioners, and counselling is apt to include rather pragmatic advice. On the other hand, in order to be able to help the patient deny reality—and that is the essence of Christian Science healing—the practitioner must keep well "prayed up;" that is, she must spend a great deal of time alone reading and meditating. In short, the practitioner is a combination physician, holy person, and friend, a role description typical of most the women's religions.

CONTINUITY, NOT TRANSITION

A pattern has emerged in this chapter: Women's religions are embedded in everyday life, sacred and profane are intertwined. The focus of women's religions is this-worldly rather than other-worldly; religion straddles the public and domestic domains. The most obvious explanation for this pattern is the social reality that constrains women more than men, and prevents them from engaging in the violent ruptures and conversions that men describe and experience. Women—and especially mothers—cannot get up and walk away from regular life in the way that men can.

It seems to me that additional factors come into play here, and in order to expand our discussion I will return to the topic of initiation (see Chapter 6). According to Mircea Eliade, girls' initiation rituals have to do with the mysteries that are natural to women: menstruation, fecundity, fertility. Boys' initiation rituals, in contrast, are concerned with the revelation of a Divine Being, sacred object, origin myth, or an event that took place at the beginning of the tribe's sacred history. "For boys initiation represents an introduction to a world that is not immediate—the world of spirit and culture. For girls, on the contrary, initiation involves a series of revelations concerning the secret meaning of a phenomenon that is apparently natural—the visible sign of their sexual maturity" (1958, 47). Put differently, girls' initiation has to do with the gradual revelation of sacrality within the natural world; boys' initiation involves revelation of sacrality outside of the natural world.

With some modification, Eliade's insight into the difference between boys' and girls' initiation ceremonies is of the utmost relevance to the thesis developed in this book. Where I disagree with Eliade is in treating the foci of boys' and girls' rituals (transcendent and immanent) as "polar opposites" [his term]. The entire point of Sande initiation, for example, is to show girls the transcendent that is immediately accessible within the immanent, not to show them that the transcendent and the immanent are two absolutely different experiential modes.

Bruce Lincoln has reached similar conclusions in his recent work entitled *Emerging from the Chrysalis: Studies in Rituals of Women's Initiation*. Lincoln argues that women's initiation bestows cosmic significance on being a woman. "In this way, ritual makes it possible for people to derive profound emotional and intellectual satisfaction from otherwise pedestrian affairs, because it points to something cosmic, transcendent, or **sacred concealed within the tedium of mundane existence**." (1981, 107, my emphasis)

Lincoln asks whether Arnold van Gennep's well-known morphology of rites of passage (separation from the former status, liminality, reincorporation into the group as a person with a new status) accurately describes what happens at female initiations. This question is of interest to us because van Gennep's model implies that the actual change or "passage" occurs during the period of liminality—when the initiate is outside of his or her "real world." Significantly, Lincoln concludes that this model does not work for girls' initiations. There is no separation (there may be isolation in her own house, but not separation) so there is no return. The passage does not occur during an extraordinary liminal stage, but while the initiand is embedded in her everyday surroundings.

In critique of anthropologist Victor Turner's (and van Gennep's) model of religious experience as liminal (i.e., outside of the ordinary, "betwixt and between"), historian of religion Caroline Bynum writes that "the themes [in the life stories ·of medieval Christian women] are less climax, conversion, reintegration and triumph, the liminality of reversal or elevation, than continuity. Moreover, women's images and symbols—which, according to [Victor] Turner's model, should reflect either inversion . . . or elevation . . . do not quite do either. They rather continue or enhance in image (e.g., bride, sick person) what the woman's ordinary experience is, so that one either has to see the woman's religious stance as permanently liminal or as never quite becoming so" (1984, 108). Whereas medieval men describe themselves as women (role reversal) to assert humility or spiritual prowess, women do not describe themselves as men but as either androgynous or as female. Margery Kempe (an English fifteenth-century saint) saw herself as mother to the baby Jesus and bride to the human Christ "carrying such images to heights of literalism by actually feeling Jesus's toes in her hands. . . . In her own eyes, Margery achieves spiritual growth not by reversing what she is but by being more fully herself with Christ" (Bynum 1984, 113). Drawing on Nancy Chodorow's ideas (see Chapter 3), Bynum suggests that "Girls' more continuous self-development, involving no fundamental need to develop a concept of 'other,' may help explain women's avoidance of dichotomous imagery and their tendency to elaborate as symbols aspects of life closer to ordinary experience (eating, suffering, lactating)" (1987, 293).[9]

Other scholars have reached parallel conclusions regarding the internal continuity of women's religious lives. Janice Boddy shows that Sudanese men afflicted by *zār* spirits tend to follow a pattern of a single spirit entering their lives at a crucial point, helping with a specific problem, and conferring a lifelong benefit; whereas for women *zār* possession is much more of an ongoing dynamic relationship (1989, 261). Laurence Moore, writing about Spiritualist mediums, notes that "almost all who began their careers as adults had felt that the first signs appeared when they were younger."

Bynum maintains that in comparison to Christian holy men's lives, the pattern of Christian holy women's lives shows few ruptures; "[I]nstead, there is gradually dawning vocation, voiced earlier and consolidated far more slowly." Moreover, women are less likely to use images of gender-reversal or to experience life-decisions as sharp ruptures because women are raised by women and develop a continuous self whereas boys must undergo the basic and intense reversal from wanting to be their mothers to accepting being fathers. If Bynum (and Nancy Chodorow) are correct in their argument (and I believe that in many cultural contexts they are), the profound sense of continuity in women's experiences would logically be deepened in matrifocal and matrilocal societies, where young women do not even undergo the rupture of leaving their natal homes to live with their husbands. Ironically, this is where the parallels between Bynum's study of women in male-dominated religions and my study of female-dominated religions ends. **The medieval women mystics described by Bynum belong to a male-dominated religion and a patrifocal culture; they at least partially reject the female role (through adopting celibacy), and they ultimately affirm a transcendent religion. In contrast, women in most female-dominated reli-**

gions embrace the female role, and preach doctrines and perform rituals of immanence.[10]

MORALITY, PARTICULARISM, AND SITUATIONAL ETHICS

According to Carol Gilligan, as a result of men's and women's different life experiences, men and women often speak in different "moral voices." Whereas men tend to stress universal rights and justice in making moral decisions, women tend to see morality as embedded in webs of specific interpersonal relationships. In my previous work among elderly Kurdish Jews in Israel, I indeed discovered that "good" religious men were expected to pray, study, and properly perform appropriate rituals, whereas "good" religious women were expected to feed the poor, care for the sick and elderly, and help their neighbors. Based on Gilligan's work and my own field experience, I expected to find that female-dominated religions emphasize correct moral behavior, and that they define moral behavior in terms of being kind and helpful.

I was startled when I discovered that my expectations were totally unfounded! Over and over I read descriptions of women's religions in which the ethnographer or historian wrote:

> The actions that the [Afro-Brazilian] *encantados* [spirits] are thought to punish are primarily connected with obligations or the failure to follow the law of the cult. Except in unusual circumstances, the Batuque spirits are expected to be indifferent to infractions of the moral code of the larger society. Robbery, theft, murder, assault, and incest are regarded as major crimes that merit imprisonment or other retributions by civil authorities, and that will also be punished by the Christian supernaturals. Malicious falsehood, dishonesty, quarrelsomeness, disrespect to parents, neglect of children, friendship with bad companions, excessive consumption of alcohol—all are regarded as serious personal shortcomings. . . . However, none of these activities is thought to bring punishment by the *encantados* (Leacock and Leacock 1972, 74).

> Supernatural rewards [on Okinawa] . . . are contingent, first and foremost, upon proper ritual action and, to a lesser degree, upon proper conduct in specific social roles and situations (Lebra 1966, 32).

> This [Korean women's] religion teaches people that they are not responsible for their suffering, and so they do not need to do anything to eradicate suffering. It does not teach a sense of moral responsibility (Suh 1989, 19).

At first glance it indeed seems that women's religions do not emphasize what we call moral behavior, and especially not that brand of moral behavior defined in terms of helping other people. A closer look, however, suggests that the moral frameworks of women's religions so differ from those of the male-dominated world religions most of us are familiar with that we are deceived into misrecognition. The dissimilarities in the moral frameworks are not only on the level of content (even if in our own culture behaving rudely to mentally confused elderly people is not considered immoral, we can easily recognize a rule of "be polite to all elderly people, even senile ones" as a "moral" rule when we come across it in another culture). The dissimilarities are also on the level of structure. I would argue that the "looser" structure of moral expectations in women's religions seduces Western researchers into describing many of these religions as focused on ritual (which appear to them to be clearly spelled out) rather than moral behavior (which appear to them not clearly spelled out), even when in actual fact proper moral behavior is treated with reverence.[11]

Karen Brown illustrates this point in regard to Haitian Vodou. "Vodou morality is not a morality of rule or law but a contextual one. It is tailored not only to the situation but also to the specific person or group involved. A moral person, in Vodou, is one who lives in tune with his or her character, a character defined by the spirits said to love that person" (1991, 240). To an observer raised in the "Thou Shalts" and "Thou Shalt Nots" of the Ten Commandments, this sort of morality may indeed be unrecognizable.

Morality in women's religions tends to be a matter of appropriate behavior in very specific contexts, rather than a matter of official or universal laws and commandments. While many male-dominated religions codify or even reify notions of how people should treat each other (Do not kill, Do not steal), women's religions tend to preach rather vague ideologies of avoiding strife or getting along with one's kinfolk. As we saw in Chapter 6, most of the women's religions accentuate messages of mutual responsibility and peaceful relations; however, the content of mutual responsibility and peaceful relations is assumed to be situational rather than universal. Thus North American Spiritualists accepted the Golden Rule as the highest statement of ethical principles, yet rejected group-imposed standards that would limit individual freedom and responsibility (Jacobs and Kaslow 1991, 78).

This is indeed consistent with Carol Gilligan's observation that in official tests of moral development, tests that reflect male moral modes, women's answers are often characterized by a lack of decisiveness or clarity. Women are often more likely to think in terms of process, interdependence, and conflict resolution, rather than justice or law.

Feminist Spirituality: A Case Study

Spiritual Feminist Starhawk has written an eloquent and thoughtful response to those who criticize Goddess religions (Feminist Spirituality) for lacking a conception of justice or system of ethics. Since most of her ideas apply to other women's religions as well, I will quote her ideas at some length.

Starhawk argues that the "conceptions of justice in the western, patriarchal religions are based on a worldview which locates deity outside the world. Of course, within each tradition there are exceptions, but in the broad view of Christianity, Judaism, and Islam, God is transcendent, and his laws are absolutes, which can be considered in a context removed both from the reality of human needs and desires and the reality of their actual effects" (1985, 194).

Starhawk illustrates this through the example of the attitude of the Catholic Church to artificial birth control. Although Catholics do not believe that God wants people to be poor and hungry, the Church is opposed to birth control even in instances in which the result of unchecked procreation is poverty and starvation. According to Starhawk, "such is the effect of this absolute morality. Because when we believe that what is sacred—and, therefore, most highly valued—is **not** what we see and sense and experience, we maintain an inherent split in consciousness that allows us to quite comfortably cause pain and suffering in pursuit of an unmanifest good" (1985, 194).[12]

In Goddess religions, on the other hand, the divine is regarded as immanent, as manifest in nature and in the needs and desires of human beings. Thus, "justice is not based on an external Absolute who imposes a set of laws upon chaotic nature, but on recognition of the ordering principles inherent in nature" (1985, 194). What discourages us from breaking "natural law" is not hellfire or Judgment at the end of days, but the fact that the consequences are also inherent in the structure of this world. "The Goddess is manifest not just in human life, but in the interwoven chain of relationships that link all forms of life" (1985, 195). Therefore, according to Starhawk, "Diversity is highly valued [in goddess religions]—as it is in nature—in a polytheistic worldview which allows for many powers, many images of divinity. In ecological systems, the greater the diversity of a community, the greater is its power of resilience, of adaptation in the face of change. . . . Diversity is also valued in human endeavors and creations" (1985, 195). As a result, in Spiritual Feminism, "Ethics are concerned with fostering diversity rather than sameness, and they are not concerned with enforcing a dogma or party line. Individual conscience—itself a manifestation of the Goddess—is the final court of appeals, above codified laws or hierarchical proclamations" (1985, 195).[13] Isn't there danger of anarchy in this sort of idiosyncratic morality? No, answers Starhawk, because in Goddess religion the individual self is never seen as separate from the entire human and biological community. "The Goddess is manifest in the self—but also in every other human self, and the biological world" (1985, 196).

As we saw in Chapter 6, many of the women's religions teach that the one who suffers is not necessarily the one who committed an immoral or improper act. Similarly, Spiritual Feminism proclaims that "Consequences [of immoral behavior] may not be distributed fairly on an individual level; it is not the owner of the chemical company who will give birth to a defective child, nor are we comforted by the belief that he will burn eternally in an afterlife. Consequences are suffered collectively, because it is our collective responsibility as a society to change those practices that destroy the lives of individuals. . . . No external God, Goddess, angel, or convoy of visitors from another planet will do this for us; *we* must create justice and ecological and social balance; this is the prime concern, the bottom line, the nitty gritty of ethics in a worldview that sees deity as immanent in human life and the world we live in" (1985, 199).

Women and Morality

The absence of dogmatic and firm moral doctrines in many of the women's religions is coupled with a nontranscendent view of divinity and a primary concern with people rather than rules. While there is no necessary link among these characteristics, there certainly is an internal logic. Concern with the here and now not only has a metaphysical dimension (immanence) but also a moral dimension (specific people rather than people in the abstract).

What I would like to ask here is whether this constellation of concerns is more associated with women's experiences than men's. Philosopher Nel Noddings argues that women's affinity to an ethic of caring is rooted in the experience of motherhood. Mothers quickly learn that absolutes are useless in dealing with the vagaries of intimate human relationships (1984).

Historian of religion Sally Purvis has described one of the attributes of mother-love that sets it apart from other types of relationships: It is independent of the specific characteristics of the particular child—the mother loves that child without knowing what kind of person that child will turn out to be, and her love is neither dependent on nor canceled by the behavior of the child. To put it differently, mother-love is a matter of relationship: I love this child because I am tied to this child in incalculable bonds of nurture and responsibility, not because he or she followed the rules.

While I basically agree with both Nodding's and Purvis's accounts, I find them a bit romanticized. In most cultures women do care deeply for their children, yet the content of that caring varies, and in all cultures some mothers have a difficult time loving all or certain of their children. What I would stress in the maternal relationship is **particularism**. By virtue of becoming a mother most women do not suddenly love **all** children, or love children as an abstract category. Rather, they love particular children—their own children. Motherhood may well make one more sensitive to the sufferings of other children, but it may equally well make one determined to protect one's own children even at the expense of other children.[14]

Particularism is where I see the notions of morality that characterize female-dominated religions as fitting in with women's life experiences as mothers. Although the matter is far from black and white, I do believe that it is accurate to say that women's religions tend to shy away from general moral codes; rather, they leave it up to the individual to behave properly in specific situations. In the next chapter we will see that most female-dominated religions also preach particularism in the supernatural sphere.

Notes

1. Ever since Max Weber's *Sociology of Religion*, this terminology has been used by students of religion. It has recently fallen into disfavor among some historians of religion and has been refined by others (in particular, to differentiate between temporal and spacial axes). But I do believe that it continues to have use in directing attention to the major orientation of particular religions. It is, however, crucial to clarify that classical scholarly assessments of religions as other-worldly versus this-worldly generally have looked at

religion from the point of view of the literate elite. It is far from clear that distinctions between this and other worlds ever have much meaning for laity—male or female.

2. "Supernatural" is another concept that some contemporary theologians and historians of religion find problematic. For the limited purposes of the present chapter, however, I do find it to be a helpful term.

3. Both Spiro (1971) and Wijeyewardene (personal communication 1992) draw attention to the fact that Buddhism incorporates certain this-worldly elements. However, I do believe it is accurate to describe the thrust of Buddhism as other-worldly, versus the thrust of the various women's religions that are this-worldly.

4. This episode in ethnographic ignorance naturally leads one to wonder whether other women's religions have also gone unnoticed by anthropologists. The well-documented tendency to "mute" women in ethnographic study, combined with the inclination to assume that the domestic sphere is cross-culturally uniform and thus uninteresting, may well have resulted in the invisibility of other women's traditions.

5. On the other hand, Wijeywardene cautions against setting up a strict polarity of spirit cults as this-worldly and Buddhism as other-worldly. In a fascinating analysis of the rhetoric of spirit mediums and Buddhist monks, he found that the monks expressed concern with the social and political stability of this world, while the spirit mediums were concerned with the fate of spirits and deities in the other world (1984b, 331).

6. Teigo Yoshida has kindly shared with me the following anecdote: "When I visited Kudaka Island several years ago, the village headman of Kudaka guided me around the island and the village. We came to the most sacred place covered by thick forest, the headman said 'Don't go inside. Men are prohibited to enter.' When I was anxious to see inside, there was a woman in our group. Pointing to her, the headman said, 'You can go in' " (personal communication 1992).

7. The *kaminchu* (priestesses), on the other hand, wear special white robes, a ceremonial headdress and necklace, and carry a special box containing the cups and incense used in the offerings (see page 233).

8. In the cities there are some full-time shamans, who earn quite a bit of money serving a wide clientele.

9. In line with Bynum's ideas, Hanks concludes that life-cycle ceremonies in Northern Thailand show that "Women achieved compassion and maturity through their sexual role, while men achieved these qualitites by denying their masculinity [becoming monks]" (1963, 81).

10. I am indebted to R. J. Z Werblowsky for this insight.

11. Please note that the Shakers and Christian Science are exceptions to almost all my general observations regarding morality and women's religions. The Shakers in particular developed detailed codes of behavior. (See Chapter 12.)

12. Starhawk's depiction of absolute moral codes in male-dominated religions is probably a bit exaggerated. Neither liberal Protestant denominations nor liberal Jewish denominations are quite so extremely rule oriented.

13. Not all feminist ethicists would agree with Starhawk's privileging of the individual conscience.

14. In cultures in which the one-on-one type of mothering familiar to Westerners does not exist—typically because the responsibility for childcare is split with other women in the kin-group—particularism has somewhat different connotations. In cultures in which a person's identity as an is individual is subsumed to his or her identity as a member of a community or kin-group, particularism has more to do with care and responsibility than with Western notions of the individual as an autonomous social unit and as a unique personality.

8

No Father in Heaven
ANDROGYNY AND POLYDEISM

GODS, SPIRITS, AND ANCESTORS
IN WOMEN'S RELIGIONS

Notions of the supernatural are what differentiate religious from secular belief systems. Given the importance that religious devotees accord their deities, we will look at the gods and spirits of each of the key examples of women's religions, even those for which data are sparse. In the previous chapters I argued that the rituals of women's religions are concerned with interpersonal relationships and reflect an essentially this-worldly, immanent orientation. Concern with relationships and this world also characterize the supernatural beings who are worshipped and addressed in women's religions. With the exception of that one statement, the variations among the supernaturals are more noteworthy than their similarities.

Burmese Nats

There is no one simple definition of *nats*—the term includes a wide variety of entities. The two main categories of *nats* are nature *nats* and the Thirty-Seven *Nats* who were human beings who died violent deaths.[1] Only a small number of the *nats* are known by an average villager. "Burmese conceptions of the *nats* (like many of their other conceptions) are marked by inconsistency, contradiction, and by what might be called cognitive looseness" (Spiro 1967, 41). Melford Spiro found that a particular *nat* might be called by several names, and that some people treat a name as specific to a certain *nat* while others treat it as a generic name.

June Nash explains that "The landscape surrounding the village and cultivated fields is alive with nats. . . . Nat propitiation enters into every significant phase of the villagers' life" (1966, 118). Nature *nats* have power over specific sections of the potentially dangerous world—wild and cultivated—in which humans live out their lives. The nature *nats* are often quite amorphous—not all are named and different people recognize different ones. Individuals perform many minor rituals to avoid immediate and personal problems caused by *nats*. Often, misfortune is caused by nature *nats* who are angered by humans trespassing on their turf or by humans who neglected to perform offerings (typically food offerings). The nature *nats* are both easily angered and potentially protective on condition of humans propitiating them. In general, Burmese tend to be more concerned with the dangerous side of the *nats* than with the protective side; most rituals are oriented toward placation.

The most important *nats* are the "Thirty-Seven *Nats*." Each of these *nats* has a name and a myth. Official lists of the thirty-seven have varied throughout the centuries, and even the number thirty-seven seems to be a classificatory category rather than a precise counting.

The best-known of the Thirty-Seven *Nats* is Min Mahagiri who is believed to guard the house. In most Burmese houses a coconut hung from the southeast pillar represents Min Mahagiri. The coconut is replaced every few months, at which times offerings of bananas, rice, tea, and other foods are made to Min Mahagiri. Min Mahagiri's myth goes as follows: A long time ago, Mahagiri lived as a human blacksmith, and he was the most powerful man in the kingdom. The king, afraid the blacksmith would raise a rebellion, took Mahagiri's eldest sister as his queen. One day the king asked his queen to summon her brother to the palace. When he arrived, the king ordered him to be thrown into a fire burning under a jasmine tree. The queen then threw herself on the flames with her brother, and they both died. The brother and sister, having become *nats* living in the jasmine tree, took to punishing anyone who came into the shade of their tree. After more adventures, a different king honored the two *nats* and ordered everyone in Burma to hang a coconut inside the house in their honor. Nowadays, Min Mahagiri is propitiated when people use anything made of metal (because he had been a blacksmith). Members of the household are perpetually aware of the proximity of the *Nat,* who dislikes the presence of birth or death in the house. When a family member is seriously ill, the coconut is removed in order not to offend Min Mahagiri. Min Mahagiri also dislikes sexual intercourse and fire, and does not like offerings of cooked food.

"Nats are petty and irascible tyrants, quick to take offense or to feel jealousy if any member of the household or the other household *nats* receive special attention. Nats require constant attention—some housewives even fan them during the hot season as well as keep their water offering and flowers fresh" (J. Nash 1966, 122). Spiro describes the relationship between people and *nats* as similar to the one between lord and subjects—a despotic relationship. "Being despotic they evoke the same sentiments evoked by government. These sentiments can be easily expressed. Since they cause trouble, avoid them; if they cannot be avoided, placate them; if their assistance is desired, bribe (propitiate) them" (1967, 138).

Village *nats* guard the village against strange *nats* and human invaders, just as the house *nat* serves as a warning to anyone who wishes to harm members of the household. Personalized *nats* seem to receive more attention than ones that do not have names and legends. The villagers' relationship to the *nats* is parallelled by their other social relations. Women have similar types of relationships with husbands and with *nats*—both must be cared for and deferred to. Adults treat children similarly to *nats*—both must be appeased and humored. People treat each other similarly to the way in which they treat *nats*—avoiding conflict and exhibiting consideration. While people may consider *nats* in general as irascible and harmful, many individuals have a personally chosen *nat* whom they feel to be a constant and helpful companion (Sarah Bekker, in a personal communication quoted in Spiro 1967, 53).

Spiritualist Spirits

Spiritualism, like other religions, begins with the God idea. Spiritualism, however, does repudiate the belief in the idea of a personal God dwelling some place in the heavens, looking down upon His children below, and waiting for them to end their earthly existence in order that they may receive their rewards and punishments. . . . God is not an overriding personality, but an **indwelling animation of all life, manifesting in illimitable ways, reached from within, rather than brought to us, from external sources** [my emphasis]" (*National Spiritualist Association Yearbook* 1953, quoted in Jacobs and Kaslow 1991, 77).

Spiritualists have professed to a variety of theological beliefs. One of the most widespread has been in the existence of an androgynous deity (see below). In actual practice, however, Spiritualists were and are much more concerned with the heavily populated spirit world than with the one God.

Communication with the spirits is frequent—through seances, possession, and dreams. Spirits talk, play music, move furniture, give advice, and make requests. In general, Spiritualist spirits are not regarded as awesome. Most spirits are helpful, and most are friends or kin of members. According to Vieda Skultans (1974, 33), the link between the spirit and physical worlds is believed to be one of mutual interdependence, and help flows both ways.

American Indian spirits have been particularly admired by Spiritualists, who see Indians as closer to natural forces and less spoiled by civilization. Two well-known theories could help account for this admiration. First, I. M. Lewis (1975) has submitted that there is a connection between women's marginal status in sexist societies and women's interest in peripheral (including foreign and nature) spirits. Spiritualist women may have been attracted to Indian spirits because both they and the spirits were "peripheral" in white, male-dominated society. Second, Sherry Ortner (1974) has argued that women universally are seen as closer to nature, while men are associated with culture (see Chapter 10 for a critique of her theory). In line with Ortner's ideas, we would expect to find that nature spirits are prevalent in a religion dominated by women.

While both Lewis's and Ortner's points have merit, I would prefer to situate the discussion of Indian spirits in the specific historical context of nineteenth-century America. Although Spiritualist women were of European ancestry, American Spiritualists lived on **American** soil. American Indian spirits, spirits of people who had lived in the American countryside and hunted and gathered in the American forests, were perceived as eminently **here,** as fundamentally immanent. By embracing American Indian spirits, nineteenth-century Spiritualists were making a theological statement rejecting transcendence (even the very concrete transcendence of "across the ocean") and were reinforcing their conception of the spirit world as co-existent with the material world.

In addition, I would venture to say that an added allure of unspoiled Indian spirits for nineteenth-century Spiritualist women lay in the (perhaps subconscious) realization that white-male-dominated technology had already begun to irrevocably ruin the planet and decimate entire populations. Spiritualism, as an American movement, took off in the wake of the Civil War. It seems likely that many Americans saw, for the first time, how machines could be used as tools of destruction on a far greater scale than had been possible in a pre-industrial age.[2] As we will see in Chapter 10, this same idea has been central to the political and spiritual consciousness of the twentieth century Feminist Spirituality Movement, which has been critical of modern technology.

Ryūkyūan Kami

Among Spiritualists, spirits are highly individualized, bearing clear personalities, names, and relationships to the people communicating with them in ritual. The Burmese *nats* also have names and stories, even if people are a bit vague regarding which *nat* is which. Unlike both the spirits of Spiritualism and the *nats* of Burma, Ryūkyūan *kami* (loosely translated as gods) generally do not have myths associated with them, nor are they highly differentiated among themselves.

The people of the Islands believe that the entire universe, both animate and inanimate, is occupied by **indwelling spirits** or *kami*. *Kami* have been described as a sort of impersonal, mystical power resident in gods, trees, people, nature, animals, storms, swords, tools, and sacred places (Haring 1964). The *kami* are associated with a wide variety of natural elements, places, occupations, ancestral spirits, and living human beings. On many of the islands, the hearth *kami* serves as a link between the household or community and the higher *kami*.

The *kami* are superhuman, nonpersonalized beings who mete out rewards and punishments. The *kami* are not omniscient or omnipotent, good or bad, yet they do have the power to supervise and influence events of this world. The function of ritual is to harness the power of the *kami*. As in Burma, lay people are more interested in avoiding trouble with the *kami* than with actively enlisting their support.

Afro-Brazilian Encantados

The various Afro-Brazilian religions have somewhat different theological approaches and posit somewhat different pantheons. The similarities are, however, sufficient to warrant treating them as a group. Afro-Brazilian cult members believe in God, Mary, and Jesus who live far away with the saints and angels. Closer to humans, physically and spiritually, are many thousands of other spirits. These spirits (*encantados*) can live on earth, and so contact with them is unavoidable. The spirits have characters similar to people—both good and bad traits.

Afro-Brazilian possession rituals teach that communication between humans and gods is possible. This communication takes place through human mediums who are in an ecstatic altered state of consciousness or trance. Most human misfortune and suffering can be explained and cured by contact with the supernatural world. Devotees believe that gods and spirits like and need to possess humans, and must be given regular opportunities to do so. Thus, possession is the supreme expression of worship.

The large pantheon of gods and spirits may include (depending on the particular cult) African gods and goddesses, Catholic saints, Indian gods and goddesses, dead slaves, dead Indians, and an assortment of demons. In Umbanda, for example, there are four major types of possessing spirits: Indians (who are stern and aloof and give advice in matters requiring quick and decisive action), Old Blacks (bent over from slavery, gentle and easy to approach, good at long and intricate personal problems, knowledgeable about herbal remedies), children (who died young, and cause the medium to be playful and innocent), and Exus (evil spirits that may make the medium engage in antisocial acts).[3] Also, each Umbanda member has an *orixa* (African deity who is syncretized to a Catholic saint) who protects him or her.

In certain cults each priestess is a votary of one god; in other cults mediums become possessed by a number of gods. In those cults in which a medium has a special spirit who consistently possesses her, this relationship is described in familial terms: the spirit is the father or mother and the medium the son or daughter, "and the spirit is expected to keep as close a watch over his devotee as a good human parent does over his offspring, as long as the devotee keeps his part of the contract and fulfills his ritual obligations" (Leacock and Leacock 1972, 60). These obligations may include food and sex taboos, ceremonial costumes, and tending a household shrine. The spirits are credited with maintaining the economic well-being of the household in the face of frequent financial crisis. Spirits can make other people behave in a way that will benefit their devotees. The spirits are also credited with maintaining their devotees and their devotees' families in "reasonably good health" (Leacock and Leacock 1972, 65).

North African Zār

Zār spirits (*zayran*) differ from *nats, kami,* and Afro-Brazilian spirits in many important ways. One similarity lies in their sheer numbers. The *zār* pantheon varies from society to society, even from ritual group to ritual group. Each *zār* (unlike *kami* but not unlike *nats*) has an individual identity. *Zār* are divided according to basic human categories of age, sex, social class, education, religion, and ethnicity. In Ethiopia, for example, they are organized in a social hierarchy similar to the Amharic social hierarchy; some are powerful lords and others are servants. Some *zārs* are intellectual, and some are benevolent healers. People tend to be possessed by *zār* spirits from the same social class as themselves.

The goal of *zār* rituals is to negotiate with a *zār* who is causing problems, and to transform him into a protective *zār*. *Zār* spirits seek opportunities to have fun in the human world. The *zār* spirits are capricious and selfish; they do not bring illness and infertility in order to harm the woman, but to convince her to supply their needs. Although *zārs* can be troublesome, most *zārs* are not exorcised; rather, they are accommodated. In some situations the *zār* spirits are seen as evil. Since the typical *zār* cult member had previously tried other healing methods—all of which had failed—turning to the *zār* ceremony can be an acknowledgment that the evil entities have won.

Zār spirits are typically perceived as having originated outside the community. Northern Sudanese, for example, recognize spirits of Muslim saints, Turkish administrators, Europeans, Hindus, Chinese, Ethiopian kings, slaves, sorcerers, prostitutes, Syrian gypsies, West Africans, nomadic Arabs, Westerners (including an archeologist), military officers and doctors of the Ottoman empire, and Southern Sudanese—in short, everyone with whom villagers have had contact during the past 150 years—everyone, that is, who is not one of them!

Unlike Allah the *zār* spirits are not eternal. They are born, age, die, and are gendered; they marry and have children and have relatives and friends and occupations and specific habitations. "Like humans, *zayran* are social beings" (Boddy 1989, 274).

Northern Thai Phii Puu Njaa

In Northern Thai villages many kinds of spirits populate the paths, gardens, fields, and houses. One kind of spirit—matrilineal clan (or descent group) spirits—are envisioned as the summation of all the spirits of houses in which the eldest women are of the same clan. These spirits are, simultaneously, independent beings who are related through female ties in the same way as their votaries are. In addition, these spirits are, in a vague manner, the nonspecific spirits of former male and female members of the matriline, and the spirits who were worshipped by former members of the matriline.[4] Typically, they occupy a corner of the bedroom next to the eldest female's bed, where they are continually present in their disembodied way. The spirits are not named (no matriline records are kept) and are divisible, but the spirit of each clan is distinct from the spirit of other clans. This entire belief system seems not to be very elaborated.

"The spirits offer a conditional protection to the people under their care: they protect if they are politely treated, receive offerings, and are formally informed of every important family event or change of status of a family member. . . . Like living relatives, they are offended if they discover that they were the last to know anything of interest or importance" (Potter 1977, 116–117). They then withdraw their protection and cause family members to fall ill. The spirits are benevolent and protective, and serve as useful disciplinarians who punish with sickness but not death. (However, some Northern Thai claim that clan spirits can get other spirits to give out harsher punishments, Turton 1984, 280).

The matrilineal descent group spirits differ from other Thai spirits in two ways that are significant for our inquiry. First, Thai spirits—except matriline spirits—are generally seen as frightening and malevolent. In this regard the matrilineal spirits are more similar to most of the other gods and spirits of women's religions; the supernatural beings of women's religions are often capricious or demanding of attention, but not evil or terrifying. And second, while most of the spirits in the broad Thai pantheon are connected to land and objects, the descent group spirits are not particularly concerned with property, a fact Turton (1976, 246) interprets as reflecting the concern of the descent group with people and not land. Again, this interpersonal focus is similar to most of the other supernatural entities we have met in women's religions. One way in which Thai matrilineal spirits differ from many of the other spirits found in female-dominated religions concerns their ethnic identity. Spiritualist, *zār*, and Afro-Brazilian spirits are often foreign (in Lewis's terms, peripheral). The Thai spirits, on the other hand, are the sum of the matrilineal ancestors (rural cults) or figures from Thai history (urban cults), in both cases, local.

The *caw* (spirits) of urban Thai spirit mediums are highly elaborated and associated with complex and specific epic legends (Wijeyewardene 1986). It strikes me as noteworthy that these spirits are inordinately concerned with revealing their individual identities to people. Rituals typically focus on figuring out which *caw* is responsible for the client's misfortune or the medium's possession.

Korean Household Gods and Restless Ghosts

In Korean women's *kut* ritual, possessing ancestors are vocal, weepy, angry, excited, and full of emotion. Women grieve for their dead ancestors, and also bicker and negotiate with them. In contrast, in male Confucian rites the ancestors are silent and awesome, and the men are solemn.

Possessing gods, spirits, and ancestors who appear in *kut* have clear identities and names. The gods of Korean shamans are not distant beings. Like petty officials, gods are fallible, greedy, and open to bribes and flattery. Janelli and Janelli (1982) describe how the gods (speaking through the possessed shaman) act like corrupt and rapacious officials, trying to get better offerings, while the villagers refuse to be intimidated and cajole, negotiate, and match wits with the deities. Korean *kut* is one of the clearest examples of direct interaction between deities and humans.

In the official Confucianist system only the ancestors of the husband's family are worshipped. Women's rituals, on the other hand, relate to ancestors from both the maternal and paternal lines. Laurel Kendall (1983) found that ghosts and ancestors from the Korean woman's family are not felt to be any more malevolent than ghosts and ancestors from the husband's family.

During the *kut* ritual, ancestors who appear do not identify themselves, nor do they appear in any particular order. The participants must figure out which ancestor is speaking. Therefore it is usually close kin who appear, otherwise no one would be able to recognize the identity of the particular ancestor. By identifying ancestors and listening to their complaints, participants gain information that helps them determine the cause of misfortune. But the ancestors never give enough information to unequivocally fix the cause of misfortune. "Even after a *kut* is finished, participants come away with different conclusions" (Janelli and Janelli 1982, 153).

The dead need the same things as the living (money, food, sex). Equally important, in Korean women's religious view, the dead need to be related to— they continue to have psychological and emotional needs. At men's Confucian ancestor rituals the dead, although benevolent, do not have strong personalities. At women's rites the dead are not so benevolent, but they have stronger personalities. From the perspective of women, ancestors "are still enmeshed in their former social relations" (Janelli and Janelli 1982, 174). Because different people have different social relationships with any particular person, they have different images of that person as a supernatural being.

Black Carib Ancestors

Black Carib prayers are addressed to God, the Virgin Mary, and deceased ancestors. Most of the ritual activity is directed toward ancestors. The song sung in the crucial dance of propitiation at the *dügü* ritual begins and ends with the refrain "Oh my grandmother, we are placating you," whether the actual ancestor is male or female (Kerns 1983, 163; Taylor 1951, 121).

Ancestors care a great deal about the interests of their earthly kin. When displeased, they withdraw protection and cease serving as mediators between their kin and the supreme authorities of the universe. Displeasure results when the living neglect religious duties, ignore the moral code, or deviate from traditional ways of life. A lower class of spirits, *hiuruha*, function as mediators between diviners and ancestral spirits. Catholic saints are also worshipped, although they are believed to be somewhat more remote from human affairs.

Black Caribs also recognize a large number of wicked or frightening supernatural entities. The *agaiumǎ* appears as a crocodile, crab, or green-haired woman. The *faialanda* is an eerie light seen by fishermen. The *umeu* are small sea creatures who harm children. The *ogoreu* is a malignant supernatural being, usually seen as a blue lizard, which attaches itself to women and is transmitted in the female line. Many sorts of fantastic animals roam the outskirts of the villages. Ruy Galvao de Andrade Coelho's (1955) description gives the impression that many but not all the evil supernatural entities are female.

Ideas concerning the human soul are also well elaborated by the Black Caribs. The human soul is understood to consist of three parts: the *anigi*, which is a kind of physical vital force located in the heart, the *iuani* whose seat is the head, and the *áfurugu*—an astral body that reproduces the material shape of a person but is composed of a substance similar to that of supernatural entities

(Coelho 1955, 137–138). This astral body is the intermediary between the supernatural and everyday realms of reality.

Sande Ancestresses

Writing about Sande in a chapter on theology is a difficult task. Like Black Carib religion, it is ritually oriented. Unlike Black Carib religion, it is a secret religion and the uninitiated do not know what Sande women are taught during their time in the bush. What can be ascertained from the ethnographic record is that Sande teaches girls how to behave, and enforces that behavior through the threat of natural and supernatural sanctions. The natural sanctions are carried out by Sande leaders, and the supernatural sanctions are carried out by the founding ancestresses of the Sande chapter, who are sometimes represented by Sande women wearing masks. Each Sande chapter has a different founding ancestress who oversees human behavior.[5]

WOMEN AND POLYDEISM

As we have seen, most women's religions relate to many spirits, gods, or ancestors. In general, these beings are not all good or all bad. There are no great benevolent lords or thoroughly evil devils. Most are somewhat "fair to middling" sorts of divinities—depending on how they are treated.

The weight of the evidence brought here indicates that women who belong to female-dominated religions are attracted to religions that offer interaction with multiple supernatural entities, even though many of these women live in societies in which monotheistic beliefs are known. I have chosen to gloss as "polydeism" a range of beliefs in more than one supernatural entity; polydeism characterizes almost all women's religions. In some women's religions the supernatural entities are close to what Westerners think of as gods, and scholars have indeed translated the native term for the supernatural entity as "god." In other women's religions spirits or ancestors direct the fortunes of human beings, but, again, I stress that a great deal of the terminological distinction reflects how Western scholars have elected to translate native terms. What seems to me significant is that even in situations in which members of the women's religion are also Catholics or Muslims (and so officially monotheistic), in the framework of the female-dominated religion, rituals address many supernatural beings. Similarly, ethnographers have been struck by the predominance of Jewish, Christian, and Muslim women at shrines of saints. Thus, we have reason to suspect that women in male-dominated religions also tend to be attracted to polydeism.

Ronald Stover and Christine Hope (1984) conducted a statistical analysis of 312 societies around the world to determine whether gender status affects religious beliefs or whether religious beliefs affect gender status. For the purposes of their study they focused on one aspect of religious belief, monotheism—which is almost always the belief in one **male** god. Significantly, they found a clear relationship between monotheism and male dominance.[6]

In a very different sort of study, Judith Ochshorn has shown an interrelationship between the rise of monotheism and gender inequality in ancient Near Eastern religions. Comparing Sumer, Elam, and Athens, she discovered that "where there was a polytheistic pantheon and cultic practices directed toward its propitiation, the presence of both sexes in the priesthood, in cult, and in popular religion was almost universal" (1981, 108; see also Lerner 1986).

And finally, writing about the Greco-Roman world, Ross Kraemer suggests that "there is conceivably some relationship between monotheism and the exclusion of women from Jewish and Christian priesthood, an exclusion that carries over to monotheistic Islam as well. When divinity is perceived to be one, and the gender of that divinity effectively presented as masculine in language, imagery, and so forth, perhaps only the sex which shares that gender is perceived as able to perform priestly functions. Conversely, among the Greeks and Romans both the gods and their clergy came in two genders" (1992, 197).

In short, it seems that monotheism is not an attractive religious option for women. In making that claim, I am not saying that men and women are born with inherently different theologies. Rather, I am suggesting that women's life experiences may lead them to prefer more than one deity. (Given the assortment of supernatural beings recognized in women's religions, I use the word deity in a very loose sense.)

We could propose a variety of means of interpreting women's affinity for polydeism. Freudian psychoanalysts could probably explain to us that the resolution of little boys' Oedipal complex leads to the development of a superego (i.e., monotheism) while girls' infantile experiences do not. Some psychologists have asserted that women's cognitive styles are more diffuse than men's, allowing us to postulate that women's theologies are also more diffuse (i.e., polydeistic). Other psychologists would tell us that women as mothers know that they are not all-powerful, so that even if as children they had fantasized an all-powerful parent/deity, as adults they know that reality is far more complex. Men, on the other hand, might still harbor a fantasy of mother/god as omnipotent.

Sociologists and anthropologists argue that in most cultures women's place in the social structure is in small, domestic units—of which there are many, rather than in the overarching institutions that tie together the individual domestic units. Men who run state level institutions could be presumed to imagine single, all-powerful deities, while women in their domestic units would tend to see many, smaller deities. Or, as David Suh claims regarding Korean society, women and other helpless and oppressed people have no other place to turn "except to the invisible spirits of their ancestors. After all, parents and relatives are the only reliable support, dead or alive, in this world of political suppression and economic exploitation" (1989, 17). In other words, the rich and powerful (and by implication we may also say men) enjoy more "public" support in the form of governments, armies, and courts, whereas women and the poor have only familial support. Translated to the spiritual sphere, the rich and men have transcendent "public" deities, while the poor and women have personal spirits.

Historians might contend that monotheism is part of a political ideology linked to the notion of divine kingship and leading to totalitarianism. Max Weber connected political processes (the rise of a world empire in China, the extension of the power of the Brahmin caste in India, and development of the Persian and Roman empires) to the rise of universalism and monotheism (1966, 23). It is suggestive that none of the women's religions are linked to either divine kingship or totalitarian social structures.[7]

One could show that monotheism is connected to a transcendent view of the divine. As I have demonstrated in previous chapters, women have an affinity for—or more precisely, an aptitude in—immanence, thus, female-dominated religions do not need transcendent monotheism. One could elaborate upon this idea by demonstrating that in the "great" monotheistic religions—Judaism, Christianity and Islam—"the mother's domination over individual birth and child care fades in significance with the great cosmic birth and transcendent care that men in connection to the great male God are envisioned to give" (Combs-Schilling 1989, 264). Or finally, one could join feminist philosopher Nel Noddings who writes that "It seems to me quite natural that men, many of whom are separated from the intimacy of caring, should create gods and seek security and love in worship. But what ethical need have women [mothers] for God? . . . What I mean to suggest is that women have no need of a conceptualized God, one wrought in the image of man. All the love and goodness commanded by such a God can be generated from the love and goodness found in the warmest and best human relations [i.e., motherhood]" (1984, 97).

All these hypotheses are food for thought, and many are likely to be true. In light of what we know about other aspects of female-dominated religions, however, I am inclined to look for the connection between women and polydeism in a somewhat different direction. In Chapter 5 I showed that women's religions often carve out a niche of expertise in addressing the problem of suffering. I demonstrated that most of these religions offer highly convincing explanations for why people suffer, and varied and eclectic solutions to suffering. I also advanced suggestions as to why women in particular are attracted to religions that elaborate this-worldly responses to suffering. Women in sexist societies are indeed sick a great deal, and women as mothers who love their children are anxious to ensure that their children survive. It is highly significant that in many situations described in this book, women who do have other religious options have turned to polydeistic and female-dominated religions because of illness, misfortune, or death of their children. It seems to me that monotheism may be too final, too absolute, to answer the needs of religions whose raison d'etre is the alleviation of suffering in this world. Monotheism leaves little room for negotiation, and it offers fewer healing options than religions with myriad supernatural entities whose neglect may mean illness and whose appeasement can mean recovery. Polydeism, in contrast, offers endless possibilities for explaining, dealing with, and (hopefully) healing suffering and illness.

A final remark is in order here. So far we have avoided looking at three out of the four North American women's religions. Two of these religions, Shakers and Christian Science, do not fit my portrayal of women's religions as polydeistic. Not surprisingly, both religions are situated in a broader cultural setting that considers monotheism to be more spiritually and intellectually advanced than polytheism. What does characterize the Shakers and Christian Science is the rejection of a purely **masculine** monotheism. We turn to the gender of the deities in the next section.

IN SEARCH OF THE GODDESS

Stover and Hope's study suggests that it is not simply the belief in one god, but the belief in one **male** god that women do not find compelling. The second half of this chapter explores the gender of the deities worshipped in female-dominated religions. In many male-dominated religions (including Judaism, Christianity, and Islam) the deity is known by masculine names and described as possessing masculine attributes (see Ruether 1974). Feminist scholars have shown how male deities both reflect and strengthen patriarchy. Mary Daly has explained, "The symbol of the Father God, spawned in the human imagination and sustained as plausible by patriarchy, has in turn rendered service to this type of society [patriarchy] by making its mechanisms for the oppression of women appear right and fitting. If God in 'his' heaven is a father ruling 'his' people, then it is in the 'nature' of things and according to divine plan and the order of the universe that society be male-dominated" (1973, 13).

In some male-dominated religions goddesses are worshipped alongside gods. Western scholarship, a product of religious traditions that lack goddesses, has tended to look at goddess worship from a psychoanalytic perspective— implying, perhaps, that goddesses are psychological anomalies in need of scientific explanation (see, e.g., Fromm and Maccoby 1970). Freud, for example, posited that devotion to goddesses reflects an infantile desire for reunification with the all-powerful mother.[8]

Fortunately, recent scholarly studies of goddess worship have begun to move beyond psychoanalytic approaches. Sifting carefully through ethnographic and textual evidence, James Preston, in a wonderful book entitled *Mother Worship,* has identified a number of common characteristics of goddesses around the world. These include antiquity (fertility goddesses were the first deities formally worshipped by human beings), a connection to motherhood, ambivalence (encompassing such opposites as love and anger or forgiveness and vengeance), a protective function vis-à-vis their devotees, an association with the resolution of human problems—especially illness, and virginity or virgin motherhood. Since Preston's study looked at goddesses in male-dominated religions, one of my goals in the present section is to verify whether these attributes are also true of the supernatural entities of female-dominated religions.

As I said earlier, feminist scholars have argued that male gods in patriarchal religions reflect and reinforce patriarchal social structures. On the whole this seems to be true, yet there are occasional situations in which male gods have been found to empower women, or goddesses to restrict women. "The existence and power of a goddess . . . is no indication or guarantee of a high status for human women" (Frymer-Kensky 1992, 80). I will limit my comments here to two brief examples. Mormonism is so patriarchal that it is inconceivable for God to perform "female" tasks. Thus, Mormon theology requires a Goddess—Mother in Heaven—to perform women's specific functions (Heeren, Linsey, and Mason 1984). The Mormon Goddess clearly is not an empowerer of women. In a very different situation, Julia Esquivel makes an impassioned plea to poor Guatemalan women to encounter the "God of the poor"—the God for whom all people are equal, and who accepts "poor women, peasants, Indians, servants, and factory workers . . . as [His] daughters" (26). Once women open their eyes to this God and to their own human dignity, women will be empowered to struggle for social justice. Esquivel's male deity, unlike the Mormon female one, does empower women.[9]

Several sociological and psychological studies of American men and women have called into doubt simplistic models of the relationship between gender roles and gods and goddesses. Tamayo and Dugas (1977) found that among both male and female college students, God (who is referred to by masculine names: Lord, King) is described in terms more similar to those in which the students describe mothers than those in which they describe fathers. Similarly, Nelsen, Cheek, and Au found that American men and women choose the word "father" over the word "mother" to describe God, but their description of God is supportive (maternal) rather than punishing (paternal). We now turn to several examples of how women in female-dominated religions portray the gender of the deity.

The Goddess Within

> For me the divine/Goddess/God/Earth/Life/It symbolizes the whole of which we are a part. . . . To poison rivers and seas and the ground on which we stand so that we can have televisions and air-conditioning, to engage in wars of conquest in order to exploit other people's labor and take the resources of their land, is to forget that we are all connected to the web of life" (Christ 1989, 320–2).

> "God is inside of you and inside of everybody else. You come into the world with God. But only them that search for it inside find it. And sometimes it just manifest itself even when you not looking, or don't know what you looking for" (Walker 1982, 177).

Despite convincing evidence that there is no necessary or simplistic relationship between women's status and the gender of deities, I was astonished to find that very few of the women's religions worship goddesses. The one exception is Feminist Spirituality.

Feminist Spirituality draws on various ancient civilizations as sources for

Goddess imagery and myths, yet "these [ancient] traditions are filtered through modern women's experiences. . . . Ancient traditions are tapped selectively and eclectically. . . . The Goddess symbol has emerged spontaneously in the dreams, fantasies, and thoughts of many women around the country in the past several years" (Christ 1979, 276).

"I found God in myself and loved her fiercely"[10] is perhaps the clearest declaration of the Goddess within the Feminist Spirituality Movement. The Goddess, unlike the Gods of Judaism, Christianity and Islam, is not "out there." Rather, goddess nature and human nature overlap, or according to some theologians, are identical. Goddess is immanent in the extreme—she is the spiritual expression of sisterhood. For some Spiritual Feminists, Goddess is a metaphor for women's spiritual power. Others believe in a more traditional female deity, albeit one whose names and traits are drawn from diverse religious traditions.[11] For all Spiritual Feminists, a female Goddess consciously enhances and reflects their own identities as women.

Carol Christ (1979, 277ff.) elaborates on the meanings of the Goddess: (1) the acknowledgment of the legitimacy and beauty of female power as a beneficent and independent power; (2) an affirmation of the female body and cycles; (3) the personification or manifestation of energy that flows between living beings and the natural world; (4) the embodiment of women's heritage, of sisterhood. Naomi Goldenberg (1979), in addition, stresses the use of the goddess concept to give women positive self-images in all stages of life: as girl (maiden), mother, and old woman (crone).

Mother-Father Deity

Several Western women's religions have modified traditional Christian male god imagery, replacing it with a male-female deity. Androgynous deities in women's religions, unlike the androgynes in Indian tradition, are not associated with androgynous **physical** characteristics (cf. O'Flaherty 1980). It is their moral and spiritual characteristics that make them androgynous.

In Christian Science God is androgynous, and referred to as "Father-Mother." Christian Scientists believe in the equality of the sexes, both in this world and in Spirit. Mary Baker Eddy, the founder of Christian Science, felt that her own sex was essential to the nature of her mission—it had been given to her to reveal the Motherhood of God. "In divine Science we have not as much authority for considering God masculine, as we have for considering Him feminine, for Love imparts the clearest idea of Deity" (*Science and Health* 1903, 517). In Eddy's own words, "God could not be less loving than my mother" (Peel 1966, 23). The Christian Science God is wholly good—Eddy rejected the classic Christian explanation of evil, claiming instead that it is impossible that the good God would have made man capable of sin, then punished him for sinning (Gottschalk 1973, 65). Christian Science opposes any anthropomorphic view of God; therefore God is described through language of negations (not this and not that).

Like most Protestant theologies, Christian Science understands God as distinct from His creation—God and man are not the same. But whereas most Protestants see man as not only separate in existence but also in nature from God (our senses tell us that man, unlike God, is finite and imperfect), Christian Science says that our senses deceive us—God is the Principle of all real being, and that "in Science" man and the universe are, like God, perfect, spiritual and eternal (Gottschalk 1973, 58).

Susan Setta (1977) has shown how Christian Science theology offered an alternative both to societal views of women and accepted religious views of God as male. According to the nineteenth-century view of women, a normal woman was passive and dependent, and Calvinism offered few options to women seeking transcendence. Women were not even allowed to speak or pray out loud in church. The Christian Science Father-Mother God, who incorporated both such "masculine" qualities as strength and such "feminine" qualities as tenderness, could allow Mary Baker Eddy and other women to become active and strong. By positing a Father-Mother God, Eddy could proclaim that masculine and feminine, men and women, are equally important within society. Just as God has masculine and feminine properties, men and women should have a balanced combination of masculine and feminine attributes.

Like Christian Scientists, Shakers attributed theological significance to the gender of their leader. Shakers believed that Ann Lee's femaleness was necessary to complement the maleness of Jesus. And like Christian Scientists, Shakers believed in a Mother-Father deity. The source of this image seems to lie in two rather different directions. Among the Shakers the notion of dual male-female leadership (see Chapter 11) developed before the notion of the Mother-Father deity (Procter-Smith 1985, 6). This is a case in which a relatively egalitarian social structure encouraged the development of a relatively egalitarian theology.[12] In addition, the characteristic traits of the female aspect of the Shaker God—Holy Mother Wisdom—seem to have been influenced by nineteenth-century notions of femininity—motherhood, passivity, love, forbearance, chastity, meekness, and virtue. However, Sally Kitch makes the interesting point that in Shaker theology gender traits are not consistently associated with male or female aspects of Divinity; for example, wisdom is sometimes associated with Holy Mother and sometimes with Father (1989, 173). Let us note that the dual gender composition of Shaker divinity should not be confused with divinity that is bifurcated in terms of good and evil. The Shaker God was held to be wholly good and merciful to human beings, and to enlighten everyone without distinction of sex or class.

During the mid-nineteenth century, Shaker communities experienced an intense and ecstatic spiritual flourishing known as Mother Ann's Work. In this period the female aspect of the Deity—Holy Mother Wisdom—was the most fully developed. When Holy Mother Wisdom communicated, a woman was needed to be her instrument or medium. This served to reinforce and legitimate the role of women in Shaker worship. "As women became increasingly prominent as instruments [mediums], female symbols became increasingly prominent in the symbol-system of the sect" (Procter-Smith 1985, 196). Yet Procter-Smith has suggested that the prominence given to the female deity did not really serve women's interests. "Although the prominence of a powerful female aspect of God undoubtedly was an empowering experience for many Shaker women, especially the instruments [mediums], it had the effect of reinforcing the strict division of labor and sexual stratification which made women peripheral in the first place" (1985, 208).

Rosemary Ruether, on the other hand, has argued that although female divine figures do not automatically further the status of women, in religious groups founded by women—such as the Shakers and Christian Science—they do promote the equality of women. In fact, we know of so few examples of women's religions with either goddesses or androgynous deities that both Procter-Smith's and Ruether's hypotheses remain unprovable.

It is important to ask why androgynous deities were attractive to many nineteenth-century North American women (and some men). I see the answer as lying in two directions. First, in nineteenth-century North America religion was increasingly deemed to be a female concern. Even male ministers were suspect for entering a profession that was "too feminine" (Welter 1974). During the nineteenth century even the mainstream Protestant denominations exhibited a tendency to emphasize the more "maternal" aspects of Jesus. It may be that an all-male deity was incompatible with a cultural assessment of religion as feminine. On the other hand, femininity in nineteenth-century America was defined as weak and passive. It also may be that an all-female deity was incompatible with a cultural assessment of women as powerless. In such a situation, an androgynous deity was a perfect solution. It could incorporate the "desirable" aspects of culturally construed femininity with the "desirable" aspects of culturally construed masculinity, while remaining faithful to Christian monotheism.

Ross Kraemer suggests that the association between women religious leaders and androgynous deities may have a long history in the Christian world. Drawing on what is known of Gnostic groups from the first centuries of the Christian era, Kraemer finds that "there seems to be some correlation between the perception of God as androgynous and the view that women could exercise Christian office" (1992, 197).[13]

The three nineteenth-century North American women's religions (Christian Science, Shakers, Spiritualism) related to benevolent, androgynous deities who embodied all the best qualities of mortal parents (cf. Becker 1990 on Christian Science and Tenrikyo). This vision had important implications. "Nineteenth-century women refused to believe that a benevolent deity would cause precious sons and daughters to be born knowing all along that he would condemn some, if not most, of them to eternal punishment in hell" (Braude 1989, 39). I see it as far from coincidental that all three of these religions offered essentially positive visions of both this life and of the next world; such visions were fitting for a parental deity.

Table 3. *The Gender of the Deity*

In Burma there are both male and female *nats*, but more male ones. There is good evidence that goddesses were preeminent in Southeast Asia before Buddhism penetrated the area (cf. Ferguson 1982).

On the Ryūkyū Islands the hearth *kami* is female. Whoever wields *kami* is *kami*, by Ryūkyūan thinking, so that priestesses and even wives and sisters are seen in some way as divine. According to Ryūkyūan cosmogony, humans were created when a brother-sister divine couple descended to earth and produced offspring. The emphasis on brother-sister pairs is common in women's religions (see Chapter 10), and we may conjecture that brother-sister deities are a variation of androgynous deities.

In Afro-Brazilian cults there seem to be fairly even numbers of male and female possessing spirits.

Male and female *zār* spirits behave differently. According to Yael Kahana (1985) hysteria is usually believed to be caused by possession by female *zār* spirits who are silly and irresponsible and cause the woman to behave in an infantile manner. Male *zār* spirits cause apathy and catatonic states. It seems that possessing spirits are more often male than female.

Korean gods and ancestors include both males and females, yet from the reports of *kut* that I have read in the ethnographic literature I get the sense that possession by female ancestors may be more common than by male ones.

Spiritualist spirits are male and female (possibly more male spirits); the deity is androgynous.

Sande ancestresses are female.

Black Carib ancestors are male and female, but are addressed in ritual singing as "grandmother."

Northern Thai matrilineal spirits are not personalized, but may possibly be thought of as female (I cannot be certain from the available ethnography). The spirits (*caw*) that possess urban mediums seem to be mostly male.

Shakers imaged a Mother-Father deity.

Christian Science has a Mother-Father deity.

Feminist Spiritualists relate to a variety of Goddesses.

THE GENDER OF THE DEITY

We will now briefly return to the polydeistic women's religions to review the gender of the deities (Table 3). We immediately see that the gender of deities in polydeistic women's religions is split fairly evenly; there is no overall preference for female or for male supernatural entities.

CONCLUSION

What we cannot say about the deities of women's religions is possibly more interesting than what we can say. None of the women's religions worships a single, omnipotent male deity. In light of the insights of Mary Daly and other feminist scholars regarding the connection between patriarchy and the "Great King in Heaven," I do not find this surprising.

On the other hand, none of the women's religions worships a single great goddess.[14] Even the Goddess "created" by Spiritual Feminists is far from being an all-powerful sovereign. Nowhere have we found the type of great mother goddess described by Preston (see page 172 above). In light of the emphasis on **mortal** motherhood in women's religions, this finding is certainly noteworthy. My guess is that mortal mothers realize that maternity does not make them omnipotent. The realities of motherhood lead women to diverse sorts of deities that "fit" the diversity of mothering experiences. Motherhood is not a matter of absolutes, but of particular sorrows, joys, decisions, and personalities. The same factors that encourage the development of immanent deities in women's religions discourage the development of either a male omnipotent god or a female great goddess. Grounded in the here-and-now, in particular relationships, the deities of women's religions tend to be as ambiguous as life itself.

A last point bears notice here. In most women's religions, supernatural entities—both male and female—appear at rituals in the bodies of their almost exclusively female spirit mediums. Since the deities who possess human beings **look like** the humans they possess, even male spirits, gods, and ancestors **look** female when the mediums are women. As we will see in the next chapter, it would be a grave mistake to underestimate either the psychological or theological implications of spirit possession.

Notes

1. In addition, Buddhist *devas* are sometimes referred to as *nats,* although they are not part of the *nat* cultus.

2. This does not negate that other aspects of science had a great attraction for Spiritualists.

3. There are other spirit types besides these four. These are the four major types.

4. If this description seems unclear, it is because the descriptions given by the native informants and recorded by the ethnographers are also unclear.

5. According to Harris and Sawyerr (1968), the Mende have a belief in some kind of one high god. In addition, they believe in and relate to a large assortment of ancestral and nature spirits.

6. They were not able to determine which causes which; the relationship seems to be reciprocal and subsistence patterns affect both.

7. On the other hand, some historians might simply claim that monotheism is so rare in the world (after all, there are only three truly monotheistic religions) that explaining why female-dominated religions are polytheistic is not even an interesting question; most religions are polytheistic. Other historians of religion disagree with the claim that monotheism is rare. Commonly cited examples include primitive monotheism (high gods in African religions) and certain streams in Greek and Hindu religion.

8. I recommend David Wulff's paper "Prolegomenon to a Psychology of the Goddess" for an acute critique of the Freudian view of goddesses.

9. A deeper inquiry into goddesses should take into account the affects of specific social conditions. Jane Harrison (1955, 260–261), for example, sees a link between matrilineality and independent goddesses, and between patrilineality and subordinate goddesses. Other scholars have argued that there is some correlation between women's status and the presence of goddesses, yet are vague about exactly how that correlation works. For example, according to Tikva Frymer-Kensky, an expert in ancient Near Eastern religion, "The eclipse of the goddesses was undoubtedly part of the same

process that witnessed a decline in the public role of women, with both reflective of fundamental changes in society that we cannot yet specify" (1992, 80).

10. This is a line from Ntosake Shange's play *For Colored Girls Who Have Considered Suicide When the Rainbow Is Enough*.

11. In *The Grandmother of Time,* Z. Budapest explores and meditates on a different goddess for each month of the year. The goddesses she chose reflect the range of traditions from which Feminist Spirituality self-consciously draws its symbols: Greek goddesses, Swedish goddess, Japanese goddess, Celtic goddess, Egyptian goddess, and more.

12. Neither Shaker belief nor social structure were wholly egalitarian (see the discussion of Shaker gender ideology in Chapter 10, and Brewer 1992, 612).

13. Moving to Japan, we learn that the female founder of the new religion Tensho-kotai-jingu-kyo proclaimed her own body to be the dwelling place of both a goddess and a god who unite with her to form an androgynous trinity (Nakamura 1980, 140).

14. The closest we come to this is the Tetum earth mother (see Appendix), out of whose vagina humanity climbed and into whose womb the dead return. Yet even among the Tetum there is a passive, masculine deity who resides in the sky. Unlike the earth mother, he is uninterested in the affairs of humans, and humans likewise are devoid of interest in him (Hicks 1984, 6).

9 ⚞⚞

Summoning the Spirits

The possessed woman herself was unaware of everything. She was taken by her god against her will, and so when the god first started to ride her, she bucked like a wild horse. Her face set rigidly, her body jerked wantonly, she lost her balance, and she conveyed a general atmosphere of tension and pain. . . . But soon the horse [medium] was tamed and began to execute superbly, in deep trance, the dance of her god. And now, animated by the deity, she **was** the deity, and the *ekedi* [priestess] led her off to dress her in the luxurious clothes of divinity. For the next twelve hours or so, . . . the woman lived in a trance, harnessed by the injunction to dance for the drums, forbidden to eat, drink, or relieve other wants. I never saw one cough or scratch, yawn or stretch, or go to the closet. The entranced creatures responded only to signals from the mother [chief priestess] and the drums (Landes 1947, 54).

Alourdes [a Haitian Vodou priestess] invariably diagnoses the origins of her clients' problems as disturbances in relationships of one sort or another. . . . Most problems are diagnosed as supernatural, and because they fall into the realm of the spirits, something can be done about them. . . . [In Alourdes' words] "You read the Bible, you read about God. But spirit you don't read about. The spirit come in people' head [possession], and you see them, you talk to them. They help you"

(Brown, 346–347).

WOMEN, TRANCE, AND POSSESSION

Many religious traditions embrace the belief that spirits or gods can enter the bodies of individuals who are in states of trance and then engage in activities typical of their personae. Possession trance is a pivotal component in the majority of women's religions. In nine out of our twelve key examples, possession trance occurs either frequently or occasionally in the context of ritual. Yet lest we are tempted to exaggerate the import of that statement, we must point out that the ethnographic record reports the presence of trance states in **most** cultures (52% in Bourguignon's 1976 sample). Trance is like prayer or sacrifice—a type of ritual behavior that occurs in many or possibly most religions and so is not in need of special explanation in women's religions. Both male-dominated and female-dominated religions utilize techniques of dancing, swaying, spinning, drumming, meditation, and singing to induce trance.

Erika Bourguignon does, however, comment on one interesting gender difference. Trance—an altered state of consciousness induced by a number of well-recognized techniques and **not** involving possession—is reported more often for men. Possession—the belief that supernatural beings can enter human beings, that humans can temporarily **become** gods, spirits, demons, or ancestors—is reported more often for women (1976, 1983). Put differently, what is more common among women is not a dissociative state known as trance, but a cultural interpretation known as spirit possession.

While spirit possession is an essential element in the ritual complexes of many women's religions, it by no means occurs in all our examples (Table 4). At various ritual occasions Sande members wear masks and costumes representing Sande ancestresses. Spirit possession, if it occurs, is rare during the rituals.[1] In the Feminist Spirituality Movement techniques such as meditation, dance, and chanting are used to induce altered states of consciousness, and rituals that dramatize the goddess-nature of mortal women are common. Spirit possession, however, has not been reported in the vast ritual literature of the Movement. And spirit possession is most definitely not a part of Christian Science ritual, where the emphasis is on rational discourse. In short, it is legitimate to argue that women have some sort of affinity for spirit possession (or that spirits have some sort of affinity for women) but that this affinity is neither absolute nor universal.

THEORIES OF WOMEN AND SPIRIT POSSESSION: CONCEPTUALIZING GENDER

In many cultures women are believed to be particularly skilled at, or prone to, possession trance. Anthropologists have offered a number of explanations for this propensity. As early as 1966, I. M. Lewis argued that where women are a disadvantaged and subordinate group (and that is the case in most societies), possession trance is a tool for them to obtain material, emotional, or social benefits that would otherwise be unavailable. Possession allows them to protest their lowly position as women in sexist society. Women are frequently possessed by male spirits that may allow women, at least temporarily, some of the advantages of being a man. Lewis has refined this argument in his 1986 book *Religion in Context,* but not substantially changed it.

Other writers have stressed the sexual element of possession trance: The possessed women, often with abandoned and ecstatic facial expressions and body movements, is said to have sexual intercourse with the possessing god or

Table 4.   *Women's Religions That Embrace Spirit Possession*

Burma *Nat* Cult	Ryūkyū Island Religion
Zār Religion	Korean Shamanism
Afro-Brazilian Religions	Northern Thai Spirit Cults (urban)
Spiritualism	Black Carib Religion
Shakers	

spirit. In cultures in which a sexual double-standard means that many women are sexually deprived for large portions of their lives, possession is a way for some women to seek sexual satisfaction (Spiro 1967).

Both the sexual deprivation explanation and the social deprivation explanation embody all the problems with deprivation theory in general that I outlined in Chapter 2 (I will not repeat them here.) Still other anthropologists have claimed that women's propensity for possession trance is a biochemical matter; that trance symptoms are in fact the symptoms of calcium deprivation suffered by pregnant and lactating women in societies in which women have limited access to calcium-rich foods (Kehoe and Giletti 1981). Bourguignon, Bellisari, and McCabe utterly discredit this hypothesis, and show that "although impressionistic accounts suggest that women often predominate in possession trance cults, the simple equation women = possession trance, is not justified by the available data" (1983, 414). I would add that the voluntary nature of possession trance—women attend rituals so as to induce trance and call down the spirits—argues against physiological explanations that assume spirit possession is involuntary.[2]

Another school of thought focuses upon cultural notions of gender-appropriate behavior. Kevin Neuhouser (1989) for example, argues that spirit possession cults attract more women than men in Brazil because it is not "masculine" to be submissive to a dominant spirit. Similarly, Melford Spiro notes that Burmese men have other alternatives that may be functionally equivalent to being a shaman—for example, monasticism (1967, 224). On the whole, I also lean toward those sorts of interpretations that carefully situate spirit possession in particular cultural contexts, and that presuppose intelligent and **religious** motives on the part of women involved in spirit possession.

Given the predilection of women for spirit possession, the high incidence of spirit possession in women's religions, and the rather rigid cultural conceptions of gender in many of the societies in which spirit possession occurs (see also Chapter 10), we note with interest that women are often possessed by male spirits. In the Afro-Brazilian cults, for example, the typically female medium **becomes** the sometimes female, sometimes male spirit. According to Seth and Ruth Leacock (1972), Brazilian Batuque women mediums often engage in "male" behavior such as smoking cigarettes or cigars, drinking alcoholic beverages, and shouting vulgarities. (The entranced medium is unaware of all this and so cannot possibly be enjoying herself!)

Vieda Skultans cites a 1886 study showing a preponderance of Spiritualist mediums to be female, but a majority of possessing spirits to be male. "In other words, the typical spiritualist experience involves a female medium and a male spirit or control" (1983, 17). It may well be that some female mediums enjoyed the opportunity to take on a male role during trance. Favorite controlling spirits included swearing, highly sexed, formally educated, and physically strong men, who gave the mediums a chance to break out of the conventional and often stifling nineteenth-century female role. Laurence Moore argues that part of the satisfaction felt by women mediums derived from "their assumption during the trance state of an otherwise forbidden male social role. Time and again under the influence of their spirit controls, they turned into swearing sailors, strong Indian braves, or oversexed male suitors" (1977, 111).

Janice Boddy has developed a subtle and fascinating interpretive analysis of role play in *zār* spirit possession. She argues that *zār,* when viewed as an aesthetic genre, serves to open thought, to free it from limitations of prior associations, to pose challenging problems, and encourage reflection on the everyday. "Symbolic inversion . . . or negative metaphor . . . is its essence: during possession rites women become men; villagers become Ethiopian, British, Chinese; the powerless and impoverished become powerful and affluent. Essentially irreversible processes—genderization, aging—become reversible; established categories are undermined. Hierarchical orderings are telescoped and undone when Islamic holy men and pagan prostitutes possess the same [Sudanese] woman" (1989, 306).

The entranced woman ceases being herself; instead, she experiences the world the way her possessing spirit does. Boddy quotes one of her informants: "When it descends into you . . . you see through the eyes of the European. Or you see through the eyes of the West African, whichever spirit it is. You see then as a European sees—you see other Europeans, radios, Pepsis, televisions, refrigerators, automobiles, a table set with food. You forget who you are, your village, your family, you know nothing from your life. You see with the eyes of the spirit until the drumming stops" (1989, 350).

In the course of a *zār* ritual, and over years of participation in *zār* rituals, a woman both observes and experiences trance and so both observes and experiences other cognitive and behavioral possibilities. "*Zār* (as both possession and performance) is a powerful medium for unchaining thought from the fetters of hegemonic cultural constructs" (1988, 23). When a woman is possessed she forgets who she is, she temporarily steps outside her usual world, she sheds her culturally constructed personhood. "In proportion to her subjective experience of otherness, her everyday reality is made to appear as one of many [possible realities]—less naturalized, less unquestionable, indeed, less subjectively real" (1988, 19).

Why is this process particularly attractive to women? Boddy contends that in the cultures where *zār* occurs, gender, for women, is overdetermined. A woman is never "just" a person; the social facts of gender determine all her daily activities, life events, and interpersonal interactions. Thus women, more than men, enjoy stepping outside their social identities to experience other human possibilities.

In an insightful review of Boddy's book, I. M. Lewis has pointed out that although her theory is attractive, she "presents no evidence to show that, as a result of the intellectual re-focusing or re-framing . . . possessed women do think and feel differently" (1990, 590). I accept Lewis's critique, and sincerely hope that future studies will rectify this deficiency. On the other hand, I believe that Boddy is justified in her claim that spirit possession has the potential to teach that "gender is not a natural attribute but a cultural construct" (Boddy 1988, 21). At the very least, in contrast to Islamic and Christian rituals that tend to present unambiguous cultural norms and hierarchies, possession rituals allow participants and audience to engage in "the dialectic expression of an entire range of often contradictory elements which form the socio-cultural universe of the society" (Giles 1987, 250).

SPIRIT POSSESSION IN FEMALE-DOMINATED RELIGIONS

Women's religions offer two chief models of spirit possession: specialist possession and lay possession. In Korea, Burma, the Ryūkyū Islands, Thailand, Shakerism[3], Black Carib religion[4] and Spiritualism there are women who are experts or professionals at contacting the spirits or gods, and who use their expertise to divine, heal, solve problems, or contact the ancestors or gods on behalf of other people. In *zār* cults and Afro-Brazilian religions, possession trance occurs at group rituals in which some, most, or all participants become possessed. These two models do not constitute an absolute dichotomy. In the Afro-Brazilian cults and the *zār* cult there are women who are "lay" mediums, and other women who are expert priestesses or "Mothers". Even within the specialist model we can identify a variety of levels of expertise, ranging from the spontaneous possession of young Shaker women during the period of Mother Ann's Work, to the cultivated and highly controlled possession of urban Thai spirit mediums. Still, I do think it is useful to acknowledge the difference between mediums who become possessed in order to teach or heal other people, and mediums who become possessed as part of a group religious experience.

Two other types of spirit possession do not occur in women's religions. In some male-dominated religions, women become possessed by evil spirits who must be exorcised by male specialists—the entire process underscoring female inferiority and male power (cf. Bilu 1987 on Eastern European dybbuks). In certain other male-dominated religions, possessed woman serve as oracles whose words are interpreted by men (e.g., Delphi). It is significant that these models are not found in female-dominated religions.

Spirit possession in women's religions incorporates both sacred and medical dimensions (Csordas 1987). Possession by the spirits offers a culturally recognized and meaningful interpretation of and solution to chronic misfortune. The healing function of spirit possession should not be taken to mean that female-dominated religions are havens for maladjusted, neurotic, or psychotic women. In women's religions (and in some male-dominated religions) overtly wild behavior during rituals is seen as a sign that the person is drunk or insane, not possessed. Because a spirit must make sense to those whom it encounters, "successful negotiation of the possession context requires the patient to have or develop considerable cultural awareness. It is thus inapplicable to those who suffer severe psychological disturbance" (Boddy 1989, 146).

A final comment about spirit possession in women's religions is one that may be self evident, but nonetheless critical. **The audience at spirit possession events is predominantly female.** Spirit possession may fruitfully be interpreted as a ritual drama with women—not men—as the audience. Possession in female-dominated religions has a great deal to do with relationships among women. This may include competition for status or resources (cf. Wilson's 1967 argument that spirit possession is correlated with social situations which give rise to tension between members of the same sex), enhancement of social or kinship bonds that are not always recognized by the dominant male culture, and healing of the many physical and emotional hurts from which women *qua* women suffer.

Janice Boddy has reached a similar conclusion regarding the *zār*. "[O]nce the idiom of possession has been invoked, people are freer to communicate in ways antithetic to the harmony-preserving tactics of everyday discourse. Close kin, spouses, affines, might indirectly discuss issues which otherwise could not be broached without injuring their relationship. And this is possible because of the potential for obfuscation inherent in the possession idiom: the distinction between human self and *zār* self is not rigidly drawn, even during possession trance. Responsibility can be assigned to *zayran,* to humans, to both. It is this latent confusion . . . that permits vitally important messages of a sort not normally countenanced to be transmitted without permanent rupture to the social fabric" (Boddy 1989, 236).

SHAMANS AND MEDIUMS

Throughout this book I have been repeating the nomenclature for religious leaders used by the experts upon whose work I draw. With the exception of Melford Spiro who directly transliterates the native word *natkadaw*, most other scholars seem to use the terms "medium" and "shaman" in a somewhat vague manner.

In descriptions of shamans in diverse cultures, one of the common features (although not, as I. M. Lewis has informed me, a necessary feature) is an ecstatic flight of the soul to a different world (plane, dimension, etc.) in which the individual undergoes unusual experiences and learns portentous information that she or he brings back to this world, and which allows him or her to be a healer.[5] The pervasiveness of ecstatic flight makes it crucial to point out that it most definitely is not a feature of religious specialist roles in women's religions. In none of the women's religions described in this book does the specialist experience an ecstatic flight in which the soul travels to other realms, even if the western ethnographer used the word "shaman" to describe the religion.

Instead, what the so-called shamans in women's religions seem to do is incorporate into their own bodies other personae (gods, spirits, ancestors, *nats,* etc.). This process is what in the anthropological and religious studies literature is known as being a medium—a channel for a supernatural being who wishes to communicate with beings in this world. Cross-culturally, there does seem to be compelling evidence to associate women with spirit possession (mediumship) and men with ecstatic flight of the soul (shamanism). For example, in Janelli and Janelli's overview of spirit communication in East Asia, we learn that in Korea, Japan, and parts of China female specialists become possessed, whereas in Taiwan male specialists travel to the other world to speak to ancestors (1982).

In his recent book, I. M. Lewis proposes a new way of looking at spirit possession and ecstatic flight of the soul. "All these features, which others have seen as separate self-sustaining styles of religiosity, are in reality constituent elements in the composite shamanistic complex" (1986, 85). In other words, they are serial phases in the assumption of the shamanistic career. Lewis cites several examples from the ethnographic literature demonstrating that spirit possession and astral voyages often overlap. Even more important, he argues that the shamanistic career typically begins with unsolicited and uncontrolled possession, yet with practice and experience the possessed individual learns to "master" the spirits and become a true shaman. Lewis concludes that both historically and in particular situations, "It does not matter how the balance between possession and soul-flight is pitched" (1986, 92).[6]

While I am tempted to agree with Lewis on this, I am not sure that I can, in good conscience, assent to his entire thesis. The essence of Lewis's argument seems to be that there is no real distinction between descent of spirits and ascent of the soul. However, the very examples that he cites to prove his case seem to suggest that this distinction does in fact exist, and is at least to some extent linked to gender. For example, quoting Carmen Blacker's study of Japanese shamanism, Lewis tells us that in feudal Japan "it was common to find . . . an ascetic [what Lewis calls shaman] husband married to a female medium" (quoted in Lewis 1986, 87).

Rather than extinguishing the ecstatic flight versus possession controversy, Lewis's analysis sharpens it. If, as Lewis claims, the same individuals are capable of both possession and ecstatic flight, **why is it that religious specialists in female-dominated religion consistently opt for the former and not the latter?**

I do believe that there is a significant difference between flight and in-dwelling, between what in other chapters I label transcendence and immanence. Whether that difference is ontologically pure or whether it is merely a matter of accent is beyond the scope of our present inquiry. In sum, despite my inclination to be swayed by Lewis's recent work, I am unwilling to gloss leaving one's body with sharing one's body. The implications of this distinction will become apparent in the following section.

GENDER, EGO FORMATION, AND SPIRIT POSSESSION

Laurence Moore has observed regarding Spiritualists, "The success of spirit communication depended on the ability of mediums to give up their own identity to become the instruments of others" (1977, 106). The essential trait of the medium (and not only in Spiritualism) is the ability to loosen her (or his) ego boundaries and literally share her or himself with another (or many other) beings. It seems to me that an individual must be extraordinarily comfortable with interpersonal relationships in order to do so. This realization brings us back to the argument I have been making throughout this book concerning gender and modes of relating. Yet before I continue, I wish to reiterate a point that frequently gets lost in discussions of gender and psychological development: Theorists such as Nancy Chodorow and Carol Gilligan do not claim that men and women are essentially different; rather, they assert that in specific (albeit very common) cultural circumstances, men and women are socialized into different behavioral modes, different moral voices, and different emotional proclivities. Thus, what follows should not be taken as a discussion of sex (biologically given) but as a discussion of gender (culturally constructed).

Sharon Conarton and Linda Silverman argue that "The developmental cycle of women must be viewed with the awareness that women's primary striving is for relatedness and connection. . . . Ego formation is different for a male because he is more aware of his boundaries. **The boundaries of the feminine ego are very thin** [my emphasis]. After experiencing herself as an extension of the mother, it is hard for the girl child to know where she stops and the other begins" (1988, 46). Drawing on Nancy Chodorow's writings and her own clinical practice, Lillian Rubin postulates that the normal development of gender identity in a girl requires no wrenching breaks with the past. As a woman she will have ego boundaries that are less rigid, **more permeable** [Rubin's words] than a man's, because she does not need defenses against feeling and attachment. Girls never need to separate themselves as completely as boys do. Girls experience themselves as more continuous with others. The capacity for participating in another's inner life is more developed among women. For the same reasons, a girl develops a more complex inner life than a boy (1983, 58–59). All of these ideas were influenced by David Gutmann's definition of two types of ego: the allocentric masculine ego that tends to objectify and experience its own separateness from others, and the autocentric feminine ego that is characterized by more permeable boundaries between self and others and between self and environment (1965). "Indeed, naturalistic observation might indicate that female domestic and maternal competence requires those very qualities of impulsivity and personalization which violate our criteria for ego adequacy. For example, careful observation of the mother-child relationship might show that the tendency to personalize the world, to abolish self-other boundaries, is essential to good mothering. . . . Indeed, when women maintain firm ego boundaries and treat their children as men treat the impersonal objects of the geometric-technical world, we call them either rejecting or schizophrenogenic" (Gutmann 1965, 239).

The developmental process described by Gutmann, Chodorow, Rubin, Conarton, and Silverman is highly relevant to understanding spirit possession. Unlike in non-possession trance or in classic shamanism, the essence of spirit possession is the willingness to share one's body with another being. In spirit possession, as Janice Boddy has observed, "[A]lthough the identities of host and spirit are distinct and even here remain functionally independent, it appears that they coalesce in possession trance. Both host and spirit are present in the host's body to varying degrees" (1989, 151). The classic (typically male) shaman, on the other hand, transcends his body—a role Nancy Chodorow and others would surely see as suitable for individuals who are raised to develop their gender identity and sense of self as negation rather than connection.

The etic (scientific) argument I have outlined above is strengthened by the various emic (native) explanations for why women are possessed more frequently than men. In many cultures in which women are believed to be particularly skilled at, or prone to, possession trance, the indigenous interpretation is that women are softer, easier to penetrate, and that is why gods or spirits choose women as their vehicles ("horses"). This is the case in Brazil, for example. Writing about Thailand, Stanley Tambiah notes that although men fill almost all ritual specialist roles, there is an opening for women in roles involving possession because women are seen as more prone to possession; spirits possess them because they are soft and vulnerable and therefore effective hosts (1970, 283). In the Northern Thai matrilineal spirit cults women predominate as mediums, and women are believed to have an inferior sort of "soft soul" that makes them more susceptible to the effects of spirits (Tanabe 1991, 189). Similarly, in certain Japanese religions, "Women are more fitted to be mediums than men, because they have stronger feelings, better intuition, and more sensitive emotions" (Offner and Van Straelen 1963, 124). I am struck by the similarity between the emic explanations of women's preponderance in spirit possession, and psychological explanations of gender differences in ego formation.

In the Burmese case the difference between the female *natkadaw* and male exorcists is instructive. The women religious specialist works by propitiating *nats*, soliciting their help, asking them to possess her, and acquiescing to their power. The male exorcist combats and attempts to drive away *nats*, using Buddhist power to do so. The *natkadaw* is a person **through** whom the *nats* speak, while the exorcist is one **with** whom the *nats* speak. The *natkadaw* shares her body with the *nat;* the exorcist remains separate—confronting the *nat* (1967, 243).

One could argue that the possessed medium does not "relate" to the spirit; instead, her own identity disappears and is replaced by the spirit. However, a careful reading of ethnographic accounts of spirit possession suggests that it is only inexperienced and unskilled mediums who totally disappear. More skilled mediums, in the words of one Black Spiritual minister, "entertain" the spirit. "When I'm in the spirit, if I'm dancing in the spirit, I'm asking [the spirit to intercede on my behalf]. I'm working with my spirit. I know what to say, what to work with. See, when I finish dancing, I know what's going to happen" (Jacobs and Kaslow 1989, 132). Writing about the bori cult, Murray Last makes a similar observation: "What is being taught by this training in possession is how to put on, like a suit of clothes, a further social self, while not putting in jeopardy one's own identity" (1991, 55).

I simply cannot close this section without reference to the obvious parallels between pregnancy and spirit possession. Hilary Graham has argued that the two phenomena are indeed homologous. I cite several of the analogies identified by Graham: "In both, the individual's body is seen to be invaded by and to interact with an alien being, by virtue of which both actor and being occupy marginal, indeterminate social positions. . . . In both, the presence of this alien provides a sufficient explanation of the actor's behavior. . . . In both, society typically manages instances of possession not by expelling the spirit (aborting the foetus) but by domesticating it, by channelling its demands into socially expected forms" (1976, 296). In short, I speculate that the same socialization process that constructs adult women who seek to share their bodies with their babies, also sometimes constructs adult women who willingly share their bodies with spirits, ancestors, or gods. The process of pregnancy—of sharing one's body—may be a suitable training process for spirit mediumship. Let us recall that in several women's religious situations (Spiritualism, Cantonese shamanism) the spirit guides are actually the dead children of the women mediums.

Ross Kraemer has suggested that it is useful to view spirit possession as a gendered, embodied metaphor rooted in women's physical experiences of heterosexual intercourse and pregnancy. That is, women seem to experience possession as an analogue of heterosexual intercourse, pregnancy, and more broadly, marriage and relationships with men: "It's not inherently bad, it has its advantages and disadvantages, and you can usually find some way to accommodate it!" (personal communication, 1993). If Kraemer's argument regarding the inherently gendered nature of spirit possession is correct, it could well explain why men often treat spirit possession as demonic, and why possessed men are often concerned with exorcism rather than accommodation; men would experience possession as "unnatural." Since my own inclination is to avoid essentialist, biologically based arguments, I find it more helpful to emphasize the socialization process that produces women who are willing (and often desperately eager) to accommodate "possession" by men, by babies, and sometimes by spirits.

MEETING THE DEITIES

If we take stock of the explanations of women and spirit possession that we have seen in this chapter, an interesting pattern becomes evident. All the theories I summarized in the beginning of the chapter (social deprivation, sexual deprivation, calcium deprivation, and overdetermination of gender) start from the assumption that possession trance is an abnormal phenomenon. Therefore, the explanation for women's involvement with spirit possession necessarily lies in some form of divergence from normal, healthy human experience. I would like to raise a different possibility. Is it possible that possession trance is one of a range of normal human abilities or talents, in much the way that musical ability or athletic ability is? Could it be that in many cultures male socialization prevents most men from developing the ability to embrace the enriching, exciting, **normal** experience of spirit possession? Is it perhaps the case that the vast majority of men, for a variety of psychosocial reasons, are so preoccupied with guarding their ego boundaries or their sense of self from the threat of "invasion" that they reject, or refuse to recognize, a religious experience that involves melding one's being with another entity?[7] As Janice Boddy writes, "It is imperative to ask why so many Western scholars . . . are committed to viewing possession as a consequence of women's deprivation rather than their privilege, or perhaps their inclination" (1989, 140). The answer to her question, it seems to me, lies in the double-barreled intellectual weaknesses of ethnocentrism and androcentrism.

I have chosen to look at spirit possession in detail for a number of reasons. First, I am struck by the uses to which possession trance is put in women's religions: to build and strengthen interpersonal relationships[8], to deconstruct gender, and to heal. Spirit possession encapsulates the particularistic, this-worldly orientation of female-dominated religions.

A second reason has to do with the role of the audience at spirit possession rituals. From the perspective of the audience (mostly female in women's religions), the essence of spirit possession is the willingness to interact with one's deities face to face (see Finkler 1986, 638). Such willingness reflects a high level of ease with interpersonal relationships, and a facility for perceiving the sacred in the midst of everyday reality.

Michael Lambek has studied spirit possession in Mayotte, an island in the Indian Ocean off the coast of Africa, between Madagascar and Mozambique.[9] On Mayotte more than one third of adult women are possessed, while only one tenth of adult men are possessed, and more non-possessed women than men assist at curing ceremonies and are spectators in public ceremonies. Lambek emphasizes the social nature of relationships with spirits. A host and spirit can have a relationship that lasts for many years. According to Lambek, **"Spirits rise precisely in order to interact with people"** (1981, 3, my emphases). The point of spirit possession is not worship—Mayotte women do not pray to the spirits. The point of possession is social interaction between humans and spirits. On Mayotte spirit possession occurs not only in public ceremonies, but also at home in informal settings. When a woman enters into a relationship with a spirit, her husband also becomes involved with the spirit. In time, a spirit may rise on its own volition outside of ritual contexts, or the husband may decide to call it up. "[Mayotte] spirits are not merely classified, they are socialized; they develop particular identity relationships with particular people, and they are taught the norms of social intercourse" (1981, 149–150).

More than any other kind of ritual, spirit possession dramatizes an ideology of the immanence of the divine: In possession trance the god, spirit, or ancestor is actually present on earth—incarnate and able to engage in dialogue with devotees. Recalling that mediums typically add a bit of their own personalities to the spirits whom they enact, what we are describing is an interactive model of the supernatural—the medium and the spirit reflect one another's personalities.

Thomas Csordas suggests that spirit possession "can be seen as a pure form of ritual drama, where the parts of deities are not played by humans, but where the deities in effect play themselves" (Csordas 1987, 6). With this in mind, we turn here to one last example.

A noteworthy aspect of Ryūkyūan belief is the pattern of treating certain individuals as if they were gods, even to the point of calling them by the god's name (see Chapter 11). Yoshinobu Ota (1989) cites the traditional *oaroari* rite to transform a woman into a priestess: During the rite the spirit of the deity possesses a woman who has three grains of rice on her head, while she chants the deity's name three times. According to Ota, the essence of becoming a priestess is the act of personifying the deity. The implications of spirit possession among Ryūkyūan priestesses are vividly recounted by Shinobu Orikuchi (quoted in Kamata 1966, 61), "Since there is no clear-cut distinction in Okinawa religion between the gods and the priestesses and female functionaries, they are often directly referred to with the divine names."

I quote here at some length from Hisako Kamata's description of ritual specialist women known as *uyigami*—women of around fifty years of age who inherit their position from mothers or mothers-in-law.

> [T]he *uyigami* have come to possess a sacred nature in the consciousness of the islanders; **they are gods during the period of the feast,** at least in their imagination. Thus, they call them *uyigami,* ancestor-gods. The old women, in their turn, regard themselves as more than human beings, and if they see a human being approaching them, they utter words, "uru-uru-uru," and scare him away. They are in a state of divine possession, wearing a crown made from a vine" (1966, 65, my emphases).

I have cited these passages to underscore an issue raised earlier: From the point of view of the audience, the possessed individual **is** the deity. Deities are seen to be physically present on earth, and seen to look like—to wear the bodies of—women.

Notes

1. According to Carol MacCormack, Sande masked ancestresses do not become possessed, but occasionally a member (usually a younger woman) goes into a state in which she communicates with the watery underworld of the ancestresses, sometimes bring up a new mask or other object (personal communication 1993).

2. In most women's religions (e.g., the *zār* cult) a woman is not diagnosed as possessed because she became entranced; rather, she initially seeks trance to find out who is possessing her. Later on, trance gives her spirits a chance to play around in the human world.

3. I am referring here specifically to the period of Mother Ann's Work when mediums possessed by Holy Mother Wisdom (and other spirits) transmitted messages, prayers, and rituals to the larger group. During other periods many if not most Shakers experienced various forms of religious ecstasy, but I would not consider these other forms to fall within the accepted definition of spirit possession.

4. Possession by ancestors is part of Black Carib rituals, especially important rituals such as *dūgú*. Ancestors temporarily use the bodies of the living to enjoy themselves and to speak. More women than men are possessed. According to Taylor (1951), most women who become possessed are between the ages of eighteen and twenty-five. There also are shamans who contact the spirits to determine why someone is sick or suffering

misfortune, and why the ancestors are unhappy. The shaman enters some type of trance during the ritual. Today all practicing shamans in Belize are women (Kerns 1983). In the past, however, it seems likely that more shamans were male (Taylor 1951).

5. Anthropologists and historians of religion have devoted a great deal of attention to defining what is a shaman and determining whether the category "shaman" is cross-culturally applicable or whether it describes a very specific type of religious specialist found in and near Siberia.

6. Lewis's book (1986) includes a careful and interesting discussion of shamans versus mediums. He begins by summarizing and critiquing Mircea Eliade's view that possession by spirits is a later and diluted form of the authentic and archaic shamanistic celestial ascent. He also cites and disproves Pater Schmidt's contention that spirit possession (what he called "black shamanism") was associated with early matriarchy, while superior "white" or true shamanism developed under later patriarchy.

7. Additionally, one might argue that external social institutions prevent men from experiencing possession trance. For example, Lambek explains the predominance of women in spirit possession in Mayotte in terms of men's involvement with Islam, which restricts their participation in spirit possession (1981).

8. To take one short example, according to Jacobs and Kaslow's study of the Black Spiritual churches of New Orleans, "the bonding which develops in the group is reinforced by the flurry of activity with which members come to one another's aid either to prevent injuries or fan and comfort an individual in the aftermath of possession" (1981, 108).

9. Lambek sees Mayotte spirit possession as part of the same general phenomenon as the *zār* cult (1981, 35 and 194 n. 3). Mayotte fits in well with our general picture of women's religions being associated with matrifocal societies in which women's status is relatively high. On Mayotte, "women gain autonomy though their status as village owners, their rights to productive land, ownership of houses and household goods, and equal control with the husbands over subsistence crops. . . . A woman should remain a virgin until her first marriage, and indeed it is in her best interests to do so, but from this point she has as much control over her sexuality as a man has over his. The wedding is a celebration of the bride's emergence into womanhood as much as it is anything else, and ease of divorce means that women are not pawns in an exchange controlled by men but can act as independent agents on their own behalf. . . . By means of judicious marriages and child fosterage over time a woman can develop a coterie of followers. . . . In addition, women are politically organized among themselves, have certain rights and responsibilities in village affairs, and select their own leaders" (Lambek 1981, 23–24). Because a bride typically receives a gift of a house from her parents, initial residence of newly married couples is likely to be in the wife's village. On Mayotte, barren women and women in polygynous marriages (i.e., deprived women) are **not** possessed by spirits more than other women.

10 🌊

Gender Ideology

Religions in which men are structurally dominant have developed elaborate ideologies that endeavor to explain, justify, cause, or apologize for women's subordinate status. Examples of such ideologies include claims that women are more prone to sin—especially sexual sin, that God chose to become incarnate as a male, that woman (Eve) brought sin into the world, and that women's souls or intelligences are inferior to men's. These ideologies both reflect and give form to patriarchal social structures.

Can we expect to find that women's religions offer ideologies that explain why men are inferior? Or should we expect that women's religions do not challenge broad cultural conceptions of male superiority? Late twentieth-century American experience has shown that the fact that women create or control an organization does not necessarily mean the organization will advocate female dominance or even gender equality. Women of the New Right, for example, have formed organizations with explicitly anti-feminist agendas.[1]

During the past two decades, as feminist anthropologists have searched the ethnographic record for universals concerning gender role and ideology, the most ubiquitous finding is that no matter what the actual **content** of the traits that a society attributes to men and women, the **level of affect** concerning those traits is singularly high. For example, whether a particular culture regards men as strong and women as weak, or men as weak and women as strong, one thing remains the same—members of that society are ardent, earnest, and zealous regarding that belief. Thai scholar Nancy Eberhardt has pointed out that "what makes gender beliefs, images, and expectations so compelling to the people who live with them is their privileged position as part of the society's moral order; violations of the gender system are experienced not as harmless eccentricities but as disturbing transgressions, an invitation to chaos and evil" (1988, 6).

Given the high emotional charge elicited by ideas about gender, we can expect to find that members of women's religions care very much indeed about issues of gender, that gender ideologies of women's religions are not isolated from the gender beliefs of the society as a whole, and that their gender ideologies are frequently the object of attack by groups and individuals outside the female-dominated religion.

Female-dominated religions often occur in cultural settings in which women as a group are believed to be more religious than men. Brazilian women predominate numerically not only in the Afro-Brazilian cults, but also in Pentecostal and Catholic churches. In Brazil **all** religion is seen as a female activity—most worshippers at Catholic churches are women, priests are treated with some suspicion (why would a man opt for celibacy?), and the Church has difficulties recruiting enough men to be priests. In nineteenth-century North America religion became notoriously "feminized," and in twentieth-century North America women continue to attend church more often and profess greater religious faith than do men. Among the Black Caribs women predominate not only in ancestral rites, but in Catholic religious associations as well. According to Coelho, 80% of the members of these associations are women (1955, 159). In Southeast Asia women excel at Buddhist merit-making acts. On the Ryūkyū Islands women and the sacred are so thoroughly associated that certain Buddhist sects that normally have only male clergy have female clergy on Okinawa.[2] And even in the regions in which the *zār* cult is located women are more involved than men in all sorts of non- and quasi-Islamic religious activities. In all these settings, women's religions fit into rather than challenge conventional notions of sex roles. Women's religions are not making any extraordinary claims in stressing women's affinity for matters of the spirit.

In Chapter 3 I proffered several hypotheses regarding gender ideology. In light of Sara Ruddick's contention that maternal thinking tends to be "conventional," I suggested that female-dominated religions would probably not encourage women to raise children who will not conform to culturally accepted gender roles; that is, women's religions would not really challenge normative gender ideologies. This hypothesis indeed proves to be correct. Sande initiation for example, inculcates in women a strong sense of female strength and solidarity, but its main goal is to prepare women for heterosexual marriage.

According to Nancy Chodorow, boys who are raised by women eventually repudiate femaleness to develop their male gender identity. Chodorow's theory explains why ideologies of female inferiority, impurity, and subordination occur in so many cultures throughout the world. Struggling with forming a sense of self in the absence of a realistic role model (because fathers are absent so much of the day), boys come to define being male as not-being-female. This leads boys to wish to repress whatever in themselves is female, to polarize masculinity and femininity, and to accord higher status to whatever they label as male. What does this process have to do with women's religions? On the one hand, in female-dominated religions gender ideology is created and elaborated by women. Therefore, female-**inferior** ideology, which according to Chodorow is created by men, should not occur. Similarly, female-**superior** ideology should not occur because growing girls do not need to reject maleness in order to develop a positive gender identity and sense of self. In women's religions, ideologies of gender dominance and subordination should not prosper. As we will see below, this hypothesis proves to be correct.

I also suggested that because mothers bear and raise children of both sexes from infancy, women are likely to know that boys and girls are not really very different (cf. Johnson 1988, 86–87). Mothers, more than fathers, will realize that babies of both sexes kick in the womb, emerge through the cervix, breastfeed, urinate, defecate, smile, sneeze, clap hands, and crawl. Therefore, women's religions should tend to play down gender as a cultural category. This hypothesis proves to be utterly incorrect. In fact, all the female-dominated religions teach that men and women are essentially different. The Shakers, for example, went so far as to say that Ann Lee's femaleness was an inherent and necessary precondition for her role in redemption. In some women's religions the difference between men and women is seen as complementary and in others this difference leads to conflict (see below, "Ritual Tugs of War").

Female-dominated religions do not arise in cultural vacuums, and we might expect that ideologies of male superiority either infiltrate into women's religions or that the women's religions invest a great deal of energy in challenging ideologies of male superiority. One of the most consistent patterns regarding gender beliefs in female-dominated religions is apparent acceptance of widespread sexist ideas concerning women's nature and role. These ideas are, however, reinterpreted as evidence of women's greater interest in, or talent for, religious activity. As we will see in the following section, for example, nineteenth-century Spiritualists embraced contemporary stereotypes of women as passive and weak, yet claimed that passivity and weakness are ideal traits for powerful mediums!

Spiritualism: A Case Study

Nineteenth-century North American popular, religious, and scientific ideology identified men with reason, strength, and the public sphere. Women were seen as weak, impressionable, and domestically oriented. "The requirements of successful mediumship are more typical of what is or was taken to be a woman's character than of a man's—passivity and submissiveness being among the most important" (Skultans 1983, 16). And, "Mediums were weak in what were considered to be the masculine qualities of will and reason and strong in what were considered to be the female qualities of intuition and nervousness. They were impressionable (i.e., responsive to outside influence) and extremely sensitive. Above all, they were passive. After all, it was queried, what spirit could manifest anything through a medium whose own personality was strongly assertive?" (Moore 1977, 196).

The naive female mediums stand in contrast to the highly educated, wealthy (male) men of science—the researchers of psychic phenomena—with whom they sometimes teamed up in order to "prove" the existence of spirits. "It has been the habit to say that great intellect stands in the way of personal psychic experiences. The clean slate is certainly most apt for the writing of a message" (Doyle 1926, 2—quoted in Skultans 1983, 16).

According to Ann Braude, "Spiritualism made the delicate constitution and nervous excitability commonly attributed to femininity a qualification for religious leadership. If women had special spiritual sensitivities, then it followed that they could sense spirits, which is precisely what mediums did" (Braude 1985, 422). In different words, "Victorian stereotypes of femininity . . . bear a remarkable resemblance to the conception of the ideal medium. The following adjectives can equally well describe the ideal woman as the ideal medium: unsophisticated, innocent, passive, young, tender, feeling, intuitive" (Skultans 1983, 23).

In the context of Spiritualism this was a double-edged sword—the innate feminine qualities that made women good mediums (and so offered them power, mobility, and some economic independence) also bound them to the prevalent sexist ideology. The good medium, like the good woman, had to renounce her self. Thus, for Spiritualists, passivity and power converged. "And here lay the crux of the dilemma. For the very quality which supposedly made women such excellent mediums was equally construed as undermining their ability to function in the outside world. Female passivity, the leit-motif of powerful mediumship, also positioned women as individuals without social power" (Owen 1981, 10).

Female mediums, for the most part, accepted the Victorian stereotypes of women as chronically ill and long suffering. Mediums were proud of their willingness to sacrifice their own well-being for the spiritual benefit of others. "Spiritualism allowed women to discard Victorian limitations on women's **role** without questioning Victorian ideas about woman's **nature**" (Braude 1985, 422, my emphases). According to Owen, on the other hand, "What the seance promised was the ritualized violation of cultural norms" (1981, 203). Women's illness and passivity, in Spiritualist seances, came to mean power, not powerlessness. Significantly, Moore shows that women mediums took obvious joy in conquering male adversaries and scoffers (1977, 113).

Although Spiritualists seem to have accepted prevalent evaluations of women, women's rights has been part of the Spiritualist platform and Spiritualists were among the most ardent advocates of women's suffrage. Spiritualists believed that the advent of spirit communication heralded a new era and a new social order that included women's rights, and a number of leading feminists, including Susan B. Anthony, were interested in Spiritualism. "Spiritualism became a major—if not *the* major—vehicle for the spread of woman's rights ideas in mid-century America" (Braude 1989, 57).

NATURE AND CULTURE

Feminist anthropologist Sherry Ortner (1974) has argued that culture is universally valued over nature because culture is what subdues or conquers nature. Women, because of childbirth and lactation, are regarded as closer to nature. Therefore, cross-culturally men are valued over women. The root of male dominance and female subordination lies in the universal tendency to associate women with nature and men with what dominates nature—that is, culture.[3]

Male-dominated religions throughout the world utilize this chain of dichotomies to justify gender inequality: Woman is in essence different from man, and this difference is analogous to the difference between nature and culture, between self-control and chaos, between sinners and saints. Ortner's typology rings true to those of us familiar with Christian teachings that equate women with flesh and matter and the masculine principle with *logos,* the word (cf. Holden 1983, 6).

This scheme does not hold true for the gender ideologies of women's religions. In the religious ideology of the Ryūkyū Islands nature and culture are integrated: Natural sites and materials and culturally constructed sites and materials are equally sacralized in ritual. Afro-Brazilian religions see men (and not women) as so rooted in the natural world (of lust, alcohol, etc.) that they cannot open up to spirits. Korean men's ancestor religion is limited to strictly biological ties of kinship (nature), whereas women's household religion involves both broader social definitions of kinship, and worship of gods associated with the house (culture).

The nineteenth-century examples are of particular importance because in the American cultural climate of the time "the female domain was perceived as natural" (Kitch 41). Christian Science, on the other hand, does not posit that either men or women are closer to nature or culture; in fact, nature is illusory whether one is male or female. If anything, for Mary Baker Eddy the female principle is equivalent to spiritual perfection while the male principle is associated with materialism. Another nineteenth-century women's religion, Theosophy (see Appendix B) identified male with matter (in Ortner's terminology— nature) and female with spirit, and some Theosophists asserted not only the superiority of the feminine principle (spirit over matter) but of the female sex. To take another example, according to Sally Kitch, "In contrast to mainstream beliefs in an opposition between nature and culture, Shaker writing in the late nineteenth century considered both realms to be human creations that stood in opposition to true or divine nature. They classified reproductive humanity in the realm of human culture that is necessarily opposed to divine nature" (1989, 50).

In several female-dominated religions, Ortner's women and nature versus men and culture dichotomy holds true, but with a twist: Women and nature are seen as superior to men and culture! Feminist Spiritualists believe that men and culture have violently destroyed our planet, and ecological activism is crucial to the Spiritual Feminist platform. In the Spiritual Feminist vision, women who identify with nature—with the web of being—can save our planet from destruction at the hands of male culture. American historian Catherine Albanese (1990) explicitly relates contemporary Feminist Spirituality to nineteenth-century "nature religions" such as Christian Science. I see contemporary Spiritual Feminism's affinity for American Indian rituals and lore as an extension of nineteenth-century Spiritualists' partiality for messages from American Indians. In both instances, American Indians are seen as embodying the "natural" (see Chapter 8).[4] The Spiritualist attitude towards nature is eloquently expressed in the following graveside funeral service: "To Nature, the source of all, we now surrender him (or her) who has passed on before us. May all the sweet and thrilling influences of fragrant fields, of flowering plants, of bursting buds and blossoming vines, of silvery streams and genial showers, of setting suns, of jeweled nights and dawning days, melodious with the songs of birds and with all the wondrous harmonies of Nature, be with our dead" (from the *Twentieth Century Formulary of Songs and Forms* by W. C. Bowman, 1907, pp. 153–154, cited in Ward 1990). I barely need to point out how this conception of death differs from the highly transcendent vision found in Judaism, Christianity, Islam, or Buddhism: rather than leaving the transient and inferior natural world for a better and higher place, the Spiritualist dead is immersed in splendid and vigorous Nature.

The Tres Personas Solo Dios religious community in the Philippines is a fascinating example of an indigenous, quasi-Christian women's religion.[5] According to Rosemary Ruether, "Some time in the 1960's this community decided to have only women as priests, based on their view that males were not able to remain celibate. The founder and his son both married, but the community believes that celibacy is necessary for priesthood. . . . The women priests, who are called padre, celebrate a mass on the holy days" (n.d., 2–3). This highly politicized group is dedicated to "preserving the natural environment against exploitative development" (Ruether n.d., 1), and Filipino women as well as men are seen as associated with nature, in contrast to foreign colonial powers who disregard and exploit nature. Not wishing to read too much into Rosemary Ruether's brief but engrossing account of this community, what does seem to be the case is that men are associated both with culture and with the "darker" side of nature—the inability to control one's body in order to develop spiritually, while women are associated with a more benevolent natural mode.

In a similar vein, Northern Thai spirit cults sacralize women's ties to the land. Writing about Southeast Asia, Penny Van Esterik points to "a dualism linking women with fertility, nurturance, and attachment, and men with supramundane power and detachment" (1982, 5). Men do not own land, they leave their natal families, and they are involved with Buddhism, which condemns "earthly" attachments. Consistent with the most prominent pattern of gender ideology in female-dominated religions, Northern Thai matrilineal spirit cults accept the prevalent assessment of women as "worldly" while interpreting attachment to this world (land and family) as good and sacred.[6]

"Where religious visions of reality allocate at least some sanctity and durability to the natural world, what is striking is the plethora of females and female elements in their sacrifice myths. Where religious visions deny ultimate sanctity and durability to the natural world, as in Christianity, Judaism, and Islam, women fall out of the communal quests for ultimate connection, the mythic searches for communal gods that establish not only who is capable of reaching for the heavens but who is capable of ruling on earth" (Combs-Schilling 1989, 262).

The Body

Women's religions relate to bodies in distinctive ways. Unlike in many (if not most or even all) male-dominated religions, women's bodies are not seen as particularly polluted or polluting. Spiritual Feminists, for example, honor women's bodies as especially reflective of the essentially good cycles of nature. I see it as interesting that in the two somewhat ascetic religions—Christian Science and Shakers—women's bodies are not more "worldly" or more "sexual" than men's.

In many male-dominated religions, ideas concerning menstrual and childbirth pollution are used to explain women's inferiority and/or to exclude women from religious rituals. Can we expect to find that menstrual and childbirth taboos do not exist in women's religions? The answer is far from simple.

The Foundress of the new Japanese religion Tenryko called menstruation "flowering" rather than "pollution" (as it is called in many other Japanese religions; see *Tenryko: Its History and Teachings*).[7] To take another example, among the African Mende (a society in which Sande is present) a menstruating woman is described as "busy" and as "having seen the moon." According to Harris and Sawyerr, this terminology is significant: "The wife is virtually committed to another claim, supernatural indeed, with whom the husband must not compete" (1968, 96).

Among the Tetum, at birth the umbilical cord and placenta are treated as sacred; they are tied to the house ritual pillar and later ceremoniously transferred to the house of the father's clan (Hicks 1976). This sort of treatment of the effluvia of birth stands in sharp contrast to the many cultures, such as Bangladesh (see McConville 1988), where the afterbirth and bloodied clothing are buried or burned because of the extreme pollution they are believed to carry. Tetum women are so thoroughly associated with the sacred and men with the secular that all spirits are treated as feminine, even male ancestral ghosts. Women priestesses preside at almost all rituals (including wedding rituals and agricultural rites), most shamans are women, and sacred objects are kept in the "female" room of the house.[8]

Thailand, on the other hand, is characterized by extensive beliefs regarding menstrual pollution. According to Wijeyewardene, menstruation is used as a rationale for excluding women from many places and activities. The female mediums of Thai urban spirit cults turn themselves into men in possession (they are possessed by male spirits), and in their ordinary lives take on some of the characteristics of men—specifically the susceptibility to pollution through contact with menstrual blood (1986, 196). Similarly, *zār* spirits do not possess menstruating women, and a menstruating woman ties a knot in her braids to warn the *zayran* not to enter her (Boddy 1989, 275).

During their menstrual periods Black Carib women must not eat any of the products of the hunt, nor handle the hunters' weapons or dogs, lest they spoil the luck of the hunters (Taylor 1951, 94). On the other hand, women may use their own menstrual blood to fabricate charms or potions that give them power over others. "One purportedly successful way of establishing complete domination over a man is for a woman to prepare a bundle of herbs . . . and place it inside her vagina; then for a number of nights she will make her mate smell it" (Coelho 1955, 169–170). While men also make charms, their charms are deemed as less powerful than women's charms (Taylor 1951, 134). Beliefs in menstrual "pollution" in several female-dominated religions seem actually to be beliefs in menstrual "power." One wonders whether in other cultural situations similar beliefs have been misinterpreted by anthropologists who interviewed primarily men (cf. Buckley & Gottlieb 1983).

On the Ryūkyū Islands ethnographers have found evidence of the existence of beliefs in menstrual and childbirth pollution (Lebra 1966). We have reason to believe, however, that these reports misinterpret Ryūkyūan attitudes. According to Teigo Yoshida (1989), in traditional Okinawan culture menstruation was seen as an expression of divinity. It is only under Buddhist influence that pollution beliefs developed. Even today, there does not seem to be as strong an ideology of female pollution in the Ryūkyūs as in Japan. *Yuta,* priestesses, and high priestesses (*noro*) may perform ceremonies while menstruating.[9]

In Ryūkyūan tradition male and female are paired and equal, but deemed linked to separate spheres: men to the political and women to the spiritual. This binary division is reflected in almost every aspect of Ryūkyūan culture, even, as Toichi Mabuchi (1968) has shown, in the architecture of the houses. In a mirror image of beliefs in female pollution, on Hateruma Island men are not allowed to enter shrines, and during days in which priestesses stay in retreat in the shrine (usually before major ceremonies) the priestesses even avoid sewing or mending men's and boy's garments (weaving and sewing are major occupations for the priestesses during retreats). Similarly, rain chants are such important ritual events that they must not be witnessed by men (Ouwehand 1985, 258). The evidence suggests that on the Ryūkyū Islands maleness is perceived as more polluting than femaleness.

Men and Women and Life and Death

Another manifestation of the identification of women with nature is the association between women and death in Western religious and psychoanalytic traditions. This is a multifaceted association, including, for example, the idea that woman (Eve) brought death into the world, and that the womb is analogous to the tomb. Diane Jonte-Pace demonstrates that both religious and psychoanalytic theories have constructed chains of associations in which female becomes a metonym for absence and death, and male becomes a metonym for presence and life. (I will not repeat her evidence here.) According to Jonte-Pace, these associations contribute "to a deeply embedded personal and cultural misogyny" (1990, 18).

I find Jonte-Pace's exposure of the link between the metonymic association of women and death on the one hand and misogyny on the other to be highly convincing, and wish to ask whether in female-dominated religions this chain breaks down. Are women associated with death in female-dominated religions? As I explained in Chapter 6, funeral rituals receive a great deal of attention in several women's religions. Yet before we treat this as corroboration of the association of women with death, we must distinguish between the symbolic view of women as death (as is the case in western religious traditions and psychoanalysis) and the involvement of real women in ancestor rituals (as is the case in several female-dominated religions). I contend that the ancestor rituals of, say, the Black Caribs, have far more to do with life than with death. One could even say that ancestor rituals serve to keep the dead alive; they certainly serve to enlist the assistance of the dead in keeping the living alive.

In female-dominated religions food is associated with life, fertility, abundance, and women. Let us recall that the elaborate food rituals of women's religions include almost no animal sacrifice (i.e., death symbolism; see Chapter 6). This point comes across dramatically in Shigeharu Tanabe's (1991) description of an elaborate ritual of a large Northern Thai matrilineal descent group. The space inside the sanctuary where the ritual takes place is divided into female and male sides. The polluted (in Thai terms) animal sacrifice takes place on the male side, while the female side remains pure.

On the Ryūkyū Islands feminine is associated with fertility, and masculine with hunger and scarcity. Priestesses are prohibited from attending funerals or coming into contact with the dead.[10] Buddhism on Okinawa is basically a cult of the dead, and men are much more involved in Buddhist funeral rituals than they are in other sorts of rituals, and even predominate at certain death rites. Women (daughters and wives), however, wash the bones of the corpse after the seventh anniversary of the death. "People say that it is always women who act intermediary roles between this world and other worlds" (Yoshida, personal communication 1992). In this case, the distinction seems to be between contact with death (which men do) and contact with the supernatural (which women do).

An even more striking instance is provided by the Tetum. As I said earlier, among the Tetum women preside at almost all religious rituals. The one significant exception is death rituals at which men are more active than women. The most dramatic figure in death rituals is the "lord of death" who is a senior male of the dead person's hamlet. This is Hicks' description of the role of the "lord of death": "[A] tremendous cry erupts from somewhere in the depths of the death house and, brandishing his own sword high in the air, the lord of death, galvanized into action, leaps onto the frontal veranda, in a ritualized attempt to keep the corpse among its kin" (Hicks 1984, 120–121).

To take a few more quick examples, Janice Boddy has observed that in the Northern Sudan (home to the *zār*) women preside over births but are not allowed to attend burials (1989, 70). And according to Gehan Wijeyewardene (1986), urban Thai mediums (almost all women) are also subject to taboos regarding death—many will not even attend funerals; male monks, on the other hand, do attend funerals.[11]

The sorts of binary images found in women's religions are not what Sherry Ortner's theory (or Jonte-Pace's analysis) would lead us to expect. At the risk of both reductionism and overgeneralization, I suggest that binary equations in female-dominated religions include the following pairs, some of which associate men with nature and some of which associate women with nature.

female	(is to)	male	(as)
life	(is to)	death	(and)
fertility	(is to)	hunger	(and)

harmony	(is to)	war	(and)
spiritual	(is to)	earthly	(and)
sacred	(is to)	profane	(and)
intuitive	(is to)	rational	(and)
ritual expertise	(is to)	administrative expertise	

RITUAL TUGS OF WAR

Although my intellectual instinct is to reject, as overly universalistic and simplistic, the sort of binary scheme I have laid out above, the available information on the cultural contexts of women's religions does seem to accentuate some form of gender opposition.[12] Northern Sudanese women, for example, demand that their value be socially recognized not through trying to be more like men, but by emphasizing their difference.

In several women's religions gender opposition is dramatized in ritual tugs of war. Throughout the Ryūkyū Islands there are annual ritual tugs of war between two groups representing the male and female principles. The female side should win in order to ensure fertility. Here is a description of one such tug of war:

> The *puru* festival continues for three days in Hatoma Island. A tug of war is played on the third day between the east and west teams. . . . From the east teams there steps out a man dressed like a warrior with a long sword and rice whisky, and from the west team a woman dressed like a peasant woman with a basket containing the heads of both rice and millet in her left hand, and with a sickle in her right hand. . . . After this the tug-of-war starts, and every year the west side wins, as it is believed that when the west wins the coming year is a bumper year (Ito 1966, 48).

A similar ritual (evidence comes from Sosu Village on Okinawa) consists of a sumo wrestling match in which a masked adult male and an old woman fight each other. It is believed that a rich harvest can be expected when the old woman wins, and so she always wins (Ito 1966, 45).

Among the Northern Thai there is an annual ritual tug of war in which men and women compete. As in other ritual tugs of war in female-dominated religions, the women—together with the spirits—always win (McMorran 1984). Among the Northern Thai, in situations in which women hold ritual authority men are likely to display aggression toward the women and their spirits, and incidents of men damaging shrines have been reported by a number of researchers.[13] Similarly, women possessed by the spirits during cult rituals sometimes display aggressive behavior toward men.

Many West African societies are fairly egalitarian in terms of economic rights, yet men and women are not identical in terms of roles. "In virtually every aspect of Kpelle [a society in which Sande is active] life, ranging from secret society activities to the most mundane interactions, sexual differences are expressed" (Bellman 1979, 40). The rather fierce structural opposition of men and women in Mende society (another one of the societies in which Sande is located) is made manifest in a ritual tug of war between men and women that the women win by pulling the men out of the women's ritual site. According to M. C. Jedrej (1976), the separation of women from men is like the separation of sacred from profane. The sacred is associated with the forest (where girls' initiation takes place), fertility, potency, danger, and the supernatural—and so men must be excluded.

Recalling Nancy Chodorow's contention that exclusive female mothering leads **men** to develop ideologies of gender antagonism, how can we explain the friction or even enmity embodied in these ritual tugs of war in **women's** religions? I believe that Chodorow herself gives us the critical clue. Chodorow has observed that especially sexist ideologies tend to arise in societies in which the father is absent, in other words, in societies in which the most salient emotional bonds are between mothers and children rather than between mothers and fathers. In such societies boys spend their earlier years exclusively or predominantly with women. In societies characterized by "father-absence" or "low father-salience," boys and men engage in what Chodorow calls "compulsive assertions of masculinity" (1971, 280). At this point, it is essential to bear in mind our discovery in Chapter 2 that women's religions tend to occur in matrifocal societies—that is, in societies with very "low father-salience." **Women's religions—with ideologies and structural manifestations of female strength, tend to co-exist with ideologies and structural manifestations of extreme "violent behavior, male narcissism, pride, and phobia toward mature women"** (1971, 280). This is amplified by the fact that girls in matrifocal societies also grow up with "low father-salience," perhaps leading them to feel that males are drastically "other." What we seem to be describing are cultural situations characterized by deeply rooted gender conflict or, returning to the terminology we used in Chapter 2, gender dissonance. Periodic ritual tugs of war are certainly one way of expressing (and temporarily resolving) gender conflict.[14]

In the following sections we look more closely at the ideological strategies of several women's religions. By far the most common strategy is to reinterpret rather than challenge the prevailing view of women. This is not to say that women's religions do not seek to correct structural manifestations of gender inequality. As we will see in Chapter 13, female-dominated religions defend and further women's individual or collective rights. What I am saying is that female-dominated religions tend to accept (exploit?) non-egalitarian views of women.

EXAMPLES

Pattern 1: Condemnation of Patriarchy—Feminist Spirituality

Spiritual Feminists have elaborated a sacred history in which gender conflict is the moving force. In brief, the sacred history of the Feminist Spirituality

Movement runs as follows: A long time ago, all over the world, people lived in harmony with nature, with their fellow human beings, and with the cosmos. They expressed their image of the beneficence, the generosity, the mystical and magical fertility of the universe through the natural symbol of the goddess-woman who brings forth and nourishes life. During this era, gender hierarchy either did not exist at all, or human orientation was matriarchal. Proof for this reconstruction can be found in archeology, ancient myths, and contemporary ethnography (see Spretnak 1982; Stone 1976; Gimbutas 1974).

At some point, for some reason (population pressures, technological and economic changes, invasions by small groups of militant men, and/or discovery of male role in reproduction) this idyllic world was turned topsy-turvy.

"Earth is the bountiful female, the ever-giving Mother, Who sends forth food on Her surface in cyclical rhythms and receives our dead back into Her womb. Rituals in Her honor took place in womb-like caves, often with vulva-like entrances and long, slippery corridors. The elemental power of the female was the cultural focus as far back as we can trace. At the moment this awe turned to envy, resentment, and fear, patriarchy was born. Why or how we do not know. . . . The objective of patriarchy was and is to prevent women from achieving, or even supposing, our potential. . . . They [patriarchy] almost succeeded" (Spretnak 1982, xii).

The apex of patriarchal oppression of women was reached during the European witch hunts of the late middle ages, in which it is estimated that millions of women were killed as witches. Women's resistance throughout the ages, culminating in the twentieth-century feminist movement, is what has prevented patriarchy from successfully erasing all vestige and memory of non-patriarchal culture.

Whether or not this historical scenario is absolutely "true" is not an issue for Spiritual Feminists. A sentiment expressed repeatedly in writings of the Movement is that "history" as an objective "something out there" does not exist; rather, history exists in the eyes, the organizing strategies, and the interpretations of particular individuals. Given the necessarily subjective nature of history, it is legitimate and even imperative for feminists to select and create *her*stories that empower them as women. "There was a time when you were not a slave, remember that. You walked alone, full of laughter, you bathed bare-bellied. You say you have lost all recollection of it, remember . . . you say there are no words to describe it, you say it does not exist. But remember. Make an effort to remember. Or, failing that, invent" (Witting 1971, 47).

Spiritual Feminists are far from unanimous in their opinions regarding gender differences. Some Spiritual Feminists stress the basic goodness, the Goddess-nature, of all living creatures—male and female; and some Feminist Spirituality groups include both male and female members. Others believe men have so distorted both their own beings and the purity of nature that women must separate themselves from men to find their own female sources and styles of power.

Although the gender ideology of the Feminist Spirituality Movement is more explicit than the gender ideologies of other women's religions, two similarities emerge. First, like most women's religions, Feminist Spirituality acknowledges the tension between the sexes. And second, Feminist Spirituality, in a roundabout sort of way, accepts and reinterprets the wider societal views of women's nature. In the writings of Spiritual Feminists, women are typically portrayed as less aggressive, more emotional, and more intuitive than men. This description of women does not differ from the highly stereotyped images of women prevalent in contemporary American culture. Where the difference does lie is in how these attributes are valued. Unlike in mainstream America, these attributes are seen as honorable and essential for the preservation of life on Earth.

Pattern 2: Gender Complementarity

Notions of gender complementarity (not gender sameness) occur in several women's religions. Ironically, the first example I bring is one that has already appeared in the section on ritual tugs of war. Carol MacCormack offers a very different analysis of West African gender relations than that developed by M. C. Jedrej (see above, page 205). "The Sherbro [one of the societies in which Sande is active] folk model presents the analogy that nature is to culture as children are to initiated and married adults. It stresses gender interdependency rather than male domination" (1980:95). According to MacCormack, secret societies function to transform (natural) children into initiated adults who understand and vow to live by ancestral laws (culture). Sande both reflects and reinforces the cultural value of gender interdependence. A men's secret society, Poro, is complementary to Sande. Officials of the two societies are responsible for different matters of importance to the community at large. Poro officials see that wells are kept clean and that disputes do not turn into full-scale fights; Sande officials treat illnesses and enforce sexual prohibitions. Men stay out of the way while Sande performs certain rituals; women stay out of the way while Poro performs other rituals. "Poro and Sande vertically polarize all of Mende society; they balance Mende men and Mende women within a complex equilibrium" (Cosentino 1982, 22).

The evidence does not allow us to determine whether Jedrej's or Mac-Cormack's interpretation is "more" correct. Instead, I would suggest that in cultural situations characterized by highly dichotomized views of gender roles, male and female simultaneously conflict and complement. If men's and women's spheres are radically different, both are necessary, yet each tends to oppose the other. Sometimes the complementary mode will be more prominent, and sometimes the conflict mode will take over. Perhaps the most important lesson to be learned from Jedrej's and MacCormack's analyses is that the identical gender ideology may be perceived as complementary or conflicting depending on the point of view of the observer.

Our next example is more clear-cut. From its inception, Theosophy sought to form a nucleus of spiritually enlightened individuals without distinction of race, creed, sex, caste, or color. Women were well represented both as leaders and as members. Theosophists believed that the body is the temporary vehicle for an eternal spirit, which in its evolutionary progress passes through all material forms from the mineral to the angelic, and reincarnates innumerable times in both male and female guises. The dynamic of the cosmic process requires the interaction of yin and yang, male and female. "Thus Theosophy provides a theoretical legitimation at the highest cosmological level for mundane notions of equality between the sexes" (Burfield 1983, 35–36).

This sort of gender ideology seems to have been especially appealing to nineteenth-century Americans. Spiritualists also believe that male and female are polar opposites that are united in the Divine. And Susan Setta argues that one of the reasons for Christian Science's success lies in the fact that Mary Baker Eddy "replaced the discriminatory separation of male and female with the liberating union of masculine and feminine" (1977, 295).[15]

On the Ryūkyū Islands gender complementarity is expressed through ideas regarding the interdependence of brothers and sisters. People believe that the spirit of the sister, either dead or living, protects her brother from malevolent influences. According to myth, the creator couple was a sister and brother. Brothers and sisters have a special relationship; he is expected to safeguard her well-being in the profane world (even after she has married), and she is expected to safeguard his well-being on the spiritual plane. The eldest sister is called by her brother "guardian spirit" or "sister-*kami*." The role of the sister is highlighted during times of danger. When the brother sets out on a journey, for example, his sister gives him a piece of cloth that she has woven, or a lock of her hair, in order to protect him. On the Yaeyama Islands (a subgroup of the Ryūkyūs) the sister plays a critical role in family rituals, and is entitled to a portion of the first fruits of the harvest, so that "her spirit will be pleased and will favor a good crop the following year" (Mabuchi 1964, 82). Married-out sisters return to their natal families annually to play the key role in family and agrarian rituals. "People say that, owing to the beneficent spirit of the sister, one remains healthy enough to work and has a good crop" (Mabuchi 1964, 82).

The spiritual relationship between brother and sister also has more prosaic implications: parents instruct brothers to treat their sisters well, so that sister's spirit will not become angry and cause him misfortune. Although women marry outside their natal families and become somewhat incorporated into their husbands' families, brothers—especially eldest brothers—are expected to help their sisters in times of need. Married-out sisters often return to help their brothers in the field at harvest time. People say that whereas wife and husband divorce, brother and sister are eternally connected. A happy marriage may be described as "They are happy as brother and sister" (Haring 1964, 45).

In a creation myth similar to the Ryūkyūan one, Northern Thais tell that the first two human beings were an elder brother and younger sister who married. It is believed auspicious for twins who were separated at birth to marry, and brother-sister incest does not incur serious ritual sanctions. Northern Thai parents, concerned about their daughters' futures, make them take care of younger brothers so that these brothers when grown up will return the favor and help their sisters. "Thai family arrangements hinge a good deal upon warmth between brothers and between sisters" (Hanks and Hanks 1963, 434).

Myths of the first couple being brother and sister, and expectations of cooperation among brothers and sisters, seem to be common throughout continental
and island Southeast Asia. These myths are often associated with social structures in which male and female are complementary rather than hierarchical.

The Shakers developed a gender ideology that was far more egalitarian
than other gender ideologies pervasive in nineteenth-century American society. Shakers seized on Darwin's hypothesis of an androgenous ancestor, and
accentuated the contention of some physiologists that each sex includes, in
undeveloped form, the organs of the other sex. Shakers believed that men's
exploitation of women for thousands of years had been one of the main
causes of failure in human history, and understood that men's exploitation of
women had been supported by the image of a male god.[16] They believed it
necessary to remake society on the basis of a new type of human relationship:
since economic evils are based on biological evils, a new kind of biological
relationship would make it possible to improve society and its economic
structure. The leadership structure of the Shakers is self-consciously egalitarian, with a man and a woman at each level of the hierarchy.[17]

In light of what we have just seen about the Shakers, it is somewhat surprising to find that they believed men and women to possess different natures—
women more spiritual, nurturing, emotional, and affectionate, and men more
worldly, physical, rational, and intellectual (Bednarowski 1980, 211; Brewer
1992, 621; Kern 1981). Shakers believed that all of nature is made up of male
and female forms, and that the distinction of sex is eternal and inherent in the
soul itself. Male and female are diametrically opposed forces that find perfection only in an all-encompassing unity, a male-female godhead.[18] Also on the
human level, both male and female are necessary, an ideology that was reflected in, for example, the insistence that men and women live under the same
roof in every house in every Shaker community (Kitch 1989, 85).

The Shakers acknowledged many of the same constitutional differences between the sexes as did the society at large, yet insisted that gender differences
and sexual separation do not mean that women should have lesser rights or
privileges (Kitch 1989, 134).[19] The Shakers did not challenge contemporary
notions of female and male nature. Instead, they insisted that female nature and
female roles are as good as male nature and roles.[20]

THE IMPORTANCE OF GENDER
DIFFERENCES

As a feminist, disappointment was my first reaction on organizing the material
for this chapter. I wanted to find out that women's religions around the world
proclaim egalitarian gender ideologies. Instead, I found that women's religions
buy into prevalent unegalitarian notions of gender and gender roles. As an
anthropologist, however, I was delighted to discover a discernable pattern.
That pleasure turned into intellectual excitement when I read Nancy Eberhardt's overview of gender relations among hill tribes in Thailand.

Eberhardt shows that among a hill tribe known as the Akha, gender is a crucial cultural category—just about every object, event, activity, and symbol is considered either male or female. Among the Shan and Yunnanese tribes, on the other hand, gender is a rather secondary cultural category. Comparing the status of women among these groups, Eberhardt found that **"in the process of subordinating gender as a cultural category, women are also devalued"** (1988, 8). In a similar vein, Tikva Frymer-Kensky has amassed evidence showing that in Mesopotamian and Old Babylonian mythology, and in Hellenistic mythology and philosophy, men and women are portrayed as essentially, ontologically different. In the Bible, on the other hand, men and women are essentially similar, the only difference being that of genitalia (1992). Although this is not the point that Frymer-Kensky was trying to make, her findings make it clear that the "egalitarian" gender philosophy of the Bible co-existed with a religious system in which women had a far smaller role than in the "non-egalitarian" religious philosophies to which she compares the Bible.

The writings of most feminist anthropologists carry either an implicit or explicit message that the blurring of gender categories is what will lead to the demise of patriarchy (cf. Rosaldo 1974; Chodorow 1974). The findings I have brought here suggest a different scenario. The very few women's religions of which we have knowledge consistently stress rather than play down gender differences. It seems to me that women's religions have in fact selected the most efficacious strategy possible considering the limitations within which they operate—none of these religions is located in a truly non-sexist cultural context. In other words, if these religions were to claim that men and women are the same, **no one would believe them anyway!** Gender differences seem to be so obviously "true," that enhancing and reinterpreting those differences offers women an ideology that is both believable and somewhat empowering (see Chapter 13). In an imperfect world, it may well serve women's interests to own a clearly bounded portion of the cultural map.

In almost all the cultural situations in which women's religions are found, women can choose between the female-dominated religion and a male-dominated religion (*nat* cult vs. Buddhism, Afro-Brazilian religion vs. Catholicism and Pentecostalism, Shakers vs. mainstream Protestantism). It is important to note that in each of these cases the female-dominated religion teaches a gender ideology that is less patriarchal than that of the parallel male-dominated religion. In other words, when women are in a position in which they can choose between a more and a less sexist gender ideology, many do opt for the less sexist one. Female-dominated religions may teach that women are passive or soft; they do not teach that women are evil or stupid.

Although most female-dominated religion, like most male-dominated religions, deem different spheres of activity to be appropriate for men and for women, **in female-dominated religions women's sphere is considered as good (if not better) than the male sphere, and women fully control the female sphere.** By way of contrast, in modern Israel where a great deal of women's religious activity involves cooking, recipes are "custom" (*minhag*) rather than "law" (*halacha*). As a result, the status of cooking as a religious ritual is lower than the status of men's prayer or Torah study. Moreover, the one aspect of cooking that falls into the realm of law is *kashrut* (food taboos and regulations), yet for pious women the male rabbi is the ultimate authority concerning *kashrut*; if an orthodox Jewish woman is not sure whether a chicken is kosher, she is expected to consult a rabbi and accept his decision. My argument here is **not** that the existence of a "female sphere" characterizes female-dominated religions; most known cultures have some sort of sexual division of labor. What **does** characterize female-dominated religions is an ideological assertion that the female sphere is as good or better than the male sphere, **and** the institutionalization of autonomy for women operating in the female sphere.

Notes

1. New Right female-dominated organizations oppose the Equal Rights Amendment, abortion rights and gay rights, and urge women to return to the home and family as caretakers and wives (Klatch 1987, 45).

2. Haring (1964) reports that in a Buddhist temple in the city of Naze (Ryūkyū) he found a woman officiating as a full priest of the Shin sect. While this would not have been permitted anywhere else, on the Ryūkyū Islands, "There was no innovation about a woman priest—this was something eminently proper and fitting that called for no comment. Perhaps Buddhism failed to gain wide acceptance in Amami despite centuries of propaganda because its priests were male" (1964, 121).

3. Many feminist scholars have offered critiques of Ortner's theory. The fact that women are able to bear children does not mean that doing so is essential to women's existential being or sense of self. If nothing else, birth control means that the ability to give birth can be suppressed. And the contention that men are further from nature seems ridiculous when we bear in mind that men, like women, eat, breathe, excrete, sleep, and die.

4. The Shakers also had a penchant for native Indian spirits (Stein 1992, 176).

5. This is a syncretic religion including elements of both Catholicism and indigenous Filipino beliefs. A central theme in this religion is the liberation of the Philippines from Western imperialistic rule. Rosemary Ruether believes that the prominence of women in this and other similar communities is at least partially an outgrowth of the indigenous Filipino tradition of female priests (n.d., 4).

6. On the Ryūkyū Islands women are equated with the spiritual and men with the material, whereas in East and Southeast Asia men are equated with the spiritual and women with the material. I do not know how to interpret this difference, but it is certainly worth noting. The answer may lie in the role of Buddhism and Confucianism as "great traditions" in East and Southeast Asia, as opposed to their marginal role on the Ryūkyū Islands.

7. Tenryko claims to believe in equality of the sexes. While they say that there is no real difference between the sexes, they also say that it is women's primary duty to give birth and raise children because men are by nature incapable of this job. Women are passive by nature and men are active. Few of the new Japanese religions preach egalitarian ideologies. For example, the True-Light Supra-Religious Organization (Sukyo Mahikari), founded by a man, teaches that the "spiritual pattern" of the male was created 20,000 years before that of the female, and is naturally associated with the general superiority of the yang principle. Winston David quotes one of their most prominent teachers as proclaiming that "if women's liberation succeeds in Japan, the country will be doomed" (1980, 199).

8. One of the more unusual traits of Tetum religion is that although the woman is the household's sacred head, the household itself is patrilineal and patrilocal. The wife performs rituals for her husband's ancestors, not for her own. When she marries she symbolically leaves behind her own ancestors (see Appendix B).

9. Anthropologist Mary Douglas has argued that menstrual taboos are more emphasized or more severe in cultures where there is an unclear message regarding gender—where male dominance is not absolute. Yoshida claims (and I agree) that gender is an extraordinarily unclear cultural category on Okinawa and so, according to Douglas, should stress menstrual taboos. However, menstrual taboos are quite unelaborated on Okinawa (1989).

10. Yoshida points out that in some cases a priestess may attend the funeral of her mother or father, but in the role of relative and not in the role of priestess (personal communication 1992).

11. In her study of a village in central Thailand, Jane Hanks found that men's and women's magical practices had different objectives. Men wield magic to gain power over spirits, people, elements, and forces. Their magic could be beneficial or malevolent. "Men had a nurturing (*liang*) role, but only for non-human beings, e.g., buffalo, pet birds, and guardian spirits of house and land. Subverting this role for hostile ends, they obtained possession of the ghost of a recent corpse by gathering the drop of oil at the chin. . . . **For men, nourishing something gave control**" (1963, 79, my emphases). Women's magic, on the other hand, was linked to her female task. It did not give power over people and it could not be destructive. There were no female sorceresses in the village, and women did not fear each other's magic. "**A woman's magic was devoted solely to promoting the processes of growth and life**" (1963, 79).

12. Whether this reflects the intellectual biases of the scholars who document them rather than of the religions is impossible to determine.

13. Richard Davis argues that the northern Thai are characterized by structural dominance of women but an ideological dominance of men. Men are associated with auspicious directions (north and right) and women with less auspicious. Davis builds a set of oppositions: north, east, male, senior, right, settlements, high things versus south, west, female, junior, left, forest, low things. "Agrarian rites are only performed by men and the aim of the rites is to give male cultivators control over the female rice deity. The phallicism evoked by erecting the 'great hawk's eye' during first-threshing suggests a triumph of male efforts to domesticate and suppress the female forces of the wild" (1974, 18).

14. Rituals that express gender conflict are also found outside female-dominated religions. Among the Greeks of Thrace and the Bulgars the Day of Babo was celebrated by married women who "while pretending to honour the midwife, worshipped the Phallus behind closed doors, introducing newly-wed young girls to the society of women; the participants, disguised as soldiers or policemen, behaved with inordinate aggressivity towards the men they met" (Anastassiadou 1976, 101).

15. A number of minor women's cults preach similar visions of the union of male and female in the age to come. Beit-Hallahmi has described a small female-dominated messianic cult in Israel. Most of the beliefs of this cult are similar to those of any number of male-dominated revitalization movements in contemporary Israel. One of the few distinguishing features of this cult is their belief that in the New Age the two sexes will become one (1992, 70ff.).

16. On the other hand, Ann Lee herself stated that "man is first, and the woman . . . second" in the "order of nature" (quoted in Brewer 1992, 612).

17. The parallel system of leadership with a man and woman at each level was most

likely introduced by a male leader, Joseph Meachum. Similarly, another male leader, Benjamin S. Youngs was responsible for developing the theology of Holy Mother Wisdom (Humez 1992, 86). It is important to bear in mind that parallel titles for leaders did not necessarily mean equal authority, and particularly in the early years the distribution of power among male and female Shakers was not fully egalitarian (I thank Priscilla Brewer for drawing my attention to this point, personal communication 1992).

18. When Ann Lee was alive she was seen as the "Queen of Heaven" by her followers. After her death the sect's theologians de-emphasized that role, and in nineteenth-century Shaker writings Mother Ann is no longer described as superior to Jesus, but as his completion (cited in Brewer 1992, 613).

19. Priscilla Brewer, on the other hand, argues that "Most Believers felt that men and women should exercise unequal power because of their distinctive traits. Wherever possible, economic and executive responsibilities were assigned to brethren. The feminization of the Society's leadership beginning in the last half of the nineteenth century came about only because of a worsening gender imbalance. The Shakers were never committed to the complete equality of the sexes" (1992, 635).

20. While much of what I have described in terms of Shaker gender ideology is also true of Christian Science, the Shakers addressed issues of gender far more explicitly. In various places in her writing Eddy contends that gender differences really do not exist, that men and women are complementary, and that women are superior.

11 ⬳

Leaders and Experts

WOMEN AND LEADERSHIP IN
FEMALE-DOMINATED RELIGIONS

Looking at Shaker history, Marjorie Procter-Smith has concluded that gender ideology and gender of leaders are firmly interlocked. She shows that "the system of dual [male and female] leadership was in place in the [Shaker] societies several years prior to the appearance of Youngs' *Testimony*, where the doctrine of a dual deity was first expressed" (1985, vii). And, during the period of Mother Ann's Work (the internal revival during the mid-nineteenth century in which messages were received from deceased Shaker leaders, God, and Holy Mother Wisdom), "As women became increasingly prominent as instruments [mediums], female symbols became increasingly prominent in the symbol-system of the sect" (1985, 196). The pattern that emerges is of women stressing female symbols after they become prominent in leadership; we can assume that this functions to validate their authority in much the same way that masculine symbols validate the authority of male leaders in other religious traditions (Catherine Wessinger, personal communication 1993).

A feature of all the religions treated in this book is that both in theory and in practice leadership roles are open to women, and women predominate in most positions of authority and prestige. Although few of the female-dominated religions claim that women are "better" than men, quite a few assert that women are more suited (or uniquely suited) to fill leadership roles. For the most part, leaders in women's religions embrace rather traditional (albeit expanded and empowered) female roles and traits. For example, when Virginia Kerns asked the Black Caribs why women are more prominent in ritual, she was told that actually anyone can participate in ritual (except children) but women are more interested, more attuned to the supernatural as they age, have better memories than men and so remember the intricate rituals, and feel more gratitude and duty toward the ancestors. As we saw in earlier chapters, many of the rituals performed by the Black Carib women involve cooking and other activities that are common parts of women's lives.

When Patricia Lerch asked her Brazilian informants why more women than men are Umbanda mediums, the qualities most often named in describing mediums were those also used by informants in discussing the attributes of a good mother or wife. Women's life experiences were said to prepare them for the role demands of spirit medium. "Men are perceived to be weak creatures unable to endure the spiritual tests and the rigors of development. Where do women get their spiritual strength? Strength comes from dealing with everyday life" (Lerch 1982, 248). Suffering trains one for mediumship, and in the words of one informant, "Women suffer more than men, both on the spiritual level and on the material level. This history of suffering makes women better suited to be mediums. Women suffer because of their husbands. . . . Women learn to suffer with patience and resignation" (1982, 249). Women's suffering typically stems from domestic problems—in particular, unfaithful husbands. Male infidelity means that men do not give enough money to their wives, so that the wives cannot educate their children and manage their households properly. This situation reflects both the economic marginality of most Brazilian women and the infamous sexual double standard. Yet the outcome is that women are deemed to be the preferable religious leaders in Afro-Brazilian cults. In addition, the actual work performed by mediums is more similar to Brazilian women's work than Brazilian men's work: According to Ruth Landes (1947), women are seen as more suited to the types of duties involved in religious ritual—cooking sacred foods and caring for the altars—because that is what they do at home.

Suffering is a theme that emerges repeatedly in the life stories of women leaders, and is used by many of the women's religions to explain why more women than men are leaders. In a study of women Spiritist healers in Puerto Rico, Koss-Chioino commented that pain seems to be more central to women's than to men's life experiences.[1] Women in sexist societies suffer from the denial of their talents and worth, in addition to the physical and psychological distress that all women undergo throughout their reproductive cycles. I would argue that **the feminization of suffering is used to justify women's religious leadership in societies in which leadership is perceived to be a male prerogative.** Pain—a female prerogative—explains why women can be religious leaders.

HIERARCHICAL RELIGIONS

Scholars have asserted that women's organizational style is less hierarchical than men's (e.g., Barfoot and Sheppard 1980, on Pentecostal churches.) According to Michelle Rosaldo (1974, 29), well-articulated systems of rank are a male rather than female mode. Emblems and insignia of rank, such as those found in armies, are rarely created by women. A range of theories have been offered to explain this gender difference. Drawing on Nancy Chodorow's ideas, Iris Marion Young (1983) argues that because boys are mothered by women, they come to relate to others in an oppositional (dichotomous) way. This leads to a mode of conceptualization that emphasizes mutually exclusive dualities (body/mind; self/other), which results in hierarchies and oppression of all kinds. Carol Gilligan (1982) has argued that men's thinking is more competitive, more concerned with winning and losing, whereas women's thinking centers more on cooperation and care (see also Johnson 1988, 94–95).

We indeed find that most women's religions preach "egalitarian" ideologies—that every human being regardless of sex, class, or age has the potential for communicating with the spirits. However, in actual fact, in all the women's religions certain categories of people are more attracted by, or attractive to, the gods or spirits. In contrast to sociological theories that show women opting for nonhierarchical organizational styles, in all these religions there is some sort of hierarchy based on spiritual development.[2] Although women's religions tend to provide equal opportunities to potential leaders with little regard to class and education, rank can be achieved through acquiring skills and followers. Unlike in many male-dominated organizations, neither wealth nor schooling determines who acquires skills and followers: ritual skills and clients often accrue to the poorest, least educated, and most unfortunate women. Still, and let me emphasize this finding, women's religious organizations do not seem to be any less hierarchical than men's. Organizational sociologists know the "iron law of oligarchy"—only the very smallest groups do not have hierarchy. Thus the fact that women's religions are hierarchical is not totally unexpected, because all groups have hierarchy. Patricia Martin's study of feminist organizations in the United States strengthens this observation: despite a myth of nonhierarchical relations, no particular internal structure seems to be a defining characteristic of feminist organizations (1990).

Sande: A Case Study

Sande initiation rituals in which all initiates are covered in white clay seem to dramatize the innate equality of all members. At the same time, Sande chapters are hierarchically organized. The route to leadership in Sande is through acquiring more knowledge. Increased adeptness is acknowledged by rites that raise some women to higher ranks. Leaders or headwomen have special skills—they are responsible for the initiates' training, and function as midwives and advisers on gynecological problems. Some women are so adept that they are known over a wide area and travel across linguistic and ethnic boundaries. The Sande leadership structure is as follows: The *Majo* is the headwoman; the *Sowei* are in charge of teaching the initiates; the *Ligba* initiate the girls; the *Ndoli* are dancers (some of whom wear masks); the *Klawa* are counselors for the initiates; the *Sowei Ligba* are in charge of providing protection for members of the Society.

This system of ranking has implications aside from ceremony. Caroline Bledsoe argues that Sande serves the interests of older women while contributing to the oppression of younger women. In that sense, Sande actually intensifies power differences among women. Sande leaders' power over female initiates' sexual and domestic services can be used to gain the loyalty of young men or those from outside lineages whom elders—male and female—seek to control. Bledsoe interprets what initiates learn in bush school as "ideological dressing on a rigid gerontocratic hierarchy" (1980, 69).

Bledsoe has observed that the skills Sande initiates learn are ones they already know—that the learning is symbolic. But unlike Carol MacCormack who explains that what the girls really learn is cooperation (see Chapter 6) or Bruce Lincoln who argues that initiates learn to see the inner cosmic significance and sacrality in everyday activities (see Chapter 7), Bledsoe claims that what initiates really learn is "absolute obedience to Sande leaders, both while they are in the bush school and in later life. Disobedience or disrespect may be threatened with infertility or even death" (1980, 68). The leaders can convincingly threaten infertility and death because they are the midwives. Both men and women fear and respect midwives whose power stems from their exclusive knowledge of obstetrics and gynecology. And despite myths to the contrary, Sande leaders actually hide more than they teach about reproduction and midwifery, and even try to keep the knowledge of childbearing secret. Women believe themselves to be utterly dependent on the midwives, and the midwives are able to use women's dependence on them during birth to extract secrets that further enhance their social power.

Other Examples

The manifestations of hierarchy vary among women's religions. The Afro-Brazilian religions are characterized by elaborate hierarchies based on spiritual talents rather than on knowledge (as in Sande). Diana Brown found that in Umbanda centers, mediums who are sought out for their consulting abilities gain great prestige and advance rapidly through the ritual hierarchy of the center. In contrast to our expectations of supportive and nonhierarchical relationships among women, most cult leaders do not want their mediums to practice outside the public sessions held at Centers.[3] (The leaders say that most mediums are not sufficiently developed spiritually to handle private sessions; the mediums claim that the cult leaders are jealous.) On the other hand, mediums wear simple white outfits and there are no class indicators such as jewelry to show socioeconomic status. In many cases poor and black mediums may outrank rich and white ones, and women may outrank men.

In Burma all the *nat* wives (mediums) attached to a particular *nat* have an internal hierarchy, led by those who are full-time devotees. Devotees feel a certain rivalry among themselves regarding whom the *nat* visits in dreams and to whom he reveals his presence. Although there is no official centralized organization of mediums associated with particular *nats,* there is an informal yet clearly recognized hierarchy based on spiritual development.

Unlike Sande leaders, the *zār* leader is a fellow sufferer, someone who deals with the same sorts of problems as her followers. Her authority does not lie in orders that the patient must obey, but in her personal charisma and her skill at the process of negotiating with the spirits. On the other hand, *zār* leaders are addressed as *shaykha* (a title of respect), and have followers (or "daughters") ranging in number from fifty to several hundred who attend annual rituals provided by the leaders for their followers. Not only is there a difference in rank between leaders and followers, but also between initiated and non-initiated followers. At *zār* rituals non-initiated women attend, but have a lower status; for example, they may not sit on the mattresses, or be served coffee.

Ironically, despite the existence of the Mother Church (see Chapter 12), Christian Science congregations are more democratic than most other women's religions. There is no clergy and officers are elected from among members of the congregation. On the other hand, and this is the essential point, Mary Baker Eddy insisted on being acknowledged and obeyed as the sole discoverer and founder of Christian Science.

The Shakers described an explicit chain of command, beginning with Almighty God and Holy Mother Wisdom, then Jesus and Ann Lee, and then the first church elders. Each Shaker community had a fully articulated hierarchy of religious and secular leaders: deacons, trustees, and elders directing the spiritual and working lives of members. Members were divided into three classes of families: novitiates, junior or second class who still owned their own property but ceased using it to join the production-consumption Shaker cooperative, and senior or third class who had renounced their property and signed a binding covenant with the Shaker community.

On the Ryūkyū Islands laypeople have rather minor ritual roles; specialists are responsible for the majority of ritual action. In the past the *noro* priestesses lived in semi-seclusion, apart from their fellow villagers, often in a special dwelling near the sacred grove. Douglas Haring quotes an informant from one of the smaller Ryūkyūan Islands, "They [*noro*] are women who live apart, wear kimono twice the usual length, with double-length combs stuck in their hair. By this costume they convince simple folk that they have come down from heaven and have alighted on a mountain top" (1953, 112). On the main island of Okinawa during the fifteenth and sixteenth centuries a strict religious hierarchy was established by the government. The hierarchy was composed of a high priestess, village priestesses, kin-group priestesses, and household ritual experts.[4] These female ritual experts were arranged into a precise, elaborated, and strict hierarchy. Today there are four different names for priestesses (the meanings of these names are not always clear) and a significant distinction between *noro* (high priestesses who are responsible for leading and preparing public rituals) and ordinary priestesses who are housewives or grandmothers.[5]

HISTORY AND PATH TO LEADERSHIP

What kinds of women become religious leaders or experts? Do they exhibit from a young age leadership abilities that are nurtured by the previous generation of leaders? Are they women who are misfits—never quite able to fulfill the role marked out for women in their particular cultures? Are they women with heightened spirituality—women who are chosen by the gods? Or are they women with an eye to personal gain and profit?[6]

In the following section we will see that the two most common themes in the life histories of women leaders are illness and an initial resistance to taking up the leader role. But since the life histories of most of these leaders are reconstructed through the leader's own memories, I wish to begin by making some general comments about autobiography. Typically, when people tell their life histories, they relate stories with plots, themes, and character development, rather than a random series of unrelated incidents. Although life in fact is made up of millions of random and unrelated incidents, when people are asked about their lives, they tend to try to make some kind of sense or order out of what they have experienced. In the case of religious autobiography this is even more true. In constructing religious autobiography—in answering the question "How did you come to be active in this religion?"—individuals sort through their life experiences and select those incidents and events that to their mind show spiritual development. The material presented below should not be treated as "objective" or factual accountings of people's lives, but rather as religious interpretations of events deemed significant by specific individuals for very specific reasons.

All of what I have just said regarding religious autobiography in general is even more true in the case of women leaders. Sidonie Smith explains that women who tell their stories "understand that a statement or a story will receive a different ideological interpretation if attributed to a man or to a woman. As a result, the [female] autobiographer . . . approaches her 'fictive' reader as if 'he' were the representative of the dominant order, the arbiter of the ideology of gender and its stories of selfhood" (1987, 48). In other words, when women religious leaders tell their life-stories they are well aware that their stories will be judged by people who, to say the least, are uncomfortable with the very idea of a woman leader. A similar point has been made by Marie-Francoise Chanfrault-Duchet: "[I]n women's life stories, the social self does not merely occupy a place within the social order; rather, its place is overdetermined by the status of woman. This means that women's life-stories, unlike men's, deal not only with the relation between the self and the social sphere, but also, and above all, with woman's condition and with the collective representations of woman as they have been shaped by the society with which the woman being interviewed must deal" (1991, 78).

In sum, I ask the reader to take the life histories of women religious leaders with a triple grain of salt: as **autobiographies**, as **religious** autobiographies, and as autobiographies of **women** religious leaders.

Illness, Visions, and Being Called by the Spirits

In Chapter 5 we saw that illness is often what leads women to become involved in women's religions. In several religions prolonged illness is a mark that a woman is destined to be a leader. For example, in Brazil signs of incipient mediumship include excessive crying, protracted illness, unexplained events, unsolvable problems, and unusual occurrences. (Psychological testing of women mediums in Brazil demonstrate that mediums tend to be reasonably well adjusted; cf. Leacock and Leacock 1972, 326–327). The path to becoming a medium usually involves a stage of sickness or other misfortune that a cult leader interprets as caused by undeveloped mediumship. Umbandists believe that the ability to be a medium is innate, inheritable, and God-given. Resistance is dangerous—it can lead to further misfortune or even death. Husbands of future mediums may object to or disbelieve in the *mediumidade* of their wives. Most women mediums and cult leaders believe that a married woman should have her husband's consent, but that if he won't give it, the spiritual order should take precedence over his resistance, otherwise her illness will worsen.

On some of the Ryūkyū Islands, priestesses are selected from certain families or lineages. On the other hand, the woman is only considered qualified to be a priestess upon experiencing *kamidari*—the mark of the divine in the form of visions, hallucinations, dreams, and abnormal behavior. Shamans (*yuta*) judge if the illness is *kamidari* or not. Only then will she learn the dances and rituals and stories of *noro*.[7] Ryūkyūan *yutas*, like Afro-Brazilian mediums, show life histories of marital discord, intrafamily conflict, chronic illnesses, and hallucinatory experiences.

Historians and anthropologists stress that many Spiritualist mediums had lost their fathers at a young age, suffered from insufficient parental affection as children, or had unfortunate experiences with husbands or male friends.[8] However, since most women in most societies have suffered from insufficient parental affection or from bad relationships with husbands or male friends, I am reluctant to pay much heed to this supposed attribute. Of greater interest is the claim by mediums themselves that they did not consciously choose to become mediums; rather, the spirits chose them. It was often at adolescence and marriage that potential mediums displayed the alarming symptoms and illnesses that would be interpreted as the call of the spirits. Still, according to Laurence Moore, "There was no consistent marital pattern among Spiritualist mediums: some were married, some had been divorced and remarried, and some remained single" (1977, 107).

Alex Owen contends that it is significant that Spiritualist mediums often experienced illness at key stages in the development of sexual maturity and adult femininity. Illness at these times offered attention and recognition, but also provided an arena for expressing conflict. "In other words, spiritualist mediumship was both expressive of an inner struggle with the problem of femininity and instrumental in reconciling that tension" (1981, 209). Again, I am not surprised to hear that women in sexist societies feel conflict at periods in their lives in which they are brought face to face with the ways in which women's freedom is restricted.

Burmese women also do not choose to become shamans. Instead, the *nat* falls in love with a woman and wishes to marry her. If she resists, she will suffer. It is said that *nats* love women who have beautiful souls. The *nat* makes itself manifest through dreams or possession. Typically, another shaman identifies the *nat* in a new devotee. Being loved by a *nat* is not sufficient to make one a shaman or "*nat* wife"; what is needed is a formal marriage ceremony. The marriage ceremony is quite expensive—costumes, orchestra, fees for shamans, and food for guests. It may take years to accumulate enough funds to carry out the ceremony.

Finally, Gehan Wijeyewardene observes that an urban Thai medium typically considers herself "called" to her role, and describes having initially tried
to escape the *caw* (spirit), who continued to persecute her until she agreed to be
his "horse."

Before going on, I wish to reiterate that the stories of illness I have just cited
do not necessarily mean that women religious leaders have been ill more than
other people; these stories **do** mean that women religious leaders tend to
attribute greater significance to their illnesses. I am struck by Joan Koss-
Chioino's observation regarding women Spiritist healers in Puerto Rico: these
women describe having felt deep **concern** for the illnesses of their family
members from an early age, and that they are especially **aware** of the illnesses
they themselves experienced as children (1992, 18). If I understand Koss-
Chioino correctly, women healers in Puerto Rico are characterized by cogni-
zance of illness, and not necessarily by actual sickness. My suspicion is that this
pattern may be true in other religions as well.

Training

One path to leadership that is rarely (although very occasionally) found in female-
dominated religions is that of a woman consciously choosing a leadership role,
and then undergoing lengthy, formal training to learn the role. The absence of
formal training is consistent with the aversion to sacred texts and official doctrines that characterize most of the women's religions (see Chapter 12).

The path to Spiritualist mediumship, for example, does not include any sort
of prescribed training or apprenticeship. Indeed, **lack** of education was seen as
conducive to successful mediumship. Many sympathetic contemporary accounts of mediums stress their naivety and lack of worldly knowledge.

A very short formal training path is found among Christian Science practitioners who must take a two-week course that allows them to be officially recognized as healers. The career of a practitioner begins when she has shown
success at healing family and friends. Then, through word of mouth her abilities gradually become known in her own congregation. As the practitioner
becomes better known, patients give testimony to her healing prowess at
church during the Wednesday meetings, and the practitioner begins to be seen
as a source of information concerning Christian Science beliefs. Finally, after
she has healed a number of serious illnesses, the practitioner applies for formal
recognition from the Mother Church as a healer. According to Margery Fox,
"Formal recognition actually means in social terms that a number of people in
the branch congregation have made the decision to depend on this person for
friendship, comfort, health, and religious instruction and advice. They have
entrusted her with the most important elements of their lives" (1989, 106).

A somewhat exceptional pattern is exemplified by the Afro-Brazilian religions in which mediumistic abilities require formal training and developing.
Once an individual decides to become a Umbanda medium she passes through
approximately four years of preparations and preparatory roles (Lerch 1982).
In Bahia Brazil, initiation requires time and money—three months of absolute

seclusion in the cult house, abstinence from sex, rich foods, and amusement. There is a large fee for initiation, which is usually paid off gradually in service to the cult center.

Mothers and Daughters

In many of the female-dominated religions, the women who become religious leaders are women whose mothers were religious leaders. For instance, when a Korean shaman dies her spirit usually possesses her daughter or daughter-in-law (Harvey 1979, 127). Among Spiritualists in South Wales today, mediums are often daughters of mediums (introduction to Spiritualism takes place in childhood, yet regular involvement does not usually happen until after marriage.) Mayotte women are much more likely to be possessed by spirits if their mothers or sisters are; this is not true for Mayotte men (see page 191). And on Okinawa it was formerly the custom that a *noro* was succeeded by her daughter.[9] And still today, in the life stories of priestesses collected by Yoshinobu Ota, we find one who was "called by the deity to succeed her mother . . . as a priestess" (1989, 117).

In Burma certain *nats* are particularly popular because they are served by *natkadaws* (*nat* wives or shamans) who go from town to town offering prayers and dances to the images of their *nats*. Typically, these women are daughters of other *natkadaws*. Two shamans interviewed by June Nash reported that they were asked by their dying mothers to become *natkadaws*, refused, became seriously ill, were advised by other *natkadaws* to join their ranks, and recovered.

According to Janice Boddy, a Sudanese woman who is interested in becoming a *shayka* (*zār* leader) learns by apprenticing, often with a close maternal kinswoman. The proclivity to be a *shayka* tends to be handed down in the maternal line. The leader learns how to call the spirits, bargain with them, and recognize their individual characteristics. She does not declare herself a *shayka*; others have to attribute this status to her as her reputation grows. Similarly, Ethiopian women *zār* leaders claim their status through transfer of power and knowledge from their mothers. Men, who do not inherit *zār* spirits from their mothers, may claim that *zār* spirits had kidnapped them during childhood (Messing 1958).

The propensity for daughters of leaders to follow in their mothers' footsteps is consistent with the emphasis on family relationships and the pattern of matrifocality in women's religions.

Korean Shamanism: A Case Study

Korean women called by the spirits to become shamans try to avoid taking on the shaman role, primarily because shamans and their families are regarded somewhat as deviants and outcasts. The path to becoming a shaman is not an easy one, and no one claims to have sought or selected this career. Potential shamans are tormented by gods and ancestors until they feel compelled to accept. The only other choice would be to deny the calling and die insane. The central event indicating the shamanistic calling is *sinbyong* or possession sickness. Once a woman accepts the role of shaman, the same spirits who had tormented her become her allies.

The spirits tend to call a potential shaman in middle life, at a time when she is suffering from a specific misfortune or more general discontent. Symptoms of *sinbyong* include a wide range of physical distresses (dizziness, headaches, digestive disorders), hallucinations and strange dreams, and inappropriate behavior (such as speaking openly about matters that are normally not discussed). The behavioral symptoms, disruptive to the family and community, are what confirms the diagnosis of possession sickness.

Youngsook Kim Harvey traces the typical spiritual development of a Korean shaman: (1) The victim feels conflict between her own needs and the housewife's role, in addition to conflict with her husband or in-laws. (2) She tries unsuccessfully to cope with these conflicts but feels trapped by them. (3) She becomes ill with vague physical symptoms, and is given a period of time to retreat from household responsibilities. (4) The symptoms persist, the woman is exempted from household duties, and her family tries to find a cure for her illness. (5) The victim recovers. (6) Old patterns of interaction within the family are resumed. (7) She becomes sick once more. This process may be repeated a number of times, until finally an experienced shaman makes a diagnosis of *sinbyong* (possession sickness), and initiates and trains the novice shaman.

Harvey documents one case in which the process continued during twenty-eight years. That particular shaman's life story, not atypical, included being forced into an arranged marriage, refusing to consummate the marriage and being raped by her husband, trying hard but unsuccessfully to accommodate herself to the housewife role, deaths of her children, illness, re-marriage to a man who became involved in extra marital affairs and who brought financial ruin on their family, abandoning her infant daughter because she did not have the financial resources to care for her properly, and—finally—a diagnosis of possession sickness.

Brian Wilson details the life story of another shaman: She was raised by a mother who supported the children because the father was ill. Her older sister was given away to another family. As a young girl she wanted to be a boy, and she resented having to obey an older brother. Her parents sent her to Seoul as a housemaid. She was married to a man not of her own choosing. Her adult life included many hardships, including the war and being financially responsible for her baby while her husband was away. One of her children died, her husband cheated on her with another woman, and she quarreled with him. Finally, she became possessed by her dead mother-in-law's spirit, which gave her a new power over her husband.

Although victims of *sinbyong* are likely to behave in ways that are both socially unacceptable and extremely disruptive to family life (e.g., they may stop performing their household duties), they are not personally blamed for their behavior because Koreans believe that spirits like to possess people who have been mistreated by their families. By allowing the victim to take on the role of shaman, her family may disprove suspicions of mistreatment.

Traits of Leaders

The life stories of Korean shamans are especially important because the shamans themselves make use of autobiographical details to demonstrate to their clients the powers of the gods and the dangers of ritual neglect. Earlier in this chapter I suggested that religious autobiographies are not objective histories. Instead, they are selections and interpretations of events that seem to the teller, at the time of telling, to explain why her life is the way it now is. I believe that illness is significant to female religious specialists **not** because they are ill more than other people, but because they themselves see their illnesses as meaningful to their religious roles. In light of the discussion of sickness and healing in Chapter 5, I do not find this to be at all surprising—women's religions excel at interpreting, sacralizing, and curing illness. The importance of a history of illness for a religious leader is not the illness per se (except insofar as it makes her more understanding of her clients' illness and suffering[10]), but rather her triumph over illness. Female religious leaders with a history of illness dramatize and personify the existential claim that suffering is not inherent to the human condition.

The reported reluctance of the leaders to take up the mantle of leadership demands a different sort of explanation. As I demonstrate later on in this chapter, the status of female religious leaders tends to be ambiguous because none of these religions is located in a truly nonsexist society. The fact that in many situations the potential leader is chosen (or even harassed) by the gods and does not herself choose the specialist role is a solution for female leaders who do not wish to openly challenge prevalent sexist norms. This is consistent with what we have said about gender ideologies in the previous chapter. I find it interesting that even in those women's religions in which leaders are highly respected, they rarely take credit for their own skills or achievements. Esther Pressel quotes one Umbanda medium as telling her that she does not know how to heal on her own, "I do things my spirits tell me, but I myself do not know how to perform them" (1974, 152). Mexican Spiritualist healers also deny credit for their healing, although they do demand that patients obey their healing instructions.

Finally, a few words are in order concerning the types of women who become religious leaders. In Table 5, I have summarized twelve of the most common character traits of leaders in women's religions. Several of these traits warrant further comment. First, many religious leaders are especially gifted musicians, orators, or actresses. These talents are necessary for religious specialists who excel at possession trance; they must be adept at portraying the various spirits and gods, many of whom are male or in other ways very different from the possessed woman herself.

Second, the leaders seem to be both especially intelligent and especially intuitive and empathetic. I find it interesting that psychologists have noted that these two attributes tend to go together, especially in girls. Sharon Conarton and Linda Silverman, in the context of a book on feminist psychotherapies, contend that: "Bright children in particular have high degrees of emotional sensitivity, and are likely to show compassion for others even as toddlers. . . . The gifted

Table 5.   *Traits of Women Religious Leaders*

Empathy: A *zār* leader is thought to be one who "really understands" (Kahana 1985, 133). Korean shamans are typically highly sensitive to intuitive cues of others, and excel at interpersonal skills.

Rapport: The most important attribute of a Christian Science practitioner is rapport with her patients. Despite the fact that practitioners send bills to their patients, the affective ties between the two are extremely important (Fox 1989).

Kindness: Afro-Brazilian mediums must be loving, kind, patient, motherly, and pure (Lerch 1980; 1982).

Intelligence: Korean shamans tend to be unusually intelligent (Harvey 1979).

Age: On the Ryūkyū Islands younger women typically show less interest in their role as *kaminchu* than older women. Older priestesses seem to have their thoughts and attention on spiritual matters, and behave and speak differently from other people.

Eloquence: Common characteristics of Korean shamans include intelligence, ability to improvise, verbal fluency and persuasiveness, goal orientation, sensitivity and intuition, calculating and manipulative interpersonal skills, a sense of justice, artistic talent, and physical attractiveness (Harvey 1979). A characteristic shared by most Christian Science practitioners is eloquence (Fox 1979). Christian Science healing is carried out through verbal exchange. Richards (1973, 72) has found that Sande leaders are women who are gifted in the traditions of the group and are great religious and moral leaders who employ myths and mysteries in explaining phenomena.

Acting ability: The Spiritualist medium role necessitated the ability to represent or speak for spirits. Many mediums were fine actresses, able to enact the personae of a large number of spirit controls—both male and female.

Musical ability: *Zār* leaders tend to be particularly talented at drumming and remembering special songs for summoning spirits, and excel at entertaining, surprising, and thrilling their audiences (Kennedy 1978).

Poise: Afro-Brazilian priestesses are known for their poise. "Under her guidance there flourishes a realm of peace and security" (Lande 1935, 388). *Zār* leaders also tend to be self-confident people who have the ability to inspire confidence and hope in others (Kennedy 1978).

Courage: The prestige of the Afro-Brazilian medium stems from the fact that it is difficult to become and continue being a medium; it requires fortitude, courage, and the ability to withstand pain and suffering.

Authority: Senior priestesses in Afro-Brazilian religions are characterized by their sense of independence and power. Among senior priestesses possession was actually discouraged as they liked to think of themselves "as mastering the deities instead of serving them" (Landes 1947, 53–54). The Afro-Brazilian religions teach that the gods use misfortune to punish people, and priestesses know how to manipulate the gods to cure. Gods are considered whimsical and unreliable (Landes 1940, 267). Priestesses ("mothers" in Bahia) are considered far more reliable, and know how to control the Gods.

Competitiveness: Modern Spiritualist mediums tend to be competitive, exhibitionistic, and manipulative (Macklin 1977).

female usually excels at taking care of others. Her antennae may be . . . [especially] attuned to the needs of others" (1988, 45–47). Given that many of the women religious leaders excel at spirit possession (see Chapter 9), it is interesting to note that David Gutmann has found that **men** whose TAT (Thematic Apperception Test) scores indicate strong ego boundaries also tend to score high on other measures of morale, social effectiveness, and mental energy. For **women,** on the other hand, he found a trend in the opposite direction: Women whose TAT scores showed weaker ego boundaries (please recall that in Chapter 9 I connected weak ego boundaries to the ability to become possessed by spirits) "often achieved top scores on interview rating of contentment and effectiveness, and they achieved notably higher scores than women with a more 'masculine' style—that is, women who approached the TAT in a reasonable, delaying and boundary maintaining fashion" (1965, 231). Put differently, women who excel at spirit possession might very well be women who are generally competent and strong—in other words, good leaders.

Third, many women religious leaders take up the mantle of leadership in old age. Regarding new Japanese religions, Kyoko Motomochi Nakamura makes the point that mature foundresses "have experienced the whole life cycle of a woman, having lived as a girl, a wife, a mother, and sometimes a divorcee or widow. . . . Nine times out of ten the women founders have lived dramatic lives of material as well as spiritual oppression; their own suffering allows them to attain a most penetrating insight into the sufferings of others" (1980, 141). It is far from coincidental that most Japanese foundresses began to preach after their children were grown and their husbands' (and, I may add, children's) demands on their time had lessened (cf. Sered 1987; Sered 1991a). As I suggested in Chapter 7, few wives and mothers are able to (choose to?) abandon their family responsibilities to pursue extraordinary religious paths.[11] Moreover, religious leadership roles (and especially healing roles) allow women to continue to use mothering skills in a postmaternal period of life (Koss-Chioino 1992, 20).

And finally, almost all of the traits I have summarized are indicative of knowledge or talent rather than of authority. In many women's religions what we seem to find is more of a specialist or expert role than a true leadership role. With the glaring exception of Sande, very few of the "leaders" of women's religions exercise much direct control over the lives of other participants. This is consistent with the growing literature on the more cooperative leadership style of American women ministers and rabbis (cf. Simon, Scanlan, & Nadell 1993). I would especially note Edward Lehman's study of mainstream Protestant ministers in which he found that men were more willing than women to use coercive power over the congregation whereas more women ministers sought to empower their congregations (1993).

LEADERS AND GAIN

A familiar theme in the literature on women and religion is that women gain—materially or emotionally—by becoming leaders. A great deal of this literature focuses on psychological issues—women use religious leadership to compensate for deprivation experienced in other aspects of life. (I have argued against this model in Chapter 2.) Some writers have proposed even narrower compensation models: Becoming a religious leader allows a small number of women to reap economic gains. I have not found this explanation convincing. Quite to the contrary, few leaders in women's religions seem to accumulate real financial benefits.

For example, Spiritualist mediumship was one of the few career opportunities open to women in the nineteenth century, and opponents of Spiritualism accused mediums of tricking clients out of money. However, according to Laurence Moore (1977, 108), few mediums became rich. Not all mediums even demanded payment in return for their services (although most were willing to accept it). Spiritualist believers were unlikely to give regular financial support to mediums, and the role of permanent minister was generally unavailable. In fact, many mediums ended their careers as paupers, alone and destitute.

Like Spiritualism, Christian Science offered women leadership opportunities at a time when almost no other religious denominations did so. Christian Science practitioners theoretically can make a living from their healing work, yet a recent study suggests that most make very little money from their healing practices (Fox 1989).

Neither do Burmese *nat* shamans make sufficient money from conducting rituals for this to be seen as a reason for a woman to become a shaman. Korean shamans, on the other hand, do charge for their services, and the money earned by a shaman is often the difference between abject poverty and some degree of financial independence. However, studies do not indicate that Korean shamans ever become wealthy.

More meaningful benefits seem to lie in the realm of relationships. June Macklin (1977) argues that being a Spiritualist medium allows one to redefine and reorganize events in a way that ensures some control over important relationships with family members. Becoming a professional medium provides an acceptable escape route to some women who are unhappy with their husbands and domestic life. Laurence Moore concludes that mediumship offers a deliverance from boredom, marital abuse, and loneliness. "Mediumship was an occupation not often pursued by women who enjoyed physical well-being, economic security, a happy family and social life, and sexual fulfillment" (1977, 129; for my critique of sexual frustration theories see "Conclusion," p. 279). Spiritualist culture gave women possibilities for attention, mobility, and status denied elsewhere, and possibilities for circumventing rigid gender norms. The professional medium had far greater opportunities for travel and adventure than other American women.

Patricia Lerch (1982) found that Umbanda spirit mediums reported satisfaction with their role for a number of reasons: listening to other peoples' problems teaches how to deal better with one's own, pleasure from being able to help troubled people, having a purpose in life, recovery from lingering illness, and a steadying influence that their possessing spirits had brought to their own lives. According to Esther Pressel, "the mastery of [their] personal difficulties is a type of self-reward" (1974, 205). Only for a very few people is the role financially rewarding, and even they do not become rich from it. The rewards are more subtle: freedom to leave the house and socialize, respect for unselfishly helping others, a social life at the Umbanda Center, the attention one receives while possessed, and the fun and drama of the rituals. Other advantages of being an Umbanda medium include prestige (clients think of them as having access to super-human wisdom), power (by being at the center of a client network a medium can offer clients practical help through reallocating resources, goods, and services), and modest economic benefits that can supplement, although not usually replace employment (Lerch 1982).

These examples indicate that three of the most important gains experienced by leaders of women's religions are **enhanced spiritual talents and insights, increased success at dealing with relationships, and the possibility of acquiring some of the social advantages normally available only to men**.

Becoming a shaman in Korea leads to a reversal of power within the family. "Such a radical role reversal is possible only where players temporarily suspend the conventional order of things in favor of a new order of reality imposed by a power transcending the man-made social order. The agent of this transcendental power is the *mudang* [shaman]" (Wilson 1983, 125). Once the diagnosis of possession sickness has been accepted, a number of changes take place in the family dynamics. First, the victim's in-laws no longer accuse the victim of faking illness to avoid work. And, once the in-laws accept her calling, the victim no longer accuses her in-laws of causing her illness. Since both the woman and her family are now seen as fellow victims of supernatural actions, they bond together to begin to deal with and benefit from the changed situation. The former dyadic relationship between the in-marrying victim and her in-laws is transformed into a triadic relationship involving the spirits who must be consulted about any actions involving the victim. The "victim," of course, is the only one who has direct access to the spirits, so her position in the family is enhanced. Further strengthening her position is the fact that the possessing spirits are often ancestral ghosts from her husband's lineage.

When a Korean woman takes on the role of shaman, other members of her family take over her former household responsibilities. In some cases the housework and childcare are assumed by female relatives; in other cases the husband needs to become involved in household chores and childcare. Typically, once a woman becomes a shaman—communicating with the spirits, financially independent, newly self-confident—roles within the family are transposed, with the shaman functioning as the household head. A Korean shaman experiences the freedom and power normally found in the male domain. According to Wilson, the shaman may wish that she could have been born a man, but "Not penis envy, she wanted power and has acquired it now as a healer" (Wilson 1983, 124). He quotes one Korean shaman: "When I die, I want to be a male spirit. I want to be a great general like the Spirit General so I can lead hundreds of thousands of people" (1983, 122).

STATUS

Leaders operate within cultural contexts that are, to a greater or lesser extent, patriarchal. Women religious leaders—women who are recognized as being in some way more powerful than most people—threaten patriarchal structures and ideologies. Thus, for example, opponents of Christian Science, both in the nineteenth and twentieth centuries, focused their attacks on Mary Baker Eddy (and especially Eddy as a woman) more than on the teachings. On the other hand, within the religion, a great deal of respect accrues to the successful practitioner, and Christian Science practitioners are well esteemed in their church communities.

Korea: A Case Study

The ambiguous position of women leaders in female-dominated religions located in patriarchal societies is illustrated by the Korean shaman. There are two words describing this role: *mansin* and *mudang*, one polite and one derogatory. The two words reflect a cultural situation in which the power of the shaman is scorned by men, but understood and utilized by women. Wilson makes the connection between the systematized oppression of women and the image of shamans in Korea. "The stereotype of *mudang* as ignorant, irrational, perverse creatures is but an extension of the Confucian stereotype for *all* Korean women. The *mudang* dares put her 'ignorance' and 'irrationality' on display, in dramatic form, for all to see and hear" (1983, 126). On the other hand, at the Korean *kut* ritual,

> Garbed in the red robes of an antique general or wielding the Spirit Warrior's broadsword as she drives malevolent forces from her path, the Korean *mansin* [shaman] claims an imposing presence. Even in everyday dress and sprawling comfortably on the heated floor of her own home, she speaks with authority. By virtue of the powerful gods who possess her, she can summon up divination visions and probe the source of a client's misfortunes, exorcise the sick and chronically unlucky, remove ill humors from those who have difficulty finding mates, and coax a reluctant birth spirit into an infertile womb. The professional shaman makes the gods and ancestors a vivid presence in the home; she spots them in her visions and gives them voice in trance (Kendall 1989, 138).

In ancient Korea there were both male and female shamans. Although ancient rulers most likely combined the roles of politician and shaman, these two functions were gradually differentiated. By the historical period female shamans outnumbered male shamans and political leaders were almost all male. Traditionally, female shamans have had three major functions: as priestesses they presided in national ceremonies, both agriculturally oriented ones and rites offered for the well-being and blessing of the royal family; as exorcists they were invited to drive out evil spirits and solicit the favor of the gods when there was a sickness in the family; and as diviners they foretold the future of the nation and of individuals.

A number of factors explain the overwhelming preponderance of female shamans in contemporary Korea. First, shamans were systematically removed from positions of national importance and driven underground and degraded. This led to the profession's becoming increasingly dominated by women; men had other more powerful and more appealing career options open to them.

Korean shamans have been able to obtain limited material and social benefits from spirit possession. Shamanism allows some women to escape from oppressive and stressful family situations, to form lucrative and satisfying careers, and to use their skills for socially recognized beneficial purposes. Women have few other ways of obtaining these (or similar) goals in Korean society. During the Yi Dynasty (1392–1910), whose founding fathers were neo-Confucianist scholars, Korean shamans were attacked for their "lewd" and deceitful practices. In the twentieth century both the Japanese colonial administration and the independent Korean government persecuted shamans for "superstitious" practices that are counter to modernity. More recently, the government once again has allowed shamanism, but shamans and their families are considered as having outcast status. Shamans, singing and dancing in public, have been disliked by Confucians, among other reasons because they do not behave in the proper, modest female manner. Officials have labeled shaman's activities as fraudulent, and endeavored to protect the public from being "duped" (Kendall, personal communication 1992).

A second reason for the preponderance of female shamans stems from the fact that within the home Korean women have been responsible for dealing with the same sorts of ghosts and spirits that shamans call on. Women—housewives and shamans—deal with the restless and potentially dangerous dead.

Despite centuries of persecution, shamans have continued to play an important role in national ceremonies. Kendall notes that in the village that she studied shamans are hired to make an annual offering to the community tutelary god, to exorcise malevolent forces, and (before water pumps became available) to petition the rain dragon during droughts (1985, 31). Her description of the activities of Korean shaman also includes numerous small-scale, institutionalized, domestic rituals (such as lunar calendrical rituals) on behalf of children and other family members. In short, Korean shamans are at one and the same time community priestesses and community outcasts.

In the following pages I present two models that describe the statuses of women religious leaders. These two models are not absolutes, however, and many leaders experience both models, either sequentially or simultaneously (one at the hands of their adherents and one at the hands of the society at large). What I see as especially interesting in both models is the role of the leader's sex in accounting for the status accorded her.

Model 1—Persecution

Social ostracism was often the fate of Spiritualist mediums, and many mediums were repudiated by their families. Professional mediums were criticized for abandoning the traditional female domestic role, and (justifiably or not) for promiscuity. The history of the latter half of the nineteenth century shows growing legal restrictions placed on mediums. Mediums were sometimes arrested (on various charges), and the increasing institutionalization of the medical profession cut into the demand for medium healers.

The life of a Spiritualist medium was not easy. "It was difficult at best to maintain professional status on traits universally recognized as qualities of physical and intellectual weakness, even if they did imply moral superiority [see Chapter 10]. . . . Seance goers often treated a private medium, because of her passiveness, as an unimportant intermediary, to be praised if things went well, but only for her strange gifts rather than for her trained skills. A good sitting might save the medium a scolding, but not necessarily the humiliation of being bound, gagged, and searched to insure proper 'test conditions' " (Moore 1977, 119). The ritualistic testing of Spiritualist mediums for fraudulence should be interpreted both in terms of sex and class. When working-class women mediums were bound with leather straps and locked in cabinets by upper-class men "the motif of male mastery surfaced. . . . Female powerlessness was especially evident in these bondage rituals and it is possible that male spirit aggression [by female mediums] was a partial response to this enforced denigration" (Owen 1981, 231).

The case of Spiritualist mediums is not unusual. According to Procter-Smith, Shaker founder Mother Ann Lee was persecuted as a **female** religious leader. She was accused of being a witch and a destroyer of families, both of which are common charges against powerful women (1985, 19; cf. Barstow 1986 on Joan of Arc; Wessley 1978 on the founder of the Guglielmites). Lee was also accused of harlotry, drunkenness, and an assortment of other crimes. She and her followers were beaten and driven out of their homes in a number of towns. Finally, Mother Ann was tied by the heels behind a wagon and dragged for several miles over an icy road. She died from these and other injuries in 1784. It is significant that much of the public criticism leveled against the Shakers focused on derogatory depictions of Ann Lee **as a woman**. "People were outraged by what they thought of as the popery of celibacy, which threatened to break up families. But they were even more incensed at the idea of full equality of women with men, which clearly struck at the roots of family and society, neither of which recognized anything approaching a legal autonomy of women" (Whitson 1983, 15). Thus, in different ways, Lee's gender was relevant both to her followers and their detractors. For her followers, Lee was the female completion to the male Jesus (see Chapter 10); for her detractors she was the epitome of a woman who rejected the subordinate role deemed as "natural" by the society of her day.[12]

In Burma, female *nat* shamans are sometimes believed to be sexually promiscuous. Being loved by a *nat* means having [metaphorical] sexual relations with him, and shamans dance in public—possessed, wildly, and with abandon. In the Burmese village studied by Melford Spiro, 60% of the male population believe that all shamans are dishonest and 30% believe that most are dishonest. Women, on the other hand, believe that shamans are honest, but still have a low opinion of them. Mothers have been known to beat their daughters to try to prevent their marrying *nats*. Shamans themselves seem to share these cultural attitudes. Again, let me stress that in the charges leveled against these shamans, the fact they that are female is central—they are accused of **sexual** promiscuity.

Model 2—Respect and Honor

In contrast to the previous examples in which leaders were accused of witch-craft, promiscuous sexuality, and breaking up families, the status of Sande leaders is consistently high. They are believed to possess powers greater than those of regular mortals. These very independent women usually have hus-bands and children in the outside world, yet disappear for weeks, months, or even years into the Sande bush schools, where their power is near absolute. When they leave the Sande bush, their elevated status carries over into village life.

Similarly, Gehan Wijeyewardene relates that nineteenth century female Thai mediums came from high-status groups, upper-class elites, and royalty. Wijeyewardene cites a description of Princess Ooboon Lawana (sister-in-law to the chief), who "was called upon to question the spirits whenever any difficulty occurred either in public or private affairs" (1986, 154). This same woman was also a large-scale trader. In modern times, urban "mediums and clients, particularly regular clients, describe the relationship as a total one, almost like that of devotee to deity" (1986, 163). Male monks in Thailand are highly respected, and on the face of it, female mediums do not seem to com-pete with or contest monks. Yet "in their own view, they seem covertly to be challenging the status of monks" (Wijeyewardene 1986, 184). Some mediums suggest that the rituals of monks are inadequate, or similar to their own rituals. The medium may even see herself as filling a role that is yet more demanding than that of the monk. A monk can leave the order, but a *caw* [spirit] may not allow his horse [medium] to leave.

Also on the Ryūkyū Islands the status of the *noro* (priestess) is high—they are a sort of peasant aristocracy. Villagers stand in awe of the *noro,* and treat them with respect. Douglas Haring conducted fieldwork on Amami Island where priestesses wear white robes and head cloths, silver and feathered ornaments, and a sacred necklace of rock crystal beads interspersed with curved semipre-cious stones believed to be magically potent. One of Haring's informants recalled that in his childhood the *noro* would ring bells on the mountains all night "and the people thought the gods had come down" (1953, 113). Priest-esses on Okinawa, according to William Lebra, are always seen as working for the benefit of the community and not in their own self-interest (1966).

On Okinawa the impressively dressed chief priestess was spiritual head of the island, and perceived as the earthly abode of one of the most important gods. The chief priestess was also involved in secular affairs of state. Lebra cites accounts by Chinese and Japanese visitors to Okinawa in which the chief priestess is described as being above the king in rank, and in which priestesses judge and punish crimes.[13] A high level of theological sophistication character-izes many priestesses: speculation about the nature of the cosmos "seem often to be objects of discussion among the priestesses who are in charge of ritual affairs" (Mabuchi 1968, 135).

During the time of the Okinawan Kingdom, the *noro* were a female theoc-racy with enormous influence at court. With privatization of land under Japanese rule during the last century, however, many *noro* lost their traditional agricultural land and economic independence. The land reforms of 1899–1903 under Japanese rule placed their land in the hands of male relatives. **The evidence indicates that it was the Japanese, not the local Ryūkyūans, who chipped away at the priestesses' power base.**

According to Ruth Landes, in Bahia, Brazilian people may complain about the high fees of the priestesses, but have no doubt about their abilities. Clients and mediums evince a great deal of respect for the priestesses, begging blessings from them, averting their gaze, and speaking very softly in their presence. "Trained to rule independently, she [the priestess] has developed into a type of matriarch that is not only unique in modern times but is anachronistic in patriarchal Brazil" (1940, 268). Priestesses call themselves by the names of their gods rather than by the names of their husbands to show their personal independence—that they belong to the god or goddess and not their husbands.

In the Brazilian case it is crucial to take into consideration issues of class. Diana Brown found that in Umbanda, lower-class women frequently become mediums and leaders and can achieve positions of considerable local influence. Lower-class men, in contrast, are relatively more powerless in Umbanda. In the middle-class sectors, leadership roles for women are rarer and men tend to predominate. This finding leads us to consider the intersection of gender and class in women's religions. In Sande, on Okinawa, and in nineteenth-century Thailand women religious leaders came from the elite classes and were treated with extraordinary respect; in Brazil, contemporary Korea, and the *zār* region women religious leaders come from lower socioeconomic classes and are treated ambivalently. This contention is strengthened by Margery Wolf's analysis of a low-status Taiwanese village woman who began to display shamanistic behavior; although she had many of the attributes of a successful shaman, she was eventually labeled crazy "because of her marginal status in the community and in the male ideology" (1990, 419).

MEN AND LEADERSHIP

Given that the theme of this book is women's religions, it is somewhat of a tautology to point out that most leaders are women. A more interesting question is whether there any men who are leaders, and if so, what are their roles. We can discern five patterns of specialist roles for men.

Pattern 1: Gender Reversal

On the Ryūkyū Islands there are male ritualists called *uranai* who are diviners and fortune tellers. When performing rituals, they dress and talk like women. In modern Korea almost all professional shamans are women; the few men are marginal and, until recently, dressed in women's clothing. Melford Spiro (1967) found that in Burma many male shamans were homosexuals. Similarly, Edison Carneiro has discovered that Afro-Brazilian priests in Bahia try to assimilate the ideal type of priestesses, acting in a feminine manner and being homosexual (1940). And Gehan Wijeyewardene notes that urban Thai male mediums are often homosexual or transvestites. Some are blatant in their adoption of women's clothing and few are married to women (1986).

In women's religions, where (as we saw in the Chapter 10) ideologies of gender difference tend to be highly elaborated, leadership is so totally associated with female characteristics that a man must "become" female in order to take on leadership roles. This pattern is particularly significant because it is not a common one (in reverse, of course) in male-dominated religions. While celibacy for women is encouraged in certain male-dominated religions, I know of no instances in which women who are religious leaders are expected to dress like men or become lesbians. In Judaism, for example, women are explicitly forbidden to wear men's clothing, and women who become religious leaders are typically women who excel at female (not male) tasks.[14]

Pattern 2: Shared Leadership

Mother Ann Lee shared leadership with her brother William and her adopted son James, and Shaker organization insists on a woman and a man at each level of leadership. At Christian Science Sunday services two readers—almost always a man and a woman—lead the service. Again, this pattern is not a common one in male-dominated religions, where women may have roles as assistants but rarely as equal partners in leadership. In Catholicism, for example, nuns are not the structural equivalents of priests, and there is no woman sharing the papal throne at the Vatican. And to take an even more extreme example, in Islam there are no formal leadership roles for women whatsoever.

Pattern 3: Secular Administrators and Scribes

In a number of the women's religions men hold important secular positions as administrators. Men in Afro-Brazilian religions serve as *ogans* (providers) who pay for ceremonies, keep the cult house in repair, and, if necessary, defend the cult before the police. Women are the spirit mediums, but men are in charge of the finances and the organization. On the Ryūkyū Islands there are men who represent the village in dealing with the priestesses—these men raise money from villagers to support the cult, and take care of the cult's finances. In Christian Science women predominate as practitioners and men predominate in the higher-paying administrative jobs in the organization. A variation on this pattern is men who specialize in writing books and religious tracts. (See Chapter 12 for a discussion of the role of sacred writings.) In particular, among Spiritualists and in the Afro-Brazilian religions, men seem to be tremendously prolific writers.

This third pattern is also uncommon in male-dominated religions, where women are typically excluded from both administrative and spiritual leadership positions. To take an example from modern Israel, women have been prohibited from serving on municipal religious councils—bodies that perform purely secular functions of allotting and overseeing finances for religious institutions.

It could be argued that if men govern the financial and bureaucratic aspects of the religion, it is not really female dominated. Therefore, I have been careful to include in this book religions with a male/female–administrative/spiritual mode of leadership only when the administrative side is not believed to be more important than the spiritual side **and** when the male administrators do not have the power to control the actions or beliefs of the female practitioners.

The absence of patterns 2 and 3 (in reverse) in male-dominated religions reflects the reality that male-dominated religions occur in cultures in which gender inequality is consistently a matter of male dominance and female subordination. Male leadership is perceived as natural, right, and complete; there is no need to share leadership with women. In contrast, women's religions occur in cultures in which there is at least some degree of male dominance and female subordination. Thus female leadership is treated somewhat ambivalently, and certain sorts of roles are reserved for men.

A somewhat unusual case is that of the Black Spiritual churches in the United States. According to Hans Baer, "Because of the disproportionate number of female members [women may outnumber men by a ratio of as high as 43:7], women in Spiritual churches generally make concerted efforts to encourage males to belong, often by granting them religious offices. Spiritual women generally are not interested in establishing matriarchal congregations, but rather sexually egalitarian ones. In order to induce males, often their spouses, sons, nephews, and brothers, to join, they may make certain concessions that may eventually culminate in males attempting to assert dominance (Baer 1993, 77). Again, we would not expect to find the reverse situation in male-dominated religions for the simple reason that in patriarchal societies men would be unlikely to make concessions in order to include women in their religious organizations. Women's presence would not be necessary to legitimate the religion; quite to the contrary, the exclusion of women (who are, by definition in patriarchal societies, of secondary status) can be used as a symbol of the high status of a religious group.

Pattern 4: Assistants

Men serve as holders of priestesses' umbrellas in Okinawa. In the Afro-Brazilian cults men drum while female mediums dance and enter trance.[15] This pattern—men as specialist assistants to women leaders—is the only one with widespread parallels in male-dominated religions. To women who have cleaned the altars in Catholic churches, arranged the flowers in Protestant churches, and prepared the cakes and cookies for *kiddush* at Jewish synagogues, this pattern is easily recognized. In women's religions the men who become religious specialists are typically men of low status, and their status is not enhanced by becoming assistants to the priestesses or shamans. Given the generally sexist orientations of the societies in which these religions are situated, assistant to a leader in a female-dominated religion is not a high-prestige job for men.

Pattern 5: Animal Sacrifice

The oddest pattern that I have discovered is that in the small number of women's religions that practice animal sacrifice, men perform the actual killing. This is true in Thailand, in certain Afro-Brazilian cults, and in *zār* initiation rituals. For example, Boddy points out that in *zār* sacrifice it is the *zār* leader's **son** rather than the leader herself who actually sacrifices the animal (1989, 129). As I argued in Chapter 10, this most likely reflects the fact that in women's religions women are so thoroughly associated with life that it is appropriate for men to deal with death.

SOME COMPARISONS

Analysis of female religious leadership takes on meaning in the context of three types of comparisons: (1) women religious leaders versus men religious leaders, (2) women religious leaders versus women secular leaders (3) women religious leaders in female-dominated religions versus women religious leaders in male-dominated religions. We will now look at each of these in turn.

Women Religious Leaders versus Male Religious Leaders

Although the differences between female religious leaders and male religious leaders are far from absolute, several trends merit comment. Women religious leaders, more than men, seem to straddle the public and the domestic spheres (Sered 1991). They use their homes as ritual spaces, they help other women deal with children and children's illnesses, and they officiate at rituals at which cooking and food are central elements.

Richard Hutch has summed up several other differences between male and female religious leaders. Women typically become leaders through a slow process of self-recognition, whereas men more often report a "once and for all" achievement during a single, identifiable stage of life. We have indeed seen that the life histories of many women leaders involve years of illness, visions, and struggling with the call of the spirits—a process that often begins in early childhood and only ends in old age (see Chapter 7). Hutch notes that women leaders are often concerned "with the internal processing of personal experience as a source of religious authority in itself" (1984, 159). For male leaders, the source of authority is more often external—education, ordination, centralized hierarchies. The material we have seen strengthens Hutch's observation. Particularly instructive is the case of the Korean shamans who use their own life stories to explicate the ritual troubles of clients.

Another difference between male and female religious leaders has been noted by Brita Gill. Writing about her own experiences as a Protestant minister in the United States, she refers to her "ministry of presence—a ministry that is oriented to individuals, not just to problems" (1985, 90). This certainly is in line with what we have described in this book. Male leaders, implies

Gill, are more concerned with rules, symbols, and knowledge. The association of women religious leaders with personal relationships rather than with
theology or organization is significant. We will return to this theme in the
next chapter.

A last way in which female religious leaders differ from male religious
leaders concerns their status in the society at large. Women who wish to
become religious leaders challenge patriarchal notions of women's place (subordinate) and women's role (familial). Not surprisingly, the model labeled above
as "persecution model" is far less common for male religious leaders (except
for founders of new religions).

Women Religious Leaders versus
Women Secular Leaders

Women religious leaders resemble women secular leaders in many ways. Both
sorts of leaders tend to attribute their success to outside factors: spirits, ancestors, easy exams, or lack of other qualified candidates, rather than to their own
innate ability or hard-earned achievements (Powell 1988, 107). This fits well
with the socialization of women to be subordinate.

For a woman to achieve a leadership position, whether religious or secular,
she needs to be known personally. Studies of gender and management have
shown that when strangers evaluate one another they consistently see men as
dominant, but when group members know one another, gender differences
tend to disappear (Powell 1988, 109). In women's religions leaders are personally known to their followers: the model of a priest who is sent or a rabbi or
minister who is invited from the outside to an unfamiliar congregation is not
one we have seen in women's religions. Female religious leaders tend to slowly
build up a clientele through word-of-mouth recognition. The example of
Christian Science practitioners illustrates this well.

Women Leaders in Female-Dominated Religions versus
Women Leaders in Male-Dominated Religions

The literature on women leaders within male-dominated religions shows both
similarities and contrasts to women leaders within female-dominated religions.
One common trait is an emphasis on healing. Illness and cure is a common
theme in the lives of women religious leaders both in female-dominated and
male-dominated religions (cf. Weinstein and Bell 1982 on Christian women
saints). Since in many cultures women are especially concerned with healing,
and healing and religion are often intertwined (see Chapter 5), this is not
surprising.

On the other hand, women leaders in male-dominated religions are, on the
whole, excluded from public leadership roles—and especially roles as ritual
officiants. The types of roles open to women in male-dominated religions tend
to be as teachers of children, assistants, nurses, and caretakers.[16] In female-
dominated religions, public ritual officiant roles **are** available to women leaders.

Studies show that women leaders in male-dominated religions often buy into the anti-female ideology of that religion. Weinstein and Bell, for instance, show that female Catholic saints "seem to have internalized the denigration of their sex's spirituality" (1982, 227). Female-dominated religions, on the other hand, typically celebrate or even exalt femininity (see Chapter 10).

Audrey Brown has conducted a particularly fascinating study of women and ritual authority in [male-dominated] African-American Baptist churches of rural Florida. In common with leaders of many female-dominated religions, the women leaders in the Florida churches are, for the most part, elderly, experts in fertility and childbirth, and involved in food rituals. On the other hand, she found that "Even though women are often better educated than males and frequently economically independent, it is their nurturing and sus-taining qualities that are glorified in church life. Female assertive behavior or aggressive leadership is discouraged and censured" (1988, 2). This is in dra-matic contrast to female-dominated religions where women leaders are typi-cally strong and articulate.

In addition, Brown found that many Baptist women leaders were aging wives of pastors. These women often had eight or more children. This clearly differs from leaders in many female-dominated religions, who more typically have lost some or even all of their children (see Chapter 4). It does seem that African-American Baptist women leaders express greater satisfaction with tra-ditional female roles than leaders of female-dominated religions do. And whereas the African-American women seem to have found Baptist theology and philosophy sufficient for interpreting their life experiences (e.g., marriage and many children), leaders of female-dominated religions do not find male-dominated theology and philosophy helpful for making sense out of their life experiences (e.g., child death).

In contrast to female-dominated religions where marital status is irrelevant, "Regardless of a woman's Christian virtue, she cannot become a [Baptist] dea-coness unless she is married to a deacon" (Brown 1988, 3). Here we note one of the most significant differences between the two categories of women religious leaders. Women leaders in female-dominated religions frequently inherit their roles from their mothers, often in the form of inheritance of the deceased mother's guardian or shamanic spirit. Women leaders in male-dominated reli-gions often acquire their roles by virtue of their husband's status: sometimes as the wife of a male leader and sometimes as the widow of a male leader. This distinction is particularly important. **The leader who inherits her position from her mother symbolizes both an independent, female chain of command and the centrality of motherhood in religious life.** As I argued in Chapter 3, this is consistent with the trend in female-dominated religious to address women primarily through their identities as mothers. **The leader who acquires her role through her husband symbolizes the tangential—even incidental—position of women on the male chain of command.** The spouse-of-the-leader model strengthens the bias toward addressing women through their identity as wife. As I argued in Chapter 3, the role of "wife" tends to be less autonomous and less empowering for women than the role of "mother."

Notes

1. Spiritism is a mixture of Spiritualism, Kardecism, folk Catholicism, and traditional folk healing.

2. The closest to nonhierarchical religions are those of the Black Caribs and the Feminist Spirituality Movement. Yet the former does seem to have a cadre of elderly women who are in charge of the rituals, and certain branches of the latter have priestesses and even high priestesses. It is of interest to note Karen Sacks's findings that among the North American Cheyenne, men's hunting societies were not hierarchical, while women's quilling and rawhide painting societies were hierarchical (1979, 80).

3. In the more traditional (more African) cults, communication with the supernatural is often through divination, which only the chief priestess knows how to do. The chief priestess divines by throwing cowrie shells into stated patterns that allow her to learn the will of the gods. Although the manner of interpretation of the cowrie shells is highly traditional, individual priestesses may prescribe different remedies.

4. The latter two roles were traditional; the first two were imposed by the government.

5. I thank Teigo Yoshida for helping me clarify the rather confusing terminology regarding contemporary priestesses (personal communication 1992).

6. A preliminary question here is which women in female-dominated religions can be considered leaders. In some religions the answer is clear: an explicit hierarchy exists and women at the top are the leaders (Shakers, Sande). A much thornier situation arises in the religions involving spirit possession. I would consider the Spiritualist medium to be a leader in the sense of a specialist with extraordinary skills and talents, although, as we see in this chapter, her status is not high and she does not organize a chapter or church. I would not consider women who dance at *zār* ceremonies to be leaders, because in many parts of Africa most women are initiated into the *zār* cult. For the *zār*, the leaders are women who are addressed by others as "leader" (*shaykha*). The most difficult decision concerns the Afro-Brazilian cults. In these cults there are certain women who are priestesses or in charge of cult centers. They are clearly leaders. Yet I am inclined to also treat the mediums as leaders, albeit on a lower level, both because (unlike in the *zār* cult) most people do not become mediums, and because mediums are consulted for healing advice.

7. Western scholars claim that the difference between priestesses and *yuta* in the Ryūkyū Islands is that the former concentrate on public rituals and the latter on private rituals. It appears, however, that there may be far more overlap between Ryūkyūan priestesses and shamans than meets the casual eye. For example, all Ryūkyūans belong to kin-groups, each of which has a woman *kaminchu* who attains office by virtue of being born on a high spiritual level. Her identity is detected by the older women of the kin-group and **confirmed by a shaman**. On the Ryūkyūs it is quite common for a woman to begin as an *ukudi* or family priestess and **then** also become a *yuta*. The priestess and shaman systems on Okinawa tend to interpenetrate in the person of the kin-group priestess, who frequently is also a shaman.

Hisako Kamata convincingly argues that the distinction between *yuta* and *noro* may be a late development. She notes that the practice of closing the eyes and shaking the head up and down is common to both *yuta* and *noro*. Even of greater interest is her discovery that because divine possession is evidence of eligibility for the *noro* role, it sometimes happens that the same women are priestesses presiding over village rituals and festivals in one village, yet are regarded as *yutas* in other villages. Evidence is also cited that suggests that in the past both men and women were *yutas,* and that the status of *yutas* was much higher than at present. They worked for the government as custodians of oral history and possessors of knowledge (1966, 62).

Similarly, Yoshinobu Ota has studied the southern Ryūkyū Islands and found that certain women experience series of traumatic illnesses that lead them to consult a shaman. The shaman may interpret the illness as a sign that the woman was born with "high *shiji*"—a sort of enhanced spirituality. "This shaman will tell her that, in order to put an end to the recurring sickness, she must become either a priestess or else a shaman" (1989, 115). Ota relates life stories of three priestesses and one shaman, and all the stories are rather similar in terms of illness and initial resistance to the calling.

8. Skultans (1983, 18), on the other hand, suggests that the connection between the death of one's father and mediumship may well have been financial—young women deprived of the economic support of their fathers were more in need of pursuing paying careers. Few other paying careers were open to women in the mid-nineteenth century.

9. It then became customary for a *noro* to be succeeded by her brother's daughter. In more recent times the position is succeeded by the son's wife (Shimabukuro Gen'ichiro quoted in Kamata 1966, 59).

10. For example, Korean shamans explain that their own personal deprivations as women allow them to identify with their clients—clients' problems are similar to ones they themselves have already worked through (see Wilson 1983).

11. I. M. Lewis interprets the high involvement of older and infertile women in possession cults in terms of their cultural status of "half-men" (since, non-fertile, they are no longer fully female). According to Lewis, this is what underlies the androgynous character frequently attributed to the leaders of peripheral cults (1971, 95). While I agree with most of Lewis's ideas, in this case I am far from convinced by his interpretation. It seems to me more likely that women without small children are able to become leaders because they have greater control over their time. I am also not convinced that women religious leaders are androgynous in any very deep sense. Rather, because in most cultures leadership is defined as a male trait, when a woman becomes a leader she looks as if she has adopted a male role. However, the data that I present in this book demonstrate that women religious leaders do not copy male modes of leadership, male identities, or male character traits.

12. Humez argues that even among Lee's followers gender was a problematic issue. "Shaker manuscript records for the first thirty years of the nineteenth century abound in evidence of continuing male rebellion against female headship" (1992, 89).

13. "It was apparently this state of affairs that led a Chinese traveler in 1683 to assume that there were no courts of law, since he observed no male judges" (Lebra 1966, 102).

14. Catholic nuns do in a sense abandon their femaleness, but they do not acquire male gender roles. Among the Bimin-Koskusmin of New Guinea, some older women ritually become men (or really androgynous) in order to be ritual leaders (Poole 1981).

15. According to Esther Pressel, the few male Umbanda mediums tend to be young, and as they age either drop out or become center directors looking after the financial affairs of the center. In some newer Afro-Brazilian groups there are men who are in charge ("fathers") who have a very low status both socially and religiously and who do not command the respect that the "mothers" command. In centers run by a man, women still retain important functions. It is telling that criticism about "fathers" is always more venomous than about "mothers" and priests are often accused of being insincere, dishonest, or evil (see Carneiro 1940).

16. In certain male-dominated religions there are other roles—for example, ascetic, temple dancer—that are sometimes available to small numbers of exceptional women.

12 ⨪

Women, Sacred Texts, and Religious Organization

UNCENTRALIZED AND UNSTANDARDIZED

None of the women's religions is nonhierarchical, and, as we have already seen, many have well-articulated systems of internal ranking. On the other hand, very few of the religions are organized around a central authority or even a roof organization that incorporates all chapters, temples, branches, or groups. Related to the absence of centralized authority, there is frequently an absence of obligatory rituals, sacred scripture, and uniform dogma. I will argue that interest in preserving and enforcing compliance to written doctrines is linked to a political agenda (missionizing) and a theological vision (transcendence), neither of which is meaningful to women's religions, and both of which are often associated with patriarchal rule.

Women's religions, on the whole, do not emphasize members' exclusive compliance to one specific set of doctrines. A number of the religions dealt with in this book are one alternative within a culture in which it is common for individuals to participate in the rituals of, and believe the theologies of, more than one religion (Korean shamanism, Burmese *nat* religion, Spiritualism). In addition, many of these religions are internally eclectic, easily and consciously absorbing new ideas or deities (Feminist Spirituality, Spiritualism, Afro-Brazilian religions).

A case in point is North American Spiritualism. The Fox sisters, who are commonly referred to as the "founders" of Spiritualism, were not particularly involved in organizing the movement, nor were there other people who organized on their behalf or in their name. Nineteenth-century Spiritualism spread like wildfire with no institutional backing. Ironically, it seems likely that the efforts of journalists and Christian clergy to persuade the public **not** to participate in Spiritualist rituals actually served to publicize Spiritualism and entice people to try their hand at contacting the dead in many communities where there were no ongoing Spiritualist groups or high-powered mediums. "Not only did the [Spiritualist] movement have no orthodox doctrine; it had no membership because it had nothing for adherents to belong to. It had no official leadership because it had no offices for leaders to hold. Mediums received no training and no ordination" (Braude 1989, 8). The one attempt at national organization during the 1850s—the Society for the Diffusion of Spiritual Knowledge—did not succeed. According to Alex Owen (1981), Spiritualists were noted for their commitment to individualism and anti-authoritarianism. They were never interested in or successful at establishing central organizations.[1]

Scholars assert that Spiritualism never developed a genuine theological creed (cf. Macklin 1974). Spiritualists back away from official dogmas and compulsory laws; they stress the individual conscience and individual experience, and try to avoid authority over member's beliefs and behavior. Spiritualist theology is vague, nondogmatic, and constantly revealed and developing. The spirits themselves profess varying beliefs, and teach varying doctrines to different individuals and groups.

Within Spiritualist groups it has been common to add to resolutions a proviso that the resolution itself is not binding on anyone who does not like it. "Lacking coherence, most gatherings that claimed to explore the truths of spiritualism simply made diversity a virtue" (Moore 1977, 14). The history of Spiritualism underscores the connection among respect for the needs of the individual, absence of official doctrine, and lack of central authority or organization.

Afro-Brazilian cults are also characterized by a lack of centralized structures, and attempts to unify the movement have been weak and unsuccessful. It is of interest that men predominate in the external leadership positions within the various federations governing Umbanda activities in the cities and states. According to Patricia Lerch (1982), Umbanda's flexible organizational style allows local cult leaders and spirit mediums to adapt rituals to the specific needs of their cult followers. Among Umbanda leaders, there is frequently animosity and even attacks on each others' doctrines and rituals.[2] The real functioning units of structure in Umbanda are the individual ritual centers or temples. Again, we note that the absence of centralized organizational structures is associated with lack of mandatory rituals and beliefs. According to Diana Brown, "The ambiguities and complexities of Umbanda's cosmology, which form part of the ongoing dialectical process of its development, give it enormous flexibility of interpretation and permit different sectors with different interests to identify with it in different ways" (1986, 76).

The Afro-Brazilian cults are nonliterate religious systems (even if particular members and leaders know how to read), and each priestess constructs her ritual repertoire according to her own experiences, ideas, and inspirations. "The [Afro-Brazilian] Batuque today is far from being a completely systematized body of beliefs, and, at the rate it is still changing, this condition seems likely to continue. Batuque members seem rarely to be troubled by the lack of a highly rationalized theology, since their interest is usually pragmatic rather than philosophical. The lack of philosophical coherence may limit the Batuque's appeal to individuals with intellectual pretensions, but of course the very looseness and lack of rigid systematization of its theology provide one explanation for the ease with which new themes are absorbed" (Leacock and Leacock 1972, 320).

We will now look briefly at a few other examples that illustrate the lack of centralization which characterizes women's religions. In Northern Thai matrilineal spirit cults, fission is common when descent groups reach a large size (ten or more households). The new group has its own spirit, shrine, officiant, and its members are no longer "of the same spirit" as the old group. To ensure this separation, the new group holds its annual sacrifice on the same day as the original group, thus preventing double attendance. Parenthetically, we may add that by preventing double attendance, any kind of larger organizational system is avoided. "There are no nesting, hierarchical, or segmentary structures, nor any superordinate genealogical structures" (Turton 1976, 221). Let us recall that even the descriptions of the spirits in this religion are vague and contradictory (see Chapter 8).

Among the Black Caribs no one tries to compel conformity in beliefs about the dead. There is no formally organized priestly hierarchy, nor an officially defined dogma. Although ritual obligations are enforced, there is a great deal of variability in the manner of performance of rituals for the dead. Details vary according to the wishes of the ancestor who requested the ceremony and the resources of the sponsors. Dream experiences, for instance, are highly valued by the Black Caribs as a source of prophetic knowledge and a means of communicating with the dead. Inspiration for religious songs and all sorts of esoteric and non-esoteric knowledge comes from ancestral spirits through dreams (Coelho 1955, 139–140).

In a similar vein, *zār* ceremonies vary considerably according to the idiosyncrasies of the leader and the type of illness being treated. There is no central organization of any kind (Kennedy 1978). According to one observer, *zār* adherents and leaders emphasize that there are a variety of *zār* traditions, beliefs, and rituals (Kenyon 1991, 101).

This sort of self-conscious non-institutionalization also characterizes Korean women's religion. Whereas Confucianist ritual manuals have enabled male ancestor worship to become quite standardized[3], Korean women's rituals and shaman lore are learned through observation and oral transmission, and variation occurs from place to place. Korean shamans are initiated by and trained by more experienced shamans, but there is no official (or even unofficial) roof organization of shamans.

Each Sande chapter is autonomous, there is no centralized Sande organization, and cooperation among chapter leaders is informal. (Because local officials participate in rituals in other chapters, there is some informal integration.) The noncentralized organization of Sande is even more interesting when we learn that one of the most striking differences between Sande and Poro (the men's secret society parallel to Sande in almost all ways) lies in structure. According to Donald Cosentino, the structure of Sande is apt to be more pluralistic than that of Poro. A medium-sized town is likely to have several Sande chiefs, each conducting her own initiation classes, often at different times of the year. Poro structure, on the other hand, is far more centralized (1982, 23). This example is particularly important because it defuses the potential counter-argument that women's religions are noncentralized because so many of them are situated in societies in which **all** religion is noncentralized. If we review the examples I have presented, we see that a number of the noncentralized women's religions are situated in societies in which men's religions are highly centralized. The clearest examples are the women's religions that coexist with Catholicism or Buddhism.

Skipping both geographically and chronologically, we discover that "The beguines, the only [Christian] movement created by women for women before the modern period . . . [were characterized by] *lack* of leaders, rules, detailed prescriptions for the routine of the day or for self-regulation, *lack* of any overarching governmental structures" (Bynum 1984, 116). Please note the contrast to many other medieval monastic movements, with their detailed codes of behavior, vows, and organizational hierarchy.

Among Spiritual Feminists there is no central organization; small, even intimate, circles are the basic units of the Movement. The following remark by a Spiritual Feminist writer well sums up what I have demonstrated thus far: "In order to keep our theology supple and responsive to individual differences and changes, we must remember that all theology—all thinking about deities and godly powers—is done by individual people in particular situations. Human beings of different sexes, ages, races and environments have different experiences of spirituality and religious phenomena" (Goldenberg 1979, 115). Among Spiritual Feminists the organizational structure is, to say the least, loose. According to Naomi Goldenberg (1979, 140), "[P]eople probably do not have to enforce a standardized set of religious images on everyone in order to feel a sense of community." This preference for noncentralization is also true, for the most part, of the secular feminist movement. As Patricia Martin explains, feminist organizations tend to be local, and many discussions of feminist organizations suggest that only small organizations can be truly feminist. Face-to-face interpersonal exchange—one of the key ideological components of feminism—is more possible in organizations with fewer members (1990, 199).

In Chapter 6 I demonstrated that women's religions tend to be characterized by an accent on ritual rather than official doctrine. So far in this chapter I have shown that even the ritual complexes of women's religions are nonstandardized and idiosyncratic. The pivotal role of spirit possession in women's religions further contributes to the focus on individual experience instead of organization. I am impressed with the countless descriptions of spirit possession in which the observer writes that although the possessed woman (or man) enacts a standardized character, the individual injects a bit of her or himself to the role. For example, in the less traditionally African of the Afro-Brazilian religions, each medium adds personal touches (behaviors, bits of costumes, etc.) to the spirit or deity by whom she or he is possessed. Similarly, although each *zār* spirit has its own attributes (its own beat on the drum and sometimes its own costume), each host brings something unique to her performance, "For a spirit reveals different aspects of itself in various women" (Boddy 1989, 303).

Case Study: The Shakers

We will look at the Shakers at some length because they present a more complex case than the previous examples. Shaker history—which is far better documented than the histories of any of the other women's religions—exhibits a certain tension between centralized authority and local autonomy. Unlike the other examples I have cited, the Shakers did aspire to a centralized organizational structure; the community at New Lebanon had the status of "Mother Church;" and a great deal of time, energy, and resources were dedicated to travel and communication between Shaker villages (Stein 1992). Moreover, early Shakers (although not later Shakers) did not demonstrate the tolerance toward other beliefs and groups that characterizes most other women's religions. For example, Ann Lee's incarceration in Manchester followed her adamant condemnation of Anglicanism and her attempts to disrupt Anglican services. Two other points should be noted: During their early American period Shakers engaged in a great deal of missionizing, and Shakers have generated enormous amounts of written material.

Internal standardization of belief has not, however, always been a priority for the Shakers. Clarke Garrett has commented on one of the most important differences between the Shakers and earlier ecstatic Christian groups. "Other groups . . . were as dedicated to following the guidance of the Spirit as the Shakers were, but all of them . . . were constrained by a tacit biblicism that not even their prophets and visionaries overstepped. . . . The Shakers, on the other hand, had from the outset believed that the messages sent by the Holy Spirit could be in any form and could entirely supersede anything that Scripture had commanded for earlier generations. The fact that their techniques of inducing ecstacy in their worship services affected everyone present meant that everyone present had access to the prophetic 'gifts' that the Lord rained upon them" (1987, 195–196).

With the death of Ann Lee the Shakers experienced a shift from mixed female and male leadership (Ann Lee, William Lee, and James Whittaker) to male leadership—James Whittaker became her successor, together with a new emphasis on legalism and organization and the construction of a formal meetinghouse.[4] Writing about Whittaker's leadership, Garrett explains that "While he [Whittaker] accepted the power of the spirit that operated in the night-long meetings and fully believed that Ann Lee was divinely inspired, he was also concerned with creating a framework of order and discipline in which the Spirit would operate" (1987, 211). As Marjorie Procter-Smith shows, this had portentous implications for women. "Early Shaker worship was a matter of intimate and spontaneous contact with the Divine, manifested through various signs such as dancing and jumping. Shaker worship gradually became more institutionalized. In the beginning there was no preaching, sermon, little reading, no public prayer—just the Holy Spirit. Then, a sermon—only given by men—was added. Then a tune sung in unison was added. Then dancing in unison. Then a hymnbook. All this happened together with increasingly strict sexual segregation during worship. . . . **With the establishment of ordered**

worship came a corresponding reduction of women's public roles in Shaker worship" (1985, 139, my emphases).[5]

After Whittaker's death, Joseph Meacham took over Shaker leadership. According to Stephen Marini, "Consciously designed Shaker institutions were the creation of Joseph Meacham" (1982, 127). Under Whittaker's rule the Shakers were organized into an elaborate and all-inclusive hierarchy of members based on spiritual merit. "Father Joseph elaborated Mother Ann's practices into formal norms" (Marini 1982, 129). And Stephen Stein argues that "Meacham played the principal role in formulating the rules and regulations that governed membership in the society and the activities of the gathered Shakers" (1992, 45). In short, the evidence seems to suggest that standardization of Shaker ritual was implemented by men, to the detriment of women.[6]

Still, the Shakers never developed the strict uniformity of worship familiar to most Christians and Jews. The first collection of Shaker hymns, *Millennial Praises*, published in 1813, included in the Preface a note of warning that these songs should not be regarded as eternally useful, "for no gift or order of God can be binding on Believers for a longer term of time than it can be profitable to their travel in the gospel" (quoted in Stein 1992, 104).

Lucy Wright, who succeeded Meacham to Shaker leadership, "stubbornly refused" to gather "scattered rules into one set of regulations" (Stein 1992, 95). (This does not mean, however, that Wright was averse to issuing rules. According to Priscilla Brewer, Wright "continually issued new and revised directives, even from her death bed," personal communication 1992). Less than six months following her death in 1821, the new central ministry (which consisted of two men and two women) began circulating manuscript copies of the "Orders and Rules of the Church at New Lebanon." In the years following Wright's death, males increasingly dominated the Shaker central ministry (Stein 1992, 133).[7]

Yet even with the publishing of hymn books and rules, "Shakerism did not produce mindless conformity. Believers were able to establish a healthy individualism within the society" (Stein 1992, 149). Shakers were among those who embraced Spiritualism in the mid and late nineteenth century, and Shaker spiritualists "welcomed insight wherever it was found, whether in Eastern religious traditions, Christian Science, or harmonial philosophies" (Stein 1992, 323). Significantly, it seems that the period in which Shakers most clearly embraced eclectic beliefs coincides with the period in which "women were increasingly prominent in all aspects of the Society's life and leadership" (Stephen Stein, personal communication 1993).

Am I arguing that the greatest thrusts toward institutionalization in Shaker history occurred during the relatively brief periods in which men were the leaders? I am reluctant to make such a bold statement. The fact is that in the history of new religious movements it is common to find that the first generation of leaders makes use of personal charisma, leaving it to the second generation to standardize and codify (see Weber's 1966 [1922] discussion of charisma). Thus, one could argue that Whittaker's and Meacham's sex is irrelevant; rather, their place in Shaker chronology is what prompted them to work toward institutionalization of worship, beliefs, and interpersonal relationships.

On the other hand, I see it as extremely significant that although Lucy Wright sanctioned the **collection** of Shaker laws, she did not sanction their **publication**. While this difference may sound trivial, I insist that the importance of **written** codes should not be underestimated. Once laws are written down, they take on a life of their own; they become eternal, immutable, universal, and (often) more consequential than the individuals who live by and with them. Moreover, as we saw earlier (page 248), regarding the nineteenth century when the Shakers became much more of a truly female-dominated religion than they had been in earlier periods, historians have noted both a deceleration of the institutionalizing process and a new openness to other religious beliefs.

Men and Centralization in Women's Religions

The historical record shows over and over again situations in which the impetus for centralization and standardization in women's religions comes from the (often small number of) men. This was true for North American Spiritualism. It was also true in the Black Spiritual churches of New Orleans, where in the early days each congregation—almost always headed by a woman—was autonomous. In the early days Black Spiritual religion had been almost exclusively a woman's religion under women's leadership. When male leaders emerged in the 1930s, they (the men) formed national organizations in which men dominated. Today women still outnumber men at the level of local ministers, but the national organization is headed by a male archbishop and men outnumber women on the Executive Board (Jacobs and Kaslow 1991, 184). Jacobs and Kaslow attribute men's rise to organizational power in terms of their literacy at a time when formal education was unavailable to most women (1991, 185). According to Hans Baer, "It appears that men have headed the largest and most institutionalized associations in the Spiritual movement. . . . My ethnographic data suggest that women tend to serve as the heads of relatively small Spiritual associations, consisting of several congregations or independent congregations" (1993, 79).

Turning to an example we have not yet met, in the Harrist Movement in Ghana, "From the beginning, it was Nackabah [the male leader], rather than Madame Tani [the female leader], who was fascinated with the modes of organization, symbols of material progress, and activities of teaching and preaching" (1979, 111). Moreover, Paul Breidenbach notes that "Literacy is essential to the preaching master, while, in fact, I did not encounter a single healing prophetess who was literate" (1979, 111). We will return to the issue of texts and gender later on.

Two women's religions do not fit neatly into the pattern of noncentralized authority: Okinawan religion and Christian Science.[8] Until the Japanese annexation in 1879, the entire Okinawan kingdom was organized for religious as well as political ends, with an official, centralized hierarchy of hereditary priestesses (*noro*) in the villages, districts, and regions, and the chief priestess who was a close relative of the ruler and virtually his equal in rank.

This centralized hierarchy began with the unification of the Okinawan kingdom in the fourteenth century. Until that time, the religion was kin based and noncentralized. Based on the available historical sources, I speculate that the *noro* hierarchy was established as a means for implementing political centralization of the Okinawan kingdom. Evidence shows that **the move toward centralization did not come from the priestesses but from the male, secular leaders.** It is suggestive that despite centuries of official centralization, there continues to be a great deal of variation regarding the exact order to the principle rituals. Even within each island—often from house to house—there is diversity in terms of the precise enactment of the ritual cycle. Certain ceremonies only are observed in particular villages, and it is rare that the annual cycles of two villages completely coincide. Each village is believed by Okinawans to be unique, with its own god and customs. And Garland Hopkins (1951) has noted that Okinawans easily appropriate parts of new religions and rituals that meet their fancy.

SACRED WRITINGS

An Exception

The other centralized women's religion is Christian Science. Christian Science churches around the world belong to an organization that is controlled by the Mother Church in Boston, Massachusetts. Mary Baker Eddy founded the Mother Church so that Christian Science would be centralized, and she herself presided over the transformation from a charismatic into a bureaucratic church. Unlike most other women's religions, Christian Science strongly discourages experimentation with, participation in, or even study of other religions and healing paths. Christian Science is the final revelation and that is all people need to know.

Christian Science's centralized organizational structure is associated with an emphasis on sacred writings. The Mother Church publishes selected texts from Mary Baker Eddy's *Science and Health* and from the Bible, and these selections are read at all local churches on specific Sundays.[9] Church members are expected to study these texts during the preceding week—a set part of the text each day. Thus, not only do all Christian Scientists hear the same texts at the same time, but there is an expectation that individual members will devote time to developing a high-level understanding of Christian Science beliefs. Christian Science healing is often effected through study of *Science and Health*, and Christian Science Reading Rooms are located in many cities and towns.

As we said earlier, Mary Baker Eddy herself organized Christian Science around the central Mother Church. On the other hand, the current administrative leadership of Christian Science is almost all male. Margery Fox shows that while women predominate in the therapeutic roles of practitioner and nurse, men predominate as both administrators and lecturers (1989, 100). We may speculate that many of the differences between Christian Science and other women's religions stem from the fact that in Christian Science, unlike in most other women's religions, men are in charge of both administration and formal teaching.

Aversion to Sacred Texts

With the exception of Christian Science, women's religions are characterized both by an aversion to centralization and a lack of authoritative sacred texts. Let us bear in mind that despite the lack of emphasis on texts, almost all these religions exist in societies in which many (or most) people are literate. Northern Thai matrilineal cults, for example, have no written records of any kind, although literacy and papermaking technologies have been known in Thailand for many generations.

Similarly, Spiritualism arose in a highly literate culture, yet Spiritualists have no sacred scripture. Religious beliefs and practices are learned from more developed Spiritualist mediums. "In fact, there is a stigma attached to learning about spiritualism, especially mediumship and healing, from published material" (Skultans 1974, 3). In light of our discussion of how women's religions tend to reinterpret rather than challenge prevalent notions of gender (Chapter 10), it is of interest to point out that among nineteenth-century Spiritualists lack of education was treated as a "female" characteristic that made women especially suitable for mediumship. While it was certainly the case that formal education was unavailable to many if not most nineteenth-century women, it was also the case that women's ignorance was turned into a virtue by Spiritualists. An "empty slate" was considered the finest instrument for spirit communication.

The Ryūkyū Islands provide a particularly interesting case study here. William Lebra (1966) notes that small pieces of paper bearing written characters obtained from the male Buddhist priest and ashes from the hearth of the chief priestess are used as charms. Put differently, male Buddhist ritual specialists ward off misfortune through sacred writing; female indigenous ritual specialists ward off misfortune through cooking accouterments.[10]

Feminist Spirituality, on the other hand, is a highly literate religious movement. Each year dozens of new books—both novels and nonfiction—are published by feminist and mainstream presses. For many women who identify with Spiritual Feminism yet live in small towns where there is no Spiritual Feminist group, books and magazine articles serve as the sole means of participation in the Movement. Thus it is especially significant that there is no official sacred scripture or a required litany of rituals that must be performed in a standardized fashion. The prolificacy of Spiritual Feminism is not part of a campaign to create uniformity of belief.

As we already have seen, in their early days the Shakers did not have any printed prayers, songs, or regulations, because they believed that a static tradition would prevent the continuing inspiration of the Spirit. Shakers felt themselves to be in the process of developing important new doctrines—even their theology was treated by them as inherently changeable. They believed that during their worship services people received direct messages from the spirit world. The Bible was not their only source of revelation, and Biblical texts were not used to prove their doctrines. Shakerism is centered on religious experience and not doctrine or creed, and it is of theological significance to Shakers that founder Ann Lee was illiterate. According to Sally Kitch, "Lee's illiteracy was sometimes seen as a possible link to Jesus; like her, Jesus left no written expressions of his message. To some believers, Lee's illiteracy only enhanced the legitimacy of her role: an illiterate who cannot study religion must receive her faith directly from God" (1979, 78). On the other hand, Shakers have produced a great deal of writings about their beliefs, and records of their lives, poems, testimonies, journals, letters, and tracts.

Literacy and Orality: Theoretical Perspectives

Anthropologists and sociologists have argued that literacy actually affects how people think. W. J. Ong, for example, has written that "More than any other single invention, writing has transformed human consciousness" (1982, 78). Jack Goody specifically connects writing to the transition from concrete (particular?) to abstract thinking (1977). These ideas are certainly consistent with my findings in Chapter 7 regarding particularism and morality in women's religions. Yet I am tempted to phrase the process somewhat differently from Goody's formulation: Women's religions, characterized by "concrete" thinking (Goody's word), **choose** to avoid literacy. Given that most of these religions are situated in societies in which literacy is known, I suggest that the lack of emphasis on sacred texts is at least to some extent volitional, and not only shapes but also reflects a variety of aspects of these religions. I concur with Ruth Finnegan that one cannot assume the uses of literacy to be the same in all situations, "For printing can be—and has been—used for enlightenment *and* for mystification; for self-expression or rebellion *and* for repression; for systematic analysis and the development of knowledge on the one hand *and* for obfuscation, dogma and the propagation of prejudice and intolerance on the other" (1988, 163; see also Schousboe and Larsen 1989). Finnegan's important insight allows us to give even greater weight to the avoidance of **sacred** texts (as opposed to optional books and literature) in most women's religions.

Shmuel Eisenstadt has shown that highly articulate theological traditions generally develop within literate cultures that are interested in producing and preserving sacred texts, commentaries, and legal and philosophical treatises. Catholicism and Judaism exemplify this trend: in both religious traditions elite [male] groups produced complex, written theologies (1982). **Literate, centralized, standardized, transcendent religious cultures are often the religious cultures that are the most male dominated.** The history of Islamization in Africa during the past century, for example, shows that in many instances growing emphasis on religious literacy coincides with the lowering of the status and participation of women in religious life (see also McGilvray 1988 on Sri Lanka).

There is indeed a logical correlation between sacred texts and centralization— they are complementary techniques for ensuring uniformity of religious belief and practice. As I have argued in Chapter 5, such uniformity is anathema to women's religions that use diverse means to address and alleviate problems of real, immediate, and emotionally charged suffering in this world. **A pragmatic, particularistic, and eclectic approach to human misfortune is inconsistent with either a central authority or a sacred text—because central authorities and sacred texts typically declare that "only our way is legitimate" and thus work to enforce conformity.** Jack Goody has made a similar point in his discussion of the effects of literacy: According to Goody, literacy aids the development of large-scale, impersonal organizations and states with universalistic rather than local (particular?) outlooks. Orality, on the other hand, according to Ruth Finnegan, is more linked to the **context** in which it takes place, and thus tends to encourage pragmatic face to face interaction (1988, 165).

RANK VERSUS CENTRALIZATION

At first glance, it would seem that rank and centralization should go hand in hand because both reflect status-conscious, classificatory, and dichotomous thinking (Young 1983). Yet in women's religions we have discovered highly articulated internal systems of rank co-existing with an almost total lack of centralized authorities.

I suspect that this finding can be explained in terms of what we have already learned about women's religions. On the one hand, these religions are characterized by a this-worldly orientation and concern with interpersonal relationships. It is consistent with both these characteristics that **human** organization in the religion is elaborate and consequential. On the other hand, we have seen that women's religions are characterized by an absence of transcendent monotheism and a de-emphasis of sacred texts. It is consistent with these characteristics that **suprahuman** organization is unelaborated. In women's religions, the nearby, the known, the particular, and the personal are the foci of interest.

It is striking that in the same religions in which no one is quite sure which deity does exactly what or how, everyone is quite sure which human individual does exactly what and to whom. A similar contrast can be made between internal rank and centralized authority. Internal rank has to do with relationships among specific and known people; organizational centralization is the profane parallel to monotheism—a declaration that the "transcendent" is somehow better than the particular, a declaration that only one way is correct and everybody must adhere to it. I am impressed by William Lebra's observation that although Ryūkyūan **deities** are not highly differentiated, among **people** in the religious organization there is a precise specification of roles "down to the level of a horse holder or a ladler" (1966, 205). Lebra comments that "This rigid differentiation of roles surely reflects a basic concern with human relationships" (1966, 205).

Feminist sociologists and psychologists have devoted a great deal of thinking to questions of organization, gender, and power, yet the currently available data are far from clear-cut. In her classic book on men and women in organizations, Rosabeth Kanter cites studies showing that women do not handle power

differently from men: men are not more competitive, dominant, or instrumental, and women are not more naturally cooperative. According to Kanter, there
is no evidence of sex difference in leadership style (1977, 199). What differs are
men's and women's opportunities for access to leadership, not their inherent
leadership techniques. [11]

On the other hand, Stamm and Ryff (1984) have looked at women's exercise
of power in a variety of cultural situations, and concluded that women's power
operates differently from men's. It is more often personal than positional, it
tends to be situationally oriented, and is frequently exercised outside the traditional authority structures of a society. [12]

The contrast between Kanter's and Stamm and Ryff's conclusions are disturbing to those of us who like neat answers. Yet I think that both studies shed
light on the organization of women's religions. On the one hand, as Kanter
would expect, they are hierarchical—they have leaders whose styles do not
seem to differ appreciably from men's (see Chapter 11). On the other hand, as
Stamm and Ryff would suppose, they consistently display an aversion to
centralization—there is a leaning toward personal rather than positional
power, leadership is highly situational, and the religions generally exist outside
the dominant power structures of the society.

A common pattern in the history of religions is a new religion or religious sect
inspired by a charismatic woman, which then becomes institutionalized through
the efforts of men (Hutch 1984). This pattern has been documented in Africa,
Japan, and the United States (Jules-Rosette 1979; Hardacre 1986; Ruether 1974).
The literature on these religions generally claims that the transition in leadership
occurred as the religion became institutionalized. Yet the definition of institutionalization is typically vague, encompassing **both** the development of internal
rank **and** the development of centralization. A closer look at the evidence proves
that women's leadership often persists long past the point at which hierarchy
emerges. Where women's power declines seems to be precisely at the point in
which individual chapters or groups form into a centralized association.

To explain why that is the case, I would like to propose two lines of reasoning. To begin with, as I have described throughout this book, women's religions do not occur in feminist utopias; they occur in societies which are, to
some extent, patriarchal. Thus, I would argue that the lack of centralization is
due to the fact that in male-dominated societies women's access to the public
domain is restricted. Leadership of a small group is far less problematic than
leadership of a nationwide or international corporation. We may conjecture
that noncentralized organizations are the only conditions under which women
can get and keep power in a patriarchal society. Once a religious movement
moves toward centralization, men take over.

The second line of reasoning I wish to propose starts from the opposite
direction. It may be that women's religions are noncentralized not because
centralized organizations exclude women from leadership, but because women
themselves have no need or desire for a centralized organizational structure. If
we look at male-dominated religions, we can ask what function a central
organization serves. The answer is clear: Central organizations are vehicles for

power and conquest, for bringing in new members, and for ensuring that old members do not leave. Yet, as I showed earlier in this chapter, women's religions tend not to preach exclusivist theologies, and they are not missionary religions.[13] Eisenstadt (1982) and others have demonstrated that the centralization of religious functionaries seems to be connected to the rise of political centralization—the development of the state. In many cases, including that of the Ryūkyū Islands during the Okinawan kingdom, religious centralization was actually implemented by political authorities in order to facilitate governmental centralization. There is convincing evidence that the rise of states is a process in which women generally have very little part. The development of a state-level political system (whether an indigenous monarchy or through foreign imperialism) has been shown to have a detrimental affect upon women's religious status (cf. Frymer-Kensky 1992 on the ancient Near East; Silverblatt 1980 on the Andes).

To my mind, what we are dealing with here are complex interactions of theology and organization. On the one hand, the rather flexible theologies of women's religions follow and justify their noncentralized organizational structures. On the other hand, nondogmatic, supple theologies do not demand a centralized organization to spread or enforce them. Codification can be seen as a response to the need for maintaining power and domination—and this **may** be where an important difference between men and women lies. Whether that difference is rooted in maternal thinking (as Sara Ruddick claims) or in social structure (as Rosabeth Kanter claims), I leave up to the intellectual inclinations of the reader.

Issues of organization have important implications for the ways in which female-dominated religions do or do not serve women's interests. Lack of centralization decreases the potential impact these religions can have on the society as a whole, both because each chapter preaches a slightly different set of beliefs and because adherents to the religion cannot easily be mobilized to work together for a unified cause. In the next chapter we will turn to the secular consequences of women's religion.

Notes

1. As we saw in the previous chapter, there were unofficial leaders. And Spiritualists did attempt numerous times to build enduring national organizations, with women among the leaders of these attempts. For example, in the 1870s Victoria Hull was three times elected president of a national spiritualist association.

2. I do not know if infighting is characteristic of other Afro-Brazilian religions or if it is connected to the higher presence of male leadership in Umbanda.

3. In men's ancestor worship the emphasis is on correct performance. There are all kinds of ritual manuals and etiquette books with step-by-step instructions.

4. Lee had wanted Lucy Wright to succeed her, and she eventually did.

5. Garrett has pointed out another difference between Lee's and Whittaker's leadership. "Ann Lee had always manifested in herself and elicited in others a great range of ecstatic experiences and possessed behaviors, but most of the time the prevailing mood seems to have been one of celebration, of rejoicing in the presence of the divine. Under

Whittaker's leadership, the gifts of the Spirit were generally those of mortification, forcing believers to confront and overcome their own sins, especially those of sexuality" (1987, 212).

6. The argument I am making here is far from undisputed. Priscilla Brewer, the expert in Shaker history who has been the most helpful to me in writing this book, feels that I have overstated the case and that the sex of the sect's early leaders was not as relevant as I claim. I choose to go ahead and make the argument anyway, largely in hope of inspiring experts in other religions to take a new look at gender and institutionalization.

7. Women continued to play important roles. Brewer particularly points to the power exercised by Ruth Landon and Asenath Clark (personal communication 1992).

8. Since many of the new religions of Japan are highly centralized (McFarland 1967, 84ff.), it is important to stress that these religions, after the first generation, are typically dominated by male leadership.

9. Christian Scientists claim that God authored *Science and Health*—Eddy was but the scribe. Cynthia Read has told me that Christian Science scriptures are printed in a standard size so as to fit into the standard book racks with which their churches are outfitted (personal communication).

10. Buddhism is a literate tradition; the indigenous religion is not (although people know how to read). On Okinawa there are male ritual specialists who deal with divination and geomancy and derive their knowledge from books.

11. Kanter's ideas are based on patterns of women's and men's leadership in "masculine" institutions (American corporations). Thus, her work is not a test of "authentic" female leadership styles, and may have only marginal relevance to women's religions that are "feminine" institutions.

12. Of course, all of these may be traits of the leadership styles of subordinate groups rather than specifically women's leadership traits.

13. For example, Cosentino has noticed that although Sande and Poro are very powerful, the Mende showed a high level of tolerance to new religions that have been introduced into the area (1982, 31).

13

Spiritual Gifts and Secular Benefits

RELIGION AND SOCIAL STRUCTURE

Religion is never isolated from other elements of the cultural system. Max Weber has claimed that religion is the form in which people worship society by creating a supernatural world that mirrors human social structure, including gender arrangements. Other scholars have shown that male-dominated religions not only mirror gender discrimination but actually cause the subordination of women in the economic sphere (cf. Silverblatt 1980; VanEecke 1989). Can we then expect to find that female-dominated religions not only reflect women's identities (e.g., as mothers), but also actively serve their interests?

Before we begin to address this question, I wish to underscore that I do not believe women participate in religion primarily in order to reap social, psychological, economic, or political profit. Women, like men, join religious groups and perform religious rituals for fundamentally religious reasons—in Clifford Geertz's terms, in order to grapple with the ultimate conditions of their existence. On the other hand, since religion is always integrated with other aspects of the social structure, even the loftiest and most mystical matters of spirit are clothed in the prosaic garb of rules, codes of behavior, and organization. The factors that draw particular people to particular religions, and the advantages that accrue to them through that membership, are multifaceted and include both sacred and profane elements. Put differently, even though women become active in female-dominated religions for essentially "religious" reasons, this does not negate the "secular" results and functions of these religions.

In most contexts in which female-dominated religions occur, individual women have some amount of free choice. Women's religions are rarely the only available religious option. As we saw in Chapter 4, for example, Korean women who wish to become religious specialists can choose between becoming shamans or Buddhist nuns. This point is even clearer in North America, where women have many religions—including many Protestant denominations—to choose from. Membership in women's religions must be treated as volitional and members must be assumed to have some awareness of the advantages of membership.

What happens once women join female-dominated religions? Do these religions offer ecstatic rituals that allow women to temporarily forget their suffering? Is religion their opiate? Do religious leaders tell poor women, women whose children are hungry, that they will eat "pie in the sky when they die"?

The answer to these questions is—No! Social deprivation and personal crises undoubtedly lead some individuals to seek a "better" or more convincing belief system—one that more adequately explains why things are the way they are. Spiritual solutions do not, however, preclude action designed to change an unsatisfactory status quo. In Chapter 5 we saw that theological explanations and ritual solutions for the problem of suffering in this world are the foci of most women's religions. In the following pages we will see that many of the women's religions offer, in addition, more concrete help with suffering. Given the this-worldly orientation of women's religions, spiritual and earthly benefits tend to be intertwined.

Many kinds of nonreligious organizations can meet women's needs for social interaction, group support, networking, empathy, even healing. Yet it does seem that religious organizations have a unique role—even in terms of meeting women's **secular** needs and furthering women's **secular** interests. This connection has been made explicit by Spiritual Feminists. A cornerstone of the Feminist Spirituality Movement is that intellectual understandings of feminist principles are not sufficient to bring about real changes in consciousness. As Mary Daly has written, "we have seen that patriarchy is designed not only to possess women, but to prepossess/preoccupy us, that is, to inspire women with false selves which anesthetize the Self" (1978, 322). Having grown out of the secular feminist movement, Feminist Spirituality has transferred political concerns to the spiritual sphere. The motto "The personal is political and the political is personal" is reflected in almost all Movement writings. For many Spiritual Feminists, religious ritual plays a key role in assisting women to liberate themselves from the thought patterns of patriarchy. "Magic . . . can be called the art of evoking power-from-within" (Starhawk 1987, 24). And indeed, sociologist Nancy Finley has documented the links between religious beliefs, a sense of personal efficacy, and political activism among Dianic Wiccans—one branch of the Feminist Spirituality Movement. Rather than functioning as an "opiate," religious involvement may empower women to work for social change in this world.[1]

It is important to distinguish between the proclaimed ideology of the religion and the actual advantages that accrue to members. As we saw in Chapter 10, almost all women's religions preach nonpatriarchal gender ideologies. Given the consistently "feminist" credos, it is of interest that certain religions have provided short-term advantages for specific women, whereas others have also resulted in long-term, structural benefits for women. We will look at these patterns in detail below.

In addition to spiritual satisfaction, enjoyable rituals, and deeper existential understanding, female-dominated religions offer women concrete, secular benefits in the here-and-now. As Michelle Rosaldo has shown, extra-domestic ties with other women are an important source of power and value for women in societies that hold to a firm division between male and female roles (1974, 39). And indeed, all the women's religions provide women with extra-domestic ties and with some sort of improved personal circumstances. What I wish to focus on here is why, if all (or almost all) female-dominated religions provide transient help for specific women, certain religions **also** offer (or at least work toward) long-term advantages to women as a group. In the remainder of this chapter we will look more closely at these two patterns, and try to understand the structural conditions that allow short-term benefits to lead to long-term advantages. I believe that attention to this question can provide important insights into a variety of issues that impact on women's secular and religious status.

Let me say from the outset that these two models are not mutually exclusive; they should be visualized as more of a continuum. I have placed Christian Science and Spiritualism in Model 1 (only short-term benefits) even though both have been vocal supporters of women's suffrage (a long-term benefit)[2], because it seems to me that the **emphasis** in both religions has been on temporary relief. Once women's suffrage had become reality, neither of these religions remained at the forefront of other feminist struggles. In contrast, the other two North American religions—Feminist Spirituality and the Shakers—have invariably supported women's rights and have also provided long-term advantageous alternatives for women as a group. It seems reasonable to argue that even in the case of religions that ostensibly provide only transient benefits for specific women, there is likely to be some sort of wider carryover. Thus, while I claim that the *zār* cult, for instance, provides benefits to the individual possessed woman and not to women as a group, I find it hard to believe that the knowledge that **all** women are potentially possessible has no generalized impact on gender relations in the society as a whole.

MODEL 1: *Only or Primarily Temporary Relief for Individual Women*	MODEL 2: *Temporary Relief for Individual Women* **and** *Long-term Benefits for Women as a Group*
Christian Science	Northern Thai Spirit Cults
Spiritualism	Sande
zār	Shakers
Afro-Brazilian Cults	Feminist Spirituality
Korean Shamanism	Ryūkyū Island Religion
Burmese Shamanism	
Black Carib Religion[3]	

MODEL 1—TEMPORARY RELIEF FOR
INDIVIDUAL WOMEN
Zār

In the *zār* cult of Ethiopia most members are married women "who feel neglected
in a man's world in which they serve as hewers of wood and haulers of water . . .
Married women in the predominantly rural culture are often lonely for the
warmth of kinship relations for typical residence is in an exogamous patrilocal
hamlet" (Messing 1958, 1120–1121).

Researchers explain women's participation in *zār* cults in light of women's
social and cultural disadvantages, and their virtual exclusion from formal Islamic rituals. In Islamic societies a female is placed under the care and authority
of males throughout her life. Legal practices, institutional mechanisms, belief
systems and social codes separate females and males in Muslim societies.
Women's access to public places and public roles is restricted, and women have
no formal role in political or economic decision making, although they may
have informal influence. (See also Chapter 2 for a discussion of the social
context of the *zār*.)

Women's participation in the *zār* cult has been interpreted by anthropologists as a function of all these factors. Other conditions scholars have cited as
laying the groundwork for women's attraction to *zār* include: cultural assessments of women as weak, treacherous, inferior beings (Lewis 1969); genital
mutilation (Boddy 1988); patrilineal and patrilocal marriage that causes women
to be isolated from their natal families, coupled with marital insecurity—easy
divorce and polygyny (Kennedy 1978); and socialization that trains girls to be
submissive to males (Kennedy 1978). Still other authors have argued that *zār*
possession is a response to women's sexual deprivation, and human situations
that attract *zārs* include opportunities for the spirit to have sexual intercourse
with a human victim of the opposite sex (Messing 1958).

How does *zār* cult participation redress any of these problems? "Lacking
full-status economic and political roles in the society at large, many women [in
Islamic societies], often with unconscious intent, struggle for control and
power through a 'manipulation of the supernatural' " (Beck 1980, 51–52). In
addition, women's religious activities create links between and among women
that sometimes override kin and status group barriers. While patriarchal,
patrilineal, and patrilocal social patterns restrict women to the domestic
sphere, *zār* cult participation gives women a set of activities that are not restricted to the domestic sphere, and that allow women some measure of control over their time, activities, and lives.

The *zār* cult has multiple curing, religious, and social functions, and different women utilize it for different reasons. Some women attend *zār* rituals to
induce possession trance, while others attend just for fun. Lucie Saunders
(1977) has found that socioeconomic class tends to determine what kind of
relationship women have to *zār*. Wealthy women, who are more restricted to
their houses for reasons of modesty and family honor, use *zār* rituals as oppor-

tunities for socializing with other women. Poor women, who may go out more freely, are less involved with the *zār* cult. Women who have migrated to the cities and so suffer from the loss of their traditional village and kin-based female support networks actively use the *zār* network to form friendship and patron-client relationships, and to offer and gain services (Constantinides 1982). Rural women, on the other hand, have plenty of other opportunities to get together with and receive support from other women.[4]

A woman possessed by a *zār* spirit becomes sick, increasingly unable to function in the home. Eventually her husband grudgingly agrees to pay for a *zār* ceremony. The path to healing, according to I. M. Lewis, is paved with gifts provided by the patient's husband or other relatives. Gifts include perfume, silks, clothing, and gourmet foods. Lewis has analyzed the *zār* cult in terms of gender hostility. Somali women have a strong sense of sexual solidarity, coupled with antagonism toward men. Men see women's possession as a strategy for attaining their goals at men's expense[5] and explain that women are more likely to be possessed because of their inherent moral weakness. The relative secrecy of the cult arouses suspicion and interest among the men. They suspect that immodesty and heresy are part of the rituals, yet they are afraid that if they do not pay, their wives will remain ill and unable to carry out household tasks. "Thus men are highly skeptical of women's sprite [*zār*] afflictions which they regard at best as malingering, and at worst as a pernicious extortion racket through which men are led to indulge their wives' insatiable demands for new clothes and delicate foods" (Lewis 1969, 208). Although men ridicule the *zār* cult, they pay substantial bills for their womenfolk's cures by the cult.

Lewis, Saunders, and Constantinides have stressed the social and economic benefits that accrue to women through *zār* participation. John Kennedy, on the other hand, points to the role of *zār* ritual in cathartic discharge of emotions, and the relief of sexual and aggressive tensions generated by the stressful conditions of Nubian women's lives. Unlike in Somalia (where Lewis did his fieldwork), the Nubian women of Upper Egypt studied by Kennedy do not obtain much material gain from *zār* possession; instead, they gain attention. In a similar vein, Yael Kahana (1985) argues that *zār* patients and leaders can "get away" with deviant behavior because no one ever knows if it is the person or the *zār* acting that way. *Zār* cults allow women to put their emotions first and their duties second. During rituals, household work and childbearing and rearing become secondary duties, while individualism becomes most important. In addition, a husband or kinsman's willingness to pay for a woman's *zār* activities is a public affirmation of her importance to him.

Most scholars feel that despite elements of gender antagonism, the *zār* cult serves to maintain the status quo rather than to change it. "The zar cult is not a deviant cult, its significance in maintaining the status quo in society has traditionally been greater than improvement of social status. Zar membership does not serve to raise or enhance the social status of its participants" (Messing 1958, 1125). Entranced women may be able to take on male prerogatives (such as drinking alcohol and smoking) during the *zār* ceremony yet "[T]he new social relationships formed [through zar cult associations] do not in any substantial way threaten the basic premises and mores of . . . society. These are the dominance by men of the formal political, economic, and religious sphere of social organization, the segregation of the sexes, and the seclusion of women" (Constantinides 1982, 201). The *zār* cult confronts **individual men** and not **patriarchy**.

Other Examples of Model 1

We now turn to several other examples of women's religions that offer assistance to individual women without seriously challenging patriarchal social structures. In a series of case studies Patricia Lerch (1980) illustrates the multifaceted assistance that women receive from the Afro-Brazilian Umbanda cult. A young mother who had been deserted by her husband came to a Umbanda center for advice. The medium told her that in her past life she had been a man who had also deserted his wife and family, and her punishment was to be reincarnated as a woman in the same situation. Umbanda provided this woman with an interpretation of her suffering that made the suffering explicable and so easier to bear. In another case a woman's husband was cheating on her. The medium (or actually the medium's spirit guide) warned her in advance so that she could confront him and tell him to leave before he had a chance to desert her. A third case concerned a woman who was deserted by her husband and became so ill and upset that she lost her job. The medium's spirit guide told her to go the center secretary who would give her some money to tide her over. In a final incident the medium hooked up an unemployed woman with another client who needed a domestic worker.

Another way in which women benefit from Umbanda participation has been noted by Esther Pressel: "Cecilia [an informant] once observed that her religion had made her a 'free woman.' By this, she explained, she meant that she could go out without her husband to private spirit sessions and afterward to restaurants with Umbandists" (1980, 168–169). According to Pressel, Afro-Brazilian rituals may come into play when tenuous male–female relationships break down. For example, a single woman may be anxious that her lover is not planning to marry her so she threatens him with black magic. Or a wife may find it difficult to act out her role as a faithful spouse and turn to Umbanda for psychological solace.[6]

Afro-Brazilian cults generally ignore the usual prejudices of Brazilian society, and the cult centers protect criminals, homosexuals, prostitutes, and single women who are no longer virgins (Carneiro 1940). In words almost identical to those used to analyze the social impact of the *zār* cult, Leacock and Leacock argue that **"From the perspective of the members, the appeal of the Batuque is not that it promises to change the world in which the members live, but that it will help them to survive in that world"** (1972, 326).

A similar theme emerges when we look at the effect that twentieth-century Spiritualism has on women's lives. In Spiritualist circles in contemporary Wales, emotional problems are worked out within the confines imposed by the traditional female role. "Indeed, this is where the contribution of spiritualism lies. For the weekly repetition of healing activities and the exchange of messages 'from spirit' constitute a ritual of reconciliation to a situation which does not permit any radical alternatives to itself. . . . [It] helps women to accept a traditionally feminine role, which they frequently find frustrating and difficult" (Skultans 1974, 4–5). The messages of these spirits reinforce traditional values and family arrangements. Vieda Skultans interprets Spiritualist ritual as rites of reversal (cf. Gluckman 1963)—rites that appear to be a protest against the established order but actually reflect an overall acceptance of that order. Rites of reversal allow individuals to let out frustration and ultimately submit to and accept the social order. It seems to me that Skultan's analysis holds equally true for both the *zār* cult and the Afro-Brazilian religions.

An even clearer example is Mexican Spiritualism, which, according to Kaja Finkler, "promotes well-being on the individual level, but tends to perpetuate a societal status quo that is rejected by the actors themselves and may also be illness producing" (1986, 628). Religious rules and temple leaders explicitly discourage political activism. The Mexican Spiritualist God recognizes that His followers are poor, but tells them that if He were to give them material benefits they would abandon Him. On the most immediate level, temple attendance often results in loss of economic productivity—healers sometimes spend two days a week working (without pay) at the temple. On the other hand, Mexican Spiritualism does not tell adherents to passively accept suffering—rituals do aim to alleviate individual illness (although not the underlying social causes of illness).

Mexican Spiritualism provides certain benefits to the wives of male adherents. Spiritualist men tend to abstain from alcohol and behave in a less "macho" manner. In Finkler's sample, 33% of male adherents had been alcoholics when they first became involved with Spiritualism. "In becoming adherents, men relinquish their drinking habits and thereby become unlike the majority of Mexican men whose drinking patterns define them as men" (1986, 633). In contrast to the dominant local gender ideology in which heavy drinking, promiscuity, and wife-beating are what define maleness, Spiritualist men avoid drinking, exhibit few macho traits, and are more likely to spend their leisure time with their families. Clearly, individual women benefit from their husbands' spiritualist participation.

The most extreme instance of Model 1 is the new Japanese religion Tensho-kotai-jingu-kyo. The foundress of Tensho taught that women (like herself) who have known much suffering are very close to the Kingdom of God, and that in the coming Age of God women will play a more significant role than they have in the past. In the present man-centered age power rules the earth, while in the better forthcoming age women will be in the vanguard. On the other hand, she encouraged women to continue to obey their husbands and elders and she preached highly conventional, sex-linked social roles (Nakamura 1980). Since Tensho deals with healing and many Tensho members have recovered from illness or other forms of suffering, it is undeniable that individual women do receive certain benefits from Tensho membership, although Tensho in no way challenges patriarchy.

MODEL 2—SHORT-TERM AND LONG-TERM BENEFITS FOR WOMEN

Sande

Sande is a "social and religious association that would promote an egalitarian position for women and ensure for them a more favorable status and an active participation in the socio-religious life. . . . In addition, women wanted considerable freedom for their sex, and the creation or adoption of a powerful secret society with a wide range of powers was an effective way to guarantee this right" (Richards 1973, 71).

In Chapter 6 we explained that Sande initiation teaches girls domestic skills they will need as adults. These tasks are not new to the girls, who have already helped their mothers care for the house and younger siblings. What they really learn in Sande are **attitudes** toward work: in particular, cooperation with other women.

Both the fun and the pain of initiation serve to bind the girls together into a united society. At the end of the initiation period they swear an oath never to reveal any fault in another Sande woman. The emphasis on cooperation enables women to deal with the many problems they are likely to encounter in the polygynous households they marry into. "This solidarity training helps to mitigate co-wife rivalry and the potential divide-and-rule powers of polygynous husbands" (MacCormack 1977, 99). In many societies, virilocal residence means that a woman is cut off from her own kin and isolated from any group that could empower or support her, yet Sande provides a woman with group support throughout her life. Sande rules state that respect must be shown to women. Sande organization safeguards the rights and position of women, and punishes men who mistreat their wives.

Sande women about to give birth prefer to return to the chapters in which they were initiated. Carol MacCormack explains that individual women link their mother's and mother's-in-law Sande chapters. "Contrary to the Levi-Straussian model of women as passive objects transferred between groups of men, in Sande, women link corporate groups composed exclusively of women" (1977, 96). The same official who performed the clitoridectomy will serve as midwife; the same women who supported her during the clitoridectomy will support her during childbirth. Women are also buried by the chapters in which they were initiated, and so become Sande ancestresses.

Earlier in this chapter I made the claim that almost all women's religions benefit specific women on an immediate level. On the face of it, Sande does not seem to fit into this pattern—clitoridectomy can hardly be said to serve women's secular interests. On the other hand, the collective effect of Sande membership clearly strengthens women's economic, political, and family situations. While I am not fully satisfied with this argument (see Chapter 6), it is what the anthropologists who have studied Sande report.

During the initiation rituals, sponsoring mothers and Sande officials may stay in the grove for weeks or months. Sande provides women an alternative space not controlled by men. Sande women have a special vocabulary that they use for talking about women's business. This vocabulary contributes to the mystique of power and secrecy surrounding Sande. Throughout the year Sande women meet to air common grievances, which certainly enhances their political position in society.

Belonging to Sande gives women a great deal of power, both in the community and within the marital relationship. Sande women know that they control a scarce and important resource: offspring. Sande women can withhold that resource if their husbands violate Sande laws. And men know that Sande women have knowledge of medicines that can cause impotence. A constellation of Sande laws seem designed to protect women's privacy: Men are not allowed near women's bathing areas, men travelling alone must announce their presence by means of an appropriate noise. Sande rules also serve to control male violence against women: a man who strikes his wife in the presence of her mother is obligated to placate both her and her Sande group (Harris and Sawyerr 1968, 105).

Sande ritual may not be contravened by any man, and even a chief who attempted to do so would be punished in a show of authority by Sande women. Sande laws affect the entire community, and the sanctioning power of Sande is recognized by the community. When at the end of the initiation season masked ancestral figures appear in the village, one of the "ancestresses" publicly shakes a bundle of switches at men and women who have violated Sande rules. All who watch are reminded of the power of Sande officials to catch and punish transgressors.

For women who have migrated into cities, Sande furnishes neighborhood chapters that offer women companionship and social support in life-crisis situations. In the nineteenth century, women in Sierra Leone took advantage of Freetown's growing population to become traders. Membership in the women's secret society provided business connections and personal protection in the absence of kinship ties. Sande sisters could certify that stranger-traders could be trusted in commercial relations and Sande held the traders to certain standards of behavior that were locally acceptable.

The group solidarity encouraged by Sande has had broader economic and political implications. West African men and women normally engage in different economic pursuits. However, when other sources of income are not available to West African men, they compete with women for agricultural resources. This is problematic for women because men are at an automatic advantage in that they have jural rights to the land. Sande gives women an organized forum for protest in this and other situations. MacCormack (1979, 35) argues that, "Because Sande women are organized into effective corporate groups and enjoy female autonomy in all matters pertaining to Sande's sphere of interests, their political position in the larger society is enhanced."

According to David Rosen, the Women's War of 1929—a tax rebellion led by peasant women against colonial authorities—developed from women's Sande activities. Again in 1971 Sande women protested against men who neglected their families in favor of personal economic gain, and against the abuse and corruption of local authorities. Rosen documents how in 1971, in the wake of economic changes threatening the agricultural, marketing, and economic autonomy of women, "Women began parading down the streets, not bearing the symbols and signs of the Sande, but dressed up in potato leaves, and other representations of agricultural activities. Women claimed that the donning of agricultural symbols would bring them good luck. As the dancing and parading became more widespread, women began to accost and hurl abuses at men of authority [who backed up the jural and economic advantages enjoyed by men]. . . . two subchiefs were dragged from their porches and beaten. Even the arrest of several of the demonstrators failed to quell the demonstrations. Women claimed that their activities were protected under the ritual umbrella of the Sande association" (1983, 39).

Despite the culturally acknowledged interdependence of men and women, the societies in which Sande women live are not egalitarian. But because a woman's allegiance to Sande—to other women—is seen as equally or more binding than her allegiance to her husband, women are guaranteed a measure of independence lacking in many other cultural systems. Sande societies endow women as a group with long-term, structural benefits, and women as individuals with short-term pragmatic benefits.

Shakers

Unlike Sande, which is more or less an automatic part of life for women in many parts of West Africa, Shaker membership was much more a matter of choice for individual women. Economic distress, among other factors, motivated many individuals to join the Shakers. Facing poverty or bankruptcy, men and women saw in Shaker communities a financially safe life-style centered around values of pacifism, work, thrift, celibacy, and cleanliness for both sexes.

Undoubtedly, part of the appeal of Shakerism—especially to women—was the neat and ordered houses in the quiet countryside, away from the noise and economic and sexual exploitation of industrializing cities. Organized into "families" of celibate men and women, Shaker villages offered a standard of living more comfortable than many members had known in their former lives. Shakers invented numerous technical improvements to simplify household chores (pot handles, clothespins, machines to cut fruit and shell peas) and economize agricultural work. Less popular tasks (such as cooking) were rotated. Working conditions for both men and women were humane and pleasant. "Life in a Shaker society offered [women] economic security, meaningful activity, and a supportive sisterhood; for a few women, it offered the opportunity to exercise gifts of leadership which would hardly have been tolerated in the outside world or in any other religious institution" (Procter-Smith 1985, 220). The neat and clean Shaker life-style had clear benefits—Shakers were healthier and lived longer than the general population (Bainbridge 1982, 359).

The religious experiences of Shaker men and women were equally respected, both men and women wrote articles in the Shaker newspapers, and women predominated in spiritual gifts such as testimonies and writing hymns and poems. Particularly when Shakerism expanded into the West in the early nineteenth century, increased leadership and travel opportunities opened up for Shaker women (Desroche 1971).

Shaker society legislated extreme sexual segregation. This had both positive and negative implications for women. In the economic sphere Shaker women, like non-Shaker women, cleaned, cooked, sewed, and engaged in small manufacture, while men worked in agricultural production. In general, men were in charge of business and temporal matters. Shaker women cleaned the men's rooms and cared for their clothing (but not in the presence of men).

Interactions between the sexes were for the most part forbidden. Relations between women and men were limited to co-presence at meals and meetings. Men and women did not shake hands or touch, they worked in separate workshops, ate at separate tables, prayed and danced in separate groups, and rarely spoke to one another. Even Shaker architecture reflected their notion of the sexes as equal, distinct, and separate: buildings often had two outside doors and two sets of staircases.

Unlike in non-Shaker society, both men and women participated in the care and education of children (men cared for boys and women for girls). In light of the emphasis that feminist scholars have placed on the sexist repercussions of women's predominance in childrearing (see Chapters 3 and 10), the significance of this aspect of Shaker life should not be underestimated.

In trying to assess how Shaker sexual segregation affected women, it is crucial to bear in mind the following points. On the one hand, it limited women's options in terms of work. On the other hand, it protected women from the dangers of childbirth and allowed women to exercise leadership over their own activities. It seems to me that in comparison to the lot of poor and working women in eighteenth- and nineteenth-century America, the lot of Shaker women—particularly in terms of economic and sexual security—was enviable. Especially after 1860, as male membership declined, the Shakers moved toward more complete gender equality (Brewer 1992, 611). Although Shaker communities never attracted more than several thousand women, for those women Shakerism did offer ongoing, collective benefits.

Sanctificationists

The nineteenth-century Sanctificationists—an all-female Christian communal sect—were critical of the sexist economic implications of traditional relationships in which the husband controlled the family finances, including money and property that the wife had brought into the marriage or earned on her own. In protest against discriminatory family arrangements, these women formed their own cooperative businesses and living arrangements. The Sanctificationist sisters established a system of communal housework and childrearing that alleviated the isolation and boredom of women's work in mainstream society. And according to Sally Kitch, there is evidence that "some of the sisters sought refuge from the dominance of abusive or drunken husbands who, in mainstream society, were still deemed women's superiors, even when inebriated or violent" (1989, 66). It is of interest to note that although most of the Sanctificationist sisters left middle-class families to join a community in which they worked at unskilled, working-class labor, "The sisters reported new levels of self-esteem from the discipline and integrity of their menial but independent work" (Kitch 1989, 152). As Kitch shows, they transformed the typical tedious household labor of women "from an endless round of ill-defined tasks to a four-hour workday in which tasks were defined, professionalized, and rotated. Outside of those specific hours, a woman's time became her own. Their collective efforts enabled them to travel extensively" (1989, 152). In addition, Sanctificationist sisters supported women's suffrage and other struggles for women's rights.

Although the Sanctificationists began as a religious group, and only created their communal work and life-style in order to survive once their celibacy had estranged them from their husbands, they eventually became primarily a secular community. According to Kitch, "having served its purpose, religion faded away. Celibacy rose in symbolic importance over the religious beliefs that had spawned it. Sanctified spiritual power was reinforced by female secular efficacy. Any group of women who could succeed and prosper as they had done must be in tune with divine will, the sisters reasoned" (1989, 157). Like the Shakers, Sanctificationist sisters constructed a new, less patriarchal, total life-style.

Northern Thai Matrilineal Spirit Cults

The *phii puu njaa* cult is a ritual complex possessed by, oriented toward, and controlled by women. The cults arbitrate moral and interpersonal behavior, determine inheritance and household membership, and allocate land resources. The cults sacralize and legitimate women's land ownership. All family members—male and female—are obligated to participate in the cult offerings and behave in accordance with cult expectations. Richard Davis argues that male power, which derives from knowledge of Buddhist texts, is strongly balanced by female power deriving from the tutelage of domestic spirits (1984, 267).

While some ethnographers have argued that the main function of the cults is to limit the sexual behavior of female cult members, Ann Hale believes that the fact that men must pay fines for sexual transgressions means that the cults furnish women with a way to restrain male sexuality—a means that women in many other cultural situations would surely envy (1979, 147).

The cults encourage women to live in close proximity with their own kin, and offer women with protection in the case of divorce and male mobility—both very common in Northern Thailand. To summarize, Northern Thai Matrilineal Spirit Cults provide institutionalized economic, sexual, social and religious independence for women.

A COMPARISON OF THE TWO MODELS

Women reap spiritual, intellectual, personal, social, economic, and political benefits from women's religions. These benefits include nonpatriarchal gender ideologies (Chapter 10) and rituals that address women's gravest existential concerns (Chapter 5). In this chapter we have seen two models of material advantages that accrue to women. Model 1, as exemplified by the *zār* cult, helps individual women overcome isolation and assists them in negotiating with their husbands. On the other hand, only minor long-lasting collective benefits for women can be attributed to participation in *zār,* Spiritualism, or Afro-Brazilian cults. On the whole, these minor benefits are the result of the cumulative affect of short-term benefits rather than any real structural improvement. In Model 1 religions what we typically find is that short-term advantages actually end up disempowering women as a group because the religion reconciles individual women to powerlessness.[7] Model 2, as exemplified by Sande, Shakerism, and Northern Thai Matrilineal Spirit Cults, not only provides short-term assistance for women, but also gives them a permanent power base for protecting their collective interests. In these religions individual benefits lead to group empowerment. Five sets of factors enable us to understand why these very different models occur.

Sisterhood Is Powerful

Whereas Model 1 consists of women who meet periodically to form a ritual group, four of the five examples of Model 2 are comprised of women who either live together (Northern Thailand, Shakers) or who have a lifetime association with one another (Sande, Ryūkyū Islands).[8] It seems that women who have ongoing, multifaceted relationships with one another reap more extensive benefits from female-dominated religions.

I find it interesting that in all the Model 2 religions **sisters** are crucial ritual actresses (see Chapter 10). In Northern Thai matrilineages, for example, groups of sisters (and their children) constitute the cult group. In other Model 2 religions fictitious "sisterhood" relations are created. The Shakers forged a new community of "brethren" and "sisters," and conjugal love was seen as far inferior to sibling love (Kitch 1979, 51). Feminists, including Spiritual Feminists, praise the universal sisterhood of women, declaring that "Sisterhood Is Powerful!" Sande women refer to one another as Sande sisters, and adopt an attitude of mutual support among themselves. And on the Ryūkyū Islands, unlike in almost any other known religion, women gain their spiritual power through their role as sisters. Sisters, not mothers or wives, perform the most critical annual rituals. It is useful here to recollect the discussion of Karen Sack's work (Chapter 3) in which the argument is made that for African women the role of sister is far more empowering than that of wife. In women's religions "sisterhood" is a symbolic expression of ongoing unity. While motherhood is what draws women to female-dominated religions, sisterhood is what empowers them to translate religious participation into secular benefits.

Perhaps the greatest evidence for the importance of sisterhood comes from two religions in which there is an urban and a rural variety. Concerning both the *zār* cult and the Northern Thai spirit cults, I would make the case that the rural cults—in which members are part of an ongoing, multifaceted community—serve women's interests as a group (at least to some extent), whereas in the city the cults are much more a matter of short-term assistance for individual, unrelated women. Regarding the *zār,* this is precisely the argument made by Janice Boddy. Boddy has tried to understand why I. M. Lewis's findings concerning the secular implications of the *zār* cult are so different from her own findings. She concludes that Lewis "extrapolates from urban cult to rural situation without paying adequate heed to the specific social and economic configurations of these locales within Sudan" (1992, 3). Her central observation is that unlike in urban Sudan where women are indeed socially isolated, in rural Sudan "women daily walk, unchaperoned in village lanes and visit freely in each others' homes. Indeed, they are morally enjoined to witness the life transitions and crises of neighbors and kin, even when the latter reside in distant villages or towns" (1992, 4). Boddy shows that in Sudanese villages there is a considerable overlap between kin ties and *zār* cult ties. And whereas official kinship ideology is patrilineal, because of the typical pattern of intravillage marriage (endogamy), individuals tend to be related to each other both through patrilineal and matrilineal ties. The secular effect of rural *zār* cult involvement, in which related females compose the membership, is to provide "an embodied counterpoint to officially articulated kinship; it activates matri-group understandings, mobilizes matri-kin support" (1992, 7). In short, what Boddy shows is that in a rural context— where cult members are related to one another through kinship ties ("sisterhood") *zār* religion involvement serves to strengthen matrilineal bonds and ideology. This is very different from the scenario painted by Lewis and others regarding urban Sudan.

Economic Independence

In the societies in which women have little or no economic power (Islamic Africa, urban nineteenth-century North America, and contemporary Brazil) women's religions serve only temporary, individual women's interests.

The interrelationship between economic organization and women's status has been investigated at length, particularly by Marxist-feminist anthropologists. The conclusions are clear: Where women are excluded from economic roles that allow them to produce and control items of exchange value (rather than items for private use), women's status is low (see, e.g., Sacks 1974). We expect to find, and indeed find, that Model 2 religions occur in societies in which women not only work, but in which they produce items that receive social value. The important role of women in the markets of Thailand and West Africa has been noted by many anthropologists (see Chapter 2), and is certainly relevant to the argument I am making here. In Shaker communities women, like men, produced items for sale. And in the contemporary United States women who identify with the Feminist Spirituality movement tend to work at salaried, socially valued jobs. In contrast, when we look at the Model 1 religions we see that Brazilian women tend to be limited to domestic work for private families; Korean women (particularly in urban areas) are increasingly seen as "mere consumers" (Kendall, personal communication 1992); Black Carib women are dependent on their out-migrating children (especially sons) to send them money; and nineteenth–century Christian Science and Spiritualist women had few economic opportunities open to them.

That economic independence has an impact on women's religions is not surprising. As I said at the beginning of this chapter, religion is never isolated from social structure. In intensely patriarchal societies women do not have opportunities to form lasting, public alliances that empower them to effect permanent benefits for women as a group. In fact, in societies in which women's economic role is extremely marginal, we do not find that female-dominated religions occur at all. A certain measure of economic freedom seems to be a precondition for women to form autonomous religious organizations. Even the most transcendent religious beliefs necessitate some sort of expression on the earthly plane; otherwise, there can be no community of believers. My argument is simply that earthly expressions require material resources. Without access to those resources, women cannot develop or maintain female dominated religions.

The interesting question is why a higher degree of economic independence— and specifically the opportunity for women to produce items that have market value—correlates with the occurrence of female-dominated religions that serve women's **communal** interests (Model 2). It seems to me that the answer most probably has to do with whether women's lives have an important public component, or whether their activities are limited to domestic realms. As Rosaldo (1974) has argued, women's status tends to be the lowest in societies in which there is a sharp division between the domestic and the public, and in which women are associated solely with the domestic sphere. In Model 2 societies women either move freely in and out of the domestic and the public realms (West Africa, Northern Thailand, contemporary United States), or there is no radical distinction between the two realms (Shakers[9]). I suggest that the social location of women in the public realm is one of the preconditions for numerous kinds of organizations and ideologies—such as female-dominated religions—that offer structural advantages to women.

The model I am offering here is circular: economic independence leads to religions that offer women long-term benefits including greater economic independence. Thus, one of the roles of female-dominated religions in the Model 2 scenario is to protect and legitimize women's economic freedom. In the Northern Thai cults this is clear—the cults sacralize women's control of land. The Shakers also present an unambiguous case in point: Shakerism actually constructed the female economic realm, and ensured that women (because of sexual segregation) had some measure of autonomy in running it.

A last comment that is in order here concerns Peggy Sanday's observation that a correlation exists between the presence of female deities and female contribution to subsistence.[10] While further research is needed to substantiate this claim, it may well be that when women have an important subsistence role, women are perceived as "cosmically" powerful. On the symbolic level that power is imaged as goddesses; on the structural level that power leads to women's religions that enhance women's communal status.

Control of Sexuality and Fertility

A third factor that is relevant to understanding the two models concerns fertility and sexuality. Model 2 religions empower women to control their own fertility, whereas Model 1 religions do not.

To begin with Model 1, we see that the *zār* is located in societies in which women's sexuality and reproductive powers are perceived as extremely important and a great deal of emphasis is placed on **men's** control of those powers. Women are carefully watched to ensure that they do not damage their families' honor. Sexual segregation, the authority of fathers and brothers, and rigid norms of female modesty all help to ensure that women will have a minimum of contact with unrelated males. Virginity at marriage is vital, and its lack is a cause for divorce and disgrace. *Zār* rituals do not challenge this cultural ideology, nor do they give women control of their own bodies.

Similarly, Brazilian women are expected to be virgins at marriage, and no man will marry a nonvirgin. A married woman's behavior is restricted to ensure that she does nothing that her husband can interpret as inviting the attentions of other men. There are cultural sanctions against a woman who is unfaithful to her husband, and her husband may beat or even kill her and her lover. Legal birth control and abortion are unavailable in Brazil. Until 1977 divorce was not permitted, and in a marriage that broke up a woman had no chance for remarrying, although the man was expected to take a concubine. For men, early and frequent sex is regarded as healthy and masculine, and marriage does not restrict a man's sexual activities. Participation in Afro-Brazilian cults does not challenge this system; it does not give women control over their own sexual or reproductive processes.

In short, **membership in *zār* and Afro-Brazilian cults helps an individual woman negotiate with the particular men who have power over her fertility and sexuality; it does not shift the balance of power in any real way.**

Northern Thai women, on the other hand, have traditionally been in control of their own fertility. They embraced modern birth control methods in the 1960s, and until then knew and approved of folk methods.[11] The spirit cults ensure that men outside the family do not trespass on the sexuality or fertility of cult members, but, in contrast to North Africa and Brazil, there is no sense that women's bodies belong to the men of their family. Similarly, Sande takes fertility out of the sphere of nature, and places its control squarely in the hands of the female group. Among the Mende a woman who has given birth is expected by Sande rules to stay away from her husband until the child is weaned, a period that often extends to three years (Harris and Sawyerr 1968, 96). In societies with high infant mortality rates, extended post-partum sexual taboos allow mothers to avoid becoming pregnant during the time that the baby needs her milk. A prolonged sexual separation also prevents her body from becoming depleted through constant pregnancy. Sanctions of various sorts are exercised against those who doubt that Sande gives women jurisdiction over sexuality and reproduction.

To take a last example, political activism of contemporary feminists, including Spiritual Feminists, has centered around issues directly related to women's control of their bodies (e.g., rape crisis centers, battered women's shelters, pro-choice organizations, and self-help health groups). Spiritual Feminism grew out of a cultural climate in which women were fighting to control their own bodies, and it sacralized that control.

Control of fertility and sexuality reaches its apex in voluntary celibacy. Cross-culturally, celibacy is a two-edged sword: it can be used to promote an image of women as carnal and polluting, or it can offer liberation from the bonds of marriage, motherhood, and dependence on men. In the few women's religions that preach celibacy, the second of these rationales emerges. In female-dominated religions, celibacy has served women's interests by giving women authority over fertility (cf. Kraemer 1980). Shakerism, for instance, provided women with dominion over their fertility at a time in which motherhood was a physically and emotionally devastating experience for many women (Kitch 1989).

In the past, high-ranking Okinawan *noro* (priestesses) could not marry or have sexual relations (Mabuchi 1964). Some villagers explain that *noro*, as the potential wives of male deities, must keep away from pollution and mortal men.[12] The celibacy of Okinawan *noro* makes sense in light of the tradition of *noro* owning their own land: Celibacy and land ownership were two aspects of the institutionalization of independence for *noro*. Unmarried and economically secure, priestesses were in full control of their own bodies. Descriptions of the ritual roles of Okinawan priestesses display a great deal of time spent traveling from holy site to holy site. Children were undoubtedly a hindrance to the mobility of priestesses. **Yet even more important, absolute control of their own fertility ensured a level of independence and power to Ryūkyūan priestesses that has rarely been equalled in any known society.**[13]

I would like to refer here to Ruth Bleier's analysis of sexuality as the "kingpin in the patriarchal formations that serve to oppress women" (1984, 164). Bleier argues that underlying all forms of patriarchal oppression—political, economic, religious—"are the assumptions of the institution of heterosexuality or heterosexism: specifically, the assumptions that men own and have the right to control the bodies, labor, and minds of women" (1984, 164). She contends that sex, partly because of its association with intimacy and love, "is by its very physical nature the most seductive, private, intrusive, direct, and possessing way to exert power and control" (1984, 181). Bleier shows how Western religion (especially Catholicism) and Western medicine and psychoanalysis have served to master women's sexuality in the interests of male dominance. Both sets of institutions establish, express, embody, or enforce "a set of power relationships between the participants: one, the authority who compels, questions, prescribes, judges, punishes, forgives, deciphers, and interprets; and the subject who sins, speaks, and receives interpreted truth" (1984, 177).

There are three aspects of male control of women's sexuality that Bleier sees as especially significant. First, from a young age girls are taught to be appealing to men. Second, from a young age girls are also taught to fear rape. And third, violent sex is used as a means of punishing women who "get out of line" sexually or who otherwise disobey or displease men. In light of these three components, we can see again how the two models of women's religions differ. To take the Model 2 religions, in the Northern Thai Spirit Cults the spirits punish a man who transgresses on a woman's body. In Sande, the ancestors and sisters punish a man who trespasses on a woman's body. Feminists, including Spiritual Feminists, have made a point of not only demanding stricter enforcement of anti-rape legislation and expanding legal definitions of rape to include marital and date rape, but of legitimizing nonheterosexual sexual expression. And the Shakers, as we saw earlier, broke the bonds of heterosexuality by demanding celibacy for both sexes. These kinds of themes are absent from Model 1 religions.

Not all female-dominated religions give women control over their own fertility or sexuality. On the other hand, no female-dominated religions ritually bestow on men institutionalized control over women's fertility or sexuality. Since in so many cultures the role of religion is to legitimize and enforce male control of women's sexuality and fertility, I am struck by the absence of wedding ceremonies or other ceremonies in which ownership of a woman's body is transferred from one man (e.g., father) to another man (e.g., husband) in female-dominated religions.[14] I believe it is fair to say that all the key examples of women's religions implicitly (if not always explicitly) encourage some measure of independence and power for women regarding fertility. The degree of that independence varies, and is reflected in the ability of the religion to, in the long-term, promote women's secular interests.

Spirit Possession

In Model 1 religions spirit possession plays a very central role. Certain Model 2 religions include spirit possession, but its role is very much a minor one.

An eloquent discussion of the inability of spirit possession to substantially affect women's status has been presented by Roger Gomm in his study of the Digo of south Kenya. First, according to Gomm, spirit possession—in that it is an **involuntary** affliction—rarely leads a woman's kinfolk to grant her any real, meaningful favors. The most that she can hope for are token conciliatory gestures. In the context of the possession ritual, women may challenge current sex roles and norms. However, not only is there no direct carryover to the "outside" world, but this challenge occurs while the woman is in trance and so in fact renouncing personal responsibility (cf. Skultans 1974 on Spiritualism). In short, the possessed woman is not acting from a position of power.

Second, according to Gomm, the concept of spirit possession mystifies the true sources of tension and discontent in the society, and those who "suffer from possession are set in a system of rewards and punishment which enables them to be manipulated to confirm a theory. The privileges permitted and the gifts granted to possessed women are part of this matrix. . . . [S]pirit possession attacks may redress the disadvantages of a lowly and deprived status, but at the same time the way in which this amelioration is obtained ensures that deviants confirm a mystifying theory which is an essential element in the control system which maintains them as lowly and deprived persons" (1975, 135).[15]

I am not sure that I agree with all of Gomm's ideas. In particular, he seems to ignore the distinction we made in Chapter 9 between lay and professional possession. His description fits well the experiences of a lay housewife who becomes possessed in the wake of illness or marital problems, but it sheds no light whatsoever on professional shamans who voluntarily and expertly beckon and manipulate the spirits throughout a long and socially recognized career. Indeed, Gomm defines spirit possession as an "involuntary affliction," a description that hardly fits the religious work of an experienced Afro-Brazilian "Mother."

Regarding lay spirit possession I believe that his points are well taken. The very essence of the role conveys a sense of weakness: the woman herself did not challenge or demand, she was merely a vehicle or "horse" of the spirits. On the other hand, I beg the reader to bear in mind the argument I made in Chapters 8 and 9 concerning the cognitive impact of seeing one's gods, spirits and ancestors consistently embodied in **female** form (through spirit possession).

Illness

In Model 1 religions women almost always join the religion because of illness. Model 2 religions have little, if anything, to do with illness.

Anthropologist Mary Douglas has proposed that bodies serve as social maps onto which cultural categories and boundaries are projected. If we concur with Douglas (as most contemporary anthropologists do), how are we to interpret a model that shows that in order to join a religion a woman must be ill? And even more to the point, a lay member simply joins through illness, but a leader typically has suffered and then dramatically overcome long, painful, debilitating diseases and misfortune (see Chapter 11). Drawing on Douglas's ideas, I would argue that in Model 1 religions the cultural categories that are "mapped" onto women's bodies are weakness, suffering, and powerlessness. In Model 2 religions, the social "map" reads very differently. Illness is, at most, peripheral; sisterhood, economic independence, and control of fertility are central.

The connection between illness and women's oppression has been well demonstrated in Barbara Ehrenreich and Deirdre English's expose of the sexual politics of sickness in the United States. Ehrenreich and English show how nineteenth-century culture fostered among middle-class women a "morbid cult of hypochondria" together with fervent dependence on medical practitioners (1973, 17). The medical view identified all female reproductive functions as inherently pathological, a view that surely weakened women's structural status. Sickness became synonymous with femininity, female disorders were traced to women's sexual, athletic, or mental exertions, and women were counseled to rest and refrain from public activities.

I quote here from Ehrenreich and English: "[L]ate nineteenth century medical treatment of women made very little sense as *medicine*, but it was undoubtedly effective at keeping certain women . . . in their place. As we have seen, surgery was often performed with the explicit goal of 'taming' a high-strung woman. . . . The more the doctors 'treated,' the more they lured women into seeing themselves as sick" (1973, 35–37).

Ehrenreich and English do point out that women were sometimes able to turn the sick role to their own advantage, both as a form of birth control and as a way of gaining attention within the family. This is consistent with what we have seen in female-dominated religions. Illness often allows women a certain measure of respite from an intolerable family situation (e.g., Korean shamans) or an opportunity to leave the house for short periods of time and find comfort in the company of other women (Afro-Brazilian religions).

On the other hand, in contrast to sisterhood (symbolic or biological) that communalizes women and thus allows women to achieve collective benefits, illness individualizes women's problems and women's solutions. A sick woman is treated as a private invalid, not as a victim of structural oppression. As a result, healing—even in the context of a female-dominated religion—tends to cure the individual woman and not the societal ills that may well have been responsible for her illness to begin with.

CONCLUSION

Having laid out and analyzed these two patterns of secular benefits, it is worth noting that the opposite patterns do not seem to occur: There are no female-dominated religions in which individual women suffer immediate disadvantages yet women as a group benefit in the long-term[16], and there are no female-dominated religions in which women are harmed both in the long term and the short term. The absence of the second pattern should not be surprising: As I said in Chapter 10, women's religions preach relatively egalitarian gender ideologies; it would be odd to find that egalitarian gender ideologies go together with entirely disadvantageous effects on women. The absence of the first pattern warrants more thought. We could easily imagine a religion in which individual women choose to sacrifice themselves for the greater good of womankind; martyrdom is certainly a well-known theme in religious history. I can only guess why this pattern does not occur. It seems to me that an ideal of individual martyrdom is inconsistent with the immanent character of women's religions (see Chapter 7). Women's religions tend to focus on the here-and-now and not on the hereafter, regardless of whether that hereafter is in the next world or in this one.

In this chapter I have argued that while it is incorrect to assume that women join female-dominated religions solely because of social and psychological deprivation, it is clear that participation in these religions serves women's secular interests in a variety of ways. On the whole, female-dominated religions provide women with short-term assistance. In certain circumstances, that short-term assistance either leads to, or is complemented by, long-term benefits. Those circumstances all involve power and autonomy. Economic independence (cf. Sacks 1974), control of sexuality and fertility (cf. Bleier 1984), and ongoing extra-domestic ties (cf. Rosaldo 1974) all set the stage for long-term advantages. Lack of power as embodied either by spirit possession (the spirit rather than the woman is the real power) and illness tends to limit secular advantages to the short term.

It is crucial to realize that both models I have presented are circular rather than linear in nature: Sisterhood and autonomy are prerequisites for the development of Model 2 religions, but when we look at the ways in which Model 2 religions benefit women, we see that autonomy and an ongoing collective power base are among the chief benefits. Similarly, concerning Model 1 religions we see that healing and spirit possession provide individual women with immediate assistance, but in that they individualize and mystify the true source of women's suffering, they undermine the ability of the religion to offer collective empowerment.

We have come full circle. We have seen in what cultural contexts women's religions arise, the content of women's religions, and how women's religions serve women's interests. I will now bring together the themes that have emerged from this study and present some more general conclusions.

Notes

1. Women's religions do not have a monopoly on serving women's interests. An apparently sexist ideology can sometimes encourage women to take political action that serves their interests as people and as women. This is certainly the case in Latin America where many liberation movements are grounded in Catholic ideology.

2. Mary Baker Eddy publicly supported suffrage and legal equality for women, and treated these issues as both political and theological ones. Christian Science in the late nineteenth and early twentieth century saw in the women's rights movement a reflection at the human level of the concept of divine womanhood explicated by Mary Baker Eddy. Also many leaders of the movement for women's suffrage were active Spiritualists.

3. I moved Black Carib religion back and forth between the two columns before I finally decided that it belongs with Model 1. The ancestor rituals of Black Carib women help individual women, for example, grandmothers, to get their sons and absent daughters to send them money. The so-called "love magic" rituals aid specific younger women to negotiate their relationships with husbands and lovers. It is difficult to see how either set of rituals affects women as a group.

4. "In the [Sudanese] village women do not need a 'support group' that is supplied by belonging to the cult. Just about every woman in the village is possessed, and even if not they still attend ceremonies. Every woman is closely related to every other; they live in each others' pockets, as they say. Support—moral, financial—is not hard to find" (Boddy, personal communication 1992).

5. Some men claim that women deliberately seek to waste their husband's financial resources to prevent his taking a second wife.

6. Ruth Landes has mentioned another way in which some women benefit from participation in the cults: One purpose of the cults in Bahia was to give the women a striking stage setting in which they look beautiful and exciting. The temple women had no lack of male admirers, "It was a duty of the men to look on and admire" (1947, 144).

7. I thank Judith Lorber for this insight.

8. Feminist Spirituality is the exception to this pattern. The North American middle class of the second half of the twentieth century is characterized by unusually high geographic mobility. It would be rare indeed to find Spiritual Feminists who have lifelong associations with one another.

9. Since the Shakers chose to live in isolated communities, it is legitimate to consider the Shaker village as both the result of and the background to Shaker beliefs.

10. Sanday's findings are of a great deal of interest, yet because women's religions do not tend to particularly worship female deities, more work needs to be done on the triple connection between goddesses, women's religious status, and women's economic status.

11. Peter Kunstadter does not make the connection explicit but it is there in his writings: The other ethnic groups in Northern Thailand (Lua', Karen) do not have matrilineal spirit cults run by women. In these groups men perform various sorts of rituals and healing and divination. And, according to Kunstadter, the Northern Thai (as opposed to the Lua' and Karen) have lower fertility rates, more women in prominent public roles, and more women than men visiting the birth control clinic (1978, 209).

12. Okinawan men believed that a husband from the same village as the highest priestesses (*noro*) would not live long. (Lower level priestesses are housewives or grandmothers and do marry.) Until recently, the marriage of *noro* was illegal and the children illegitimate. A *noro* who wished to marry would continue living with or near her brother, and her husband would come to "visit." During the last century *noro* have been permitted to marry, and almost all do so. Still, before major festivals they sleep apart from their husbands.

13. In recent times their economic independence has been eroded by loss of land, **and** celibacy has declined.

14. An example here is a Spiritualist marriage ceremony found in the *Twentieth Century Formulary of Songs and Forms* by W.C. Bowman (1907), cited in Ward (1990). The ceremony carries no hint of men's control of women's sexuality or fertility, and the introduction to the ceremony actually acknowledges that marriage is a product of present political and social conditions, and "the mere fact of its having been made venerable thus far by law, custom and religion is no conclusive evidence either of its perfection or its perpetuity" (p. 130). The ceremony itself addresses the couple in these extraordinarily egalitarian terms: "And recognizing equal rights and equal dignity on the part of man and woman, the marriage vows you plight to each other are not separate and distinct, but mutual and equal" (p. 132).

15. Digo spirit possession, as described by Gomm, differs considerably from *zār*. Among the Digo, women who court chronic spirit possession are accorded low status and considered to be mad. The *zār* cult, on the other hand, is made up of women who initially were possessed involuntarily, but then chose to pursue further possession experiences.

16. Field reports indicate that for Sande women the individual benefits outweigh the pain of clitoridectomy.

Conclusion

CRITIQUE OF PREVIOUS SCHOLARSHIP

I am indebted to the ethnographers and historians who collected and published information on the examples this book is based on. I wish to reiterate my thanks, before I continue with a necessary, feminist critique of a great deal of what I have read.

I have already discussed how deprivation theory—one of the most common theories used to "explain" women's religiosity—both reduces women's vibrant existential quests to such banal factors as sexual frustration (cf. Kern 1981) and fails to do justice to the rich variety of forms of women's spiritual expression. It is particularly important to address the issue of sexuality, because over and over in the literature I find scholars using it to rationalize women's religiosity. Erik Erikson, for example, claims that there are deep existential implications to the anatomical fact that in sexual intercourse the male penis penetrates the female vagina.[1] It seems to me however, that with the exception of rape (and that is not what Erikson is talking about), the similarities in the ways that men and women experience sexual relations (and religion) are surely far more significant than the differences. I find it absurd to interpret such patterns as the belief that suffering is not necessary to the human condition and can and should be alleviated (see Chapter 5) in terms of the anatomical organization of heterosexual intercourse. And indeed, scholars who use physiological and anatomical models rarely (if ever) look deeply at women's theological and philosophical stances.[2]

In light of the data presented in this book and the (to my mind unfortunate) attraction of anatomical and physiological models, it is ironic that few scholars interpret women's religiosity in terms of motherhood. Accounts of women's religions, my fieldwork among Kurdish women, and my own personal experiences as a mother all lead me to conclude that the loves, sorrows, and responsibilities of mothering have a much profounder impact than the rather brief sex act does on one's religious life. Evaluating the lack of attention given to motherhood in contrast to the surplus of attention given to sexual intercourse, I suspect that we have uncovered a lurking phallocentric obsession in western scholarship.

It strikes me as significant that so many scholars have seen women's religiosity as standing in special need of psychological explanation. It also strikes me as significant that so many scholars have seen goddesses as standing in special need of psychological explanation. Does a pattern emerge? I am reminded of the revolting joke told among gynecologists: Why are there so many gynecologists in the world? Because the very fact of being female is an illness! What seems to underlie both the scholarly literature and the joke is a perception of female as exceptional, other, not normal, and so in need of explanation.

To take one brief example, according to Alex Owen, "Spiritualist mediumship was both expressive of an inner struggle with the problem of femininity and instrumental in reconciling that tension" (1981, 209). I would like to raise the question of why women's religious participation is so often explained even by feminist scholars as a function of cultural definitions of womanhood, while men's religious participation is almost never explained as a function of cultural definitions of manhood!

It seems to me that previous scholars have devoted disproportionate attention to the personal histories of the leaders of women's religions. Indeed, for several religions I easily found volumes purporting to "analyze" the foundress, but I had trouble finding any detailed descriptions of theology or rituals. In particular, scholars have been impressed by the apparent central role of illness in the life stories of leaders. Yet, as I pointed out in Chapter 11, it seems far more likely that these stories, a form of literary device, are constructed to "prove" the key beliefs of the religion—that suffering is not inescapable in this life. One wonders whether so many modern scholars would explain Islamic monotheism in terms of Mohammed's (hypothetical) illnesses, relationship with his parents, or sexual frustrations.

In Chapter 7 I suggested that the morality of women's religions tends to be invisible to Western scholars. When I read that Okinawans have little interest in religious and philosophic speculation (Kerr 1958, 217), I am led to ask whether the truth was that many of the scholars who reported about Okinawan culture could not believe that mere women did in fact think about such things. At least in the Okinawan case, given that men are not allowed to enter the sacred groves, we can also assume that the majority of ethnographers who studied Okinawan religion were denied access to key information. Yet we find no mention in their published treatises of the possibility that they might have missed out on essential elements of women's religious beliefs and rituals.

In a similar vein, in Chapter 1 I critiqued the use of the term "love magic" to describe certain religious rituals performed by Black Carib women in order to preserve family relationships. When I first began looking for women's religions, I found very few—because so few were called "religions" by western scholars. Healing cults, magic, superstition—but not religion. Do we, as scholars, get lost in our own terminology?

Feminist thinker Carol Christ has critiqued Mircea Eliade's "conception of religion as providing release from the 'chaotic and dangerous flux of things' "

(1991, 91). Eliade, Christ explains, valorizes the spiritual progress shown by detachment from the "immediate" and the "concrete" (his words). As Christ asks: Who says that the transcendent is "better" than the immanent? An issue that must be addressed by feminist scholarship is the tendency among academics to treat interest in the other world as more noble, virtuous, and estimable than interest in this world. The models for "pure" spirituality whom many of us read about in college were, for the most part, mystics who dramatically devalued the concerns of this world. Once we fall into the trap of judging transcendent religiosity to be "better" than immanent religiosity, it is but a short step to believe—as have critics of Spiritualism—that women's religions are this-worldly because women are less intelligent or less capable of abstract thinking than men. (And indeed this is an easy trap because the so-called "great world religions" are both male–dominated and other-worldly.) A feminist critique must begin with a broad proclamation that recent studies of sex differences show no gap between men's and women's intelligence (see Hyde 1990). Women's religions are not characterized by a this-worldly orientation because women are just not quite as smart as men. Whether or not my suggestion of interpreting the this-worldly orientation of female-dominated religions in terms of women's emotional and day-to-day experiences of mothering is correct, I am convinced that this sort of socio-cultural interpretation is a step in the right direction.

As a feminist anthropologist I am uncomfortable writing a book about women and religion until I see a few books that are explicitly about men—that use uniquely male experiences to interpret men's religious lives.[3] My fear in writing this book is that readers will join me in exploring these extraordinary women's religions, yet will abandon me when I ask how religion looks when we treat the female as normative. For example, could it be that possession trance is a normal and healthy part of human experience, but men have trouble with it because they have a problem with relationships?

A LACK OF CONCLUSIONS

I opened this book by asking whether women's religions are in any way "womanly"; whether there is anything distinctively feminine in the theological, symbolic, or ritual content of female-dominated religions. I argued that I would not expect religiosity to be an automatic function of sex: ritual preferences are not carried on the x or y chromosomes, and the ethnographic record does not warrant our making many generalizations about women and men.

To recapitulate some of the non-universals we have seen: In most female-dominated religions leaders are old women, except in Spiritualism where they are young. Women's religions do not engage in missionizing, except for the Shakers who dedicated a great deal of time and resources to seeking converts. In most women's religions food rituals are very important and elaborated, except in Christian Science. Animal sacrifice is anathema to women's religions, except for the *zār* cult. On the Ryūkyū Islands almost all rituals are performed by priestesses, the ritual role of laity is marginal, and rituals are highly standardized and unemotional; among Spiritual Feminists all participants have crucial

ritual roles, ceremonies tend to be innovative and personal, and demonstrations of emotion are respected. Women's religions do not usually itemize and
codify rules of moral behavior, except for the Shakers who spelled out what
one should do and how one should do it every hour of the day and night.

When we turn our attention to the supernatural entities addressed in
women's religions, the differences among the religions leap off the page. In
some of the women's religions the deities insist that people behave morally to
other people; in other religions the deities are concerned primarily with ritual
proficiency. In some the deities are associated with famous myths and easily
identifiable personalities; in others they are not (and in the Northern Thai
matrilineal spirit cults it is near impossible to discern who or what the spirits
even are!). In some of the religions the deities are foreigners or peripheral; in
others they embody the very essence of the community and its native land.

Throughout this book I have demonstrated how women's religions enhance
and glorify interpersonal and familial bonds, and provide support and nurturance for ill and suffering women. Yet Tensho-Kotai-Jingu-Kyu teaches that the
most common cause of illness is *innen*—a Karma chain, fate, or bondage that is
transmitted from one individual to another through family links. In Tensho,
healing is effected by breaking chains of *innen*! Unlike in mainstream Japanese
culture in which a sick person is closely cared for and seen as especially righ-
teous, in Tensho the sick role loses all legitimacy. Members are told to stay
away from sick people so as not to catch the spirit causing the illness. In
contrast to most other women's religions, Tensho teaches that strong interpersonal bonds are not desirable, that sick people should not be nurtured, and that
illness does not lead to righteousness.[4] Indeed, one of the first acts of the
foundress was to order her followers to throw away their ancestors' tablets and
break off with the Buddhist temples whose cemeteries held their family tombs
(Nakamura 1980, 182).[5]

The specific historical and cultural contexts of the religions go a great way
toward explaining their differences. Beginning with the global statement that
women's religions are rare, we can identify a variety of circumstances in which
they are more likely to occur. First, when a new and powerful religion conquers a tribal or village level society, women may end up in charge of what
used to be the religious system in which both men and women participated.
This model is true, for example, of Korean shamanism. A second model
concerns male migration and resulting matrifocality. When men are absent a
great deal of the time (for a variety of possible reasons including war and
economic necessity) women become more independent in terms of religious
choice. This model is relevant to the *zār* cult and the religion of the Black
Caribs. In other cultural situations the mainstream, male-dominated religion
does not provide adequate explanations for and solutions to problems that are
particularly acute for women. If the society tolerates alternate religious
choices, women may become involved with "fringe" cults. For example, we
saw how some scholars explain women's dominance in nineteenth-century
North American Spiritualism as an outgrowth of women's dissatisfaction with
Calvinist belief that their dead babies were going to hell rather than heaven.

None of the women's religions originated in a cultural vacuum. All developed within contexts of sexist cultures, and most emerged out of (or in reaction to) non-female-dominated religions. The Afro-Brazilian religions are syncretic cults in which Catholicism (clearly not dominated by women) is a major component; Christian Science and Shakers identify with the Christian tradition; Korean shamanism was not dominated by women in the past. It could be argued that each of the women's religions reviewed in this book has more in common with men's religions of the same time and place than with women's religions located on different continents.

The dissimilar histories of the women's religions, together with their very diverse cultural contexts, partially account for the lack of universal patterns. But again, I wish to stress that I do not really think that the absence of universal patterns needs explanation: We would hardly expect all men's religions to be similar, so why should we expect all women's religions to be?

A final factor to consider is social roles versus sex as a shaper of religiosity. We saw in Chapter 3 that recent studies have linked sympathy and nurturance to the **social** role of caring for children. Since most of the themes we have discovered in women's religions seem to be functions of social role (primary responsibility for children), we should not be surprised to find that just as patterns of parenting vary from culture to culture, so do patterns of women's religiosity. In a similar vein, in an important study of spirit possession in contemporary Egypt, Soheir Morsy found that "when other dimensions [besides sex] of persons' identities are taken into account by reference to status within the household, and the developmental cycle of the family, the significance of power differentials beyond those associated with gender identity are brought into focus. Thus, the higher frequency of *uzr* [spirit possession] among the male category of brother of household head contrasts with the low frequency of the illness among relatively powerful females, notably the mothers of married sons" (1991, 205). In brief, I am left wondering which of the patterns we have discovered in this book are gender linked and which are role or status linked.

SUMMARY

In the Introduction I proposed two conditions sufficiently widespread to account for the patterns or motifs that we might uncover in women's religions situated in dissimilar cultural contexts. These two conditions are patriarchy and motherhood. **Very few of the patterns we have uncovered can be interpreted primarily in terms of women's oppression in patriarchal cultures.** As I argued in Chapter 2, women's religions tend to occur in societies characterized by a relatively high level of autonomy for women.

Most of the patterns that I have described in this book can be understood as functions of women's social role as mothers in societies in which that role is granted both esteem and structurally recognized authority. Cross-culturally, women give birth to children and are primary caretakers of children. This cross-cultural reality leaves its stamp on all women's religions. Motherhood is a central point of self-definition for women in the cultures with which I am dealing in this book. In all these cultures, girls are socialized from a young age to be mothers; in all these cultures motherhood shapes the lives of almost all adult women. Even celibate Shaker and infertile Luvale women were part of cultural contexts in which motherhood fashioned women's life experiences. If there are women's religions in which motherhood is not a pivotal motif, I have not been able to discover them in the available ethnographic or historical literature.[6]

Motherhood does not have automatic consequences for women's religiosity—that is one of the themes that has repeatedly surfaced in this study—and that in part explains why each of these religions is different from the others in many significant ways. On the other hand, if one wishes to understand why there are certain traits that characterize almost all women's religions, if one wants to write about women and religion from a cross-cultural perspective, it is helpful to look at motherhood, which is, after all, the human experience that most clearly impacts on women differently than on men. My focus on motherhood is neither a literary device nor an ideological stance; rather, it is an accurate and pervasive reference point for the study of women's religions.

The first trend that has emerged is that women's religions are more likely to occur in societies that are matrilineal, matrilocal, or matrifocal than in societies that are not. A number of factors account for this trend. To begin with, matrifocality in the context of an otherwise patriarchal culture leads to a situation of gender disjunction in which "cracks" may open up into which women's religions can then fit. In matrifocal societies women's identity as mother (an active identity) is emphasized more than their identities as wives or daughters (passive identities). In matrilocal societies women tend to be freer to meet together with other women. In matrilineal societies women are more likely to control their own fertility. Not surprisingly, women's religions tend to further enhance women's roles as mothers. This is the place to clarify that Nancy Chodorow's ideas do not explain **why** women's religions arise; they simply help us interpret the content of these religions. However, it does seem relevant that women's religions cluster in matrifocal, matrilocal, and matrilineal societies—that is, in situations in which all the implications of women's mothering (as explained by Chodorow) are especially potent.

Drawing on Chodorow's theses, we have suggested that women—who themselves were raised by women—develop an ease with and affinity for interpersonal relationships. This is manifested in the ritual constellations emphasized in women's religions. Food rituals, ancestor rituals, and initiation rituals all function to strengthen communal bonds.

Ongoing, intense, and intimate relationships between mothers and children lead many women to seek religions that offer persuasive interpretations of child death and provide effective and eclectic means of alleviating illness and suffering. Women's religions excel at both these tasks, often filling a gap left by the male-dominated religions of their day.

Perhaps the most important implication of motherhood involves particularism. Women as mothers love and nurture specific children, and they seek out the divine within the profane "real" world of relationships and nature. Very few women are able to simply pack up and leave their families to pursue ascetic or other extraordinary religious paths.

Comfortable with other people, women are willing to meet their gods and goddesses face to face and even share their bodies with divinities (in spirit possession). Transcendent, monotheistic male deities have little meaning for mothers who daily confront existential issues of birth, suffering, and death. One of the clearest patterns to emerge from this study is really a "non-pattern": none of these religions worships a single, all-powerful, male deity.

None of the women's religions teaches that women are inherently inferior. Many of these religions explain why women are more suited for religious leadership (they understand suffering better, their souls are softer, etc.). These religions teach that men and women are essentially different, and that while both male and female are necessary in this world, the two are often in tension. In many cultures in which we find female-dominated religions women have primary responsibility for raising children, yet are dependent on (all too often erratic) economic contributions of men in order to raise children properly. A philosophy of gender tension fits in well with women's actual experiences.

Focused on people, women's religions tend to be internally hierarchical within the individual chapters or congregations—they care a great deal about who does what to whom. Uninterested in transcendence and neglected by the powers-that-be, women's religions display an aversion to centralization and institutionalized doctrine. A lack of codified moral laws, however, does not mean a lack of morality. Moral behavior in women's religions is situational, rooted in particular relationships, yet perceived as having implications for the entire community.

Women's religions serve women's secular interests. In situations in which women enjoy economic independence, control over their own bodies, and ongoing relationships with their fellow members, female-dominated religions can obtain permanent, collective benefits for women. In situations in which women are economically and socially isolated, female-dominated religions pro-vide specific women with short-term support vis-à-vis specific men.

A last pattern, and the sole pattern that does seem to be truly ubiquitous in women's religions, concerns militarism. None of the religions engages in any sort of *jihad* or holy war. Although most of the religions welcome new mem-bers, none carries out any sort of forcible conversion.[7] The epitome of this pattern is the Shakers. Despite their interest in drawing in new members, even being raised in a Shaker community did not automatically translate into Shaker membership. Moreover, the Shakers were pacifists who refused to fight in America's wars. Can we deduce from this that women are more tolerant of alternative beliefs, that women are less violent than men? Sara Ruddick and many other feminist writers certainly think that is indeed the case. Personally, I am reluctant to make such grandiose claims. On the other hand, it may well be that through the experiences of raising children women come to grips with issues of power and lack of power in ways that most men do not. The dilemma of mothering—that we possess far more power than we dare to use but that all our power cannot protect or mold our children exactly as we wish—could very well translate into an aversion to forcible proselytizing. Women, as subordinate members of sexist societies, are unlikely to have access to, be socialized into, or attracted by military power. Most women know all too well what it means to be victims of violent coercion.

As we review these patterns and once again highlight the implications of motherhood, it is critical to reiterate that the social rather than the biological aspects of motherhood have emerged as most salient to women's religions. Ornate fertility rituals, myths of mother goddesses who give birth to the world, and ceremonies that extol the wonders of lactation are almost totally absent from women's religions. What does receive attention and elaboration in these religions is women's social roles as nurturers and healers, women's rights and responsibilities as primary childcare providers, women's emotional experiences of pain at the illness and death of children, women's social ties with other mothers, matrifocality, and women's proclivity for discovering the sacred which is immanent in this everyday world of care and relationship.

Most readers of this book grew up in male-dominated religious traditions, and probably have been tempted to compare their own religious traditions to those presented here. I want to clarify that the patterns outlined above are not unique to women's religions; they simply are easier to see in women's religions. I surmise that many of these patterns can also be found, to some extent, in women's religious activities within male-dominated religions.[8] The difference between the two types of situations is that in female-dominated religions these patterns are institutionalized and esteemed. In male-dominated religions, on the other hand, these patterns tend to be subsumed under the categories of "folklore," "superstition," "syncretism," "heresy," or simply "ladies' auxiliary."

Notes

1. Erikson, like Freud, tries to define the "intrinsically feminine" and "intrinsically masculine" essence of women and men in terms of the anatomical differences of their genital organs. According to Erikson, men and women organize space according to the morphology of their bodies, and this affects psychosocial development and orientation to "inner" and "outer" space. Men and women follow the spacial morphology of their bodies in their psychic, social, cultural, and religious lives. Women's womb is an "inner productive space" that men do not have. Women tend to a fear of being left empty or deprived of treasures or unfulfilled or drying up. This is manifested in their spiritual experience.

2. Spirit possession and ecstatic mysticism are generally the favored phenomena explained by proponents of physiological and anatomical models.

3. I am not referring to books **implicitly** about men. Almost all available studies of religion are in fact about men and religion; it is just that the authors do not make that fact clear and do not use maleness as an analytic category.

4. A second "exception" are the nineteenth-century Sanctificationists, who strictly regulated relationships among the all-female membership. According to Sally Kitch, group by-laws forbid members to become especially close to particular co-members, and even overly intensive mother-child ties were discouraged (1989, 108).

5. According to Nakamura, however, maternal ties are not condemned in the way that other familial ties are (1980). This fits in more closely with other women's religions.

6. The closest I can come to a women's religion that does not emphasize motherhood is the religion of the Ryūkyū Islands—sisterhood is at least equally if not more fundamental to Ryūkyūan women's religious perceptions and roles.

7. Most women's religions even allow members to belong to other religions concurrently (see Chapters 5 and 12).

8. The one pattern rarely if ever found in male-dominated religions is strategies to serve women's secular interests, particularly what I have called "Model 2"—long-term structural benefits for women as a group.

APPENDIX A

Alphabetical Summaries of Key Examples

Afro-Brazilian Religions Syncretic religions combining elements of African tribal religions, Amerindian religions, Catholicism, and Kardecism (French Spiritism). Known by such names as Candomblé, Umbanda, Batuque, Xango, and Macumba. Two main features are curing and public rituals in which mediums are possessed by spirits. Most people who attend Afro-Brazilian rituals do so in order to be healed of illness or misfortune.

Black Carib Religion Main feature is numerous mourning and ancestor rituals organized by old women. Black Caribs live in Central America. The religious life of the Black Caribs of Belize is especially well documented.

Burmese *Nat* Religion The indigenous Burmese religion centers on the appeasement of *nats* (spirits/gods). *Nats* are propitiated to prevent and cure illness, at key stages in the agricultural cycle, at births, deaths, marriages, and Buddhist initiations. Elaborate myths are associated with *nats*. At large festivals female *nat* shamans become possessed by their *nat* "husbands." Smaller *nat* rituals are carried out by housewives.

Christian Science Founded in the United States in the nineteenth century by Mary Baker Eddy. Main tenet: matter is illusory, therefore illness is illusory. Healing comes about through study and prayer, which lead one to truly understand the nonreality of matter.

Feminist Spirituality Movement A contemporary American religion that has grown out of the secular feminist movement. Spiritual Feminists draw on myths and symbols of many cultures, emphasize the spirituality of female energy and bodies, relate to goddesses, and perform rituals that empower women. **Womanism** is the name used by African-American feminists for their own women's spirituality movement.

Korean Household Religion Korean women make food offerings to the gods of their households and consult female shamans to divine why misfortune has struck their households. At the elaborate *kut* ritual, shamans become possessed by various gods, spirits, and ancestors.

Northern Thai Matrilineal Spirit Cults Northern Thai kinship organization is matrilineal and matrilocal. Spirits that are understood as belonging to the descent (or cult) group are propitiated at various ritual occasions. All the matrilineal descendants of a founding ancestress constitute a cult group.

Ryūkyūan Island Religion The official, mainstream religion of the Ryūkyū Islands (the main island is **Okinawa**) is totally dominated by women. Priestesses (*noro*) at the household, family, and village levels (and formerly at the state level) perform multitudinous rituals that seek the assistance of the *kami* (gods). Shamans (*yuta*), who are also women, perform personal healing and divination rituals.

Sande Secret Society In much of West Africa adolescent girls are initiated into the women's Sande secret society (also known as Bundu). Sande initiation teaches about childbirth and other skills and attitudes women need to know. Sande chapters protect their members by punishing men and women who infringe on Sande rules.

Shakers Ann Lee led a group of eighteenth-century English Shakers to America where they founded rural communes dedicated to agriculture, celibacy, and worship. Shakers believed that Ann Lee had come to finish the work of Jesus Christ, and that the Messianic era had already begun. Their worship was characterized by ecstatic dancing and "shaking."

Spiritualism Beginning in the nineteenth-century United States, Spiritualists believed that individuals continue to exist after death, and that the living can communicate with the dead at seances. Mediums (mostly women) were channels for this communication. Currently, Spiritualist groups exist in the United States, Great Britain, and Mexico (where the emphasis is on healing rather than communication with the spirit world).

Zār In parts of Africa and the Middle East, individuals (mostly women) suffering from a variety of ailments are diagnosed as possessed by *zār* spirits. In order to be healed and resume functioning, the individual must undergo initiation into the *zār* cult. The *zār* is not exorcised; rather, the woman learns to accommodate the *zār*. Members meet periodically at possession trance rituals.

APPENDIX B

Alphabetical Summaries of Auxiliary Examples

Beguines The movement of celibate Christian women known as Beguines originated during the thirteenth century in the Low countries and the Rhine Valley. These women lived in small communities and dedicated their lives to charitable acts. For a variety of reasons, including the fact that they lived outside of monasteries, they did not receive papal approval.

Black Spiritual Churches New Orleans Spiritual people trace their origins to a woman named Leafy Anderson, who came from Chicago to New Orleans in the 1920s. Spiritual churches are linked to numerous older religious traditions, including Protestantism, Folk Catholicism, Pentecostal Movement, nineteenth-century American Spiritualism, and Vodou practices of the African diaspora. Spiritual people have a widespread eclectic belief system. During church services, many Spiritual people may enter into trance or other ecstatic states that include periods of dancing, spinning, uttering "coos," violent seizures, writhing on the floor, etc. Recent studies show fifty Spiritual churches in New Orleans today.

Guglielmites This thirteenth-century Christian "heresy" considered women to be the only hope for the salvation of humanity. They announced that the third person of the trinity had been incarnated in the female Guglielma of Milan and would establish a female-ruled church with female cardinals. Churchmen viewed the Guglielmites as fools and Guglielma was condemned as a heretic.

Luvale of Zambia Women's ritual expertise is passed down through matrilineal lines. The Luvale believe that female ancestors afflict their outmarrying female descendants with illness and infertility to remind them of their matrilineal obligations. Involvement in women's rituals and participation in the women's healing cult cures women afflicted by ancestral spirits.

Sanctificationists Also known as the Woman's Commonwealth and as the Sanctified Sisters. This all-female group became an official community in 1890 in Belton, Texas. The women broke off from the Methodist church, primarily because of their belief in celibacy and ecumenism. Although they began as a worship group, so many of the women became estranged from their husbands (because of their religious beliefs) that they found it necessary to form a commune to ensure their economic survival. The group never had more than 100 members. According to Sally Kitch, "Although they left no record of a belief in either a female God or a female Christ, court testimonies, interviews, and the group's constitution reveal a feminist approach not only to the economic and social independence of women from men, and to the personal autonomy of individual women, but also to a female-identified source of spiritual authority" (1989, 14). Kitch notes that the group experienced violent resistance to their celibate communism (1989, 63). Over the years the religious focus of the group declined, and the economic focus took precedence.

Tenrikyo   This Japanese religion was founded in 1838 when God revealed himself to the foundress Miki Hakayama. Tenrikyo teaches that sickness originates from mental attitudes. God is referred to in Tenrikyo as "God the Parent" and associated with parental love. Diseases are seen as an opportunity to improve oneself because God informs humans of his true intentions through disease. In recent years approximately half of the priests are women, and two-thirds of the members are women.

Tensho-Kotai-Jingu-Kyu (also spelled **Tensho-Kotai-Jingukyo**)   This new Japanese religion was founded in 1945 when Mrs. Sayo Kitamura discovered that she carried God in her abdomen. She became the spokeswoman of a *kami* [deity], known as the Tensho Kotai Jin (Absolute Almighty God of the Universe). The Tensho cult draws on Buddhist, Shinto, Confucianist, and Christian concepts. There is a worldwide membership of approximately 360,000 people, most of whom are Japanese.

Tetum Religion   In this Indonesian society women are associated with the sacred and men with the secular. Women preside over most rituals and most ghosts are female. The clan shrine is attended by a priestess. Birth symbolism is highly developed in Tetum religion; the first ancestors emerged from the earth womb, and birth rituals are complex and lengthy.

Theosophy   The Theosophical Society was founded in New York in 1875, and in the 1880s spread to London and Madras. Theosophists taught that the human body is a temporal home for the eternal spirit and this spirit goes through evolutionary stages and reincarnates itself both in male and female guises. This evolutionary process involves the interaction of both matter and spirit, *yin* and *yang*, male and female.

Vodou   The leaders of Haitian Vodou are mediums who lend their bodies and voices to a large and variegated pantheon of mostly African spirits. In rural areas of Haiti most leaders were male; in contemporary urban America most are female. The essence of Vodou is healing: healing between people and healing between the living and the spirits. Rituals involve drumming and possession trance.

REFERENCES — KEY EXAMPLES

Afro-Brazilian Religions

Bastide, Roger. 1978 [1960]. *The African Religions of Brazil*. Baltimore: Johns Hopkins University Press.

Brown, Diana DeG. 1986. *Umbanda Religion and Politics in Urban Brazil*. Ann Arbor, Michigan: UMI Reseach Press.

Brumana, Fernando Giobellina, and Elda Gonzales Martinez. 1989. *Spirits from the Margin: Umbanda in Sao Paulo*. Upsala, Sweden: Acta Universitatis Upsaliensis.

Burdick, John. 1990. Gossip and Secrecy: Women's Articulation of Domestic Conflict in Three Religions of Urban Brazil. *Sociological Analysis* 50(2):153–170.

Carneiro, Edison. 1940. The Structure of African Cults in Bahia. *Journal of American Folklore* 53:271–278.

Herskovits, Melville. 1943. The Southernmost Outposts of New World Africanisms. *American Anthropologist* 45(4):495–510.

Landes, Ruth. 1940a. A Cult Matriarchate and Male Homosexuality. *American Anthropologist* 35:386–397.

———. 1940b. Fetish Worship in Brazil. *Journal of American Folklore* 53:261–270.

———. 1947. *City of Women*. New York: Macmillan .

Leacock, Seth, and Ruth Leacock. 1972. *Spirits of the Deep: A Study of an Afro-Brazilian Cult*. New York: Doubleday Natural History Press.

Lerch, Patricia. 1980. Spirit Mediums in Umbanda Evangelizada of Porto Alegre, Brazil: Dimensions of Power and Authority. In *A World of Women*, ed. Erika Bourguignon, 129–159. New York: Praeger.

———. 1982. An Explanation for the Predominance of Women in the Umbanda Cults of Porto Alegre, Brazil. *Urban Anthropology* 11(2):237–261.

Merrick, Thomas, and Marianne Schmink. 1983. Households Headed by Women and Urban Poverty in Brazil. In *Women and Poverty in the Third World*, ed. Mayra Buvinic, Margaret Lycette, and William McGreevey, 244–271. Baltimore: Johns Hopkins University Press.

Neuhouser, Kevin. 1989. Sources of Women's Power and Status among the Urban Poor in Contemporary Brazil. *Signs* 14(3):685–702.

Pressel, Esther. 1974. Umbanda Trance and Possession in Sao Paulo, Brazil. In *Trance, Healing, and Hallucination*, ed. Felicitas Goodman, Jeannette Henney, and Esther Pressel, 113–221. New York: John Wyley and Sons.

———. 1980. Spirit Magic in the Social Relations between Men and Women (Sao Paulo, Brazil). In *A World of Women*, ed. Erika Bourguignon, 107–127. New York: Praeger.

Scheper-Hughes, Nancy. 1989. Death Without Weeping. *Natural History* 10:8–16.

Simpson, George E. 1978. *Black Religions in the New World*. New York: Columbia University Press.

Willems, Emilio. 1953. The Structure of the Brazilian Family. *Social Forces* 31:339–345.

Black Caribs

Bolland, O. Nigel. 1977. *The Formation of a Colonial Society: Belize, from Conquest to Crown Colony*. Baltimore: Johns Hopkins University Press.

Bullard, M. Kenyon. 1974. Hide and Secrete: Women's Sexual Magic in Belize. *The Journal of Sex Research* 10(4):259–265.

Chernela, Janet M. 1991. Symbolic Inaction in Rituals of Gender and Procreation among the Garifuna (Black Caribs) of Honduras. *Ethos* 19(1):52–67.

Coelho, Ruy Galvao de Andrade. 1955. *The Black Carib of Honduras: A Study in Acculturation*. Diss. Northwestern University.

Gonzalez, Nancie. 1983. Changing Sex Roles Among the Garifuna (Black Carib) and their Implications for the Family. *Jounal of Comparitive Family Studies* 14(2):203–213.

———. 1969. *Black Carib Household Structure*. Seattle: University of Washington Press.

Helms, Mary W. 1981. Black Carib Domestic Organization in Historical Perspective: Traditional Origins of Contemporary Patterns. *Ethnology* 20(1):77–86.

Kerns, Virginia. 1980. Black Carib Women and Rites of Death. In *Unspoken Worlds: Women's Religious Lives in Non-Western Cultures*, ed. Nancy A. Falk and Rita M. Gross, 127–140. San Francisco: Harper and Row.

———. 1983. *Women and the Ancestors: Black Carib Kinship and Ritual*. Urbana: University of Illinois Press.

———. 1992a. Preventing Violence Against Women: A Central American Case. In *Sanctions and Sanctuary: Cultural Perspectives on the Beating of Wives*, ed. Dorothy Ayers Counts, Judith K. Brown, and Jacquelyn C. Campbell, 125–138. Boulder: Westview Press.

———. 1992b. Female Control of Sexuality: Garifuna Women at Middle Age. In *In Her Prime: New Views of Middle-Aged Women*, ed. Virginia Kerns and Judith K. Brown, 94–111. Urbana: University of Illinois Press.

Munroe, Robert. 1980. Male Transvestism and the Couvade: A Psycho-Cultural Analysis. *Ethos* 8(1):49–59.

Sanford, Margaret. 1974. A Socialization in Ambiguity: Child-Lending in a British West Indian Society. *Ethnology* 13(4):393–400.

Staiano, Kathryn. 1981. Alternative Therapeutic Systems in Belize: A Semiotic Framework. *Social Science and Medicine* 15b:317–332.

Taylor, Douglas MacRae. 1951. *The Black Carib of British Honduras*. Viking Fund Publications in Anthropology, no. 17. New York: Wenner-Gren.

Burmese Nat Religion

Furnivall, I. C. S. 1911. Matriarchal Vestiges in Burma. *Journal of the Burma Research Society* 1:15–30.

Goswami, M. C., and H. Kamkhenthang. 1972. Mother's Brother in Paite Society. *Man in India* 52(1):21–38.

Khaing, Mi Mi. 1962. *Burmese Family*. Bloomington: Indiana University Press.

Nash, June C. 1966. Living with Nats: An Analysis of Animism in Burman Village Social Relations. South East Asia Studies, Yale University. In *Anthropological Studies in Theravada Buddhism*, 117–136. Cultural Report Series, vol. 13. New Haven: Yale University.

Nash, Manning. 1965. *The Golden Road to Modernity*. New York: Wiley.

———. 1966. Ritual and Ceremonial Cycle in Upper Burma. South East Asian Studies, Yale University. In *Anthropological Studies in Theravada Buddhism*, 97–115. Cultural Report Series, vol. 13. New Haven: Yale University.

Spiro, Melford. 1967. *Burmese Supernaturalism*. Englewood Cliffs, N.J.: Prentice-Hall.

———. 1971. *Buddhism and Society*. London: George Allen and Unwin.

———. 1977. *Kinship and Marriage in Burma*. Berkeley: University of California Press.

Christian Science

Becker, Carl B. 1990. Religious Healing in 19th Century 'New Religions': The Cases of Tenrikyo and Christian Science. *Religion* 20:199–215.

Eddy, Mary Baker. 1903. *Science and Health, with a Key to the Scriptures*. Boston: Published by the Trustees under the will of Mary Baker Eddy.

Fox, Margery. 1989. The Socioreligious Role of the Christian Science Practitioner. In *Women as Healers: Cross-Cultural Perspectives*, ed. Carol Shepherd McClain, 98–114. New Brunswick: Rutgers University Press.

Gottschalk, Stephen. 1973. *The Emergence of Christian Science in American Religious Life*. Berkeley: University of California Press.

Peel, Robert. 1966. *Mary Baker Eddy*. New York: Hold, Rinehart and Winston.

Setta, Susan. 1977. Denial of the Female—Affirmation of the Feminine: The Father-Mother God of Mary Baker Eddy. In *Beyond Androcentrism: New Essays on Women and Religion*, ed. Rita M. Gross. Missoula, Montana: Scholars Press.

Stark, Rodney, William Sims Bainbridge, and Lori Kent. 1981. Cult Membership in the Roaring Twenties: Assessing Local Receptivity. *Sociological Analysis* 4(2):137–162.

Trevett, Christine. 1984. Women, God and Mary Baker Eddy. *Religion* 14:143–153.

Williams, Peter W. 1980. *Popular Religion in America*. Englewood Cliffs, New Jersey: Prentice-Hall Inc.

Wilson, Bryan R. 1961. *Sects and Society*. Berkeley: University of California Press.

Feminist Spirituality

Adams, Bert N. 1969. *Kinship in an Urban Setting*. Chicago: Markham Publishing Company.

Adler, Margot. 1979. *Drawing Down the Moon*. Boston: Beacon Press.

Baruch, Grace, and Rosalind Barnett. 1983. Adult Daughters' Relationships with their Mothers. *Journal of Marriage and the Family* 45:601–606.

Bernard, Jessie. 1975. *Women, Wives, Mothers: Values and Options*. Chicago: Aldine Publishing Company.

Budapest, Zsuzsanna E. 1989. *The Grandmother of Time*. San Francisco: Harper and Row.

Christ, Carol. 1979. Why Women Need the Goddess: Phenomenological, Psychological, and Political Reflections. In *Womanspirit Rising*, ed. Carol P. Christ and Judith Plaskow, 273-287. San Francisco: Harper and Row.

———. 1989. Rethinking Theology and Nature. In *Weaving the Visions*, ed. Judith Plaskow and Carol Christ, 314–325. San Francisco: Harper and Row.

———. 1990. Symbols of Goddess and God in Feminist Theology. In *The Book of the Goddess Past and Present*, ed. Carl Olson, 231–251. New York: Crossroad.

Daly, Mary. 1978. *Gyn/Ecology: The Metaethics of Radical Feminism*. Boston: Beacon Press.

Finley, Nancy J. 1991. Political Activism and Feminist Spirituality. *Sociological Analysis* 52(4):349–362.

Gimbutas, Marija. 1974. *The Gods and Goddesses of Old Europe, 7000–3500 B.C.: Myths, Legends and Cult Images*. London: Thames and Hudson.

Iglehart, Hallie. 1982. Expanding Personal Power Through Meditation. In *The Politics of Women's Spirituality*, ed. Charlene Spretnak, 294–304. Garden City, New York: Anchor.

Morton, Nelle. 1989. The Goddess as Metaphoric Image. In *Weaving the Visions: New Patterns in Feminist Spirituality*, ed. Judith Plaskow and Carol P. Christ, 111–118. New York: Harper and Row.

Porterfield, Amanda. 1987. Feminist Theology as a Revitalization Movement. *Sociological Analysis* 48(3):234–244.

Rabuzzi, Katheryn Allen. 1988. *Motherself: A Mythic Analysis of Motherhood*. Bloomington and Indianapolis: Indiana University Press.

Sanders, Cheryl J. 1989. Christian Ethics and Theology in Womanist Perspective. *Journal of Feminist Studies in Religion* 5(2):83–91.

Sjoo, Monica, and Barbara Mor. 1987. *The Great Cosmic Mother: Rediscovering the Religion of the Earth*. San Francisco: Harper and Row.

Solovitch, Sara. 1990. Witchful Thinking. *Philadelphia Inquirer*, 28 October, 29–32.

Spretnak, Charlene, Editor. 1982. *Politics of Women's Spirituality*. Garden City, New York: Doubleday.

Starhawk. 1985. Ethics and Justice in Goddess Religion. In *Women's Consciousness, Women's Conscience: A Reader in Feminist Ethics*, ed. Barbara Hilkert Andolsen, Christine E. Gudorf, and Mary D. Pellauer, 193–200. San Francisco: Harper and Row.

———. 1987. *Truth or Dare*. New York: Harper and Row.

Stone, Merlin. 1976. *When God Was a Woman*. New York: Dial Press.

Walker, Alice. 1982. *The Color Purple*. New York: Washington Square Press.

Williams, Delores S. 1989. Womanist Theology. In *Weaving the Visions: New Patterns in Feminist Spirituality*, ed. Judith Plaskow and Carol P. Christ, 179–186. New York: Harper and Row.

Korean Shamanism and Household Religion

Harvey, Youngsook Kim. 1976. The Korean Mudang as a Household Therapist. In *Culture-Bound Syndromes, Ethnopsychiatry and Alternative Therapies*, ed. William P. Lebra, 189–198. Honolulu: University of Hawaii Press.

———. 1979. *Six Korean Women: The Socialization of Shamans. American Ethnological Society Monographs*. Vol. 65. St. Paul: West Publishing Company.

———. 1980. Possession Sickness and Women Shamans in Korea. In *Unspoken Worlds: Women's Religious Lives in Non-Western Cultures*, ed. Nancy A. Falk and Rita M. Gross, 41–52. San Francisco: Harper and Row.

Janelli, Roger, and Dawnhee Yim Janelli. 1982. *Ancestor Worship and Korean Society*. Stanford: Stanford University Press.

Kendall, Laurel. 1983. Korean Ancestors: From the Woman's Side. In *Korean Women, View from the Inner Room*, ed. Laurel Kendall and Mark Peterson, 97–112. New Haven: East Rock Press.

———. 1984. Korean Shamanism: Women's Rites and a Chinese Comparison. In *Religion and the Family in East Asia*, ed. George A. De Vos and Takao Sofue, 57–73. Berkeley: University of California Press.

———. 1985. *Shamans, Housewives, and Other Restless Spirits: Women in Korean Ritual Life*. Honolulu: University of Hawaii Press.

———. 1989. Old Ghosts and Ungrateful Children: A Korean Shaman's Story. In *Women as Healers: Cross Cultural Perspectives*, ed. Carol Shepherd McClain, 138–156. New Brunswick: Rutgers University Press.

Kim, Yung-Chung, Editor. 1982. *Women of Korea: A History from Ancient Times to 1945*. Seoul, Korea: Ewha Women's Press.

Koh, Hesung Chun. 1984. Religion and Socialization of Women in Korea. In *Religion and the Family in East Asia*, ed. George A. De Vos and Takao Sofue, 237–257. Berkeley: University of California Press.

Lee, Kwang Kyu. 1984. Family and Religion in Traditional and Contemporary Korea. In *Religion and the Family in East Asia*, ed. George A. De Vos and Takao Sofue, 185–199. Berkeley: University of California Press.

Mattielli, Sandra, Editor. 1977. *Virtues in Conflict: Tradition and the Korean Woman Today*. Seoul: Royal Asiatic Society.

Suh, David Kwang-sun. 1989. Shamanism: The Religion of *Han*. Paper presented at the First Interfaith Dialogue; Asian Women's Resource Center for Culture and Theology. Kuala Lumpur, Malaysia.

Wilson, Brian. 1983. The Korean Shaman: Image and Reality. In *Korean Women, View from the Inner Room*, ed. Laurel Kendall and Mark Peterson, 113–128. New Haven: East Rock Press.

Ryūkyūan Island Religion

Anzai, Shin. 1976. Newly-Adopted Religions and Social Change on the Ryūkyū Islands (Japan). *Social Compass* 23(1):57–70.

Haring, Douglas G. 1953. The Noro Cult of Amami Oshima: Divine Priestesses of the Ryūkyū Islands. *Sociologus* 3(2):108–121.

———. 1964. Chinese and Japanese Influences. In *Ryūkyūan Culture and Society*, ed. Allan H. Smith, 39–55. Honolulu: University of Hawaii Press.

Hopkins, Garland Evans. 1951. Okinawa Religion. *International Review of Missions* 40:179–184.

Ito, Mikiharu. 1966. Rice Rites in Japan Proper and the Ryūkyūs: A Comparative Study. In *Folk Cultures of Japan and East Asia*, 37–55. Monumenta Nipponica Monographs, no. 25. Tokyo: Sophia University Press.

Kamata, Hisako. 1966. Daughters of the Gods: Shaman Priestesses in Japan and Okinawa. In *Folk Cultures of Japan and East Asia*, 56–73. Monumenta Nipponica Monographs, no. 25. Tokyo: Sophia University Press.

Kerr, George H. 1958. *Okinawa: The History of an Island People*. Rutland, Vermont: Charles E. Tuttle Company.

Kreiner, Josef. 1968. Some Problems of Folk-Religion in the Southwest Islands (Ryūkyū). In *Folk Religion and the Worldview in the Southwestern Pacific*, ed. N. Matsumoto and T. Mabuchi, 101–118. Tokyo: Keio University.

Lebra, William P. 1966. *Okinawan Religion*. Honolulu: University of Hawaii Press.

Mabuchi, Toichi. 1964. Spiritual Predominance of the Sister. In *Ryūkyūan Culture and Society*, ed. Allan H. Smith, 79–91. Honolulu: University of Hawaii Press.

———. 1968. Toward the Reconstruction of Ryūkyūan Cosmology. In *Folk Religion and the Worldview in the Southwestern Pacific*, ed. N. Matsumoto and T. Mabuchi, 119–140. Tokyo: Keio University.

———. 1976a. Optional Cult Group Affiliation Among the Puyama and the Miyako Islanders. In *Ancestors*, ed. William H. Newell, 91–103. Hague: Mouton.

———. 1976b. A Note on Ancestor Worship in 'Cognatic' Societies. In *Ancestors*, ed. William H. Newell, 105–117. Hague: Mouton.

Matsui, Hiroko, Kazuya Horike, and Hideshi Ohashi. 1980. Rorschach Responses of Okinawan Shamans 'Yuta'. *Tohuku Psychologica Folia* 39(1–4):61–78.

Matsuzono, Makio. 1976. A Note on the Enshrinement of Ancestral Tablets at Zamami Island, Okinawa. In *Ancestors*, ed. William H. Newell, 231–240. Hague: Mouton.

McCume, Shannon. 1975. *The Ryūkyū Islands*. Harrisburg: Stackpole Books.

Noguchi, Takenori. 1966. The Japanese Kinship System. In *Folk Cultures of Japan and East Asia*, 16–36. Monumenta Nipponica Monographs, no. 25. Tokyo: Sophia University Press.

Ohashi, Hideshi, Shinsuke Sakumichi, and Kazuya Horike. 1984. A Social Psychological Study of Okinawan Shamanism (1)—Approach and Some Findings. *Tohoku Psychologica Folia* 43(1–4):66–79.

Ota, Yoshinobu. 1989. Creating the Experience of a Sacred Elite: An Examination of the Concept of *Shiji* in Southern Ryūkyūan Religion. *Contributions to Southeast Asian Ethnography* 8:111–125.

Ouwehand, C. 1985. *Hateruma: Socio-Religious Aspects of a South-Ryukyuan Island Culture*. Leiden: E. J. Brill.

Sasaki, Kokan. 1984. Spirit Possession as an Indigenous Religion in Japan and Okinawa. In *Religion and the Family in East Asia*, ed. George A. De Vos and Takao Sofue, 75–84. Berkeley: University of California Press.

Spencer, Robert Steward. 1931. The Noro, or Priestesses of Loo Choo. *Transactions of the Asiatic Society of Japan* 8:94–112.

Yoshida, Teigo. 1989. Lecture. International Cultural Center for Youth. Jerusalem, 23 March.

———. 1990. The Feminine in Japanese Folk Religion: Polluted or Divine? In *Unwrapping Japan*, ed. Eyal Ben-Ari, Brian Moeran, and James Valentine, 58–77. Honolulu: University of Hawaii Press.

Sande Secret Society

Bellman, Beryl L. 1979. The Social Organization of Knowledge in Kpelle Ritual. In *New Religions of Africa*, ed. Bennetta Jules-Rosette, 39–56. Norwood, New Jersey: Ablex Publishing Corporation.

Bledsoe, Caroline H. 1980. *Women and Marriage in Kpelle Society*. Stanford, California: Stanford University Press.

Cosentino, Donald. 1982. *Defiant Maids and Stubborn Farmers: Tradition and Invention in Mende Story Performance*. Cambridge: Cambridge University Press.

Harris, W. T., and Harry Sawyerr. 1968. *The Springs of Mende Belief and Conduct*. Freetown: Sieera Leone University Press.

Hoffer, Carol P. [MacCormack]. 1972. Mende and Sherbro Women in High Office. *Canadian Journal of African Studies* 4(2):151–164.

———. 1974. Madam Yoko: Ruler of the Kpa Mende Confederacy. In *Women, Culture, and Society*, ed. Michelle Z. Rosaldo and Louise Lamphere, 173–187. Stanford: Stanford University Press.

Jedrej, M.C. 1976. Structural Aspects of a West African Secret Society. *Journal of Anthropological Research* 32:234–245.

Lamp, Frederick. 1988. Heavenly Bodies: Menses, Moon, and Rituals of License among the Temne of Sierra Leone. In *Blood Magic*, ed. Thomas Buckley and Alma Gottlieb, 210–231. Berkeley: University of California Press.

MacCormack, Carol. 1982. Health, Fertility and Birth in Moyamba District, Sierra Leone. In *Ethnography of Fertility and Birth*, ed. Carol MacCormack, 115–139. London: Academic Press.

———. 1977. Biological Events and Cultural Control. *Signs* 3:93–100.

———. 1979. Sande: The Public Face of a Secret Society. In *The New Religions of Africa*, ed. Bennetta Jules-Rosette, 27–37. Norwood, New Jersey: Ablex Publishing Corporation.

Margai, M. A. S. 1948. Welfare Work in a Secret Society. *African Affairs* 47:227–230.

Richards, J. V. O. 1973. The Sande and Some of the Forces that Inspired its Creation or Adoption with Some References to the Poro. *Journal of Asian and African Studies* 8(1-2):69–77.

Rosen, David M. 1981. Dangerous Women: "Ideology," "Knowledge" and Ritual Among the Kono of Eastern Sierra Leone. *Dialectical Anthropology* 6:151–163.

———. 1983. The Peasant Context of Feminist Revolt in West Africa. *Anthropological Quarterly* 56:35–43.

Tonkin, Elizabeth. 1983. Women Excluded? Masking and Masquerading in West Africa. In *Women's Religious Experience*, ed. Pat Holden, 163–174. London: Croom Helm.

Shakers

Bainbridge, William Sims. 1982. Shaker Demographics, 1840–1900: An Example of the Use of U.S. Census Enumeration Schedules. *Journal for the Scientific Study of Religion* 21(4):352–365.

Bednarowski, Mary Farrell. 1980. Outside the Mainstream: Women's Religion and Women Religious Leaders in Nineteenth-Century America. *Journal of the American Academy of Religion* 48(2):207–231.

Brewer, Priscilla J. 1986. *Shaker Communities, Shaker Lives*. Hanover: University Press of New England.

———. 1992. "Tho' of the Weaker Sex": A Reassessment of Gender Equality among the Shakers. *Signs* 17(3):609–635.

Campion, Nardi Reeder. 1990 [1976]. *Mother Ann Lee: Morning Star of the Shakers*. Hanover: University Press of New England.

Desroche, Henri. 1971. *The American Shakers: From Neo-Christianity to Presocialism*. 1955. Amherst: University of Massachusetts Press.

Foster, Lawrence. 1981. *Religion and Sexuality*. New York: Oxford University Press.

Garrett, Clarke. 1987. *Spirit Possession and Popular Religion: From the Camisards to the Shakers*. Baltimore: Johns Hopkins University Press.

Humez, Jean M. 1992. "Ye Are My Espistles": The Construction of Ann Lee Imagery in Early Shaker Sacred Literature. *Journal of Feminist Studies in Religion* 8(1):83–104.

Kern, Louis J. 1981. *An Ordered Love: Sex Roles and Sexuality in Victorian Utopias—the Shakers, the Mormons, and the Oneida Community*. Chapel Hill: University of North Carolina Press.

Kitch, Sally L. 1989. *Chaste Liberation: Celibacy and Female Cultural Status*. Urbana and Chicago: University of Illinois Press.

Klein, Janice. 1979. Ann Lee and Mary Baker Eddy: The Parenting of New Religions. *Journal of Psychohistory* 6(3):361–375.

Marini, Stephen A. 1982. *Radical Sects of Revolutionary New England*. Cambridge: Harvard University Press.

Procter-Smith. 1985. *Women in Shaker Community and Worship: A Feminist Analysis of the Uses of Religious Symbolism*. Lewiston, New York: Edwin Mellen.

Stein, Stephen J. 1992. *The Shaker Experience in America*. New Haven: Yale University Press.

Whitson, Robley Edward, Editor. 1983. *The Shakers: Two Centuries of Spiritual Reflection*. New York: Paulist Press.

Spiritualism

Braude, Ann. 1985. Spirits Defend the Rights of Women: Spiritualism and Changing Sex Roles in Nineteenth-Century America. In *Women, Religion and Social Change*, ed. Yvonne Yazbeck Haddad and Ellison Banks Findley, 419–432. Albany: State University of New York Press.

———. 1989. *Radical Spirits: Spiritualism and Women's Rights in Nineteenth-Century America*. Boston: Beacon Press.

Dye, Nancy S., and Daniel B. Smith. 1986. Mother Love and Infant Death, 1750–1920. *Journal of American History* 73:329–353.

Finkler, Kaja. 1985a. Symptomatic Differences Between the Sexes in Rural Mexico. *Culture, Medicine and Psychiatry* 9:27–57.

———. 1985b. *Spiritualist Healers in Mexico*. South Hadley, Massachusetts: Bergin and Garvey.

———. 1986. The Social Consequence of Wellness: A View of Healing Outcomes from Micro and Macro Perspectives. *International Journal of Health Services* 16(4):627–642.

Macklin, June. 1974. Belief, Ritual, and Healing: New England Spiritualism and Mexican-American Spiritism Compared. In *Religious Movements in Contemporary America*, ed. Irving Zaretsky and Mark Leone, 383–417. Princeton: Princeton University Press.

———. 1977. A Connecticut Yankee in Summerland. In *Case Studies in Spirit Possession*, ed. Vincent Crapanzano and Vivian Garrison, 41–85. New York: John Wiley.

Moore, R. Laurence. 1977. *In Search of White Crows: Spiritualism, Parapsychology, and American Culture*. New York: Oxford University Press.

Nelson, Geoffrey K. 1969. *Spiritualism and Society*. London: Routledge and Kegan Paul.

Owen, Alex. 1981. *The Darkened Room*. London: Virago Press.

Skultans, Vieda. 1974. *Intimacy and Ritual: A Study of Spiritualism, Mediums and Groups*. London: Routledge and Kegan Paul.

———. 1983. Mediums, Controls and Eminent Men. In *Women's Religious Experience*, ed. Pat Holden, 15–26. London: Croom Helm.

Smith-Rosenberg, Carroll. 1985a. The Female World of Love and Ritual. In *Disorderly Conduct*, 53–76. New York: Oxford University Press.

———. 1985b. The Cross and the Pedestal: Women, Anti-Ritualism, and the Emergence of the American Bourgeoisie. In *Disorderly Conduct*, 167–181. New York: Oxford University Press.

————. 1985c. Puberty to Menopause: The Cycle of Femininity in Nineteenth-Century America. In *Disorerly Conduct*, 182–196. New York: Oxford University Press.

Ward, Gary L., Editor. 1990. *Spiritualism II: The Movement.* New York: Garland Publishing.

Northern Thai Matrilineal Spirit Cults

Cohen, Paul T. 1984. Are the Spirits Cults of Northern Thailand Descent Groups? *Mankind* 14(4):293–299.

————, and Gehan Wijeyewardene. 1984. Introduction. *Mankind* 14(4):249–262.

Cook, Nerida. 1981. *The Position of Women in Thai Buddhism: The Parameters of Religious Recognition.* Master's Thesis. Australian National University.

Davis, Richard. 1974. Tolerance and Intolerance of Ambiguity in Northern Thai Myth and Ritual. *Ethnology* 13:1–24.

————. 1984. Muang Matrifocality. *Mankind* 14(4):263–271.

Eberhardt, Nancy. 1988. Introduction. In *Gender, Power, and the Construction of the Moral Order: Studies from the Thai Periphery*, ed. Nancy Eberhardt, 3–12. Madison, Wisconsin: Center for Southeast Asian Studies.

Ferguson, John P. 1982. The Great Goddess Today in Burma and Thailand: An Exploration of Her Symbolic Relevence to Monastic and Female Roles. In *Mother Worship*, ed. James J. Preston, 283–303. Chapel Hill: University of North Carolina Press.

Hale, Ann. 1979. A Reassessment of Northern Thai Matrilineages. *Mankind* 12(2):138–150.

————. 1984. The Search for Jural Rule: Women in Southeast Asia—the Northern Thai Cults in Perspective. *Mankind* 14(4):330–338.

Hanks, Jane Richardson. 1963. *Maternity and its Rituals in Bang Chan.* Cornell Thailand Project Interim Reports Series, vol. 6. Ithaca, New York: Department of Asian Studies, Cornell University.

Hanks, Lucien M. 1983. The Yuan or Northern Thai. In *Highlanders of Thailand*, ed. John McKinnon and Wanat Bhruksasri, 101–112. Kuala Lumpur: Oxford University Press.

————, and Jane Richardson Hanks. 1963. Thailand: Equality between the Sexes. In *Women in the New Asia*, ed. Barbara E. Ward, 424–451. Amsterdam: UNESCO.

Heinze, Ruth-Inge. 1988. *Trance and Healing in Southeast Asia Today.* Bangkok: White Lotus Co.

Irvine, Walter. 1984. Decline of Village Spirit Cults and Growth of Urban Spirit Mediumship: The Persistence of Spirit Beliefs, the Position of Women and Modernization. *Mankind* 14(4):315–324.

Keyes, Charles F. 1984. Mother or Mistress but Never a Monk: Buddhist Notions of Female Gender in Rural Thailand. *American Ethnologist* 11(2):223–241.

Kirsch, A. Thomas. 1982. Buddhism, Sex-Roles and the Thai Economy. Occasional Paper, Center for Southeast Asian Studies, ed. Penny Van Esterik. Northern Illinois University.

————. 1985. Text and Context: Buddhist Sex Roles/ Culture of Gender Revisited. *American Ethnologist* 12(2):302–320.

Kunstadter, Peter. 1978. Do Cultural Differences Make Any Difference: Choice Points in Medical Systems Available in Northwestern Thailand. In *Culture and Healing in Asian Societies*, ed. Arthur Kleinman, Peter Kunstadter et al., 185–217. Cambridge, Massachusetts: Schenkman Publishing Company.

McMorran: M. V. 1984. Northern Thai Ancestral Cults: Authority and Aggression. *Mankind* 14(4):308–314.

Mougne, Christine. 1984a. Women, Fertility and Power in Northern Thailand. Paper presented at the International Conference on Thai Studies. Bangkok, 22–24 August.

———. 1984b. Spirit Cults and Matrifocality in Northern Thailand: Demographic Perspective. *Mankind* 14(4):300–307.

Piker, Steven. 1972. The Problem of Consistency in Thai Religion. *Journal for the Scientific Study of Religion* 11:211–229.

Potter, Shulamith. 1977. *Family Life in a Northern Thai Village: A Study in the Structural Significance of Women.* Berkeley: University of California Press.

Rabibhadana, Akin. 1984. Kinship Marriage and the Thai Social System. Paper Presented at the Conference on Marriage Determinants and Consequences. Pattaya City, Thailand: Institute for Population and Social Research, Mahidol University, 30 May–3 June.

Tambiah, S. J. 1970. *Buddhism and the Spirit Cults in North-East Thailand.* Cambridge: Cambridge University Press.

Tanabe, Shigeharu. 1991. Spirits, Power, and the Discourse of Female Gender: The Phi Meng Cult in Northern Thailand. In *Thai Constructions of Knowledge,* ed. Manas Chitakasem and Andrew Turton, 183–212. London: School of Oriental and African Studies.

Tantiwiramanond, Darunee and Shashi Pandey. 1987. The Status and Role of Thai Women in the Pre-Modern Period: A Historical and Cultural Perspective. *Sojourn* 2(1):125–149.

Turton, Andrew. 1976. *A Case Study of Jural and Political Structures at the Village Level and their Twentieth Century Transformations.* Diss. University of London.

———. 1984. People of the Same Spirit: Local Matrikin Groups and their Cults. *Mankind* 14(4):272–285.

Van Esterik, Penny. 1982. Interpreting a Cosmology: Guardian Spirits in Thai Buddhism. *Anthropos* 77:1–15.

Wijeyewardene, Gehan. 1970. The Still Point and the Turning Point: Towards the Structure of Northern Thai Religion. *Mankind* 7(4):247–255.

———. 1977. Matriclans or Female Cults: A Problem in Northern Thai Ethnography. *Mankind* 11(1):19–25.

———. 1984a. Northern Thai Succession and the Search for Matriliny. *Mankind* 14(4):286–292.

———. 1984b. Talking about Merit and Karma. In *Honouring E.F.C. Ludowyk: Felicitation Essays,* ed. Percy Colin-Thome and Ashley Halpe, 314–333. Sri Lanka: Tisara Prakasakayo Ltd.

———. 1986. *Place and Emotion in Northern Thai Ritual Behaviour.* Thailand: Pandora.

Zār

Boddy, Janice. 1988. Spirits and Selves in Northern Sudan: The Cultural Therapeutics of Possession and Trance. *American Ethnologist* 15(1):4–27.

———. 1989. *Wombs and Alien Spirits: Women, Men, and the Zār Cult in Northern Sudan.* Madison: University of Wisconsin Press.

———. 1992. Subversive Kinship: The Role of Spirit Possession in Negotiating Social Place in Rural Northern Sudan. Paper presented at the Annual Meeting of the Amercian Anthropological Association. San Francisco, 3 December.

Constantinides, Pamela. 1982. Women's Spirit Possession and Urban Adaptation in the Muslim Northern Sudan. In *Women United, Women Divided*, ed. Patricia Caplan and Janet Bujra, 185–205. Bloomington: Indiana University Press.

———. 1985. Women Heal Women: Spirit Possession and Sexual Segregation in a Muslim Society. *Social Science and Medicine* 21(6):685–692.

Ferichou, Sophie. 1991. The Possession Cults of Tunisia: A Religious System Functioning as a System of Reference and a Social Field for Performing Actions. In *Women's Medicine: The Zar-Bori Cult in Africa and Beyond*, ed. I. M. Lewis, Ahmed Al-Safi, and Sayyid Hurreiz, 209–218. Edinburgh: Edinburgh University Press.

Kahana, Yael. 1985. The *Zār* Spirits, a Category of Magic in the System of Mental Health Care in Ethiopia. *International Journal of Social Psychiatry* 31(2):125–142.

Kennedy, John G. 1978. *Nubian Ceremonial Life*. Berkeley: University of California Press.

Kenyon, Susan M. 1991. The Story of a Tin Box: *Zār* in the Sudanese Town of Sennar. In *Women's Medicine: The Zar-Bori Cult in Africa and Beyond*, ed. I. M. Lewis, Ahmed Al-Safi, and Sayyid Hurreiz, 100–117. Edinburgh: Edinburgh University Press.

Last, Murray. 1991. Spirit Possession as Therapy: Bori among non-Muslims in Nigeria. In *Women's Medicine: The Zar-Bori Cult in Africa and Beyond*, ed. I. M. Lewis, Ahmed Al-Safi, and Sayyid Hurreiz, 49–63. Edinburgh: Edinburgh University Press.

Lewis, I. M. 1969. Spirit Possession in Northern Somaliland. In *Spirit Mediumship and Society in Africa*, ed. John Beattie and John Middleton, 188–219. London: Routledge and Kegan Paul.

———. 1990. Spirits at the House of Childbirth. Review of *Women and Alien Spirits*, by Janice Boddy. *Times Literary Supplement*, June 1–7, 590.

———. 1991. Introduction: *Zār* in Context: The Past, the Present and Future of an African Healing Cult. In *Women's Medicine: The Zar-Bori Cult in Africa and Beyond*, ed. I. M. Lewis, Ahmed Al-Safi, and Sayyid Hurreiz, 1–16. Edinburgh: Edinburgh University Press.

Messing, Simon D. 1958. Group Therapy and Social Status in the *Zār* Cult of Ethiopia. *American Anthropologist* 60:1120–1126.

Morsy, Soheir A. 1991. Spirit Possession in Egyptian Ethnomedicine: Origins, Comparison, and Historical Specificity. In *Women's Medicine: The Zar-Bori Cult in Africa and Beyond*, ed. I. M. Lewis, Ahmed Al-Safi, and Sayyid Hurreiz, 189–208. Edinburgh: Edinburgh University Press.

Natvig, Richard. 1987. Oromos, Slaves, and the *Zār* Spirits: A Contribution to the History of the *Zār* Cult. *International Journal of African Historical Studies* 20(4):669–689.

———. 1988. Liminal Rights and Female Symbolism in the Egyptian *Zār* Possession Cult. *Numen* 35(1):57–68.

Rahim, S.I. 1991. *Zār* among Middle-Aged Female Psychiatric Patients in the Sudan. In *Women's Medicine: The Zar-Bori Cult in Africa and Beyond*, ed. I. M. Lewis, Ahmed Al-Safi, and Sayyid Hurreiz, 137–146. Edinburgh: Edinburgh University Press.

Saunders, Lucie Wood. 1977. Variants in *Zār* Experience in an Egyptian Village. In *Case Studies in Spirit Possession*, ed. Vincent Crapanzano and Vivian Garrison, 177–192. New York: John Wiley and Sons.

REFERENCES — GENERAL

Albanese, Catherine. 1990. *Nature Religion in America: From the Algonkian Indians to the New Age*. Chicago: University of Chicago Press.

Anastassiadou, Iphigenie. 1976. Two Ceremonies of Travesty in Thrace: The Day of Babo and the Caloyeri. *L'homme* 16(2–3):69–101.

Argyle, Michael, and Benjamin Beit-Hallahmi. 1975. *The Social Psychology of Religion*. London: Routledge and Kegan Paul.

Baer, Hans A. 1993. The Limited Empowerment of Women in Black Spiritual Churches: An Alternative Vehicle to Religious Leadership. *Sociology of Religion* 54(1):65–82.

Barfoot, Charles, and Gerald Sheppard. 1980. Prophetic vs. Priestly Religion: The Changing Role of Women Clergy in Classical Pentecostal Churches. *Review of Religious Research* 22(1):2–17.

Barstow, Anne Llewellyn. 1986. *Joan of Arc: Heretic, Mystic, Shaman*. Studies in Women and Religion, vol. 17. Lewiston, New York: Edwin Mellen Press.

Bart, Pauline. 1983. Review of Chodorow's *The Reproduction of Mothering*. In *Mothering: Essays in Feminist Theory*, ed. Joyce Trebilcot, 147–152. Savage, Maryland: Rowman and Littlefield.

Basilov, V. 1976. Shamanism in Central Asia. In *The Realm of the Extra-Human*, ed. Agehananda Bharati, 149–157. Hague: Mouton.

Beattie, John, and John Middleton. Editors. 1969. *Spirit Mediumship and Society in Africa*. London: Routledge and Kegan Paul.

Beck, Lois. 1980. The Religious Lives of Muslim Women. In *Women in Contemporary Muslim Societies*, ed. Jane I. Smith, 27–60. London: Associated University Presses.

Beech, Mary H. 1982. The Domestic Realm in the Lives of Hindu Women in Calcutta. In *Separate Worlds: Studies of Purdah in South Asia*, ed. Hanna Papanek and Gail Minault, 110–138. Columbia, Mo.: South Asian Books.

Beit-Hallahmi, Benjamin. 1992. *Despair and Deliverance: Private Salvation in Contemporary Israel*. Albany: State University of New York Press.

Belenky, Mary Field, Blythe McVicker Clinchy, Nancy Rule Goldberger, and Jill Mattuck Tarule. 1986. *Women's Ways of Knowing: The Development of Self, Voice, and Mind*. New York: Basic Books, Inc.

Bell, Diane. 1983. *Daughters of the Dreaming*. Melbourne: McPhee Gribble/ George Allen and Unwin.

Bennett, Lynn. 1983. *Dangerous Wives and Sacred Sisters: Social and Symbolic Roles of High-Caste Women in Nepal*. New York: Columbia University Press.

Berger, Iris. 1976. Rebels or Status-Seekers? Women as Spirit Mediums in East Africa.

In *Women in Africa*, ed. Nancy Hafkin and Edna Bay, 157–181. Stanford: Stanford University Press.

Bilu, Yoram. 1987. Dybbuk Possession and Mechanisms of Internalization and Externalization: A Case Study. In *Projection, Identification, Projective Identification*, ed. Joseph Sandler, 163–178. Madison: International Universities Press.

Bleier, Ruth. 1984. *Science and Gender*. New York: Pergamon.

Boserup, Esther. 1970. *Women's Role in Economic Development*. London: George Allen and Unwin.

Bourguignon, Erika. 1976. Possession and Trance in Cross-Cultural Studies of Mental Health. In *Culture-Bound Syndromes, Ethnopsychiatry, and Alternative Therapies*, ed. William P. Lebra, 47–55. Mental Health Research in Asia and the Pacific, vol. 4. Honolulu: University of Hawaii Press.

———, Anna Bellisari, and Susan McCabe. 1983. Women, Possession Trance Cults, and the Extended Nutrient-Deficiency Hypothesis. *American Anthropologist* 45: 413–416.

Breidenbach, Paul. 1979. The Woman on the Beach and the Man in the Bush: Leadership and Adepthood in the Twelve Apostles Movement of Ghana. In *The New Religions of Africa*, ed. Bennetta Jules-Rosette, 99–126. Norwood, New Jersey: Ablex Publishing Company.

Briffault, Robert. 1931. *The Mothers*. New York: Macmillan Company.

Brock, Sebastian B., and Susan Ashbrook Harvey. 1987. *Holy Women of the Syrian Orient*. Berkeley: University of California Press.

Brown, Audrey L. 1988. Women and Ritual Authority in Afro-American Baptist Churches of Rural Florida. *Anthropology and Humanism Quarterly* 13(1):2–10.

Brown, Judith K. 1963. A Cross-Cultural Study of Female Initiation Rites. *American Anthropologist* 65:837–853.

Brown, Karen McCarthy. 1989a. Afro-Caribbean Spirituality: A Haitian Case Study. In *Healing and Restoring: Health and Medicine in the World's Religious Traditions*, ed. Lawrence E. Sullivan, 255–285. London: Macmillan.

———. 1989b. Women's Leadership in Haitian Vodou. In *Weaving the Visions*, ed. Judith Plaskow and Carol P. Christ, 226–234. San Francisco: Harper and Row.

———. 1991. *Mama Lola: A Vodou Priestess in Brooklyn*. Berkeley: University of California Press.

Buckley, Thomas, and Alma Gottlieb. Editors. 1988. *Blood Magic*. Berkeley: University of California Press.

Burfield, Diana. 1983. Theosophy and Feminism: Some Explorations in Nineteenth Century Biography. In *Women's Religious Experience*, ed. Pat Holden, 27–56. London: Croom Helm.

Bynum, Caroline Walker. 1984. Women's Stories, Women's Symbols: A Critique of Victor Turner's Theory of Liminality. In *Anthropology and the Study of Religion*, ed. Frank Reynolds and Robert Moore, 105–125. Chicago: Center for the Scientific Study of Religion.

———. 1987. *Holy Feast and Holy Fast*. Berkeley: University of California Press.

Campbell, Debra. 1989. Hannah Whitall Smith (1832–1911): Theology of the Mother-hearted God. *Signs* 15(1):79–101.

Chanfrault-Duchet, Marie-Francoise. 1991. Narrative Structures, Social Models, and Symbolic Representations in the Life-Story. In *Women's Words: The Feminist Practice of Oral History*, ed. Sherna Berger Gluck and Daphne Patai, 77–92. New York: Routledge.

Chesler, Phyllis. 1989. *Sacred Bond: The Legacy of Baby M.* New York: Vintage Books.

Chodorow, Nancy. 1971. Being and Doing: A Cross-Cultural Examination of the Socialization of Males and Females. In *Woman in Sexist Society*, ed. Vivian Gornick and Barbara Moran, 259–291. New York: Basic Books.

———. 1974. Family Structure and Feminine Personality. In *Women, Culture, and Society*, ed. Michelle Z. Rosaldo and Louise Lamphere, 43–66. Stanford: Stanford University Press.

———. 1978. *The Reproduction of Mothering*. Berkeley: University of California Press.

———. 1981. Reply by Nancy Chodorow. *Signs* 6(3):500–514.

———. 1989. *Feminism and Psychoanalytic Theory*. New Haven: Yale University Press.

Christ, Carol P. 1991. Mircea Eliade and the Feminist Paradigm Shift. *Journal of Feminist Studies in Religion* 7(2):75–94.

Christian, William. 1972. *Person and God in a Spanish Valley*. New York: Seminar Press.

Clarke, Edith. 1966. *My Mother Who Fathered Me: A Study of the Family in Three Selected Communities in Jamaica*. London: George Allen and Unwin.

Claus, Peter J. 1975. The Siri Myth and Ritual: A Mass Possession Cult of South India. *Ethnology* 14(1):47–58.

Cloudsley, Ann. 1984. *Women of Omdurman: Life, Love and the Cult of Virginity*. London: Ethnographica.

Colson, Elizabeth. 1969. Spirit Possession among the Tonga of Zambia. In *Spirit Mediumship and Society in Africa*, ed. John Beattie and John Middleton, 69–103. London: Routledge and Kegan Paul.

Combs-Schilling, M. E. 1989. *Sacred Performances: Islam, Sexuality, and Sacrifice*. New York: Columbia University Press.

Conarton, Sharon, and Linda Kreger Silverman. 1988. Feminine Development Through the Life Cycle. In *Feminist Psychotherapies: Integration of Therapeutic and Feminist Systems*, ed. Mary Ann Dutton-Douglas and Lenore E. Walker, 37–67. Norwood, New Jersey: Ablex Publishing Corporation.

Crapanzano, Vincent. 1987. Spirit Possession. In *Encyclopedia of Religion*, vol. 14, ed. Mircea Eliade, 12–19. New York: Macmillan.

Csordas, Thomas J. 1987. Health and the Holy in African and Afro-American Spirit Possession. *Social Science and Medicine* 24(1):1–11.

Cucchiari, Salvatore. 1988. 'Adapted for Heaven': Conversion and Culture in Western Sicily. *American Ethnologist* 15(3):417–441.

Dally, Ann. 1982. *Inventing Motherhood: The Consequence of an Ideal*. London: Burnett Press.

Danforth, Loring M. 1982. *Death Rituals of Rural Greece*. Princeton: Princeton University Press.

Davis, Susan S. 1982. *Patience and Power: Women's Lives in a Moroccan Village*. Cambridge, Massachusetts: Schenkman Publishing Company.

Davis, Winston. 1980. *Dojo: Magic and Excorcism in Modern Japan*. Stanford: Stanford University Press.

de Vaus, David, and Ian McAllister. 1987. Gender Differences in Religion: A Test of the Structural Location Theory. *American Sociological Review* 52:472–481.

Desan, Suzanne. 1990. *Reclaiming the Sacred: Lay Religion and Popular Politics in Revolutionary France*. Ithaca: Cornell University Press.

Divale, William. 1984 [1974]. *Matrilocal Residence in Pre-literate Societies*. Ann Arbor: UMI Research Press.

Doyle, Patricia Martin. 1974. Women and Religion: Psychological and Cultural Implications. In *Religion and Sexism*, ed. Rosemary Radford Ruether, 15–40. New York: Simon and Schuster.

Dyregrov, Atle. 1990. Parental Reactions to the Loss of an Infant Child: A Review. *Scandinavian Journal of Psychology* 31:266–280.

———, and Stig Berge Matthieson. 1987. Similarities and Differences in Mothers' and Fathers' Grief Following the Death of an Infant. *Scandinavian Journal of Psychology* 28(1):1–15.

Ebaugh, Helen Rose Fuchs, and Sharron Lee Vaughn. 1984. Ideology and Recruitment in Religious Groups. *Review of Religious Research* 26(2):148–157.

Ehrenreich, Barbara, and Deirdre English. 1973. *Complaints and Disorders: The Sexual Politics of Sickness.* New York: Feminist Press.

Eisenstadt, Shmuel. 1982. The Axial Age: The Emergence of Transcendental Visions and the Rise of Clerics. *Archives Européennes de Sociologie* 23(1):294–314.

Eliade, Mircea. 1958. *Rites and Symbols of Initiation.* New York: Harper and Row.

Erikson, Erik. 1968. The Development of Ritualization. In *The Religious Situation,* ed. Donald Cutler, 711–733. Boston: Beacon Press.

Esquivel, Julia. 1987. Christian Women and the Struggle for Justice in Central America. In *Speaking of Faith,* ed. Diana L. Eck and Devaki Jain, 22–32. Philadelphia: New Society Publishers.

Finnegan, Ruth. 1988. *Literacy and Orality: Studies in the Technology of Communication.* Oxford: Basil Blackwell.

Frazer, J.G. 1911–1915. *The Golden Bough: A Study in Magic and Religion.* London: Macmillan.

Fromm, Erich, and Michael Maccoby. 1970. *Social Character in a Mexican Village: A Socio-Psychoanalytic Study.* Englewood Cliffs: Prentice-Hall.

Frymer-Kensky, Tikva. 1992. *In the Wake of the Goddess: Women, Culture, and the Biblical Transformation of Pagan Myth.* New York: Free Press.

Geertz, Clifford. 1969. Religion as a Cultural System. In *Anthropological Approaches to the Study of Religion,* ed. Michael Banton. London: Tavistock Publications.

Giles, Linda L. 1987. Possession Cults on the Swahili Coast: A Re-examination of Theories of Marginality. *Africa* 57(2):234–257.

Gill, Brita. 1985. A Ministry of Presence. In *Women Ministers,* ed. Judith L. Weidman, 89–106. San Francisco: Harper and Row.

Gilligan, Carol. 1982. *In a Different Voice.* Cambridge: Harvard University Press.

Gluckman, Max. 1963. *Order and Rebellion in Tribal Africa.* London: Cohen and West.

Goldenberg, Naomi R. 1979. *Changing of the Gods.* Boston: Beacon Press.

Gomm, Roger. 1975. Bargaining from Weakness: Spirit Possession on the South Kenya Coast. *Man (N.S.)* 10:530–545.

Goody, Jack. 1977. *The Domestication of the Savage Mind.* Cambridge: Cambridge University Press.

Gough, Kathleen E. 1968. The Nayars and the Definition of Marriage. In *Marriage, Family, and Residence,* ed. P. Bohannan and J. Middleton, 49–71. Garden City, New York: Natural History Press.

Graham, Hilary. 1976. The Social Image of Pregnancy: Pregnancy as Spirit Possession. *The Sociological Review* 24(2):291–308.

Gutmann, David. 1965. Women and the Conception of Ego Strength. *Merrill-Palmer Quarterly of Behavior and Development* 11(3):229–240.

———. 1977. The Cross-Cultural Perspective: Notes Toward a Comparative Psychology of Aging. In *Handbook of the Psychology of Aging,* ed. James Birren and K. Schaie, 302–326. New York: Van Nostrand Reinhold.

Hagestad, Grunhild O. 1984. Women in Intergenerational Patterns of Power and Influence. In *Social Power and Influence of Women,* ed. Liesa Stamm and Carol D. Ryff,

37–55. AAAS Selected Symposium, no. 96. Boulder, Colorado: Westview Press.

Hales, Mary A. 1990. Motherhood and Sex Role Development. In *Woman-Defined Motherhood*, ed. Jane Price Knowles and Ellen Cole, 227–243. New York: Harrington Park Press.

Hardacre, Helen. 1986. *Kurozumikyo and the New Religions of Japan*. Princeton: Princeton University Press.

Harris, Marvin. 1985. *Culture, People, Nature: An Introduction to General Anthropology*. 4th Ed. New York: Harper and Row.

Harrison, Jane. 1955. *Prolegomena to the Study of Greek Religion*. New York: Meridian Books.

Hayes, Rose Oldfield. 1975. Female Genital Mutilation, Fertility Control, Women's Role, and the Patrilineage in Modern Sudan: A Functional Analysis. *American Ethnologist* 2:617–633.

Haywood, Carol Lois. 1983. The Authority and Empowerment of Women among Spiritualist Groups. *Journal for the Scientific Study of Religion* 22(2):157–166.

Heeren, John, Donald Linsey, and Marylee Mason. 1984. The Mormon Concept of Mother in Heaven: A Sociological Account of its Origin and Development. *Journal for the Scientific Study of Religion* 23(4):396–411.

Hibbard, Judith H., and Clyde R. Pope. 1987. Women's Roles, Interest in Health and Health Behavior. *Women and Health* 12(2):67–84.

Hicks, David. 1976. *Tetum Ghosts and Kin: Fieldwork in an Indonesian Community*. Palo Alto: Mayfield Publishing Company.

———. 1984. *A Maternal Religion: The Role of Women in Tetum Myth and Ritual*. Monograph Series on Southeast Asia. Northern Illinois University: Center for Southeast Asian Studies.

Holden, Pat. 1983. Introduction. In *Women's Religious Experience*, ed. Pat Holden, 1–14. London: Croom Helm.

Hori, Ichiro, 1968. *Folk Religion in Japan*. Chicago: University of Chicago Press.

Horton, Robin. 1969. Types of Spirit Possession in Kalabari Religion. In *Spirit Possession and Society in Africa*, ed. John Beattie and John Middleton, 14–49. London: Routledge and Kegan Paul.

Houtart, Francois. 1977. Therevada Buddhism and Political Power—Construction and Deconstruction of its Ideological Function. *Social Compass* 24(2–3):207–246.

Hutch, Richard A. 1984. Types of Women Religious Leaders. *Religion* 14:155–173.

Hyde, Janet Shibley. 1990. Meta-analysis and the Psychology of Gender Differences. *Signs* 16(1):55–73.

Infante, Teresita R. 1975. *The Woman in Early Philippines and Among the Cultural Minorities*. Manila: Unitas Publications.

Jacobs, Claude F. 1989. Spirit Guides and Possession in the New Orleans Black Spiritual Churches. *Journal of American Folklore* 102:45–67.

———, and Andrew J. Kaslow. 1991. *The Spiritual Churches of New Orleans*. Knoxville: University of Tennessee Press.

Jamzadeh, Laal, and Margaret Mills. 1986. Iranian Sofreh: From Collective to Female Ritual. In *Gender and Religion: On the Complexity of Symbols*, ed. Caroline Walker Bynum, Steven Harrell and Paula Richman, 23–65. Boston: Beacon Press.

Jay, Nancy. 1985. Sacrifice as Remedy for Having Been Born of Woman. In *Immaculate and Powerful*, ed. Clarissa Atkinson, Constance Buchanan and Margaret Miles, 283–309. Harvard Women's Studies in Religion Series. Boston: Beacon Press.

Johnson, Miriam. 1988. *Strong Mothers, Weak Wives: The Search for Gender Equality*. Berkeley: University of California Press.

Jonte-Pace, Diane. 1987. Object Relations Theory, Mothering, and Religion: Toward a Feminist Psychology of Religion. *Horizons* 14(2):310–327.

———. 1992. Situating Kristeva Differently: Psychoanalytic Readings of Women and Religion. In *Body-texts in Julia Kristeva: Religion, Woman, Psychoanalysis*, ed. David Crownfield. Albany: State University of New York Press.

Jules-Rosette, Bennetta. 1979. Changing Aspects of Women's Initiation in Southern Africa: An Exploratory Study. *Canadian Journal of African Studies* 13(3):389–405.

Kanter, Rosabeth Moss. 1977. *Men and Women of the Corporation*. New York: Basic Books.

Kaplan, Alexandra, and Janet Surrey. 1984. The Relational Self in Women: Developmental Theory and Public Policy. In *Women and Mental Health Policy*, ed. Lenore Walker, 79–94. Sage Yearbooks in Women's Policy Studies, vol. 9. Beverly Hills: Sage.

Kehoe, Alice, and Dody Giletti. 1981. Women's Preponderance in Possession Cults: The Calcium-Deficiency Hypothesis Expanded. *American Anthropologist* 83(3): 549–550.

Keller, John W., Dave Sherry, and Chris Piotrowski. 1984. Perspectives on Death: A Developmental Study. *Journal of Psychology* 116:137–142.

Kerner, Karen. 1976. The Malevolent Ancestor: Ancestral Influence in a Japanese Religious Sect. In *Ancestors*, ed. William H. Newell, 205–217. Hague: Mouton.

Kittay, Eva Feder. 1983. Womb Envy: An Explanatory Concept. In *Mothering: Essays in Feminist Theory*, ed. Joyce Trebilcot, 94–128. Savage, Maryland: Rowman and Littlefield.

Klatch, Rebecca E. 1987. *Women and the New Right*. Philadelphia: Temple University Press.

Knowles, Jane Price. 1990. Woman-Defined Motherhood. In *Woman-Defined Motherhood*, ed. Jane Price Knowles and Ellen Cole, 1–7. New York: Harrington Park Press.

Koss-Chioino, Joan. 1992. *Women as Patients, Women as Healers: Mental Health Care and Traditional Healing in Puerto Rico*. Boulder: Westview Press.

Kraemer, Ross S. 1980a. Ecstasy and Possession: Women of Ancient Greece and the Cult of Dionysus. In *Unspoken Worlds: Women's Religious Lives in Non-Western Cultures*, ed. Nancy A. Falk and Rita M. Gross, 53–69. San Francisco: Harper and Row.

———. 1980b. The Conversion of Women to Ascetic Forms of Christianity. *Signs* 6(2):298–307.

———. 1989. Monastic Jewish Women in Greco-Roman Egypt: Philo Judaeus on the Therapeutrides. *Signs* 14(2):342–370.

———. 1992. *Her Share of the Blessings: Women's Religions Among Pagans, Jews, and Christians in the Greco-Roman World*. New York: Oxford University Press.

Ladislav, Holy. 1988. Gender and Ritual in an Islamic Society: The Berti of Darfur. *Man (N.S.)* 23:469–487.

Lambek, Michael. 1981. *Human Spirits: A Cultural Account of Trance in Mayotte*. Cambridge: Cambridge University Press.

Laub Coser, Rose. 1981. On *The Reproduction of Mothering*: A Methodological Debate. *Signs* 6(3):487–492.

Lebra, Takie Sugiyama. 1970. Religious Conversion as a Breakthrough for Transculturation: A Japanese Sect in Hawaii. *Journal for the Scientific Study of Religion* 9(3):181–196.

————. 1972. Religious Conversion and Elimination of the Sick Role: A Japanese Sect in Hawaii. In *Transcultural Research in Mental Health*, ed. William P. Lebra, 282–292. Mental Health Research in Asia and the Pacific, vol. 2. Honolulu: University of Hawaii Press.

Lehman, Edward C., Jr. 1993. Gender and Ministry Style: Things Not What They Seem. *Sociology of Religion* 54(1):1–12.

Leiderman, P. Herbert, and Gloria F. Leiderman. 1974. Affective and Cognitive Consequences of Polymatric Infant Care in the East Africa Highlands. In *Minnesota Symposia on Child Psychology*, vol. 8, ed. Ann Pick, 81–110. Minneapolis: University of Minnesota Press.

Leifer, Myra. 1980. *Psychological Effects of Motherhood: A Study of First Pregnancy*. New York: Praeger Publishers.

Lerner, Gerda. 1986. *The Creation of Patriarchy*. New York: Oxford University Press.

Lerner, Harriet G. 1989. *Women in Therapy*. New York: Harper and Row.

Lewis, I.M. 1975 [1971]. *Ecstatic Religion*. Harmondsworth, Middlesex, England: Penguin Books.

————. 1986. *Religion in Context: Cults and Charisma*. Cambridge: Cambridge University Press.

————. 1989. *Ecstatic Religion*. 2nd Ed. London: Routledge.

Lightfoot-Klein, Hanny. 1989. *Prisoners of Ritual*. New York: Harrington Park Press.

Lincoln, Bruce. 1981. *Emerging from the Chrysalis: Studies in Rituals of Women's Initiation*. Cambridge: Harvard University Press.

Lopata, Helen. 1987. Women's Family Roles in Life Course Perspective. In *Analyzing Gender*, ed. Beth Hess and Myra Marx, 381–407. Newbury Park, California: Sage Publications.

Lorber, Judith. 1981. On *The Reproduction of Mothering*: A Methodological Debate. *Signs* 6(3):482–486.

Macaulay, Jacqueline. 1985. Adding Gender to Aggression Research: Incremental or Revolutionary Change? In *Women, Gender, and Social Psychology*, ed. Virginia O'Leary, Rhoda Kesler Unger, and Barbara Strudler Wallston, 191–224. Hillside, New Jersey: Lawrence Erlbaum Associates.

Martin, Joann. 1990. Motherhood and Power: The Production of a Women's Culture of Politics in a Mexican Community. *American Ethnologist* 17(3):470–490.

Martin, Patricia Yancey. 1990. Rethinking Feminist Organizations. *Gender and Society* 4(2):182–206.

May, L. Carlyle. 1954. The Dancing Religion: A Japanese Messianic Sect. *Southwestern Journal of Anthropology* 10:119–137.

McClain, Carol Shepherd, Ed. 1989. Reinterpreting Women in Healing Roles. In *Women as Healers: Cross-Cultural Perspectives*, 1–19. New Brunswick: Rutgers University Press.

McConville, Frances. 1988. The Birth Attendant in Bangladesh. In *The Midwife Challenge*, ed. Sheila Kitzinger, 134–154. London: Pandora Press.

McFarland, Neil. 1967. *Rush Hour of the Gods*. San Francisco: Harper and Row.

McGilvray, Dennis B. 1988. Sex, Repression, and Sanskritization in Sri Lanka. *Ethos* 16(2):99–127.

Meckel, Richard. 1989. Educating A Ministry of Mothers: Evangelical Maternal Associations, 1815–1860. In *Major Problems in American Women's History*, ed. Mary Beth Norton, 139–145. Lexington, Massachusetts: Heath and Company.

Mernissi, Fatima. 1977. Women, Saints, and Sanctuaries. *Signs* 3(1):101–112.

Miller-McLemore, Bonnie J. 1992. Epistemology or Bust: A Maternal Feminist Knowledge of Knowing. *Journal of Religion* 72(2):229–247.

Moberg, David. 1962. *The Church as a Social Institution: The Sociology of American Religion.* Englewood Cliffs, New Jersey: Prentice-Hall.

Murdock, George P. 1949. *Social Structure.* New York: Macmillan.

———. 1967. *Ethnographic Atlas.* Pittsburgh: University of Pittsburgh Press.

Nakamura, Kyoko Motomochi. 1980. No Women's Liberation: The Heritage of a Woman Prophet in Modern Japan. In *Unspoken Worlds: Women's Religious Lives in Non-Western Cultures,* ed. Nancy Auer Falk and Rita M. Gross, 174–190. San Francisco: Harper and Row.

Nathanson, Constance. 1979. Sex, Illness and Medical Care. In *Health, Illness and Medicine,* ed. Gary L. Albrecht and Paul C. Higgins, 16–40. Chicago: Rand McNally.

Neel, Carol. 1989. The Origins of the Beguines. *Signs* 14(2):321–341.

Nelsen, Hart M., Neil Cheek Jr., and Paul Au. 1985. Gender Differences in Images of God. *Journal for the Scientific Study of Religion* 24(4):396–402.

Neumann, Erich. 1963. *The Great Mother: An Analysis of the Archetype.* Princeton: Princeton University Press.

Noddings, Nel. 1984. *Caring: A Feminine Approach to Ethics and Moral Education.* Berkeley: University of California Press.

Norbeck, Edward. 1970. *Religion and Society in Modern Japan.* Houston: Rice University.

O'Flaherty, Wendy Doniger. 1980. *Women, Androgynes, and Other Mythical Beasts.* Chicago: University of Chicago Press.

Ochshorn, Judith. 1981. *The Female Experience and the Nature of the Divine.* Bloomington: University of Indiana Press.

Offner, Clark, and Henry Van Straelen. 1963. *Modern Japanese Religions.* Leiden: E. J. Brill.

Ong, W. J. 1982. *Orality and Literacy: The Technologizing of the Word.* London and New York: Methuen.

Ortner, Sherry. 1974. Is Female to Male as Nature Is to Culture? In *Women, Culture and Society,* ed. Michelle Zimbalist Rosaldo and Louise Lamphere, 67–88. Stanford: Stanford Univeristy Press.

Paige, Karen Ericksen, and Jeffrey M. Paige. 1981. *The Politics of Reproductive Ritual.* Berkeley: University of California Press.

Pernet, Henry. 1982. Masks and Women: Toward a Reappraisal. *History of Religions* 22(1):45–59.

Pine, Vanderlyn R., and Carolyn Brauer. 1986. Parental Grief: A Synthesis of Theory, Research, and Intervention. In *Parental Loss of a Child,* ed. Therese A. Rando, 59–96. Champaign, Illinois: Research Press Company.

Pitts, Walter. 1989. If You Caint Get the Boat, Take a Log: Cultural Reinterpretation in the Afro-Baptist Ritual. *American Ethnologist* 16(2):279–293.

Poole, Fitz John Porter. 1981. Transforming 'Natural' Woman: Female Ritual Leaders and Gender Ideology among Bimin-Kugkusmin. In *Sexual Meanings,* ed. Sherry Ortner and Harriet Whitehead, 80–115. Cambridge: Cambridge University Press.

Potter, Jack M. 1974. Cantonese Shamanism. In *Religion and Ritual in Chinese Society,* ed. Arthur P. Wolf, 207–231. Stanford: Stanford University Press.

Powell, Gary N. 1988. *Women and Men in Management.* Newbury Park, California: Sage Publications.

Preston, James J. 1982. Conclusion: New Perspectives on Mother Worship. In *Mother Worship,* ed. James J. Preston, 325–343. Chapel Hill: University of North Carolina Press.

Purvis, Sally. 1991. Mothers, Neighbors and Strangers: Another Look at Agape. *Journal of Feminist Studies in Religion* 7(1):19–34.

Rando, Therese A. 1986. The Unique Issues and Impact of the Death of a Child. In *Parental Loss of a Child*, ed. Therese A. Rando, 5–44. Champaign, Illinois: Research Press Company.

Redfield, Robert. 1956. *Peasant Society and Culture*. Chicago: University of Chicago Press.

Rich, Adrienne. 1986 [1976]. *Of Woman Born: Motherhood as Experience and Institution*. New York: W. W. Norton and Company.

Risman, Barbara J. 1987. Intimate Relationships from a Microstructural Perspective: Men Who Mother. *Gender and Society* 1:6–32.

Rosaldo, Michelle Zimbalist. 1974. Women, Culture, and Society: A Theoretical Overview. In *Women, Culture, and Society*, ed. Michelle Zimbalist Rosaldo and Louise Lamphere, 17–42. Stanford: Stanford University Press.

Rosaldo, Renato. 1989. *Culture and Truth: The Remaking of Social Analysis*. Boston: Beacon Press.

Rosenblatt, Paul, Patricia Walsh, and Douglas Jackson. 1976. *Grief and Mourning in Cross-Cultural Perspective*. New Haven: HRAF Press.

Rossi, Alice S. 1981. On *The Reproduction of Mothering*: A Methodological Debate. *Signs* 6(3):492–500.

Rubin, Lillian B. 1983. *Intimate Strangers: Men and Women Together*. New York: Harper and Row.

Rubin, Simon Shimshon. 1984–1985. Maternal Attachment and Child Death: On Adjustment, Relationship, and Resolution. *Omega* 15(4):347–352.

Ruddick, Sara. 1982. Maternal Thinking. In *Rethinking the Family: Some Feminist Questions*, ed. Barrie Thorne and Marilyn Yalom, 76–94. New York: Longman.

———. 1983. Preservative Love and Military Destruction: Some Reflections on Mothering and Peace. In *Mothering: Essays in Feminist Theory*, ed. Joyce Trebilcot, 231–262. Savage, Maryland: Rowman and Littlefield.

Ruether, Rosemary. 1974. *Religion and Sexism: Images of Woman in the Jewish and Christian Traditions*. New York: Simon and Schuster.

———. n.d. In the Mountains of Banahaw Padre Is a Woman. Unpublished essay.

———, and Rosemary Skinner Keller. Editors. 1981. *Women and Religion in America*. Vol. 1. San Francisco: Harper and Row.

———, and Rosemary Skinner Keller. Editors. 1983. *Women and Religion in America*. Vol. 2. San Francisco: Harper and Row.

Sacks, Karen. 1974. Engels Revisited: Women, the Organization of Production, and Private Property. In *Women, Culture and Society*, ed. Michelle Zimbalist Rosaldo and Louise Lamphere, 207–222. Stanford: Stanford University Press.

———. 1979. *Sisters and Wives*. Westport, Connecticut: Greenwood Press.

Sanday, Peggy Reeves. 1981. *Female Power and Male Dominance: On the Origins of Sexual Inequality*. Cambridge: Cambridge University Press.

———, and Ruth Gallagher Goodenough, Editors. 1990. *Beyond the Second Sex: New Directions in the Anthropology of Gender*. Philadelphia: University of Pennsylvania Press.

Sanderson, Lilian Passmore. 1981. *Against the Mutilation of Women: The Struggle to End Unnecessary Suffering*. London: Ithaca Press.

Schatz, Barbara D. 1986. Grief of Mothers. In *Parental Loss of a Child*, ed. Therese A. Rando, 303–314. Champaign, Illinois: Research Press Company.

Schlegel, Alice. 1972. *Male Dominance and Female Autonomy*. New Haven: HRAF Press.

————. 1977. Male and Female in Hopi Thought and Action. In *Sexual Stratification: A Cross-Cultural View*, ed. Alice Schlegel, 245–269. New York: Columbia University Press.

Schoenfeld, Eugen, and Stjepan Mestrovic. 1991. With Justice and Mercy: Instrumental-Masculine and Expressive-Feminine Elements in Religion. *Journal for the Scientific Study of Religion* 30(4):363–380.

Schousboe, Karen, and Mogens Trolle Larsen, Editors. 1989. *Literacy and Society*. Copenhagen: Akademisk Forlag, Center for Research in the Humanities, Copenhagen University.

Schulenburg, Jane T. 1989. Women's Monastic Communities, 500–1100: Patterns of Expansion and Decline. *Signs* 14(2):261–292.

Sered, Susan Starr. 1987. The Liberation of Widowhood. *Journal of Cross-Cultural Gerontology* 2:139–150.

————. 1988. The Domestication of Religion: The Spiritual Guardianship of Elderly Jewish Women. *Man (N.S.)* 23:506-521.

————. 1990. Women, Religion, and Modernization: Tradition and Transformation among Elderly Jews in Israel. *American Anthropologist* 92:306–318.

————. 1991a. Conflict, Complement, and Control: Family and Religion among Middle Eastern Jewish Women in Jerusalem. *Gender and Society* 5(1):10–29.

————. 1991b. Childbirth as a Religious Experience? Voices from an Israeli Hospital. *Journal of Feminist Studies in Religion* 7(2):7–18.

————. 1992. *Women as Ritual Experts: The Religious Lives of Elderly Jewish Women in Jerusalem*. New York: Oxford University Press.

Seremetakis, C. Nadia. 1991. *The Last Word: Women, Death and Divination in Inner Mani*. Chicago: University of Chicago Press.

Sharma, Arvind. 1977. How and Why Did the Women in Ancient India Become Buddhist Nuns? *Sociological Analysis* 38(3):329–351.

Shimony, Annemarie. 1980. Women of Influence and Prestige Among the Native American Iroquois. In *Unspoken Worlds: Women's Religious Lives in Non-Western Cultures*, ed. Nancy A. Falk and Rita M. Gross, 243–259. San Francisco: Harper and Row.

Silverblatt, Irene. 1980. Andean Women under Spanish Rule. In *Women and Colonization: Anthropological Perspectives*, ed. Mona Etienne and Eleanor Leacock, 149–185. New York: J. F. Bergin.

Singer, Merrill. 1985. The Concept of Justice in the Religions of the Caribbean. *Phylon* 46:296–299.

Smith, Jane I. 1987. Islam. In *Women in World Religions*, ed. Arvind Sharma, 235–250. Albany: State University of New York Press.

Smith, Sidonie. 1987. *A Poetics of Women's Autobiography*. Bloomington: Indiana University Press.

Smith, W. Robertson. 1972 [1889]. *The Religion of the Semites: The Fundamental Institutions*. New York: Schocken.

Spiro, Melford E. 1984. Some Reflections on Family and Religion in East Asia. In *Religion and the Family in East Asia*, ed. George A. De Vos and Takao Sofue, 35–54. Berkeley: University of California Press.

Spring, Anita. 1976. An Indigenous Therapeutic Style and Its Consequences for Natality: The Luvale of Zambia. In *Culture, Natality, and Family Planning*, ed. John F. Marshall and Steven Polgar, 99–125. Chapel Hill: University of North Carolina, Caroline Population Center.

————. 1978. Epidemiology of Spirit Possession among the Luvale of Zambia. In

Women in Ritual and Symbolic Roles, ed. Judith Hoch-Smith and Anita Spring, 165–190. New York: Plenum Press.

Stamm, Liesa, and Carol D. Ryff. 1984. Introduction. In *Social Power and Influence of Women*, ed. Liesa Stamm and Carol D. Ryff, 1–11. AAAS Selected Symposium, no. 96. Boulder, Colorado: Westview Press.

Stark, Rodney, and William Bainbridge. 1985. *The Future of Religion*. Berkeley: University of California Press.

Stover, Ronald, and Christine Hope. 1984. Monotheism and Gender Status: A Cross-Societal Study. *Social Forces* 63(2):335–348.

Suzuki, Mitsuo. 1976. The Shamanistic Element in Taiwanese Folk Religion. In *The Realm of the Extra-Human*, ed. Agehananda Bharati, 253–260. Hague: Mouton.

Tamayo, Alvaro, and Albert Dugas. 1977. Conceptual Representation of Mother, Father, and God According to Sex and Field of Study. *Journal of Psychology* 97:79–84.

Tamez, Elsa, Editor. 1989. *Through Her Eyes: Women's Theology from Latin America*. Maryknoll, New York: Orbis Books.

Tanner, Nancy. 1974. Matrifocality in Indonesia and Africa and Among Black Americans. In *Women, Culture, and Society*, ed. Michelle Z. Rosaldo and Louise Lamphere, 129–156. Stanford: Stanford University Press.

Tavris, Carol. 1992. *The Mismeasure of Women*. New York: Simon and Schuster.

Tenrikyo: Its History and Teachings. n.d. ed. Tenrikyo Overseas Mission Department.

Thompson, Catherine. 1983. Women, Fertility and the Worship of Gods in a Hindu Village. In *Women's Religious Experience*, ed. Pat Holden, 113–131. London: Croom Helm.

Thompson, Daniel C. 1974. *Sociology of the Black Experience*. Contributions in Sociology, vol. 14. Westport, Connecticut: Greenwood Press.

Van Binsbergen, Wim M. J. 1981. *Religious Change in Zambia*. London: Kegan Paul.

Van Esterik, Penny. 1982. Introduction. In *Women of Southeast Asia*. Occasional Paper, Center for Southeast Asian Studies, ed. Penny Van Esterik, 1–15. Dekalb: Northern Illinois University.

VanEecke, Catherine. 1989. From Pasture to Purdah: The Transformation of Women's Roles and Identity Among the Adamawa Fulbe. *Ethnology* 28(1):53–73.

Wadley, Susan S. 1980. Hindu Women's Family and Household Rites in a North Indian Village. In *Unspoken Worlds: Women's Religious Lives in Non-Western Cultures*, ed. Nancy A. Falk and Rita M. Gross, 73–93. San Francisco: Harper and Row.

Walker, Sheila. 1972. *Ceremonial Spirit Possession in Africa and Afro-America*. Lieden: E. J. Brill.

Ward, Colleen. 1982. A Transcultural Perspective on Women and Madness: The Case of the Mystical Affliction. *Women's Studies International Forum* 5(5):411–418.

Weber, Max. 1966. *The Sociology of Religion*. Boston: Beacon Press.

Weinstein, Donald, and Rudolph Bell, M. 1982. *Saints and Society: The Two Worlds of Western Christendom, 1000–1700*. Chicago: University of Chicago Press.

Welter, Barbara. 1966. The Cult of True Womanhood: 1820–1860. *American Quarterly* 18:151–174.

———. 1974. The Feminization of American Religion, 1800–1860. In *Clio's Consciousness Raised: New Perspectives on the History of Women*, ed. Mary Hartman and Lois Banner. New York: Harper and Row.

Werblowsky, R. J. Zwi. 1991. *Mizuko kuyō*: Notulae on the Most Important "New Religion" of Japan. *Japanese Journal of Religious Studies* 18:295–354.

Wessley, Stephen E. 1978. The Thirteenth-Century Guglielmites: Salvation Through Women. In *Medieval Women*, ed. Derek Baker. Oxford: Basil Blackwell.

Whelehan, Patricia, and Contributors. 1988. *Women and Health: Cross-Cultural Perspectives*. Granby, Massachusetts: Bergin and Garvey.

Wilson, Peter. 1967. Status Ambiguity and Spirit Possession. *Man* 2:366–378.

Wittig, Monique. 1971. *Les Guerilleres*. Trans. David LeVay. New York: Avon Books.

Wolf, Margery. 1990. The Woman Who Didn't Become a Shaman. *American Ethnologist* 17(3):419–430.

Wulff, David. 1984. Prolegomenon to a Psychology of the Goddess. In *The Divine Consort: Radha and the Goddesses of India*, ed. John S. Hawley and Donna M. Wulff, 283–297. Delhi: Motilal Banarsidass.

Yanagisako, Sylvia Junko. 1977. Women-Centered Kin Networks in Urban Bilateral Kinship. *American Ethnologist* 4(2):207–226.

———. 1979. Family and Household: The Analysis of Domestic Groups. *Annual Review of Anthropology* 8:161–205.

Young, Iris Marion. 1983. Is Male Gender Identity the Cause of Male Dominance? In *Mothering: Essays in Feminist Theory*, ed. Joyce Trebilcot, 129–146. Savage, Maryland: Rowman and Littlefield.

INDEX

gender inequality in, 170
interpretations of, 170–72
and male dominance, 169
male god in, 169
Moore, Laurence, 183, 187, 197, 198, 228
Morality, 155–58, 280
in Feminist Spirituality, 156–57
motherhood influence, 158
particularism in, 158, 285
this-worldly nature of, 157
Mormon Goddess, 173
Moroccan women, 78
Mother Ann's Work, 151–52, 175–76, 185,
  192n3, 215
Mother Catherine, 76
Mother-child bonds, 47, 284
and child death, 99, 284
nineteenth century U.S. families, 92–93
object relations theory, 73
Mother Church, 250
Mother-daughter relationship
Belize society, 51
Burmese family, 53
and leadership inheritance, 223
United States society, 57
Mother-Father deity, 174–76
Mother goddesses, 77
Motherhood, 81–85
Black Caribs of Belize, 78–79
developmental model, 73
effect on women's thinking, 83–84, 282–83
and emotional/spiritual development, 82–85
and gender ideology, 197
genital mutilation meaning, 127–28
illness connection, 105
in Korean household religion, 74–75
and leadership inheritance, 239
in matrifocal societies, 66, 72
meaning of, 81–85, 283–85
and morality, 158
and particularism, 284–85
personality effects, 82–83, 85
power dilemma, 285–86
psychoanalytic view, 73
sacralization in women's religions, 61–62
in Sande belief, 74
in Shaker religion, 75–76, 81, 284
and spiritual intuition, 76
symbols of, 75–76
this-worldly focus, 149
valuation in Buddhist theology, 22
versus wife, status, 71
women's religion correlate, 66, 72–73, 283–85
Motherself (Rabuzzi), 77
Mourning. *See also* Child death
in Dominica Carib, 80
nineteenth century U.S. women, 93

rituals in, 130–33, 139–40
Mrs. Kitamura, 76, 86n2, 131
Mudang, 18, 123, 146, 229–30. *See also* Korean
  shamans
Musical ability, 226
Muslim women. *See* Islam

Nao, 125
Nash, June, 161, 162
Nat religion. *See also* Burmese culture
Buddhism differences, 17, 113–14, 146
characteristics, 15–17, 161–63, 289
and children's health, 90
food rituals, 134
gender of deity, 177
healing techniques, 116
hierarchical organization, 218
nat characteristics, 161–63, 177
older women in, 80
sacred and profane in shamans, 152
shaman qualities, 221
social context, 52–54
suffering explanation, 113–14
women mediums in, 189
Natkadaws, 189, 223
Nature *nats*, 161–63
Nature spirits, 163–64
Neuhouser, Kevin, 183
New Orleans movement. *See* Black Spiritual
  movement
New Right women, 195, 211n1
Noddings, Nel, 158, 171
Noro. *See also* Priestesses
fertility/sexuality control, 273, 278n12
hierarchical leadership role, 219, 250
mother-daughter succession, 223
in Ryūkyūan Islands religion, 14, 119, 221,
  240n7
status of, 233
yuta distinction, 240n7
North American religions, 22–29
Northern Sudan, 63–64. *See also* Zār cult
Northern Thai matrilineal spirit cults. *See also*
  phii puu hjaa cult
benefits, 268
blood sacrifice de-emphasis, 137
versus Buddhism, 21–22, 146, 159n5
characteristics, 19–22, 289
economic independence, 271
food rituals, 135, 137
function, 20
gender ideology, 200, 204, 212n13
group emphasis in ritual, 122, 135
and matrifocality, 48–50
matriline spirits in, 166–67
medium characteristics, 189, 222
menstrual pollution beliefs, 201

Transvestites, 235
Tres Personas Solo Dios community, 200, 211*n*6
True-Light Supra-Religious Organization, 211*n*8
Tugs of war, 204–5
Tulu speakers of India, 60
Turkic shamanism, 143*n*18
Turner, Victor, 153
Tutelary spirits, 96–97

Umbanda cult, 32. *See also* Afro-Brazilian religions
  appeal to women, 33–34
  benefits, 262
  categories of spirits, 165
  characteristics, 32–34
  hierarchical organization, 218
  illness as recruitment path, 108–9
  social benefits of leadership, 228–29
  uncentralized organization, 244
Uranai, 234
Uyigami, 192
Uzr, 283

van Genneps, Arnold, 153
Victorian stereotypes, 198
Violence, 84, 87*n*7
Virginity, 7, 272
Virilocality, 59–60
Vodou. *See* Haitian urban Vodou
Voluntary celibacy, 273. *See also* Celibacy
Votaries, 165

Walker, Alice, 27
Wasswassa, 106–7
Weber, Max, 5, 111, 141*n*2, 158*n*1, 171, 248
Wedding ceremonies, 139–40, 274
Wessinger, Catherine, 215
West Africa. *See also* Sande secret society
  matrifocality, 57
  social context, 45–46, 57–58
Whittaker, James, 25, 247–48, 255*n*5
Wicca religion, 27. *See also* Feminist Spirituality Movement
Widows, 78
Wijeyewardene, Gehan, 20, 21, 22, 49, 149, 150, 159*n*3, 159*n*5, 222, 233
Wilson, Brian, 230
Wilson, Peter, 186

Witches, 27
Wives
  inheritance of leadership, 239
  versus mothers, social status, 71
Womanism
  characteristics, 27, 42*n*13
  nurturing interpretation, 77–78
Woman's intuition, 76–78
Womb, tomb analogy, 202
Women's Commonwealth, 96
Wright, Lucy, 25, 248–49
Written codes, 249, 285
Wulff, David, 178

Xango cult, 32

Yaeyama Islands, 208
Yako, 137
Yoshida, Teigo, 202
Young, Iris, 216
Youngs, Benjamin, 213*n*17
Yunnanese tribe, 210
Yutas. See also Shamans
  healing techniques, 115
  life histories, 221
  priestess distinction, 240*n*7
  Ryūkyūan Islands religion, 14–15, 240*n*7

Zār cult, 36–39
  benefits to women, 260–62
  blood ritual, 137–38
  central role in society, 38
  characteristics, 36–39, 290
  and deprivation theory, 62–66
  gender of deity, 177
  healing techniques, 116
  hierarchical organization, 218–19
  history, 63
  human qualities of spirits, 166
  illness explanation, 124
  initiation ritual, 128
  Islam relationship, 36–38
  and matrifocality, 63–64
  men's control of sexuality, 272
  menstruation beliefs, 201
  origins, 30
  role play in spirit possession, 184
  sisterhood in, 269–70
  spirit possession, 154, 184–86
  spirits (*zayran*) in, 165–66
  uncentralized organization, 245